By the Fire
We Carry

By the Fire We Carry

The Generations-Long Fight for Justice on Native Land

REBECCA NAGLE

HARPER

An Imprint of HarperCollins*Publishers*

HarperCollins books may be purchased for educational, business, or sales promotional use. For information, please email the Special Markets Department at SPsales@harpercollins.com.

FIRST EDITION

POEM ON PAGE V: "Returning from the Enemy, Part 3," from A MAP TO THE NEXT WORLD: POEMS AND TALES by Joy Harjo. Copyright © 2000 by Joy Harjo. Used by permission of W. W. Norton & Company, Inc.

Designed by Kyle O'Brien

Library of Congress Cataloging-in-Publication Data has been applied for.

ISBN 978-0-06-311204-9

24 25 26 27 28 LBC 7 6 5 4 3

Vertigo is a terrible mode of travel.

It returns you perpetually to the funnel of terror.

I want it to stop and am furious that fear has found me here,

in the sun where people are laughing, doing ordinary things.

I want to be ordinary, I mean, with no worry that my house will
be burned

behind me, that my grandchildren will become the enemy.

Here is the gravel singing under my feet, there are gulls

weaving the sky with horizon, alligators watch from the waters.

I walk with my friend to have lunch on the pier. I panic.

I want to know that I am worthy of all this sky,

the earth, this place to breathe.

I peer out from the house I have constructed from the hole in my
heart.

I have returned to the homelands beloved by my people

who were marched to the west

by the authority of a piece of paper.

I keep warm by the fire carried through cruelty.

— Joy Harjo, "Returning from the Enemy, Part 3"

Contents

By the Fire
We Carry

Prologue

ON THE OUTSKIRTS OF NASHVILLE, TUCKED BETWEEN OPEN PASTURES
and suburban cul-de-sacs, stands a museum dedicated to the legacy of
Andrew Jackson. The building was once his home. In July of 2015, I arrived to carry out a family tradition. After going through the main house
and paying the entrance fee, I nervously guided myself to Andrew Jackson's grave. Our seventh president is buried behind a black wrought-iron
fence in a neatly kept English garden on grounds that betray their former
life as a plantation. Staff in period clothing milled about. I waited until I
thought no one was looking. And then I spat on his grave.

President Andrew Jackson's signature policy was the ethnic cleansing
of Indigenous peoples from the territorial limits of the United States to
west of the Mississippi. Fearing that Cherokees would not survive on the
land of our creation, my ancestors—against the will and government of
the Cherokee people—agreed to leave. For this, they were killed. In my
family, Andrew Jackson's betrayal is personal.

A woman had seen me spit. She started yelling. "Don't believe everything you read!" she screamed. Her statement confused me. What was she
afraid I had read? The museum texts surrounding us? The lionizing biog-
raphies available in the gift shop? The popular version of American history?

The fight over truth is so bitter because power flows from the dominant narrative—the power to shape both public sentiment and public

policy. In the telling of the American story, Andrew Jackson, like most US presidents, is a household name. In contrast, the history of Indigenous peoples is barely known and the stories that are popular are mostly wrong. Perhaps the woman was afraid of the book I would one day write.

IN THE SUMMER OF 2017, I WAS SCROLLING THROUGH FACEBOOK WHEN I saw a post from Muscogee legal scholar Sarah Deer. It was about a court case I had not yet heard of. A man on Oklahoma's death row was arguing the state didn't have jurisdiction to execute him because he was Native and the murder happened on the Muscogee reservation. Oklahoma argued that reservation no longer existed.

Before Muscogee Nation came to present-day Oklahoma, the tribe's territory spanned what is now Florida, Georgia, and Alabama. In the 1830s, the US military rounded Muscogee people up at gunpoint and forced them into exile halfway across the continent. In a letter to Muscogee leaders, Andrew Jackson promised their new home would remain theirs for "as long as the grass grows or the water runs, in peace and plenty." That promise was not kept. In violation of their treaties, Oklahoma was created on top of Muscogee land. Since it became a state, Oklahoma acted as if all reservations within its borders were abolished. For over a century, the Muscogee reservation was denied. While that might sound like a reservation no longer exists, that's not what the law says.

On August 8, 2017, the Tenth Circuit Court of Appeals—one step below the Supreme Court—upheld the Muscogee reservation. "This is a BIG F DEAL," Deer wrote in her post. "My tribal nation has a recognized reservation again!" The case would ultimately go all the way to the Supreme Court. Their decision would become one of the most important rulings of this century for Indigenous land and treaty rights.

I would spend the next six years reporting on the case—first for news articles, then a podcast, and eventually this book. I knew whatever the outcome, the case would likely determine the reservation status of my tribe too. I grew up with stories of how my ancestors sacrificed their lives for the sovereignty and land of Cherokee Nation. What I felt was the possibility that the land they died for would be recognized as Cherokee land for the first time in over a century. It was a visceral sense of justice. I felt it in my blood.

This case was fought over the Muscogee reservation. My personal connection to it is through the broader implications it had for my tribe, Cherokee Nation. This book includes both Muscogee and Cherokee history, as well as that of other tribes impacted by the eventual Supreme Court decision, including the Chickasaws, Choctaws, and Seminoles. As neighbors in our ancestral homelands and in Oklahoma, the Muscogees and Cherokees share a history that stretches back further than colonization. At times we were enemies, at times we were allies—most of the time our political relationship was more complicated. Because of our proximity, our histories share many parallels—but they are not the same. Our fates, however, remain intertwined.

In writing this book, I strove to be honest about where I come from and my personal relationship to this case, while understanding the limits of my perspective and the need to include other Indigenous voices. In my family's telling, my ancestors were heroes for signing our tribe's removal treaty. As an adult and a journalist, I have tested my childhood understanding against the historical record, and, of course, it is more complicated. I am the descendant of white settlers, Cherokee enslavers, and Indigenous people whose history on this land stretches back to the beginning of time. In a world that rewards whiteness, my proximity to it makes it easier for me to be heard. Which means that you are more likely to come across an Indigenous voice like mine. Brown and Black Indigenous writers—like Alaina Roberts, Joy Harjo, and Elizabeth Hidalgo Reese—have also contributed to the topics covered here. Suggestions for your future reading are in the back of the book.

At the center of this case about land and treaty rights are also the survivors and victims of violence. The appeals that led to the Supreme Court decision started with two convictions in Oklahoma state court. It is important to remember those convictions would not have happened without a very young survivor, her family, and the family of one murdered man pushing for justice.

The story of this lawsuit and its connected history includes accounts of murder, suicide, racial violence, and sexual violence. A guide to where those subjects appear in the book can be located in the appendix. Please take care of yourself while you read.

I wrote this book because I wanted the story of this historic Supreme Court decision to be well documented. I wrote this book because during the litigation I heard people gloss over the wrongs of history. And I wanted to catalog the cruelty of what they brushed aside. I wrote this book because I believe the American public needs to understand that the legacy of colonization is not just a problem for Indigenous peoples, but a problem for our democracy.

And, selfishly, I wrote this book because the story lived in my body and I needed it to come out.

Part I

CHAPTER I

The Crime

THE INDIAN NATION TURNPIKE IS A FOUR-LANE HIGHWAY CUTTING north to south through the bottom right corner of Oklahoma. On a cold day in November, I'm on the highway headed south. Just after Henryetta, the exit dumps me onto a shiny two-lane blacktop. After a mile, between the trees and the fence posts, I see a narrow opening on the left. Having pieced together the location from press coverage, court records, and word of mouth, I think I know where I'm going. The legal name for the road is N 3980, but everyone calls it Vernon Road, after the small town it leads to.

The stereotype of Oklahoma, from musicals or Westerns or just plain ignorance, is of a land that is flat and dry. But that's true only for the western part of the state. The fingertips of the Ozarks stretch into eastern Oklahoma, and in the spring and summer months the landscape—dotted with hills, rivers, and creeks—turns verdant. People call it Green Country.

It's fall, and the sides of Vernon Road are deep and muddy, so I drive down the middle. I'm going parallel to the interstate now—the hum of the highway still audible—but on this road there is no traffic. After two big curves and a hill, the road stretches out flat and straight in front of me. The gravel is the color of faded rust, a burnt orange teetering on beige. I pass a Muscogee cemetery on the left, then a little yellow house, before

George Jacobs memorial

reaching a spot on the road between the cow pastures and the trees that looks like any other spot except for one thing: a large, metal, white cross.

The cross stands with a lean in the ditch. Garden stones have been placed in a circle around the base. The white paint is chipping and rust curls around the edges, but in faded letters I can still read the name George Jacobs.

It was a few days after the murder, in the summer of 1999, when the Jacobs family came to his house. Over twenty years later when we speak, Anderson Fields Jr. can't remember exactly who it was, maybe a sister and a nephew. Probably through small-town talk, Anderson figures, the Jacobs family heard he was the one who found George. They wanted to put up a cross where their loved one had died, and they wanted Anderson to show them the place. And so he took them. At the time, it was an otherwise nondescript section of dirt road, except for one undeniable mark: blood. There had been so much of it, it stayed for months. "Even after it rained, you could still see that spot," he told me. "After a while, it started to look like an oil stain."

The cross commemorates George Jacobs's life. But it also marks the exact location of his murder—a fact that would become crucial evidence in the appeal of his killer. That appeal would eventually go all the way to the Supreme Court. Under US law, tribes occupy a precarious legal status which often makes it difficult for them to bring cases on their own behalf. As a result, many of the most important legal decisions about tribal land and sovereignty come from surprising places. Like this one, which started in 1999 as a small-town murder.

AUGUST 28, 1999, WAS PATRICK MURPHY'S LAST DAY AS A FREE MAN.[*] It was a Saturday—his day off. He didn't have big plans, just helping his

---

[*] The account of George Jacobs's death that I present in this chapter is based on trial testimony from *Oklahoma v. Murphy* and *United States v. Murphy*, along with interviews I conducted with witnesses, police investigators, family members, and members of the community. Specific citations may be found in the endnotes.

cousin move some furniture. Patrick woke up, took a shower, and pulled a beer out of the chilled six-pack waiting in his cooler. He drank it—all six—while he waited for his cousin to show up.* Except for a small sliver of road, the view from Patrick's front porch was trees.

That summer, Patrick was working in Henryetta as a line lead at a factory that built filters for the military. He was thirty years old and had three children from a previous marriage who were supposed to be staying with him for the weekend, but were at his mom's place a few hundred yards down the hill. His girlfriend was staying there too; they had been fighting.

Patrick's trailer, as well as his mom's house, sat on the family's land, a spot relatives still call the "home place." "It was all cousins [that] stayed down there," one aunt told me. Even the generations that came and went before Patrick were buried in the yard. Tucked into a curve of the North Canadian River, people call the small community the Bottoms; some call it the Hole. The name you might find on a map—if it's marked at all—is Ryal.

Ryal is a Muscogee (or "Creek" in English) community. The last treaty Muscogee Nation signed with the US government, in 1866, reserved over three million acres for the tribe—spanning eleven counties in Oklahoma. Some parts are urban, containing the city of Tulsa and its surrounding suburbs. But the southern half of Muscogee Nation's treaty territory, including Ryal, is rural. In these isolated communities lies the heartbeat of Muscogee culture. It's where elders still speak the language, where Creek Methodist and Baptist churches stand, and where, on Saturday nights, people still dance at Muscogee ceremonial grounds.

Ryal was small enough that the Murphy kids could walk everywhere: between relatives' houses, to the Ryal school, and to the local Creek Baptist church, Hickory Ground #1. When the grown folks were visiting,

---

* Patrick's heavy drinking is important context, but it's hard to talk about without conjuring stereotypes about Native Americans and drinking. According to national data, rates of heavy or binge drinking among Native Americans and white people are about the same. The widespread myth that Native Americans are genetically predisposed to alcoholism has been thoroughly debunked.

children were not allowed to listen or interrupt, so they played outside. The cousins spent those days cutting through the woods to the ball field, the basketball court, or another relative's house. They built makeshift go-karts and raced them down the big hill that led to the river bottom. Only when called did they return home.

Patrick was raised by his mother, a full-blood Muscogee woman. His father, a Black man, hadn't been around much. At Ryal School, Patrick was a star athlete. By the time he went to high school in Dustin, a little ways south, he'd honed in on basketball. A lot of cousins would move north to Henryetta, or even farther to places like Okmulgee or Tulsa, but after playing basketball for two years in junior college, Patrick moved back to Ryal.

By the time Patrick was sitting on his front porch that hot August morning, he had lived back home for almost a decade. Through an opening in the trees, he watched a car pull into the driveway. It was Mark Taylor, the cousin he'd been waiting on. Patrick threw a cooler of beer in the back of his green Chevy pickup truck, and both men piled in. After the cousins moved furniture and ate some barbecue, it was about six or seven o'clock. On a long, hot summer day the sun still sat high in the sky. They decided to go driving around. Not unlike the days they had spent roaming the hills of Ryal as kids on foot, except now they were roaming the back roads of McIntosh County by truck.

GEORGE JACOBS WAS OLDER THAN PATRICK, BUT FROM THE SAME COM-munity. Since it was all family down there, George Jacobs's grandma and Patrick Murphy's great-grandma were sisters, which made them cousins in a way. In his half century of life, George had seen a lot, including a tour in Vietnam. After growing up in Ryal, he moved to Tulsa, where he worked as a mechanic rebuilding motors. There, he lived in a second-story apartment above his older sister. She remembered George coming downstairs every Saturday morning and saying "It's time to eat" after cooking breakfast. "George was a younger brother, an easygoing guy who was always willing to help anyone if he could," she would later say. (The Jacobs family did not want to speak about the case—one relative told me it was still too painful. Their comments about George are taken from court transcripts and victim impact statements.)

George Jacobs also spent that Saturday driving around with his cousin, also named Mark. George and Mark Sumka met up that morning on the Okfuskee-Okmulgee county line and decided to drive around in George's black Dodge sedan. It was a normal thing to do on the weekend—back-roading, visiting friends, and dropping in on relatives. Until nightfall, the Dodge sedan would meander back and forth along the four-lane Indian Nation Turnpike and the braided curves of the North Canadian River.

One of their last stops was George's mother's house, where George grew up. Down in the North Canadian River bottom, the house sat at the dead end of the same county road that went past the Murphy place. The matriarch of the Jacobs family was a lifelong member of Hickory Ground #1 Baptist Church and a homemaker who liked to garden, can fruit, and hand-stitch quilts. But she was in her seventies now, and the house was getting run-down. That day, George told his cousin he was thinking about moving back home. He wanted to help his mom fix the place up.

When night fell, George and Sumka took back roads down to a little country bar. At about 8:30 or 9 p.m., they sat down and ordered sandwiches. Mr. G's bar sat in an old, rock building that had once been the post office for Vernon, Oklahoma. The handful of streets in Vernon, which is about nine miles south of Ryal, are named after the Southern states from which its early residents fled: Louisiana, Mississippi, Alabama. As Oklahoma was becoming a state, Black people saw it as a potential oasis from the violence and segregation of the South, and they founded over fifty all-Black towns there. Vernon is one of thirteen that still exists. In its heyday, the town hosted a grocery store, hardware store, cotton gin, cafés, a syrup mill, and a hotel. Today, the only public establishments left in Vernon are churches.

By the time they finished their sandwiches, George was pretty drunk. After Sumka helped him into the passenger seat of the Dodge sedan, George passed out. Sumka took the keys and drove back north on the only road out of town: Vernon Road.

BY THE SUMMER OF THE MURDER, PATRICK AND HIS GIRLFRIEND, AMY, had been together for five and a half years (her name has been changed here). According to Amy, Patrick would get jealous over little things, like if Amy talked to other people at work. If she read a book, Patrick would ask her "what was more important, my book or him," she remembered. But the biggest thing that made Patrick jealous was George Jacobs. Amy had dated George for three years and they had a child together. That summer their daughter, Megan, was nine years old. As an adult, Megan remembered going outside when Patrick would beat her mother.

The Thursday before the murder Amy had gone into town to apply for a job. When she got home, Patrick accused her of going to see George. According to Amy, she and George no longer spoke. But Patrick didn't believe her. He told Amy she should go back and live with George if she wanted. As the fight escalated, Patrick threatened to kill George Jacobs and his entire family. He said he was "going to get them one by one."

Driving around that Saturday, the first relative Patrick and Mark Taylor dropped in on was a young man named Billy Jack Long. Billy Jack was the baby of all the cousins and that summer had just turned eighteen. He wanted to go out riding with the older men. "There's no room for kids in this truck," Taylor replied, knowing he and Patrick had been drinking. But Patrick and Billy Jack insisted. "He looked up to Pat a whole lot," Taylor later told me. "And I sure wish he [Patrick] hadn't drug him down that road." Later, as the three cousins watched a neighbor rope calves, Taylor remembered he had told his wife he would watch their kids that night. He went home, leaving Patrick and Billy Jack to meander through the dark night without him.

Katherine King spent that Saturday painting duck decoys at a factory in Okmulgee County, and after she got off, her eyes, along with everything else, needed rest. She was asleep when Patrick's loud truck motor in the driveway woke her up. Lifting the blinds with one hand, she looked to see who was there and recognized the green Chevrolet (she and Patrick used to work together). Next to Katherine in bed was her boyfriend of three years, who, in the complicated relationships of their close-knit community, was George Jacobs's son. Through a crack in the kitchen door, she asked Patrick what he wanted. "Is he here?" Patrick replied. It

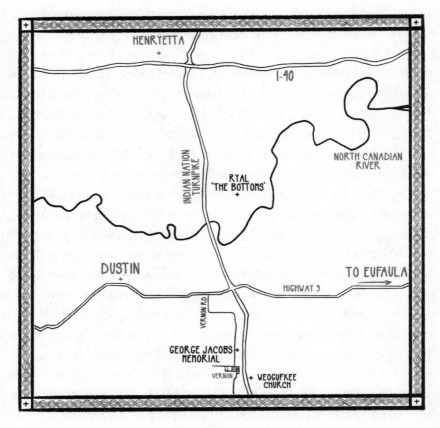

Map of Vernon Area

wasn't a friendly question. Katherine told Patrick that if he didn't leave she would call the police. But her fourteen-year-old son, Kevin, wanted to go out drinking and riding around with the older men. People who knew Kevin called him "Bear." At first Patrick wasn't sure he wanted the kid to come, but Kevin offered to bring his own thirty-pack. Patrick would later say he let Kevin tag along so he could save money on beer.

With Patrick behind the wheel, Kevin King and Billy Jack Long piled onto the long bench seat. Patrick knew a country bar he thought would let the teenagers drink. It was a little south of where he lived, somewhere in the small town of Vernon. By the time Patrick turned left on Vernon Road, it was pitch dark. He couldn't see the road curve left, then right, or the view from the top of the hill before it stretches out straight and flat. He could only see the rhythm of trees and fence posts through the moving patch of headlight beams.

On the unlit dirt road Patrick saw another car coming toward him. When the car got close, Patrick recognized it; it was George's black sedan. Mark Sumka, who was still behind the wheel, had known Patrick since the first grade, and slowed down to say hi. The two cars stopped in the middle of the road, their windows parallel. Patrick asked Sumka who else was in the car. When Sumka said it was George Jacobs, Patrick told Sumka to kill the engine. Scared, Sumka took off. On the narrow road, Patrick swung his car around and sped up. He passed the sedan, then made a sharp right, cutting Sumka off with his truck. Sumka slammed on the brakes. In a cloud of dust, three figures jumped out of Patrick Murphy's truck.

Before Sumka could put the car in park, Kevin and Billy Jack pulled George Jacobs out of the passenger seat and started punching him. Bewildered, Sumka ran around the corner of the car, but Billy Jack punched him in the face, hard. Blood gushed from Sumka's nose and he fell to the ground. The sounds of the fight and the red glow of taillights dimmed as he went unconscious from the blow. When Sumka came to, he was alone. Afraid, he started running—away from the men and the fight, and into the dark. He hid—about a hundred yards away, breathless and bloody. But as he stood there his fear turned to worry. What about George? By the time he walked back toward the headlight beams, it was too late. He saw George lying in the ditch.

THAT NIGHT, ANDERSON FIELDS JR. WAS GETTING READY FOR BED when his two sisters and niece arrived from out of town. They told him there was trouble on Vernon Road. The women had seen a group of men fighting and it looked like one of them wasn't okay. Anderson grabbed his shotgun and hopped in the back of the truck; the three women sat in the cab. When they got to the haphazardly parked cars on Vernon Road, Anderson could see someone lying in the ditch. He asked if the man in the ditch was all right. When the other men turned to face him, Anderson could see blood on their clothes. He tapped the truck to signal for his niece to pull away. They drove back into town, where Anderson left the women, got a friend, and called the sheriff.

When Anderson returned to Vernon Road, the men were gone. The black Dodge sedan was still parked on the road with its headlights on. In the light, Anderson could see the man still lying on the edge of the ditch. He tried to talk to him, but the man didn't respond. "Blood was gushing out just about from everywhere," he remembers. Anderson thought he was still alive because he could see bubbles in the blood oozing out of his neck, as if he was still trying to breathe. But by the time the McIntosh County sheriff arrived, George Jacobs was dead.

IT WAS LATE, SOMETIME AFTER MIDNIGHT, WHEN SPECIAL AGENT IRIS Dalley got the call. A decade-long veteran of the Oklahoma State Bureau of Investigation (OSBI), Dalley's job was to collect the forensic evidence at the scene of the crime. The rural crime scene wasn't near a house or a building, so Dalley wasn't given an address, just directions to drive a mile south of Highway 9 on Vernon Road. On the unlit road, she didn't note any landmarks or watch her odometer; she just drove until she saw police tape and cars. Later, Dalley remembers, when she made her report, she used those initial directions—one mile south of Highway 9—to pinpoint the location of the crime scene.

Normally as an investigator, Dalley had to order sheriff's deputies out of her workspace, but tonight was different. The sheriff's department had blocked off the road, but the deputies were huddled on the far side of the tape. They pointed to the spot still illuminated by the headlights of the Dodge sedan, and told Dalley the crime scene was that way. As Dalley walked down the dark road toward the car, she could see a body lying in the ditch.

In front of the car was a large pool of blood. From the trails across the gravel, Dalley could tell the victim had been stabbed there and then dragged to the ditch. In the middle of the pool was a fleshy object. Seeing it, Dalley understood why the sheriff's deputies wouldn't go near the scene. The fleshy object was male genitalia; George Jacobs had been castrated. Smears of blood obscured smaller injuries on George's face, but

Dalley could see that the victim's stomach was cut and his throat was slit. A medical examiner would later declare George Jacobs's cause of death was exsanguination: he bled to death.

THE MEN WERE STILL STANDING OUT ON VERNON ROAD WHEN PATRICK warned Sumka if he said anything he would kill him. The four of them—Patrick Murphy, Kevin King, Billy Jack Long, and Mark Sumka—squeezed into Patrick's truck. He took off, leaving skid marks in the orange gravel. The drive continued in the dark as the truck curved north on Vernon Road, past the cemetery and up the hill until it turned right on Highway 9. As they headed east over the bridge, they could see the painted lanes of the Indian Nation Turnpike below them.

Mark Taylor, Patrick's cousin, was watching TV on the couch while his kids slept when he noticed headlights in the front window. When Patrick stepped out of the cab of his truck, Taylor noticed he looked different from just that afternoon.

"I killed George Jacobs," Patrick told him.

"Shut up," said Taylor. "Don't bullshit me." But Patrick looked back at him, serious and cold. Billy Jack nodded. "Everybody looked a little bit shocked," Taylor remembered. Sumka looked terrified. "I didn't think he was alive," said Taylor. "He looked so pale." Taylor told the group to leave; he didn't want to be part of any trouble. He warned them that if they ever got caught, they would never get out of prison.

The men decided to go on to Kevin's house, where George Jacobs's son—who was dating Kevin's mom—was still sleeping. On the drive, Patrick told Sumka he was going to do that son of a bitch the same way he'd done the other son of a bitch. At about one o'clock in the morning, Kevin sneaked back into his house and tried to get George's son out of bed, but his mom was awake. Katherine told Kevin that nobody was going anywhere. Kevin tried to go back out to the truck, but she yelled through the front door. The fourteen-year-old listened to his mom and came back inside.

After dropping off Billy Jack Long, Patrick headed to his mom's house—where his girlfriend, Amy, was sleeping. Patrick woke Amy up to tell her what happened. "If the boys done the job right, George Jacobs was dead," he said. Patrick handed Amy a trash bag of bloody clothes and told her to wash them, but she refused. Then he asked her for a lighter. Minutes later from the bedroom window, Amy saw a flare in the dark night.

Patrick watched the rush of gasoline-fueled fire die down, got back in his truck, and drove down the hill to his trailer. He parked his truck out front; went to his bedroom; took off his pants, boots, and watch; and got into bed.

At about five or six o'clock that morning, a McIntosh County deputy sheriff pulled up to Patrick's trailer, where the green Chevrolet was still parked in the drive. He didn't knock on Patrick's door or try to go inside; he was there just to make sure nobody left while OSBI waited for a search warrant. Word travels fast in a small town, and a few people connected Patrick to the truck out on Vernon Road. Before the night ended OSBI had their main suspect. Alone, in his patrol car, the deputy sheriff watched the sun rise over the eastern hills of Ryal. At about 11 a.m., two OSBI agents, another McIntosh County deputy sheriff, and a policeman for Muscogee Nation arrived with the warrant. When police entered his home, Patrick Murphy was still asleep.

MEGAN JACOBS WOKE UP THAT NIGHT TO A BAD DREAM. SHE HAD A feeling something was wrong. In the dream, her father, George, dropped her off without saying goodbye or "I love you." When Megan got up, she walked down the hall and saw her mother with Patrick, crying. Amy's eyes were red and wet; the look in Patrick's eyes made Megan want to run. The next morning, Megan saw police cars surrounding Patrick's trailer.

The morning after the murder, the Jacobs family gathered at a relative's house. There, an aunt took Megan by the hand and led her outside. They walked down the driveway until they were alone. George's sister turned to her niece and told Megan her dad wasn't coming back. He had been killed. Megan's vision went blank and her head fell backward. Her aunt caught her before she hit the earth.

In the illogical way grief works, Megan sometimes blamed herself for her father's death. Maybe, she thought, if she had stayed with George that night none of it would have happened. In her nightmares, Patrick would come back to kill her and her entire family, just like he said.

IF YOU TURN RIGHT ON HIGHWAY 9, AWAY FROM VERNON ROAD, THE blacktop crosses the turnpike and cuts straight through fields and ranches before arcing north. The otherwise tamed landscape is dotted with hills of bushy trees. After twenty minutes or so the state highway curves back south where it lands in the small town of Eufaula—the McIntosh county seat. It was here that Patrick Murphy sat in jail for the three seasons he awaited trial.

Four months after the murder, Oklahoma issued a bill of particulars seeking the death penalty for both Patrick Murphy and his eighteen-year-old cousin, Billy Jack Long. Kevin was only fourteen* when he followed Patrick to Vernon Road that night. It would take over two years for Oklahoma courts to decide whether he should be tried as a juvenile or as an adult. In 2002, Kevin was charged as an adult, pled guilty, and was sentenced to forty-five years in prison. Billy Jack Long would also plead guilty in exchange for life in prison with the possibility of parole. That left Patrick Murphy to face Oklahoma's death penalty alone. But of the three, Patrick is the only one still alive. Both Billy Jack and Kevin died in prison.

The McIntosh County courtroom is a mismatch of drop ceilings and fluorescent lights hanging low over ornate wood paneling. In the spring of 2000—eight months after the murder—the trial of Patrick Murphy began. Patrick sat at a long wooden table with his lawyers. He listened during the proceedings, but kept his head down. The state's evidence was damning. Mark Taylor testified that Patrick told him in the hours after the murder that he had killed George Jacobs. Sumka, George Jacobs's cousin,

---

* Some reporting and court records have said Kevin King was fifteen at the time of the murder. During the federal trial his mother, Katherine King, clarified that he had not turned fifteen yet and was only fourteen.

described what he had witnessed on Vernon Road that night. It all lined up, the district attorney told the jury.

There was one piece of evidence, however, that didn't. When OSBI crime-scene investigator Iris Dalley took the stand, the prosecutor introduced state exhibit number 13. It was a map. On it, about a mile south of Highway 9 on Vernon Road, Dalley placed a black star to mark the location of George Jacobs's murder. Other witnesses also described the location of the crime scene: Anderson Fields Jr. said it was between a quarter and a half mile south of his house; a police officer with Muscogee Nation said it was two miles north of town. If anybody had plotted these points on Vernon Road—where people said the crime occurred and what Dalley marked on her map—they would have realized someone was wrong.

Patrick's court-appointed public defender had a busy year; he was going through a divorce and trying four capital cases, including Patrick's. According to Patrick, his attorney spent less than an hour with him to prepare for trial. The defense attorney told the jury Patrick had been too drunk to form the criminal intent necessary for first-degree murder—an argument that implied his client *did* murder George Jacobs, and one he did not have Patrick's consent to make. (To this day, Patrick maintains his innocence. He claims that while he was on Vernon Road that night, it was Billy Jack Long and Kevin King who killed George Jacobs, not him.) When Patrick got up from the long wooden table to take the stand, his lawyer allegedly whispered, "It's your ass. You better get up there and save it." Patrick's testimony was a disaster; he couldn't keep track of the details, so he kept contradicting himself.

At the very end of the four-day trial it was the Jacobs family's turn to speak. George's older sister, who lived in the Tulsa apartment below him, read a victim impact statement. "It hurts like hell now. I couldn't eat. I lost twelve pounds in one week after the murder of my brother," she told the jury. "They will never suffer hurt like I do. No one knows the pain, hurt, lonely, lonesome feeling within." At every family gathering she could feel George's absence and the trauma of his violent death. "I just hope and pray that these killers get the most severe punishment," she said. "There is no mercy for them." After deliberating for a few hours, the jury came back. From a small piece of paper, the foreman read, "Having heretofore found the defendant, Patrick Dwayne Murphy, guilty of murder in the first degree, [we] fix his punishment at death."

One day that fall or winter—no one can remember when, just that it was cold—Patrick rode in the back of a police car to the shores of Lake Eufaula. He was getting baptized. The pastor who officiated the outdoor ceremony remembers Patrick taking it very seriously. The Christian God provides a kind of total redemption that is rarely available here on earth. Many would say for someone like Patrick, it shouldn't be offered. Yet, in his faith, Patrick found hope. Hope that sustained Patrick the decades it took for his case to meander its way to a historic legal victory. Had Patrick given up, that victory would not have come. That fall or winter day in Eufaula, Patrick waded waist-deep into the muddy lake. He held his breath as his head plunged below the cold water.

It would take a long time, twenty years to be exact, but Patrick's case would grow beyond what anyone could have ever imagined. Like Oklahoma thunderclouds in spring, it billowed. Eventually the storm would envelop Oklahoma, Muscogee Nation, the Trump administration, members of Congress, the oil and gas industry, the governor, tribal leaders, and the United States Supreme Court. At its beginning, however, the conflict was simple. The state of Oklahoma wanted to execute Patrick Murphy for the murder of George Jacobs. But Patrick wanted to live.

CHAPTER 2

Beginning

IN MY FAVORITE PICTURE OF MY GRANDMOTHER SHE IS HOLDING A pile of dirt. Her green pants and short-sleeved yellow shirt are glowing from the day's sun. Behind her stand two headstones, almost passing her waist. They read *John Ridge, Cherokee Leader* and *Major Ridge, Cherokee Chief.* My grandmother is bent over, a trail of earth drifting down from her outstretched hand. She had taken that dirt, that earth, from where our family lived before removal, and was spreading it over our grandfathers' graves in Oklahoma.

John Ridge is my great-great-great-grandfather and Major Ridge—or ᏋᎾᏓᏟ (gah-nuh-dah-tle-gee) in Cherokee—is his dad. They lived in the same place in my child's mind as Aunt Bonnie or Granddaddy Po—the great-aunts and grandparents who passed before I was born, but were still part of family stories told around the kitchen table. Before I was old enough to know about things like US presidents and wars, I knew my ancestors had been leaders of Cherokee Nation, and in their lifetime, they had fought and died for our tribe. The way my grandmother told the story, they were heroes.

My grandmother collected the dirt she spread across their graves on a road trip with my aunt to Tsalagi Uweti—Cherokee homelands in the

Southeast. A few years later, when I was about ten years old, we repeated the trip with my dad. We stopped at a museum about the Trail of Tears in northern Georgia. There, portraits of John and Major Ridge hung on the wall. I recognized them immediately; copies of the same pictures hung in my grandmother's living room. According to my unreliable childhood memory, there was a block of museum text next to their photos explaining their connection to Cherokee history.* Only here there was a new word, one I had never heard my grandmother say: "traitors."

IN THE BEGINNING, CORN DIDN'T HAVE A GROWING SEASON. WITHOUT planting, watering, or picking, Selu brought corn to her family every day. Selu "was the first woman," says Janelle Adair, citizen of United Keetoowah Band of Cherokee Indians and traditional storyteller. Unlike Eve, who was plucked from the rib of a man, Selu "came from a stalk of corn." As she traveled down the stalk, she gathered the corn and brought it with her.

Selu's boys were curious about where all the corn came from. One day they secretly followed their mother and saw that the corn came from her body; Selu was corn. Disgusted, they decided to kill her. "Instead of being angry or feeling betrayed," says Adair, "she tried to provide for them and for everyone that would come after." Before she died, Selu gave her children very specific instructions that, if followed, would guarantee corn would continue to grow in abundance and without effort. But the boys didn't listen. And that is why corn grows only certain times of the year.

That growing season became the Cherokee calendar in a way. Our new year, our most important ceremonies, coincide with the planting, ripening, and harvesting of corn. Many white historians have tried to estimate precisely how long Cherokees were an agricultural society before Europeans arrived. But according to our stories, since there have been Cherokee people there has been the cultivation of corn.

---

* I went back to the historical site while reporting this book, and did not find the word "traitor" in the museum text. Instead the treaty that they signed was described as "fraudulent."

Into the late 1700s, Cherokee towns were built around corn. Each community had a large, central field so no one would go hungry. Houses fanned out from there, where families had their own, smaller gardens. And women, who maintained their family plots and organized the community harvests, owned it all. When hungry soldiers at early colonial forts wanted corn, it was Cherokee women they purchased it from.

Near the high point of Appalachia, a river curves past foggy peaks, through mountain valleys and soft hills until it opens onto a long, flat, fertile plain. Here, the village of Hiawassee once sat. From the town center you could hear the wide river still churn with the momentum of the mountains. This is where my family used to live.*

In 1776, the year of this country's birth, colonial militias waited until it was too late in the growing season for the corn to be replanted. And then they invaded Cherokee Nation and burned the fields of corn to the ground. In the Christian Bible, mankind was kicked out of Eden as punishment for its sins. During the Revolutionary War, the Cherokee Eden was destroyed as punishment for siding with the British.

When he heard the militias were coming, ᏚᎵ's father loaded his family into a canoe. They paddled down the Hiawassee River and then the Tennessee until they were far from the militia's reach. At about the age of five, ᏚᎵ became a refugee. When the militia reached Hiawassee, they found the town deserted. On a distant rise, a scout was still stationed to warn others. The militiamen hunted the scout down, killed him, and then burned everything they could find. After two scorched-earth campaigns, half of all Cherokee towns were leveled. The Cherokee women who used to sell their corn at colonial forts now came to the Indian Agent to beg for food.

Peace was reached in 1785, but it was precarious. Militiamen returned home with stories of the fertile, idyllic mountain valleys they had invaded. Soon illegal white squatters started pouring in. This set off another chain of violence; to defend their land, Cherokees killed or expelled the intruders.

---

*   At the time, Hiawassee referred to the town and the broader region of the river valley.

To defend the intruders, militias waged ruthless campaigns. When a frontier militia found a Cherokee family hiding under a white flag of truce, they let a white man—whose own family had been killed by Cherokee warriors—execute the women and children with an ax. When Cherokee leaders were called to a diplomatic meeting by the US president, a local militia leader attacked them. The scorched-earth campaigns became so frequent that militias had to march past towns they had already burned to reach the ones they hadn't. Nothing would ensure peace with the Cherokees, one militia leader wrote, "but their total extinction."

Cherokees were divided on how to respond. Many feared more destruction, but a group of traditionalists wanted to defend Cherokee land. In the divide, ᏍᎪᎵ chose war. As a teenager, he joined the traditionalists, killed his first person, burned down a fort, stole horses, mutilated soldiers' dead bodies, and barely escaped death himself. Once, when ᏍᎪᎵ killed a white man and his son, he returned home expecting a hero's welcome. But the Tennessee militia got there first. In retaliation, they killed eleven people. The families, in mourning, blamed ᏍᎪᎵ for their loss. War is a logical response to invasion, but whatever force Cherokees used to defend their homelands, the retaliation was always worse. As war put their survival at risk, it became untenable. ᏍᎪᎵ, along with the rest of his tribe, would never stop defending Cherokee land. But he had to find a different way.

CHEROKEE NATION'S TRADITIONAL HOMELAND SPANNED BOTH SIDES of the Appalachian Mountains, covering parts of present-day Alabama, Georgia, North and South Carolina, Tennessee, Kentucky, and Virginia. By the end of the 1700s, Cherokees had ceded about half of that land in treaties signed with the British Crown and then the United States. Some of the land cessions were small, covering the space between two rivers, others the size of a US state. Traditionally, Cherokee towns operated autonomously. Even the decision to go to war was made at the community level. In response to colonization, Cherokees formed a centralized government. It would take decades to solidify, but by the end of the eighteenth century, leaders from each community began meeting regularly in council.

Major Ridge

At this time, the United States was already pushing Cherokees to abandon their homelands. According to US leaders, Cherokees had two options: they could "go over the Mississippi" and continue their traditional lifestyle, or stay and "become industrious like the white people." In other words, Cherokees could move west or assimilate. Some traditionalists who wanted to move far from the influence and violence of white encroachment chose to leave. ᏎᎤᎵ chose to stay.

By the time he reached adulthood, ᏎᎤᎵ had settled in the community of Pine Log in the northwest corner of present-day Georgia. Unlike the steep mountains of his childhood, the high places around Pine Log were soft hills. There ᏎᎤᎵ married, started a family, and came to represent the town on Cherokee Nation's emerging National Council.

At first Cherokee leaders didn't know what to make of the young chief from Pine Log. But ᏎᎤᎵ was a great orator and quickly rose to prominence. As Cherokees were creating a new nation, in both sentiment and structure, ᏎᎤᎵ helped shape it. And the nation he helped form was one adamantly opposed to giving up their land. When an aging chief proposed moving west, ᏎᎤᎵ spoke up—defeating the proposal and removing the old man from office. When another chief agreed to an illegal cession, ᏎᎤᎵ helped assassinate him. To remove further temptation, ᏎᎤᎵ pushed the National Council to outlaw individual chiefs from selling Cherokee land. In an act that sealed his own fate, the punishment was fixed at death.

They say you're not supposed to name a baby until you know them. ᏎᎤᎵ earned his Cherokee name as a young hunter. Once, when he was lost, he used the ridgeline to find his way home; "ᏎᎤᎵ" roughly translates to mean someone who walks along the top of the mountain. Born as a refugee, coming of age in war, ᏎᎤᎵ emerged as a political strongman. At a time when he and Cherokee Nation were fighting to survive, ᏎᎤᎵ helped chart the way. He embraced change in a way that was often ahead of public sentiment. This type of leadership—taking decisive action even when it is unpopular—can be seen as brave, but it is also arrogant. Either way, it is precarious. Like the ridgeline, there is a long way to fall.

———

THE FOREBEARS OF THE MUSCOGEE PEOPLE CAME OUT OF THE EARTH.
Before then all living things lived in the darkness of mud. But they wanted
light. After emerging from the soil, they entered a thick fog—so thick
they still couldn't see. They prayed to the Master of Breath to blow the fog
away. He answered their prayers with a gentle wind that lifted the haze,
and finally they could see one another. With that sight they formed the
relationships and clans that became the foundation of Muscogee society.

Long before states or colonies had names, Muscogee land encompassed much of present-day Alabama, Georgia, and Florida. The landscape was carved up by the wide, sluggish rivers of the coastal plain that
gained speed as they fell from the Appalachian plateau. English traders
named the tribe after the most prominent feature of their homeland:
Creeks. Throughout history their confederacy, and then nation, has been
called Mvskoke, Muscogee, Creek, and Muscogee (Creek). In this book, I
will mostly use the word "Muscogee."

For millennia, the Muscogee and Cherokee peoples were neighbors, with all the diplomatic ties and territorial disputes that come with

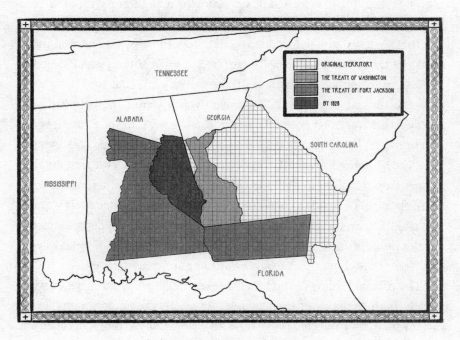

Map of Muscogee Homelands

proximity. They spoke different languages but, along with other tribes in the Southeast, shared many ceremonial practices. As the United States demanded more of each nation's land, their relationship became more complicated. At times, they united in opposition. At others, the crucible of colonization was a wedge between them.

Traditionally, Muscogee towns—like those of the Cherokee—had a lot of autonomy. The violence of colonization—raids for the Indigenous slave trade; the disease those raids brought; and military invasions from the Spanish, the British, and finally from the United States—dramatically reordered Muscogee life. To defend themselves, Muscogees came together under a political confederacy governed by a national council. Within the confederacy, however, were deep divisions. The lower towns, which were closer to the Eastern Seaboard, interacted more with white society. They began to change the way they lived, including what crops they planted, what clothes they wore, and even raising livestock instead of hunting. The upper towns, more isolated, continued to follow a traditional lifestyle. By the early 1800s, the lower towns took their annual payments in axes, plows, and spinning wheels. The upper towns took their payment in guns and ammunition.

Tuckabatchee, the political seat of the upper towns, was nestled in the banks of the wide Tallapoosa River. The flat town square was flanked by distant rolling hills. It was here, in the fall of 1811, that hundreds gathered to hear one man speak. Tecumseh was a rising Indigenous leader whose father was Shawnee and mother Muscogee. After the Shawnees had been ravaged by disease and land loss, Tecumseh's brother had a vision. In it, Native nations from different places, governments, cultures, and languages came together to fight the United States. To the gathered crowd, Tecumseh spoke of how Europeans seized their land, assaulted their women, and trampled on the graves of their ancestors. Indigenous peoples needed to reject white culture, he preached, and return to their traditional ways of life. Their only chance for survival was to fight America together.

The official leaders of the Muscogee Confederacy were closer to white society than the body of their people. When Tecumseh was done laying out his plan, they rejected it. Along with other leaders from Cherokee and Choctaw Nations, SO₊LLY was there that day. The Cherokee chiefs told

Tecumseh that if he brought his message of war to their tribe they would kill him. Before he left Tuckabatchee, Tecumseh told the crowd that when he returned home he would strike the ground so hard it would send an earthquake through the entire continent. That winter, the earth shook so violently the Mississippi River flowed backward. The Muscogee Confederacy became divided. While Muscogee leaders were still aligned with the United States, a growing number of Muscogee people wanted to fight along with Tecumseh. They called themselves the Red Sticks.

After a group of Red Sticks killed white settlers near Nashville, a US agent demanded a Muscogee Chief capture and execute the guilty. When the chief complied, the simmering divisions within the Muscogee Confederacy exploded into civil war. To reject white culture, the Red Sticks slaughtered hogs, burned cotton dresses, broke axes and hoes, and attacked assimilated Muscogee leaders. Symbolically, they even killed their own livestock. The Red Sticks did not desire direct military confrontation with the US, but Southern politicians did. They hoped war with the Muscogee Confederacy would end in defeat for the tribe and more land for them. After the Mississippi militia attacked a band of Red Sticks and the warriors retaliated, the Muscogee civil war turned into a war between the Red Sticks and the United States. Some Muscogees, mostly from the lower towns, remained loyal to the United States. But the overwhelming majority sided with the Red Sticks.

When the War of 1812 broke out between the British and the young republic, like every other nineteenth-century American war, the fighting turned into a sprawling conflict between the United States and Indigenous nations. Tecumseh's growing military alliance sided with the Crown. At first, the Cherokee National Council voted to stay neutral. But ᏍᎧᎵᎩ and other young chiefs worried that wasn't enough. The United States would not distinguish between the hostile Red Sticks and the peaceful Cherokees, he argued, and their tribe would be swept into the conflict either way. ᏍᎧᎵᎩ also worried if the Red Sticks won the Muscogee civil war, their rejection of white culture would spread—possibly to his tribe. At first, the Council rejected ᏍᎧᎵᎩ's overtures. But then he stood up and said that he would join the US forces as a volunteer. So many joined him the Council reversed its position. For the third time in his life, ᏑᎵ was going to war—but this time, he would fight with the United States.

The Tennessee militia was led by a man swiftly rising in politics. As one of Tennessee's earliest land speculators, Andrew Jackson both profited from and fought for the seizure of Indigenous land. Anxiety about Tecumseh and the Red Sticks swept the Tennessee frontier, and before receiving approval from the president, Jackson built a force of about two thousand men. In a speech to his assembled militia volunteers, he promised that "the soil which now lies waste and uncultivated may be converted into rich harvest fields to supply the wants of millions."

Jackson's campaign against the Red Sticks was marked by war crimes from its earliest days. US militiamen shot women and children "like dogs," Davy Crockett, who served in the Tennessee militia, would later write. Crockett remembered the militia setting a house on fire with women and children trapped inside. He watched a twelve-year-old boy burn alive. The militia members were so low on rations that the next day they went back to the ransacked village to look for food. Underneath the charred house, they found a cellar full of potatoes cooked in grease from the bodies that died in the fire. They ate the potatoes.

Two years into the war, in the early months of 1814, Jackson's campaign came to a complete standstill. Jackson and his troops were stuck at a southern outpost, where a drought left rivers low and cut off supplies. The governor of Tennessee implored Jackson to retreat, but the stubborn general, nicknamed Old Hickory, proclaimed he would rather die. Jackson was so low on food he reportedly survived by eating acorns. That spring, after the waters rose and supplies came, allied Muscogee, Choctaw, and Cherokee soldiers joined Jackson's forces. Together they prepared for a final battle.

At a sharp bend on the Tallapoosa River, the remaining Red Sticks sought refuge in the town of Tohopeka. To block a land assault, they built a barricade of logs running the width of the peninsula. The three other sides of their stronghold were protected by a horseshoe bend of water and the high bluff of the riverbank. Jackson himself stated he couldn't conceive of a better defense. As the battle began, ᏑᎵ, and the rest of the Indigenous forces, waited on the far side of the river. Jackson had "determined to exterminate" the Red Sticks "if management could effect it" and instructed the

Indigenous soldiers to wait on the riverbank and kill any Red Sticks who tried to escape. Jackson's troops would storm the barricade.

But Jackson's plan wasn't working. After two hours of shooting at the log fortress with rifles, muskets, and cannons, he had made no progress. A Cherokee soldier grew tired of waiting and decided to swim across the Tallapoosa. By some accounts, it was ᏐᎵ. He captured a canoe, brought it back, and soon the Indigenous troops had ferried themselves across the river. Once they infiltrated the Red Sticks' stronghold they set fire to buildings, attacked the warriors, and weakened their defenses. The diversion allowed Jackson's troops to finally breach the barricade.

The Battle of Tohopeka (or "Horseshoe Bend") ended in slaughter. As Red Sticks tried to escape across the river they were gunned down. The "river ran red with blood." The army killed an estimated nine hundred Muscogee people that day, including women and children. It remains one of the largest massacres of Native Americans in US history. To get an accurate count of the dead, US soldiers cut off each person's nose as they made their tally. From their skin, they cut long strips to make bridle reins.

By the end of the war, three thousand Muscogee people—15 percent of the population—had died. In the upper towns, crops and livestock had been largely destroyed, leaving the survivors with no food. On October 5, 1813, Tecumseh himself was killed in battle after British troops deserted him. American soldiers reportedly took his scalp and other pieces of his body as souvenirs. In the balance of power between Indigenous nations and the young fledgling republic, the War of 1812 was a sea change. For most tribes living east of the Mississippi, armed resistance was no longer viable. Sometimes I hear the sentiment that if Indigenous nations had only fought harder, colonization would have turned out differently. People who say this don't know how hard our nations fought. Or that turning away from armed conflict was a matter of survival, not will.

On August 9, 1814, Muscogee chiefs negotiated peace with Andrew Jackson. Jackson warned the assembled leaders if they didn't concede to his demands he would chase them "into the sea" along with the British. In one of the largest Indigenous land cessions in US history, the Muscogee Confederacy ceded 23 million acres, including the southern portion of present-day Georgia and much of Alabama. The Treaty of Fort Jackson left the remaining Indigenous nations in the South—the Muscogee, Cherokee, Choctaw, Chickasaw, and Seminole—more geographically isolated from one another, and surrounded by white settlers. At the end of the hostile negotiation, the US government had the audacity to frame its actions as benevolent. "From motives of humanity," the treaty read, the United States agreed to provide Muscogees the food they needed as a result of total war.

ᏌᎾᎵ and other Cherokee soldiers returned home to find their communities ransacked. To reach the southern battlefields, the Tennessee militia had traveled through Cherokee country, stealing horses and corn and hogs, and damaging property along the way. ᏌᎾᎵ and other Cherokee leaders would later fight to get the US to pay restitution for the damages, and for Cherokee soldiers to be provided with the same pensions as their white counterparts.

After the massacre at Horseshoe Bend, the US Army promoted Jackson to major general. When word spread that the British army was planning to attack the port city of New Orleans, the major general was sent south to defend it. Though his army—which included frontiersmen and Choctaws—was greatly outnumbered by British troops, they prevailed. The losses for England were staggering—over two thousand soldiers died. Unlike the Battle of Horseshoe Bend, the British bodies were not mutilated. Instead, Jackson negotiated a temporary cease-fire so the British army could bury their dead.

Peace between the Crown and the United States had actually been negotiated one month prior, but since the talks were held in Europe Jackson didn't know. The Battle of New Orleans did not help win the war, but Jackson proved skillful at crafting his public image, and the details did not tarnish his reputation as a folk war hero—then and now. As he traveled back to Tennessee, New Orleans furnished two public steamers. Fans threw a ball for him in Natchez and hosted a supper in Greenville. The groundswell would propel his career in the military, the Senate, and beyond.

In a personal letter to President Monroe in 1817, Jackson confessed that he had long viewed treaties with Indigenous nations as an "absurdity." Such treaties were necessary, Jackson wrote, when Indigenous nations were strong and the federal government was still weak, but now, "circumstances have entirely changed." Years before he had the power to enact it, Jackson laid out the direction in which he wanted US policy to go: the United States should take whatever Indigenous land it wanted.

After the Battle of Horseshoe Bend, Andrew Jackson gave ᏍᎤᎳᎩ the military rank of major. ᏍᎤᎳᎩ would take the title as his first name. Though he did not—and would never—speak English, his many inter-actions with the white world created a rough translation of his Cherokee name: Ridge. And so in history books, museums, and even our family cemetery, this is what my great-great-great-great-grandfather is called: Major Ridge.

CHAPTER 3

The Argument

ON JANUARY 7, 2004, LISA MCCALMONT WAS TRAVELING WEST ACROSS the flat plain of the interstate. It was a cold day; the temperature hovered above freezing, but the sky was clear. At the high points on the road, she could see for miles.

Lisa was at the start of a new career as a federal public defender. Her energetic personality made her seem younger than her forty-some years, but her colleagues took her seriously. When it came to fighting for clients, Lisa was relentless. Her office was in Oklahoma City, but she was spending that Wednesday driving around McIntosh County investigating one of her first cases: Patrick Murphy's. It had been almost four years since Patrick had been convicted and sentenced to death. Once Lisa got ahold of Patrick's case she started from scratch, investigating the crime from bottom to top in case his previous lawyers had missed anything. Lisa was like a reverse detective, trying to find any evidence that could save her client's life.

Lisa found an easy parking spot in front of the Muscogee Nation Lighthorse Tribal Police Department, turned off the ignition, and walked inside. Lisa and her colleague Mike Evett were collecting affidavits about Patrick's childhood and wanted to interview an officer who had testified at trial, Eldon Kelough. When they mentioned to Kelough that their next stop was the crime scene on Vernon Road, he got curious. He wanted to see where, exactly, they were headed. Mike and Lisa pulled out a map—the same map OSBI investigator Iris Dalley had shown the jury at trial—and pointed to that big, black star on Vernon Road. Kelough told them the star was in the wrong place.

Kelough wasn't at the crime scene the night of the murder, but he'd heard about it at the office the following Monday. An important piece of evidence, the murder weapon, was still missing. According to Mark Sumka's statement, Patrick had thrown the pocketknife into a field somewhere west of Vernon Road, where it might still be. OSBI had searched the field, but didn't find it. Two days after the murder, Kelough got in his patrol car and headed south.

Kelough drove slowly down Vernon Road looking for the crime scene. About a mile north of where the road hits the small grid of Vernon streets, he saw a maroon circle on the gravel. It was blood. He parked and got out. He knelt down on the gravel road and bounced a few rocks in his hands until he found a stone that felt about the same weight as a pocketknife. And then he did what Mark Sumka had described. He reared his arm back like a baseball pitcher and threw. The rock arced up, whirled through the air, and landed with a distant clack. Kelough walked to the rock, heel to toe, counting each step. The distance was about 150 feet.

That section of Vernon Road was lined by a dense row of trees. But about twenty or thirty feet south of the bloodstain there was a gap in the overgrowth providing a clear shot to the field. Kelough stood in the middle of the road and looked west through the opening. He walked, heel to toe, 150 steps out into the field. He looked down and saw the knife. It was right there, he told me years later, at his feet.

With Mike and Lisa in his office, Kelough thought back to where he had seen that bloodstain marking the scene of the crime. Vernon Road has two big curves in it. The spot OSBI marked was north of the curves, but the crime scene Kelough found years earlier was south. Kelough took out a pen and marked a second spot on Mike and Lisa's map. They left his office and got back on the highway.

A little south of Henryetta, Lisa and Mike got off the turnpike and headed west on Highway 9. As they turned left on Vernon Road, Mike tracked their progress on the map. As the car edged slowly down the gravel road, they got to the place where Iris Dalley had placed that black star. They didn't see anything. The road turned 90 degrees to the east and took another sharp turn to the south—as if it was tracing the edge of a square—before it stretched out straight and flat. When they got to the spot Kelough had marked, Lisa got out of the car. She saw something. A white cross. When she got close enough, she could read the inscription painted in black letters across the horizontal beam: *George Jacobs*. It would take nearly two decades for this discovery to change her client's conviction, but that cold January day set everything in motion. Lisa paused and looked back down the road toward where they had first stopped—where the police and prosecution said the crime had occurred. It was over a mile and a half away.

WHEN PATRICK MURPHY WAS SENTENCED TO DEATH, LISA MCCALMONT was working as a corporate lawyer in Texas. Law wasn't her first career. After spending ten years as a geologist in the oil industry, she went back to school, got her law degree, and wound up in Houston. At first it was exciting, but after a while the concerns of her corporate clients felt frivolous. By the early 2000s, Lisa wanted to do something more meaningful. When she saw a job posting for a federal public defender in Oklahoma City, she applied. In 2003, she and her husband moved about thirty minutes south of the big city to Norman, Oklahoma. She didn't know it at the time, but her circuitous route to becoming a public defender would help her out in one of her biggest cases.

In a few short years on the job, Lisa would gain national recognition for her work fighting the death penalty. Without a criminal justice background, she often took a novel approach. Her biggest fight was against lethal injection. Lisa worked with scientists and medical professionals to argue that the three-drug cocktail used in lethal injection could lead to conscious suffering, therefore constituting cruel and unusual punishment.* On the subject, Lisa became a national expert whom lawyers from California to Kentucky would call for advice. For her own clients, Lisa was a bulldog. She would do whatever it took to save their lives.

By the time Lisa took up Patrick's case, he had been trying to overturn his sentence in Oklahoma's state courts for four years. With the help of other public defenders, Patrick had filed a direct appeal and what's called an application for "post-conviction relief." He lost both. The clients who came to Lisa and her colleagues in the Federal Public Defender's office had already tried to overturn their death sentences in Oklahoma courts and failed. The team was in charge of the last thing between people on death row and the execution chamber—a petition in federal court. A federal habeas corpus petition isn't a criminal appeal; it's a lawsuit. In this case, it meant suing the state of Oklahoma—specifically the warden of the Oklahoma State Penitentiary—arguing that Patrick's detention and pending execution were unconstitutional.

When Lisa joined the capital division of the Federal Public Defender's office in Oklahoma City, it was small—only four people including her. Sometimes Gary Peterson, a patent lawyer and friend, helped out and volunteered on their cases. The small group of lawyers would often eat lunch together at a barbecue place in downtown Oklahoma City. The high-stakes, hard work made quick friends of the colleagues. Years later, when I sat at Gary's kitchen table in Edmond, he reminisced, "We were like the four musketeers."

When I asked Gary why he spent years volunteering on death penalty cases, his voice turned serious. "I think us humans aren't smart enough to decide whether other humans should live or die. I think that's almost a divine thing," he told me. "When humans try to make those decisions they mess it up."

---

* According to Lisa's research, the drugs would not always render people unconscious. One of the drugs in the cocktail was meant to paralyze people. So some people could be awake and suffering while being executed, but since they couldn't move, no one would know.

Scott Braden worked in the public defender's office at the same time as Lisa and is a citizen of Osage Nation. Seeing how capital punishment worked from the inside solidified his opposition to it. "It really is a crusade on the part of prosecutors and staff to build political careers on the backs of the poor," he told me. "The poor are the ones that get executed. The rich don't get executed."

AFTER PATRICK MURPHY WAS CONVICTED OF FIRST-DEGREE MURDER and sentenced to death, he was transported from the McIntosh County Jail to Oklahoma's death row. The Oklahoma State Penitentiary is nicknamed Big Mac after the town, McAlester, where it is located. Death row inmates at Big Mac were housed in the prison's H Unit. From the outside, H Unit looks like an earthen pyramid. Created in the 1990s during America's prison-building boom, the cells were buried underground. The unit was designed so that prisoners would have no physical contact with staff. Inmates stayed in their cells twenty-three to twenty-four hours a day.

When Patrick arrived in the summer of 2000, H Unit housed 138 men. In a state that was 76 percent white at the time, only 57 percent of the people on death row were. Except for the sky above the 23-feet-by-22-feet concrete-walled exercise room, the prisoners in H Unit did not see the outside world. When Patrick got there, he was in shock. For months, he did nothing but sleep.

The Supreme Court temporarily struck down the death penalty in the 1970s, but since its reinstatement in 1976, more than 1,500 men and women have been executed in the United States. Patrick Murphy was sentenced to death at the same time that Oklahoma was ramping up its use of capital punishment. In 1997, Oklahoma executed one person. In 2000—the year Patrick was convicted—that number had risen to eleven. By 2001, it had reached eighteen—a record high in the last half century. Oklahoma is, per capita, the country's leading executioner.

The execution chamber was on the top floor of H Unit. The condemned men lived below it. When Scott Braden attended executions in the 2000s, the procedure always started at midnight. He remembers the prisoners banging on the metal doors of their cells as if in protest.

The sound echoed through the callous concrete walls. "It was the eeriest thing," he told me. "You could hear them throughout [the] whole building." Patrick remembers banging on the heavy metal door of his prison cell at the hour he knew his friends were dying. For him, it was a way to say goodbye.

ONCE LISA LEARNED ABOUT THE DISCREPANCY IN THE CRIME-SCENE location, she had to prove it. She and her team took crime-scene photos from the night of the murder and compared them to the two conflicting spots on the road: the place where police had reported the crime had occurred, and the place where the Jacobs family had put the roadside memorial. They even hired an accident reconstruction expert to examine the photos. Their unanimous conclusion: OSBI had gotten it wrong.

OSBI's error raised the team's suspicion. Maybe it was an innocent mistake; but maybe OSBI was trying to hide something. If so, what were they hiding? It got the team thinking about jurisdiction. Police and prosecutors have authority over only specific geographical areas; a district attorney from Philadelphia can't prosecute crimes in New York and vice versa. Maybe, they thought, there was something off about the location that meant Oklahoma didn't have jurisdiction to prosecute Patrick. The team had plenty of reasons why Oklahoma shouldn't execute Patrick, like ineffective assistance of counsel. But almost none of their clients had a fair trial, and they still got executed. It was hard to win on issues with a lot of gray areas. But if they could make an argument about jurisdiction, that was black and white.

Many public defenders would not have given the discrepancy this much thought. What difference could a mile on a dusty dirt road possibly make in the life or death of a condemned man? But Lisa was no ordinary public defender. Thanks to her background in geology and oil, she knew that a mile could make all the difference in the world. Once she determined OSBI had recorded the wrong crime-scene location, Lisa dug into the land itself. She found someone to do what's called a "title examination," to look into who owned the spot on the road where the murder had actually occurred. It turned out that the land, like much of Oklahoma, had a complicated history. What you could see of the land had long been owned by non-Natives, but underneath the surface, a Muscogee family still held the mineral rights. Meaning technically—maybe—the land was still Indian country.

"Indian country" is a complicated phrase. For many Native people it evokes a broader sense of community, but because the word "Indian" comes from Columbus's mistaken belief that he had landed in Asia (called the Indies at that time) and is sometimes used by non-Native people as a derogatory term, many Native people prefer that non-Native people don't use it. In the United States Code, however, Indian country legally defines the different types of land reserved for tribes and Native people. In this book, the word will be used in its legal context.

Who is allowed to prosecute crimes in Indian country depends on the type of crime and the Native status of both the victim and defendant. Both Patrick Murphy and George Jacobs were citizens of Muscogee Nation. In Indian country, only tribes and the federal government have jurisdiction to prosecute Native defendants. States do not.

Lisa had another reason she wanted to win on jurisdiction. If Patrick's state conviction was thrown out, he would certainly be retried in federal court, but the feds couldn't execute him. The federal death penalty can be imposed in Indian country only with the tribe's consent. Of the over 570 tribes in the United States only one allows the federal death penalty on their land; Muscogee Nation does not. If Lisa could prove that the tract of land on the east side of Vernon Road was legally Indian country, it meant Oklahoma didn't have the jurisdiction to try Patrick in the first place, let alone sentence him to death. Her client's life would be saved.

TO UNDERSTAND HOW ONE SECTION OF ONE ROAD COULD BE UNDER the jurisdiction of the state, and another section—just a mile away—could be Indian country, you have to know a little about the history of Oklahoma.

Before Oklahoma became a state in 1907, it was the treaty territory of dozens of tribes. The place where George Jacobs was killed—and all three million acres around it—was owned communally by his tribe, Muscogee Nation. In the late 1800s, white settlers wanted the land, so the government came up with a scheme to transfer ownership, piece by piece. The scheme was called allotment. Henry L. Dawes—the Massachusetts senator who came up with the idea—argued that Native Americans were poor because they didn't own private property. By breaking up communally owned land and giving each tribal citizen an individual plot, the United States government—in its great benevolence—would help Native Americans climb the economic ladder. That is, of course, not what happened.

Picture a sheet cake. Before allotment, the entire cake belonged to the tribe. With allotment, the US government came and sliced up the cake into a bunch of pieces. The pieces were then owned by individual tribal citizens instead of by the tribe itself. Anytime one of those citizens lost ownership of their land—by sale, swindle, or outright theft—the cake got smaller. After a century of this policy in Oklahoma, only a few scattered pieces were left. Legally, those pieces were called "restricted allotments."

In oil-rich Oklahoma, it was not uncommon for people to sell their land but maintain rights to whatever natural resources might lie beneath. In other words, they kept the cake but sold the frosting. If oil was ever drilled there, the owners of the land's mineral rights would get the royalties. The east side of Vernon Road, just north of town, had originally been allotted to a Muscogee woman named Lizzie Smith. The land was sold, but her family kept the mineral rights. As she had kids and her kids had kids, her mineral rights were divided into fractions. Over the years, most of the fractions were sold. But in 1999, about one-twelfth of the mineral rights to Ms. Smith's original allotment was still owned by her son and another descendant.

The legal definition of Indian country includes all allotments "to which title has not been extinguished." It might sound like a stretch, but in Lisa's mind, that one-twelfth fraction of mineral rights meant the Indian title was, in fact, not extinguished. If Lisa could get a court to agree, she had what she needed to save her client's life. But first she needed help.

SHARON BLACKWELL WAS RETIRED AND WAITING FOR ANOTHER GRAND-
baby to arrive when one day, out of the blue, she got a call from a public
defender in Oklahoma. Sharon is a citizen of the Omaha Tribe and a descendant of Muscogee Nation. She grew up in Holdenville, in the southwest corner of Muscogee Nation, but at the time was living in northern
Virginia. Sharon had worked as a field solicitor, a special assistant to the
assistant secretary, and a deputy commissioner in the Bureau of Indian
Affairs, the federal agency tasked with managing the United States' relationship with Native nations. In other words, she was quite familiar with
the legal terrain of tribal land.

"Indian lawyers say the first three words an Indian child learns are:
'mama,' 'papa,' and 'jurisdiction,'" Sharon would later tell me. Being a
lawyer doesn't make you an expert in every area of the law, and Lisa had
practiced corporate litigation and criminal defense, but she was new to
federal Indian law. She asked Sharon for help. "I hung up those tap shoes,"
Sharon remembers replying. "I love court. I love trials, but it's over now.
I'm a grandmother now." She gave Lisa the names of a few other lawyers,
wished her luck, and politely hung up the phone.

A week later, Lisa called back.

"You're gonna do this, aren't you, Sharon?" Lisa told her. Lisa had
talked to the recommended lawyers and they all sent her right back to
Sharon. Sharon tried to object, but Lisa interrupted, "You know you're
gonna do this."

And to that Sharon simply said, "Yes. I guess so."

OSBI's mistaken crime-scene location had gotten Lisa thinking, but
it's not where her mind stopped. In addition to restricted allotments,
Indian country—as defined under US law—also includes "dependent
Indian communities" and reservations. Murphy's defense team would
eventually argue that the spot where the murder occurred fit all three. If
a court agreed with any one of those claims, Oklahoma couldn't execute
Patrick.

While the phrase sounds condescending, a dependent Indian community is legally defined as land that was originally set aside for tribal

citizens, and is still under some degree of federal supervision. To prove that the place where George Jacobs was killed was a dependent Indian community, the team wanted to document the presence of Muscogee people, their tribe and culture. So Scott went to a historical collection at the University of Oklahoma and got maps of Muscogee family cemeteries in the area. Sharon and the rest of the team spent a day driving around and documenting the cemeteries, which are distinct because family members place wooden houses above the graves. They looked up Muscogee churches and ceremonial grounds and found that two were within three miles of the George Jacobs memorial: the Weogufkee Indian Baptist Church and the Weogufkee Ceremonial Ground. Both are still there today.

The fire that burns at the Weogufkee Ceremonial Ground has been kept alive by Muscogee people since time immemorial. In the 1830s, when the US government forced Muscogee Nation from their homelands to what is now Oklahoma, they carried their fires. On hot summer nights, when the air is thick with sweat and the songs of cicadas, the members at the Weogufkee grounds still practice ceremonies that stretch back to before Europeans arrived.

When allotment came and Muscogee land got divvied up, Elizabeth Butler's grandfather was assigned the section where the Weogufkee grounds still sit. Elizabeth grew up there; her family home sits walking distance from the fire, and the family cemetery is just off the road. On Saturdays when they danced, Elizabeth's mother would cook all day and the whole community would come by their house to eat. Today, the land still belongs to the family, but Elizabeth doesn't live there anymore. In early 2023, I drove to where Elizabeth lives now in Okmulgee, about thirty miles north, to meet with her and the women who help run the Weogufkee grounds today. Over the generations, a lot of things change, but some things stay the same. For our visit, the women prepared a heaping pile of food.

Melody McPerryman, Elizabeth's daughter, remembers having to do all the dishes as a kid. "There was no paper plates or cups," she told me. Her parents' generation would save jelly jars to use as drinking glasses, and she remembers the sound of spoons clinking on the glass as the adults stirred sugar into their tea. The ceremonial grounds were the center of her community as she grew up during the 1970s. People didn't just stay for the dance, but would come and camp all week. Between work and school, people don't seem to have the time to do that anymore. "It seemed like everybody got along much better back then," Melody told me.

When Liza Proctor was a child, her uncle was the *mekko* (sometimes translated as "chief" or "leader") at the Weogufkee Ceremonial Ground, but her grandparents went to the Weogufkee Indian Baptist Church. As a kid on Sunday mornings, Liza would pass her grandparents on their way to church when she was coming home from dancing all night. The history of Christianity within Muscogee Nation is complicated—at one time the tribe outlawed it—but over the generations Muscogee people did with Christianity what they did with just about everything else: they made it their own. When Liza was thirteen years old, her mom converted, and Liza got baptized in the small pond the congregation used as a baptismal font.

Liza remembers, before the church got electricity, having Bible study around coal lamps. Like out at the stomp grounds, families built camps or small cabins around the church and when they came for Sunday service they stayed for days. Before church started, the deacons would round up all the children and make sure they sat quietly in the pews. Rosemary McCombs Maxey didn't have to be corralled for Sunday service—her father was the preacher. Rosemary remembers rocking on the bench she shared with Liza and listening to it squeak. In those days, the services were never in English.

Today the baptismal pond has been paved over by the Indian Nation Turnpike, and the services at Weogufkee Indian Baptist Church are mostly in English—a change that only happened in the last two decades. The hymns, though, are still in Muscogee. Rosemary speaks Muscogee (it is her first language), but doesn't like to sing in front of other people. When church members asked her recently to lead the Muscogee hymns, she was "scared to death." But hearing those old songs she grew up with felt so good that she kept doing it.

For many, it was preposterous that land could be under tribal jurisdiction when it had not been recognized in over a century. But the whole time, the sovereignty of Muscogee Nation was still being exercised. On this land, Muscogee people still spoke their language, practiced their

Weogufkee Grounds Women: (left to right) Elizabeth Butler, Keli Proctor, Georgia (Judy) Proctor, Melody McPerryman

ceremonies, maintained their government and their way of life. Despite Oklahoma's position that the land no longer belonged to them, Muscogee people never left.

IN ADDITION TO ARGUING THAT THE CRIME-SCENE LOCATION WAS A dependent Indian community, Patrick Murphy's defense team was prepared to make a far bolder claim: that the whole of Muscogee Nation's 1866 treaty territory—the tribe's entire sheet cake—was still Indian country. The state of Oklahoma had not acknowledged the Muscogee reservation, or the tribe's criminal jurisdiction on it, since it became a state. And while that is a long time, it does not mean a reservation no longer exists. "Every Indian lawyer in the country knows the cases that we rely upon. We know the treaties that we work with," Sharon Blackwell told me. "And the most important part of the case law is the disestablishment of a reservation."

The word "reservation" is not a casual turn of phrase; it is a legal term. Before the United States was a country, the land from sea to shining sea belonged to hundreds of Indigenous nations. When they ceded land to the United States through treaties, any land that was not ceded was "reserved" for the tribes. The United States signed treaties with Indigenous nations through the same constitutional process by which it signed treaties with countries like Japan or Mexico. Just like Oklahoma cannot renegotiate US treaty terms with Britain, states cannot alter the treaty rights of Indigenous nations. Only Congress can. Sharon and the defense team pored over the historical record, looking for any evidence that Congress had gotten rid of the Muscogee reservation. But they couldn't find a single act of Congress that had.

So Murphy's defense team put all three arguments on the table: that Ms. Smith's allotment was Indian country, that the Vernon area was a dependent Indian community, and that the treaty territory of Muscogee Nation—an area almost the size of Connecticut—was still a reservation. At this juncture, Patrick's case was still about whether he would live or die, but his legal team planted the seeds for it to become something much bigger. "I've never had any doubt that the treaty lands are tantamount to reservations," Sharon told me years later.

After their research was complete, Lisa filed a 146-page federal habeas petition in the US district court in eastern Oklahoma arguing that Patrick Murphy should not be executed by the state of Oklahoma on thirteen grounds—including that he had an intellectual disability and inadequate counsel, and that Oklahoma's lethal injection protocol constituted cruel and unusual punishment. The strategy in death penalty appeals is a bit kitchen-sink—any one issue can save a client's life. Staying within the law and reason, Patrick's lawyers put forward every argument they thought they could win. Ground one in the long petition was that Oklahoma didn't have jurisdiction to prosecute Patrick in the first place. "If you don't have jurisdiction, you can't execute," Gary told me back in Edmond. "You can't do anything."

AMONG LISA AND HER COLLEAGUES PATRICK GOT A NICKNAME: "THE happiest man on death row." The conditions, unbearable for most people, never seemed to get to him. According to Kristi Christopher, another lawyer in the public defender's office, Patrick was always smiling, friendly, patient, and appreciative. Every year on her birthday, Kristi would get a message. He never forgot. Like with most of her clients, Kristi didn't talk much with Patrick about the murder. Outside of updates on his appeal, Kristi and Patrick mostly talked about sports. Kristi would bring Patrick magazines and newspapers with NFL statistics, which he would use to run the fantasy football league on death row. When Kristi's office took bets on college basketball March Madness brackets, Patrick would always enter. One year, he almost won.

Prison isolates people from their loved ones. Not so for Patrick; he maintained a strong network of friends and family. At one of his many court hearings, the guards let Patrick sit and visit with his relatives—a rare moment for a man on death row. Scott snapped a picture. In it, Patrick wore a simple blue prison uniform and handcuffs. His mom hugged him, emotional but happy. It was the first time she had touched her son in five years. It would be the last time they hugged before she died.

As a quirk of the federal habeas process, Lisa had to "exhaust" all her arguments in state court before her federal petition could move forward. But as a federal public defender, she wasn't allowed to file anything in state

11/18/2004

Patrick and his mom

court. So her friend Gary Peterson filed it for her. For a while, the team had two cases going: the one Lisa filed in federal court and the one Gary filed in Oklahoma. The state case was remanded back to the McIntosh County court for an evidentiary hearing. On November 18, 2004, the whole legal team arrived in the small lake town of Eufaula and checked in to their hotel. As seasoned lawyers on death penalty convictions, they knew it would be a long process. But that courtroom in Eufaula would be the first place they tested the theory they hoped would save their client's life.

Gary Peterson was ready to prove that OSBI's crime scene was in the wrong location. He had prepared Anderson Fields Jr. (the Vernon resident who found George Jacobs), a land surveyor, and a crime-scene reconstruction expert to testify. But before he had a chance to make his case, the state admitted their mistake. When OSBI crime-scene investigator Iris Dalley took the stand, the DA asked her, "In the trial testimony, did you indicate that the location of the scene was approximately a mile or so south of Highway 9 on the Vernon Road?" Dalley replied, "Yes, sir." The DA then asked her, "Was that a correct measurement?" Dalley simply said, "No, sir." Gary was floored.

But the DA had a work-around: he argued that while George Jacobs may have died in the ditch, his fatal wounds were inflicted on Vernon Road. And the road was a right-of-way owned by McIntosh County, therefore under the jurisdiction of Oklahoma. The county commissioner even testified about how their employees maintained the gravel.

When Sharon Blackwell got up to testify, the DA objected. He said the evidentiary hearing was about the location of the murder, not about who had jurisdiction. The judge agreed. So the team's main argument was shut down before it even began. The judge did allow Gary to supplement the trial record with what's called an "offer of proof." This was necessary because parties aren't allowed to raise issues on appeal that weren't brought up in the lower court. And so Sharon wrote out an affidavit summarizing what she would have said on the stand, preserving the question of whether or not Muscogee Nation still had a reservation for higher courts to decide. According to her research and legal opinion, she wrote, "the boundaries of the Creek Nation were established by Treaty in which the Creek Nation's sovereignty and jurisdiction within its boundaries was guaranteed," and that their reservation "has not been disestablished."

The McIntosh County judge agreed with the DA that the murder of George Jacobs occurred on a right-of-way maintained by the county, therefore was not in Indian country. The allotment argument, the reservation argument, and all the other issues the team had prepared were dismissed. A year later, on appeal, Oklahoma's highest court for criminal cases would disagree with the DA, the trial court, and their interpretation of the county road. But they did not grant Patrick Murphy relief. The Oklahoma Court of Criminal Appeals said the mineral rights were too small to maintain Indian title to the land. For the Muscogee reservation, they stated, "if federal courts remain undecided on this particular issue" it wasn't their place "to step in." Patrick remained on death row. Oklahoma courts had settled the Indian country claim, but were still stuck on a separate issue: whether or not Patrick Murphy had an intellectual disability.*

* The legal term under Oklahoma law was "mentally retarded," not "intellectually disabled." Because "retarded" is often used as a pejorative for people with intellectual

IN THE PUBLIC SPHERE, WHETHER OR NOT THE GOVERNMENT SHOULD execute people is often a moral discussion. But in court, the big questions are not moral, but technical and legal. In 2002, early on in Patrick's case, the Supreme Court ruled that it was unconstitutional to execute people with intellectual disabilities. The court, however, didn't define who was or was not intellectually disabled, leaving it up to each state to decide. While Oklahoma tinkered with its own standards, Patrick's case got stuck in limbo. The delays didn't overturn Patrick's conviction, but they kept his pending execution at bay.

To prove their client had an intellectual disability, Patrick Murphy's defense team collected evidence from people who knew him. Patrick's mother admitted to drinking while she was pregnant, and one evaluation concluded Patrick had fetal alcohol syndrome. Patrick was held back in grade school, but graduated from high school and attended two years of junior college. Prosecutors pointed to Patrick's success to show that he couldn't possibly have an intellectual disability. But according to the defense team, Patrick masked his intellectual disability with help from other people. One college classmate remembers everyone helping Patrick get by so he could still play basketball. Even inmates on Oklahoma's death row described helping Patrick read and write letters.

While Patrick's case lingered, the Oklahoma state legislature passed a new law that defined who had an intellectual disability. Under the law, if a defendant scored above 76—on any IQ test, ever—their claim to an intellectual disability was waived. Patrick Murphy's IQ was tested multiple times. A few times it was below 76, but twice it was above. Finally, in 2012, Oklahoma's highest court for criminal appeals ruled Patrick was not intellectually disabled and could, in fact, be executed. It was twelve years after he arrived on death row and eight years after Lisa discovered that roadside cross. By that time, Lisa, Kristi, and Scott no longer worked at the Federal Public Defender's office in Oklahoma City, but Patrick's federal habeas petition was still working its way through federal court.

---

disabilities, I am not using it in this text.

Now—with every issue it raised settled in Oklahoma—it was the only thing left to save Patrick's life.

ON THE EVE OF HER FIFTIETH BIRTHDAY, LISA WAS HAVING A GLASS OF wine with her husband at their home on the outskirts of Norman. The air outside was still and dark. At one point in the conversation, she wandered into the other room and never came back. When her husband went to look for her, he found her body. Lisa had died by suicide.

At the time, a spokesperson for the nonprofit Lawyers Concerned for Lawyers commented, "The best and most compassionate lawyers are the most vulnerable to mental illness." Sometime after Lisa's funeral, her husband placed a headstone on her grave inscribed with both their names; one day the couple will be buried together. Engraved along the bottom of the stone rectangle is a line from a poem by Ezra Pound: "I desire only that my dust be mingled with yours, forever and forever and forever."

Sitting in Gary Peterson's kitchen a decade later, he lit up when he talked about his old friend and colleague, but grew quiet when it came time to talk about her death. "She was an extraordinary lawyer," he told me. "We'd never seen anything like her before."

A few months before her death, a federal court ruled for the first time on the habeas petition Lisa had filed for Patrick. Judge Ronald Wright for the US district court in eastern Oklahoma denied Patrick Murphy federal habeas relief on all grounds. Without citing any treaties, congressional statutes, or case law, he concluded that Muscogee Nation did not have a reservation. It would take another decade for that decision to be overturned.

CHAPTER 4

Promise

COTTON IS A VERY THIRSTY PLANT. EVEN FRESHWATER HAS A SMALL amount of salt in it. Over time, saturating the earth with all the water that cotton needs makes the soil salty—salty enough that nothing can grow there. Up and down the Eastern Seaboard where enslaved people put cotton into the ground year in and year out, the soil was dying. Southern planters needed new land. But by the late 1820s, the most fertile land for cotton was still the treaty territory of Indigenous nations.

In Georgia, the demand for Indigenous land also came from poor frontier families. There, anytime Indigenous nations gave up some of their territory that land was entered into a public lottery. Georgians became "sick with the expectation of Indian land," Major Ridge's son would write. So sick that they sang a song about it:

"All I ask in this creation," the song went,

> *Is a pretty little wife and a big plantation*
> *way up yonder in the Cherokee Nation.*

By the 1820s, one-fifth of Georgia's land was still the treaty territory of Cherokee and Muscogee Nations. The state was not alone. Choctaw

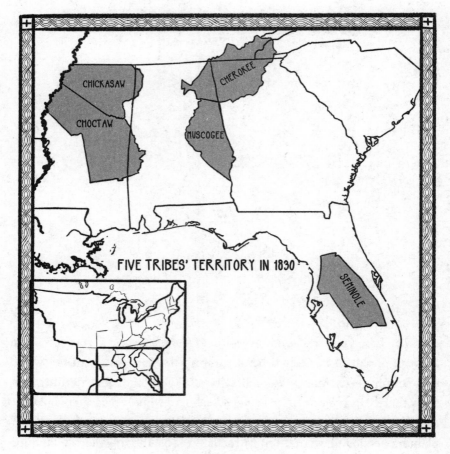

Five Tribes' Land

and Chickasaw Nations' treaty territory covered nearly half of Mississippi, and Muscogee Nation a large swath of Alabama. Southern politicians got together and came up with a plan: if Indigenous nations wouldn't agree to leave, their states would terrorize them until they had no choice.

WHILE MAJOR RIDGE CAME OF AGE AT WAR, HIS ELDEST SON CAME OF age at white mission schools. In the fall of 1818, John Ridge arrived in the New England countryside. Nestled in the foggy hills of Cornwall, Connecticut, sat a two-story clapboard school building. The Foreign Mission School, nicknamed the "heathen" school, was created to convert Indigenous youth so they—instead of white missionaries—could spread the message of Christ's salvation among their people. When John arrived, the schoolmaster was upset. The teenager used "profane" language, thought too much of himself, and was a bad influence on other students. Since John got there, the schoolmaster complained, the entire school felt less "pious."

At the time, Cherokee Nation needed leaders who could speak English and understand US law. When Major Ridge requested a spot for his son at Cornwall, he explained he wanted John to get a white education, so that "when he comes home he may be very useful to his Nation." Indigenous youth like John were also educated to prove something: that Indigenous people were just as intelligent and capable as white people. This was up for debate at the time—with many white people arguing that Native Americans, as a race, were inherently inferior, therefore less deserving of human rights. John wasn't the only Cherokee or Indigenous leader to receive his level of education, but he was one of a few. From a very young age, the weight of his nation was on his shoulders.

With his education, John did not preach the gospel to other Cherokees. Instead he would proselytize to white people about the rights of Cherokee Nation. The educators at Cornwall thought they would create Cherokee missionaries. Instead they created Cherokee diplomats.

John's white education came with a cost. From a young age, he lived away from family. At one mission school, both John and his cousin were sexually abused by an older student. It was John's father, who lived a day's journey away, not the missionaries, who found out about the abuse and stopped it. At Cornwall, at least John wasn't alone. Also in attendance was his cousin Elias Boudinot. The cousins were close—more like brothers. Elias, unlike John, was a devout student who for the rest of his life would remain committed to the message of Christ's salvation. The missionaries doted on him.

At Cornwall, John's studies improved, but his health declined. A couple years into his studies, at the age of eighteen, John had severe pain in his hip and could no longer walk. He was moved to the home of the school steward. Up a narrow, wooden staircase at the end of a short hall sat a small bedroom with one window where, far from family, bedridden, and in constant pain, the teenager stayed for two years. The steward's daughter, Sarah, was sent to care for John. Sometimes she would stay and visit. Over the years, they fell in love.

When the young couple were married, the New England public was outraged that a "heathen" had been allowed to marry a white woman. When John and Sarah traveled back to Cherokee Nation, they were mobbed by angry crowds. There were calls to close the school. Two years later, when Elias married Harriet Gold, the prominent daughter of a local politican, the public exploded. People called for Boudinot's death. In Cornwall's town square, a mob placed an effigy of Harriet on a barrel of tar and her brother set it on fire. The school didn't survive the second marriage, and closed the following fall.

To receive his white education, John endured distance from home, the scorn and discipline of missionaries, disability, chronic pain, sexual abuse, love, and rejection. Despite all this, John accepted the weight he was handed—embraced it, even. In his duty to his nation, he would never waver. To carry out that duty, John would mold himself to fit the white world. But from a young age he saw the bargain for what it was: he was fighting for equality with people who would never see him as their equal. After the public response to his marriage, he wrote, even the most educated Cherokee, in their eyes, is still "an Indian."

From the time of George Washington, US presidents promised Cherokees that if they could live more like white people—raise livestock, farm, wear cotton clothes, and adopt Christianity—they could remain on their lands. For Cherokees, the pressure to assimilate was also practical. There was not enough wild game to support subsistence hunting, so more Cherokees kept livestock. After tides of death from disease, intermarrying with white people helped Cherokees rebuild their population. Even our traditional, decentralized government had to change after US officials exploited it by coercing individual chiefs to sell off pieces of Cherokee land. So, over and over again, Cherokees adapted.

In the promise of civilization, US leaders spoke out of both sides of their mouths. In a confidential letter to Congress in 1803, President Thomas Jefferson argued that once Indigenous people had been made farmers they wouldn't need the "extensive forests necessary in the hunt-

JOHN RIDGE,

A CHEROKEE.

PUBLISHED BY F. W. GREENOUGH, PHILAD.ª

Drawn Printed & Coloured at I.T.Bowens Lithographic Establishment Nº 94 Walnut St.

Entered according to act of Congress in the Year 1838 by F. Wainwright in the Clerks Office of the District Court of the Eastern District of Penn.ª

John Ridge

ing life" and more of their land could be opened for white settlers. The real goal of civilization, then, was to weaken the ties between Indigenous people and their land. But for Cherokees it did the opposite. As Major Ridge put it, civilization rendered "our attachment to the soil more strong, and therefore more difficult to defraud us of the possession." The conflict this created would shape the next few decades of Cherokee and US history alike.

Two years after John left Cornwall, Muscogee Nation was in crisis. By any means necessary, Georgia wanted all Muscogee land within its borders. For a time, Muscogee and Cherokee Nations united against their common enemy—the state of Georgia. In that relationship, John was a bridge. With his white education, John became a diplomat for Muscogee Nation. In December of 1824, two US officials traveled to Muscogee Nation to demand the tribe give up their homelands in exchange for land out west. During the tough negotiations the Council spoke through a great orator rising in Muscogee politics: Opothle Yoholo. "Ruin is almost the inevitable consequence of a removal beyond the Mississippi," he told the officials. "We feel an affection for the land in which we were born," the Council wrote. "We wish our bones to rest by the side of our fathers." Opothle Yoholo and John would become close friends.

Rebuked by the Council, US negotiators came up with a different plan. While meeting with the official government of Muscogee Nation during the day, they started meeting secretly with one chief by night. William McIntosh, Speaker of the lower towns, was willing to sell the whole of Muscogee Nation's homeland. Under the false pretense that Muscogee Nation was again on the brink of civil war—and that those refusing to give up their land were hostile Red Sticks—McIntosh and US negotiators called a meeting at McIntosh's home in Georgia. Opothle Yoholo warned US officials that whatever deal they struck with McIntosh would not be "binding on the nation" since it was not done "in general council." Opothle Yoholo also had a warning for McIntosh. Like Cherokee Nation, the Muscogee council had outlawed unauthorized cessions of Muscogee land on punishment of death. "My friend, you are about to sell our country," Opothle Yoholo told McIntosh. "I now warn you of your danger." Moments later, William McIntosh signed the Treaty of Indian Springs.

OPOTHLE YOHOLO.

A CREEK CHIEF.

PUBLISHED BY E. C. BIDDLE, PHILADELPHIA

Opothle Yoholo

William McIntosh

According to the treaty terms, the tribe would cede all of their land in Georgia and most of their land in Alabama in exchange for the same amount of land "acre for acre" west of the Mississippi and $400,000— half of which was earmarked for McIntosh and his party. The fraudulent treaty was ratified by the US Senate less than a month later; Muscogee leaders were stunned.

Fearing for his life, McIntosh appealed to the governor of Georgia for protection. McIntosh—whose mother was Muscogee and father was white—was the governor's first cousin. But the Georgia politician was up for reelection in a tight race and desperate for any Indigenous land cession that would aid his victory. In opposition to his cousin's wishes and the treaty stipulations—which guaranteed Muscogees could remain on their land for another eighteen months—the governor sent surveyors into Muscogee territory. With axes and chains, they started marking out sections for the upcoming land lottery. For the council, it was too much.

The Muscogee council decided to execute McIntosh for treason. On April 30, 1825, more than two hundred warriors surrounded his home and set it on fire. From a second-floor window, McIntosh shot at them, but the flames forced him outside. Fleeing the burning home, McIntosh was gunned down in his front doorway. As he stumbled onto the lawn, an executioner plunged a knife through his heart.

Though it had already been ratified, Muscogee leaders hoped to escape the harsh terms of the fraudulent treaty. A delegation led by Opothle Yoholo was sent to Washington. Muscogee leaders were not fluent in English and did not trust US officials. So they employed two Cornwall-educated Cherokees to help them: David Vann and John Ridge. This was the hope of John's white education—to force the United States to deal with Indigenous nations honestly. Like Sisyphus rolling a boulder uphill, John, Opothle Yoholo, and the Muscogee delegation took on the impossible: stopping a treaty that had already been signed into law.

On his fourth day in office, President John Quincy Adams signed the Treaty of Indian Springs into law. Adams had narrowly and controversially won the presidency over Andrew Jackson, and while he wasn't as hostile to Indigenous nations as his opponent, he wasn't willing to make political sacrifices to protect Muscogee land, either. Georgia was already threatening civil war. Georgia officials wanted all Muscogee land within its borders, but at the time, the state's western boundary had never been surveyed or marked. Muscogee leaders didn't trust an imaginary line between them and their hostile neighbors. Instead they wanted a natural boundary, like a river. To the secretary of war, Opothle Yoholo demanded the fraudulent treaty "be canceled," and pleaded that the land left by the treaty was so small the nation "could not live upon it." Comparing Indigenous people to leaves on a tree in autumn, the secretary warned Opothle Yoholo that his tribe was thinning in numbers and could easily be exterminated. The negotiations dragged on for five months. Losing hope, Opothle Yoholo attempted suicide.

With authorization from the delegation, John Ridge revived the negotiations. He proposed a smaller creek as the line between Muscogee Nation and Georgia—giving Georgia more land, but maintaining a natural boundary. Under the bargain, Muscogee Nation would retain a sliver of land in Georgia and their entire treaty territory in Alabama. The Adams administration agreed. On April 22, 1826, the Treaty of Washington was ratified. Muscogee Nation's escape from the Treaty of Indian Springs marks the only time in US history a tribe renegotiated a treaty after it was ratified. It looked like John's education was working.

Georgia leaders, however, were furious. Later that year, US officials came back for the rest of Muscogee land in the state. Under the leadership of Opothle Yoholo, the council said no. The superintendent of Indian affairs came up with a plan. He saw Opothle Yoholo and John as his main opposition, and decided to turn the council against them. The superintendent accused Opothle Yoholo and John Ridge of conspiring to control Muscogee Nation's money. It worked. John Ridge was expelled from the nation and warned that if he returned he would be killed. On November 15, 1827, Muscogee leaders signed a new treaty ceding "all remaining lands" in Georgia.* Opothle Yoholo boycotted the signing.

John was livid. He publicly mocked the white official; Elias Boudi-

---

* According to John, the superintendent even offered David Vann a bribe if Vann could broker the land session.

not printed a defense of his cousin in the press; and even John's allies in Congress called for an inquiry. The months John spent fighting to save Muscogee land in Georgia were for nothing. Not only did he fail, but he had been cast as a corrupt and self-serving leader.

With no land left in Georgia, an estimated seven thousand Muscogee citizens were now refugees; the once sprawling confederacy was reduced to five million acres in Alabama. The Georgia legislature quickly passed laws forbidding Muscogee citizens from entering the state without a permit, and Muscogee leaders complained their people were being shot and killed by white Georgians. Opothle Yoholo's prediction proved correct: there was simply not enough land for the nation to live on.

AFTER GRADUATING FROM CORNWALL, ELIAS BOUDINOT MOVED TO THE new capital of Cherokee Nation. Unlike the deep valleys of old Cherokee towns, the land of New Echota is wide and flat. The small town center, laid out in neat perpendicular streets, is framed by towering Georgia pines that cast long shadows and crisp pine needles over the ground. Catty-corner from the new Supreme Court building and National Council House sat a one-room print shop, where in January of 1828, a large printing press arrived with two sets of metal typefaces: one in the English alphabet and the other in Cherokee syllabary. Elias was chosen to edit the tribe's new newspaper.

The only thing greater than Elias's faith in the Christian God was his faith in Cherokee Nation. It can be hard to think of the 1820s as a time of opportunity, but Elias was full of hope. After a century of death, war, and land loss, Cherokees had established a new writing system, a central government, and even a newspaper. Elias named the paper after the Phoenix of Greek mythology, which over and over ascends from the ashes. The paper's name in Cherokee—ᏣᎳᎩ ᏕᎭᏟᏬᎯ—literally means "it rises."

In February of 1828, Elias printed the first edition of the *Cherokee Phoenix*. Elias deftly used the paper to advocate for the land and sovereignty of Cherokee Nation. His columns were reprinted in papers across the country, shaping the national conversation. Thanks to Cherokee scholar Constance Owl and translators Tom Belt and Wiggins Blackfox, we know

Elias Boudinot

Cherokees also used their bilingual paper to have a conversation among themselves that white people couldn't understand; entire articles printed in Cherokee don't appear in English. Addressing his Cherokee readers, Elias told them (translated here), "There are only a few of us around here and they always want to take us out of our lands." But through the paper, he reassured them, "You'll hear about things just like white people do."

In the first edition of the *Cherokee Phoenix*, Elias printed Cherokee Nation's new, written constitution. As Cherokee Nation remade itself under the influence and pressures of colonization, it adopted aspects of white supremacy. Article 3, section 4 of the new constitution denied Black Cherokees citizenship. Cherokees first had contact with the European concept of chattel slavery through the Indigenous slave trade, in which Cherokees were kidnapped and enslaved by the Spanish and British. In the early 1700s, a third of the enslaved population in South Carolina was Indigenous. Since time immemorial, Cherokee identity was based on one's maternal clan; if your mother was Cherokee, you were too. In Cherokee society, "kinship, not freedom" was the opposite of slavery, writes historian Tiya Miles. "In the Cherokee understanding, to be kin meant being human, and to be human meant being free."

By the late 1700s individual Cherokees enslaved people of African descent, but Black Cherokees who had a clan through adoption or birth still had full citizenship rights. In the 1820s, all that changed. After John Ridge and Elias Boudinot married white women, they petitioned the National Council to allow children with a Cherokee father but white mother (their children) to be citizens. The Council obliged. Around that time, the Council also passed laws excluding mixed-Black Cherokees from citizenship—even if their mother was Cherokee. Four other tribes—Muscogee, Chickasaw, Choctaw, and Seminole Nations—also adopted chattel slavery from the US South. Partially for this reason, our nations came to be called the loaded moniker "the Five Civilized Tribes."

While Elias appears to have opposed slavery (by reprinting abolitionist texts in the *Phoenix*) both Major Ridge and John Ridge enslaved people of African descent and supported anti-Black policies within Cherokee Nation. In an 1826 letter, John Ridge wrote that intermarried whites were accepted because it helped the tribe with its "march of civilization," but the "few instances of African mixture with Cherokee blood" were viewed as a "misfortune & disgrace." Growing up, this part of our family history wasn't talked about. After learning it, I spent years not wanting to claim my ancestors, and then years not knowing how.

In the fledgling United States, wealth was power. And for Indigenous leaders at the time, power was survival. But wealth, of course, is also about greed. Because of the people they enslaved, the Ridges could afford fine things like china plates, silks, extensive fruit orchards, and even a white-painted plantation-style home.

Cherokees' traditional form of self-governance was not perfect, but it was a society structured to prioritize equality and maintain balance. When we left behind the clan system, we lost this. The inequality born of this time—the lower status of women, the introduction of class, the gulf between traditional and acculturated Cherokees, and the adoption of anti-Black racism—is something we have yet to overcome.

Once Cherokee Nation's new government was seated, John and Major Ridge took their places within it. John Ridge became president of the National Committee—one of two legislative bodies—and Major Ridge became an executive counselor, almost like a cabinet member.

At the heart of the Cherokee experiment in nationhood was the land. The first article of the new constitution described in great detail the boundaries of Cherokee Nation—naming each river, creek, ridgeline, and road—and proclaimed that the territory was "reserved forever to the Cherokee Nation by the Treaties concluded with the United States." In so many words, the constitution drew a line in the sand: not one more foot of land would be ceded. At the time, the tribe still held treaty territory in the states of Tennessee and North Carolina, but the majority of its land, including New Echota, lay within Georgia. Cherokee Nation's declaration of sovereignty over that land enraged the state.

In retaliation, the Georgia state legislature proclaimed jurisdiction over Cherokee Nation and passed a series of laws to harass Cherokee citizens. The state outlawed Cherokees from mining gold on their land, testifying in Georgia courts, and even convening their government. To enforce their terror, Georgia created a special militia—the Georgia Guard. In violation of federal law and treaties, Georgia opened another

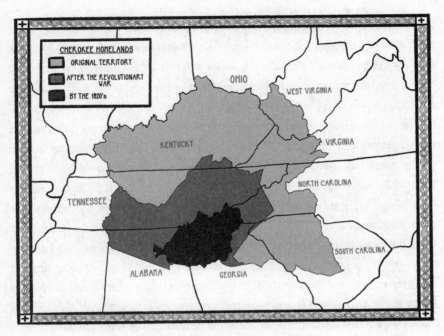

Map of Cherokee Homelands

land lottery—this time of land the tribe had not ceded. In droves, white squatters moved onto Cherokee land. When a group of warriors led by Major Ridge tried evicting some of the squatters, a mob found one of the warriors, beat him in the head, chest, and face, and left him on the side of the road to die. In 1829, things, unbelievably, got worse; news had spread that settlers found gold. Elias estimated intruders stole $1.5 million worth of gold in five months—amounting to over $40 million in today's dollars. Cherokees who tried to prevent the theft were arrested by the Georgia Guard; some were tortured. Georgians, John Ridge wrote, didn't understand treaty rights, the Constitution, or the law. They knew only "that they are poor and wish to be rich."

Overrun by white squatters, beaten and murdered by militias, life for Cherokees in Georgia was becoming unbearable. Cherokee leaders appealed to President Andrew Jackson. After the "stolen election" of 1824, Andrew Jackson had defeated John Quincy Adams in a landslide. Jackson's hostile position toward Indigenous nations was well known; in Georgia he won the vote by 97 percent. According to US law, the federal government was obligated to enforce Cherokee Nation's treaty rights in the face of Georgia's flagrant violations, but Jackson refused. "Towards this race of people, I entertain the kindest feeling," he told the Senate. But "I can see no alternative for them, but that of their removal to the west, or a quiet submission to the state laws."

In his first State of the Union address, President Andrew Jackson laid out his signature policy. It would impact not just Cherokee Nation but all Indigenous nations living east of the Mississippi. They would be expelled from the territorial limits of the United States. It was a policy of ethnic cleansing. After it was drafted in committee, the bill was named the Indian Removal Act.

Cherokee Nation fought the bill in the halls of Congress and in the court of public opinion. In speeches and editorials, Elias and John argued their tribe had an inherent right to their land which came from possession since time immemorial and was guaranteed by treaties with the United States. Cherokee leaders leveraged their relationships with Christian missionaries, and the same organizations that had established churches in their nation and ran the school in Cornwall became the backbone of opposition to removal. The opposition was big. Protesters of the Indian Removal Act started the first national petition drive in the country's young history. (Before then, most petitions were about things like tariffs, lighthouses, or establishing new postal routes.) In the first national political action organized by women in the United States, 1,500 white women signed their names to memorials protesting the act. (This too was first modeled by Cherokees, where women had organized their own petition drives a decade earlier.) Opposition to removal planted the seeds for many white Northern Christians' involvement in the abolitionist movement and, in turn, women's suffrage.* In the US, still in its infancy, you could

---

*   Harriet Beecher Stowe, the younger sister of Catharine Beecher, who organized the women's petition drive, authored *Uncle Tom's Cabin*. George Cheever—whose mother signed the first petition delivered to Congress from Hallowell, Maine—would become a prominent abolitionist minister. Senator Theodore Frelinghuysen, who spoke against the Indian Removal Act, would later organize the (albeit problematic) abolitionist group the American Colonization Society.

hear the petitioners asking what kind of democracy their country would be. Treaties were not just promises to Indigenous nations, they argued, but, according to the Constitution, the supreme law of the land. If the US didn't follow its own laws, would not this grand experiment in democracy fail? To them it was clear the majority of Americans opposed the bill. If Congress rammed it through over their protest, then their democracy would no longer govern according to the will of the people.

The outpouring of public support was overwhelming. "There is no question," John Ridge would later write, "of the Cherokees having a vast majority of the people of the United States in their favor." While it is largely forgotten, Indigenous resistance formed the first large-scale political protest movement in the United States. It would not have been possible without Cherokee leaders educated in a white world.

When the Indian Removal Act was taken up by Congress, the debate was bitter. The fault lines it carved would stay in US politics for generations. As Southerners coveted Indigenous land, Cherokees found their allies in the North. On the House floor, New Jersey senator Theodore Frelinghuysen spoke for three days. He warned his colleagues God would "call down the thunders of his wrath" if the morally repugnant bill passed. When the senator from Georgia took the podium, he spoke even longer. He mocked the women's petitions, Northern religious leaders, and Cherokee resistance. Unbelievably, he argued removal was actually best for Cherokee Nation. In the natural order of things, Southern politicians claimed, white people and Indigenous people could not coexist. The difficulties facing Cherokee Nation, therefore, did not come from Georgia's violence, but because Cherokees lived too close to white people. In the pages of the *Phoenix* Elias retorted, "In the name of common sense, we ask, who makes the difficulties?"

In the Senate, where Southern states had more votes, the bill sailed through. The House, however, was a different story. When Georgia congressman Wilson Lumpkin reached the podium, he told his colleagues, "We have been inundated with memorials, pamphlets, and speeches made at society and town meetings. But, sir, let it be remembered that weak minorities always made the most noise. Contented majorities, conscious of their strength, are never found praying for a redress of grievances." Cherokee leaders had accomplished the impossible: galvanizing the American public to their cause. But it didn't matter. In this chapter of American history, the silent majority prevailed. On May 26, 1830, the Indian Removal Act passed the House of Representatives by a margin of only 5 votes.

Most often the histories of Indigenous dispossession and enslavement in the United States are taught separately, but these two systems of oppression needed each other. What we think of as the antebellum or Deep South was built on the land Southern lawmakers fought for and won in the Indian Removal Act. And in 1830, the South had an additional 21 votes in the House, because enslaved people—who of course could not vote— were counted toward Southern states' representation. Without those 21 votes, the bill would have never passed.

People say you cannot judge history by today's standards, but there is no need; it is not possible to judge removal more harshly than the activists of 1830 did. After the bill passed, they argued the "pillars" of democracy would "dissolve" and that God would punish our country for our sins. The United States would no longer be a beacon of democracy in the world and, in words that echo today, one newspaper asked, "With what face can we curse Russia for bathing Warsaw in blood?" One observer warned that the expulsion of Indigenous people from the South would "fix a stain upon the honor of this country, which can never be washed away."

Cherokee leaders, though, had not lost faith. Having failed to defend their homeland before both the president and Congress, they turned to the third branch of American democracy: the courts. When it had been time for the tribe to elect a principal chief, Major Ridge backed a man named John Ross. As the son of a Cherokee mother and Scottish trader, Ross grew up familiar with the white world; for his ability to navigate it, he was groomed for leadership. In 1830, a Northern Christian ally introduced Principal Chief John Ross to a lawyer from Baltimore. At first this lawyer, William Wirt, was not sympathetic to the Cherokee cause, but after conversations with Ross he came to believe that Georgia's actions were unconstitutional—and that the tribe could win in the Supreme Court. In a letter informing the National Council the tribe was hiring Wirt, Ross wrote, our "nation has every thing that is sacred at stake, and Georgia nothing."

At the time, the Supreme Court had heard only one case involving tribes: *Johnson v. McIntosh*. In that ruling from the previous decade, the Supreme Court decided Indigenous nations did not own their land, but were "occupants" or tenants—and that the United States was their landlord. After the Revolutionary War, the theory went, the US inherited the land from the British, and the British had owned it by right of "discovery." Title by discovery came from the pope, who, in the early years of colonization, had declared that any land, treasure, and even people belonging to non-Christian nations were free for the taking. This "doctrine of discovery" is still the law in the US today. It was cited by the Supreme Court as recently as 2005.

Over its illegal harassment, Cherokee Nation sued the state of Georgia. The Supreme Court agreed to hear the case. In *Cherokee Nation v. Georgia*, the tribe warned the court that if Georgia wasn't stopped, Cherokee Nation and the laws of the United States would "be swept out of existence together." In a rush to end the term, the court issued its opinion a few weeks later.

While the chief justice read his decision from the bench, John Ridge sat in the audience. The court did not answer the question of whether or not Georgia's actions were constitutional. Instead it was hung up on what, legally, Cherokee Nation was. Some of the justices believed Cherokee Nation was a foreign country with powers under the treaty clause of the Constitution. Others argued that Indigenous nations could not be sovereign because they were weaker than and dependent on the United States. Chief Justice John Marshall struck a precarious compromise—one that remains part of federal Indian law today. Tribes, he argued, had the right to self-govern, but they weren't foreign countries. Instead, he concluded, Cherokee Nation was a "domestic dependent nation."

The decision meant Cherokee Nation did not have legal standing to bring their own case, and left the tribe searching for another avenue. One of Georgia's harassment laws prohibited any white person from residing in Cherokee Nation without a permit from the state. The law was meant to target Christian missionaries, whom Georgia officials believed were encouraging Cherokees to resist. On March 12, 1831, the Georgia Guard rounded up all the missionaries. In chains, Samuel Worcester—the printer of the *Cherokee Phoenix* and a close friend of Elias Boudinot—was dragged over seventy miles to a Georgia prison where a jailer told him, "Here is w[h]ere all the enemies of Georgia have to land—Here and in Hell." Most missionaries either moved out of state or signed an oath of allegiance to Georgia, but two—Samuel Worcester and Elizur Butler—refused. This time representing Worcester and Butler, Wirt filed another petition to the Supreme Court of the United States. Like Patrick Murphy's lawyers, Wirt argued Georgia did not have jurisdiction to prosecute crimes on Cherokee land.

For three days, William Wirt and his co-counsel John Sergeant argued *Worcester v. Georgia* before the court. Georgia refused to participate. The case captured the nation's attention; so many members of the House of Representatives attended, the body was adjourned. Andrew Jackson was running for reelection the following November, and since the lawyers representing Cherokee Nation were also running (Wirt for president with the Anti-Masonic Party, and Sergeant for vice president with the National Republicans), the election was largely seen as a referendum on the Cherokee cause. Building on the foundation of Cherokee activism, Wirt argued Cherokee Nation had an inherent right to self-governance on their land, recognized by treaty. As Wirt spoke at length about the violence Cherokees faced, the chief justice was reportedly so moved he cried.

On March 3, 1832, the Supreme Court issued its decision. Chief Justice Marshall (who had previously written that tribes were "domestic dependent nations" who only had the right of "occupancy" to their land) dramatically reversed his position. Indigenous nations, he wrote, were "the undisputed possessors of the soil, from time immemorial." It was "extravagant and absurd," he went on, to think Europeans by establishing "feeble settlements" hugging the Eastern Seaboard, legally acquired "the lands from sea to sea." Under the Constitution, Marshall noted, Indian affairs were "exclusively" handled by the federal government. Georgia, as a state, could not alter the rights of Cherokee Nation under US law. Furthermore, treaties were the "supreme law of the land" under the Constitution and were no less binding if made with Indigenous nations than any other government. Therefore, Georgia's actions did not just violate the sovereignty of Cherokee Nation, but also the Constitution of the United States.

In conclusion, Justice Marshall wrote, on the land of Cherokee Nation "the laws of Georgia can have no force." The prosecution of the imprisoned missionaries was declared null and void.

Justice Marshall's three decisions (*Johnson v. McIntosh*, *Cherokee Nation v. Georgia*, and *Worcester v. Georgia*—often called the "Marshall trilogy") are considered the foundation of federal Indian law today. But rather than laying out clear and consistent rules, the decisions openly contradict one another. Contradictions are not uncommon in the arena of federal Indian law; current Supreme Court justice Clarence Thomas has even called it "schizophrenic." Putting the ableist metaphor aside, there is a better way to understand the complexity, says Ojibwe legal scholar Maggie Blackhawk. "It's a battlefield." As Native people resisted colonization they shaped US law, winning some fights and losing others. Cherokee legal advocacy created a legal foundation that both subjugates Indigenous nations and recognizes our inherent sovereignty.

When the *Worcester* decision came down, Elias Boudinot and John Ridge were in Boston. They had been on a speaking tour drumming up support and raising money for the Cherokee cause, drawing huge crowds of white allies.* Like so many other important moments in their lives, they celebrated the victory together. "It is a great triumph on the part of the Cherokees," Elias wrote back home. Cherokee Nation would no longer face Georgia's terror alone; after years of refusal, the federal government would have to intervene. Elias and John had dedicated their lives to learning English, American law, and how to navigate the white world. After so many defeats, their efforts finally paid off. It was a triumph for American democracy too. Two branches of our young republic pushed through a policy of ethnic cleansing that would have forever stained the honor of our

---

* From previous land cessions, the federal government owed Cherokee Nation an annual lump sum. But Jackson didn't want the tribe to spend it on litigation, and illegally stopped paying it.

country. But the third branch said no. Back home, runners delivered the news of the Supreme Court victory to every corner of Cherokee Nation. People danced until the sun rose. At long last, Georgia's reign of terror would end. On the land of their creation and by the graves of their ancestors, Cherokees could remain.

CHAPTER 5

The Appeal

JAMES FLOYD WAS DRIVING DOWN THE INTERSTATE—HIS WIFE BEHIND the wheel—somewhere between Norman and Okmulgee when his phone rang. In the summer of 2016, the principal chief of Muscogee Nation had been in office for about six months. For the busy tribal leader, a car ride to a distant meeting was a good time to talk. And so—looking out over the monotonous rhythm of trees and pavement—Floyd picked up. The call was about a letter. Patrick Murphy's public defender had been trying to get in touch with him. The lawyer wanted Muscogee Nation to join Patrick's case and argue that they still had a reservation.

Twelve years had passed since Lisa McCalmont found that roadside cross; the old team of federal public defenders had all changed jobs, and Lisa had passed away. The case changed hands a couple of times before Patti Ghezzi—who had sent that letter—became Patrick Murphy's lead counsel. She would stay on the case until the end.

It took Oklahoma courts over a decade to decide Patrick was *not* intellectually disabled—and therefore *could* be executed. That ruling allowed Patrick Murphy's federal habeas petition to finally move forward. On January 6, 2016, the Tenth Circuit Court of Appeals announced it would hear *Murphy v. Royal* on all grounds, including the question of tribal jurisdiction.* Meaning that the appeals court could soon up-hold—or undermine—Muscogee Nation's land rights. Federal appeals courts are one step below the Supreme Court, and—unless the Supreme Court intercedes—have the final word in most cases. If Muscogee Nation wanted to weigh in on whether or not they had a reservation, Floyd had only a few months to decide.

The call Floyd answered came from the tribe's attorney general. Over the low hum of the highway, they talked through the pros and cons of getting involved in Patrick Murphy's case. Heavy on Floyd's mind was George Jacobs's family; they were also citizens of his tribe. Floyd's family is from a small community called Trenton, less than a mile south of Vernon. His family cemetery is still there, and when Floyd travels back for burials and family gatherings he sometimes drives past the George Jacobs memorial. "There's people that are living and breathing and still dealing with the trauma of this case," he told me.

It is not unusual for death penalty appeals to take a long time. But Patrick's appeals stopped being about justice for George Jacobs, or even his own fight to stay alive. And Chief Floyd was far from the first tribal leader who didn't get to choose what case would decide his tribe's land and treaty rights. By the nature of federal Indian law, tribes often don't get to pick which legal vehicle will settle important issues. The only choice is whether or not they get in.

Floyd also worried about what would happen if Muscogee Nation got involved and lost. While the state was operating under the assumption that the Muscogee reservation no longer existed, previous federal court decisions had left the door open. A loss in *Murphy* could close the door. As he watched the green trees and exit signs whir past, the statements

---

* In a federal habeas petition, the inmate sues the warden of the prison where they are incarcerated. And so, the name of Patrick's lawsuit changed every time the warden at the Oklahoma State Penitentiary changed, which—amidst a series of botched executions—happened a lot. The Oklahoma State Penitentiary would cycle through wardens Sirmons, Workman, Trammell, Warrior, and Duckworth before the Tenth Circuit finally decided Patrick's case as *Murphy v. Royal*—the case name I will use for this chapter.

Chief Floyd

of tribal citizens—especially elders—echoed in his mind. "Before I was even chief, when I was out campaigning, people would say . . . we still have a reservation and nobody seems to recognize [it]," he remembers. "You gotta do something about it," they would tell him.

Ultimately, Floyd realized he didn't have a choice; Muscogee Nation couldn't sit on the sidelines. It's like the old saying "you gotta fish or cut bait," he told me. "We couldn't just continue to let this thing ride and let those attorneys bring this case without [us]." Floyd knew the case law; he knew the content of Muscogee treaties and the acts of Congress that impacted those terms. And he knew they still had a reservation. "We felt very strongly from the outset we could win," Floyd remembers. "The law was on our side."

While Muscogee Nation had their own lawyers, appellate litigation is a special practice. The tribe needed a law firm qualified to argue in front of the Tenth Circuit that was also familiar with federal Indian law. Fortunately, such a firm was already interested in the case. Philip Tinker learned about Patrick Murphy's case when he was still in law school. After serendipitously meeting Patrick's old college classmate at a conference, Philip got in touch with Patrick's public defender. For years, he volunteered on the case. Philip is a citizen of one of Oklahoma's thirty-nine tribes, Osage Nation, and as a young lawyer was convinced the blanket assumption that there were no reservations in Oklahoma was legally incorrect. When his tribe went to the Tenth Circuit in 2010 to defend their own reservation, they lost. Philip thought, just maybe, the *Murphy* case could change the tide.

Philip was alone in his prediction. On his first day at a law firm specializing in tribal sovereignty—Kanji & Katzen—Philip tried to convince his boss to get involved in Patrick's case. From his desk, Riyaz Kanji stared back at Philip. "So this case is challenging the conventional wisdom that there are no more reservations in eastern Oklahoma?" Kanji asked. "In a case with horrible, grisly, murder facts?"

Philip nodded.

"No way in hell are we taking this case," Kanji replied.

"As an experienced litigator, you know bad facts make bad law," Kanji told me years later. The professional opinion of most lawyers Philip talked to was that a brutal murder was not the proper legal vehicle to defend a tribe's land rights against a century of wrongheaded assumptions. In other words, everyone thought Patrick Murphy would lose. But Philip didn't give up. According to Kanji, for years Philip was in his office every week to bend his ear.

When the Tenth Circuit was ready to take up *Murphy*, Philip also heard from Patti Ghezzi, Patrick's public defender. He went into Kanji's office to plead his position one last time. That day, the conversation went differently. The Supreme Court had just issued an opinion in a separate reservation case. The ruling, in Kanji's mind, dramatically changed the odds that they could win. "Okay," he told Philip. "We should talk to the Nation."

Once they got connected, Muscogee Nation hired Kanji & Katzen. For the tribe, the law firm would file all the paperwork and argue the case before the Tenth Circuit. Once everyone was on board, they had only seven months to prepare what's called an amicus brief. *Amicus* is an arcane Latin term that simply means "friend." People who aren't party to a case, but have a stake in it, can file briefs supporting one side or the other. Muscogee Nation had only 9,333 words to explain to the Tenth Circuit why—although it hadn't been recognized in over a century—they still had a reservation.

The modern Muscogee Nation, of about a hundred thousand citizens, is the fourth-largest federally recognized tribe in the United States. In 2015, Chief Floyd was elected to a four-year term to lead the executive branch of their three-tiered government, which also includes a tribal council and court system, all headquartered in Okmulgee, Oklahoma. The Muscogee Nation tribal complex is a spacious campus north of downtown. Rising from the earth, the court building is designed after the tribe's traditional mounds. The modern executive building and the office of the attorney general sit on opposite sides of a gray parking lot. Across that block of concrete, and over the space between Okmulgee and the Kanji & Katzen office in Michigan, the team worked on *Murphy*. The chief and attorney general of Muscogee Nation still had the everyday work of running a tribe on their plates, but it seemed like *Murphy* was always the last thing they did before they went to sleep and the first email they saw in the morning. Chief Floyd remembers bringing piles of documents home to read over weekends.

The *Murphy* case was specifically about the status of the Muscogee Reservation, but there was widespread recognition that whatever the appeals court held for Muscogee Nation would probably apply to all five tribes—including Choctaw Nation, Chickasaw Nation, Seminole Nation of Oklahoma, and my tribe, Cherokee Nation. During allotment, Congress passed laws that applied to all five tribes. However federal courts interpreted those laws—as upholding or ending the Muscogee reservation—would likely extend to a much bigger area. While the Muscogee reservation is three million acres, the Five Tribes' territory taken together is 19 million acres, and 43 percent of the land in Oklahoma. There was tension, Chief Floyd admitted, between recognition of the tribes' shared interests, and not wanting to feed into Oklahoma's hysterical warnings that the decision would cleave the state in half. But still, leaders of the Five Tribes worked closely together. Chief Floyd kept other tribal leaders updated, and, at the Tenth Circuit, Seminole Nation of Oklahoma added their name to Muscogee Nation's brief.

According to Muscogee Nation's Attorney General Kevin Dellinger, the simplest way to summarize the question before the Tenth Circuit was whether "the 1866 reservation boundaries of the Muscogee Nation had ever been disestablished." Oklahoma argued that Congress got rid of the reservation during allotment, when communally held tribal land was divided and assigned to individual tribal citizens. But just like private land ownership does not change the map of the United States, allotment did not necessarily change the boundaries of a reservation. And the Supreme Court has a test to determine if it did.

The *Solem* test—named after the 1984 Supreme Court decision *Solem v. Bartlett*, which amalgamated previous court rulings—is a three-step "analytical structure" used to determine whether a reservation still exists. The first and most important step is straightforward: did Congress ever pass a law that disestablished or diminished the reservation? Like we would expect in any other area of the law, for Congress to do something it has to put it in writing. And according to *Solem*, "only Congress"—not Oklahoma or any other state—"can divest a reservation of its land."

If the language Congress passed is ambiguous or unclear, the *Solem* test engages a second step. In step two, courts can also look at congressional intent through contemporaneous evidence, such as congressional debate, reports to Congress, and communication with tribes, to determine what people understood to be the case at the time. Here, the courts are asking: Was it widely understood that a reservation was being diminished or extinguished? Or, based on evidence, did tribal leaders and Congress believe the reservation would continue? And lastly, in step three, courts can look at how the land has been used since. Who lives there now? Who lived there right after allotment? And is the tribe still there?

Courts were only ever supposed to look to steps two and three if step one was ambiguous. But—as often happens in federal Indian law—US courts kept bending the rules, and not to the benefit of tribes. In numerous cases, judges would skip step one to disestablish a reservation based on evidence from steps two and three. Meaning that Congress never passed a law to get rid of the reservation, but courts would decide that somehow that's what Congress meant to do. The cruel irony being that the US created an entire legal framework to seize Indigenous land, and then didn't follow its own rules.

A 2016 Supreme Court decision in *Nebraska v. Parker* finally changed the tide—just three months after the Tenth Circuit announced Patrick's case would move forward. Without a decade of delay due to the intellectual disability proceedings, *Murphy* could have easily fallen into the judicial trend that swallowed other reservations. To Philip, the timing was an "absolute miracle." To Riyaz Kanji, it dramatically altered his calculation of whether or not they could win. In *Nebraska v. Parker*, which asked whether or not the small town of Pender was still inside the Omaha reservation, the Supreme Court unanimously ruled the Omaha Tribe's reservation had never been diminished. In a decision authored by the conservative justice Clarence Thomas, the court relied on step one of the *Solem* test—and step one only. "As with any other question of statutory interpretation," Thomas wrote, "we begin with the text." In strong language, *Parker* told lower federal courts that where step one affirmed a reservation, the question was settled.

There was one big difference, however, between *Parker* and *Murphy*: the disputed area the Supreme Court upheld for the Omaha Tribe is part of one small town in rural Nebraska. In the *Murphy* case, the disputed area covered over three million acres, large parts of Tulsa, and vast oil and gas infrastructure.

For their amicus brief, Muscogee Nation's team compiled evidence for each step of the *Solem* test. For step one, they reviewed early twentieth-century laws and found that congressional language dissolving the Muscogee reservation simply did not exist. If the courts adhered strictly to precedent, that was all the team needed, but of course they couldn't rely on it. For step two, they compiled congressional reports and debates to show Congress also didn't *intend* to get rid of the reservation.

For step three, the Murphy team had to prove Muscogee Nation had never left their reservation. At the time, more than half of the tribe's citizens lived on or near the reservation boundaries, where the tribe provided many of the same public services as any other local government—law enforcement, healthcare, transportation infrastructure, and education. The small legal team reached out to every agency and gathered a huge amount of records. Of the dozens of examples they collected, only three or four made it into the brief.

When the public hospital in Okmulgee, their capital city, was struggling, the tribe took it over. Muscogee Nation also saved a rehabilitation center in Okmulgee and another hospital in Okemah. Those facilities serve tribal citizens and noncitizens alike. If the tribe hadn't intervened, some rural residents would have to drive an hour to reach an emergency room. I spoke with a former Oklahoma state senator whose nearly ninety-year-old mother used the tribe's healthcare facility to recover from a bad fall. Another Okmulgee resident used the tribe's rehabilitation center after her toddler developed a rare brain tumor; Muscogee Nation's healthcare workers helped the young girl relearn how to talk and walk. Neither family is Native. The same year *Murphy* went to the Tenth Circuit, Muscogee Nation supported nearly nine thousand jobs in Oklahoma. In a state where jobs are hard to come by, tribes are some of the top employers. It is worth noting that Oklahoma didn't need to present evidence that its government functioned. But the tribe did.

WHERE THE SOUTH MEETS THE MIDWEST, THE SKY UNLEASHES A SPE-
cial kind of rain that covers everything in a thin layer of ice. In the middle of one long workweek on *Murphy*, when most stores and offices were
closed, and the roads were unsafe, Attorney General Kevin Dellinger still
had to go in. The stressful drive rattled him. By the time he sat down at
his desk, he was in a bad mood. But then he saw something that gave him
pause.

"I have a picture called *The Trail of Tears*," Kevin told me. The painting
in his office depicted Muscogee people during the forced removal from
their homelands in the 1830s, to where they live now in Oklahoma. The
people had not been allowed to bring adequate supplies, so they walked
through the snow without warm clothing, some without shoes. "There
were people who had no choice other than to walk in these deplorable conditions. . . . They didn't know if they were going to make it or not. Didn't
know if the person next to them was going to make it or not." When Kevin
compared his sacrifice to the sacrifice of his ancestors, he felt selfish. "I
had a car to drive in. I had a coat to wear. I had a home that was heated,"
he thought to himself. "In that moment I felt very ashamed." When Kevin
thought about what his ancestors sacrificed so that there could even be a
Muscogee reservation, he knew he had to fight for it. "I can't explain. . . .
I'm at a loss for words," he thought, searching. "But I think we had to
honor those who came before us . . . no matter what the consequences."

Muscogee Nation filed their amicus brief on August 12, 2016. In
it, they stated the Muscogee reservation could not "be abrogated by the
march of time, the weight of popular assumptions, or even . . . a century
or more of State efforts to assert jurisdiction." Muscogee Nation wasn't
asking the Tenth Circuit to right the wrongs of history or give back their
land. Their reservation, legally, was still theirs. They were simply asking
the court to follow the law.

THE TENTH CIRCUIT COURT OF APPEALS IS IN AN AUSTERE, MARBLE
building in downtown Denver. Straddling three-story white pillars, an
etched inscription reads ERECTED IN THE YEAR NINETEEN HUNDRED AND
TEN. The marble face was built with stone from the same quarry as the

Lincoln Memorial. The building hears federal appeals from six western states, encompassing seventy-six federally recognized tribes—over half of which are in Oklahoma—and is the last stop before the Supreme Court. It took Patrick Murphy's case eighteen years to reach it.

Since Muscogee Nation was not technically party to the case, they had to ask the court for time during oral arguments to defend their reservation. The court allowed them ten minutes. David Giampetroni, an attorney at Kanji & Katzen, argued the case for the tribe. To prepare, Philip and David locked themselves in a Denver hotel room for six days, practicing the argument over and over again. With only ten minutes before the judges, every sentence counted. Philip doesn't remember what time he woke up on the morning of oral arguments, just that he didn't sleep well the night before. Philip, David, and the attorney general for Seminole Nation met in the lobby of the hotel and walked the few downtown Denver blocks to the Tenth Circuit. There, they met Patti Ghezzi and Patrick's defense team in a small room where they went over everything one last time.

The courtroom was the size of a small church. Rows of wooden benches faced a little brown gate. On the other side of the bar sat two broad tables. The lawyers for Patrick Murphy and Muscogee Nation sat at one. At the other, the lawyers for the state of Oklahoma. Looking down at them from the raised bench was the panel of three judges who would decide the case. After apologizing for stumbling over the pronunciation of her last name, Chief Judge Timothy Tymkovich invited Patrick Murphy's lawyer, Patti Ghezzi, to the podium.

Patti is soft-spoken, direct, and meticulous, but never gives a simple answer—in the way lawyers are apt to do. Her first job out of law school in the late seventies was at a small nonprofit that helped tribes and tribal citizens in court. There, Patti worked on her first death penalty case. The state of Oklahoma wanted to execute a teenager who had killed another student at the Chilocco Indian Agricultural School—a federally run boarding school created to assimilate Native youth and erase Native culture and peoples. In front of Oklahoma's highest court of criminal appeals, Patti argued the state didn't have jurisdiction because the crime happened on Indian land. She won.

After bouncing around a few public and private organizations, Patti landed in the Federal Public Defender's office for the Western District of Oklahoma in 2008. When she arrived, she was immediately handed Patrick Murphy's case. Nine years later, she approached the podium in the Tenth Circuit courtroom carrying a stack of notes. Patti didn't know which of the eight issues her client's petition raised the three judges would focus on, so she was prepared to argue each one. She spent her first ten minutes arguing it violated Patrick's constitutional rights when the Jacobs family asked the jury for his execution; the Supreme Court has ruled such statements are prejudicial. The prosecutor "did that on purpose," Patti said in conclusion. "Because he needed that evidence to get the death penalty." With that, she flipped a page in her stack of notes and started her next argument. "Regarding Indian country jurisdiction," she began.

"Haven't cases like Mr. Murphy's been prosecuted in Oklahoma state courts for pretty much over a hundred years?" one judge interrupted. It didn't matter, Patti rebutted, what actions Oklahoma had taken. "Only Congress can disestablish a reservation." Patti's slow, soft voice rose at the suggestion. "When you're talking about disestablishment, you can't presume it lightly," she told the judges emphatically. "You have to have clear and plain language." The lawyer for Muscogee Nation, David Giampetroni, also pushed this point. The Creek Allotment Agreement not only didn't get rid of the reservation, but in it Congress acknowledged "continued tribal and federal jurisdiction" over "the lands of the tribe."

When the assistant attorney general of Oklahoma took the podium, she asked the judges to look at "context." Congress "wanted to create a state," she said of the allotment era. It would have made "no sense" for half of that state to still be reservation land.

For Judge Scott Matheson, context wasn't enough. He repeatedly asked Oklahoma's lawyer if she could point to a specific sentence or phrase in an act of Congress that ended the Muscogee reservation. In one of the most significant exchanges of the day, she replied, "I cannot."

At the end of their allotted time, Chief Judge Tymkovich excused the attorneys. "Thank you, counsel. We appreciate the arguments this morning," he said in conclusion. "Difficult issue."

Unlike the public deliberations of Congress, federal courts make their decisions in private. After oral arguments, the judges take an informal

vote in a closed-door meeting and assign one judge to write the opinion. After the opinion is drafted, other judges can negotiate the details
before signing on. Only after it is finalized is the opinion released to
the public. For the Tenth Circuit, none of that happens on a set schedule. All the lawyers for Patrick Murphy and Muscogee Nation could do
was wait.

EARLY ONE TUESDAY MORNING, ABOUT FIVE MONTHS AFTER THE HEAR-
ing, Philip woke to his phone ringing. Still in bed, he answered. "We
won," David Giampetroni yelled over the line. "What did we win?" Philip
asked, still groggy from sleep. "*Murphy*," David said. "We won the whole
thing."

Philip remembers being excited, but David remembers something
else. According to David, Philip could not speak for several minutes. He
was sobbing. For David, as a lawyer, the victory was meaningful. But for
Philip, as a tribal citizen, it was personal.

To Philip, the decision felt like vindication. Like finally the courts saw
what he had been fighting for since law school: that when tribes have a
legal right to their land, it is not the role of courts to rewrite the rules to
take it away. "The reason we do this is because of the history," he told me.
After "the atrocities that have been visited on tribal communities . . . the
very least we can do is live up to the promises that were made."

Kevin Dellinger was already in the office when he got the call. Before
he had time to react, Kevin and his staff were headed across the gray parking lot to the executive building. They huddled in Chief Floyd's office.
The first emotion Floyd remembers feeling was relief. To him, the opinion affirmed what he had always known: that the reservation boundaries
were still intact. His relief, however, was tempered by his knowledge of
what came next. The team had no doubt Oklahoma would appeal to the
Supreme Court.

The Tenth Circuit opinion reads like a history lesson. For more than
120 pages, the court went through every law Congress passed in the
lead-up to Oklahoma statehood, and summarized the impact each had on
the treaty territory of Muscogee Nation. Kevin read it in detail, absorbing

every word. "I just got chills," he remembers. It wasn't some five-page opinion where the court glossed over the history. The court had done their homework. That "doesn't happen very often," Kevin told me. "Congress has not disestablished the Creek Reservation," the Tenth Circuit concluded. "The most important evidence—the statutory text—fails to reveal disestablishment at step one."

At the end of the decision was an order: Oklahoma no longer had jurisdiction to execute Patrick Murphy. "We therefore reverse the district court's judgment and remand with instructions to grant Mr. Murphy's application for a writ of habeas corpus under 28 USC statute 2254. The decision whether to prosecute Mr. Murphy in federal court rests with the United States. Decisions about the borders of the Creek Reservation remain with Congress."

WHEN YOU'RE STANDING ON VERNON ROAD, LOOKING EAST TOWARD the George Jacobs memorial, you can see for a long way. Across the cow pasture in the distance is a set of trees and, beyond that, cars hum by on the interstate. In the opposite direction, a ridge rises in the distance and continues along the horizon line until it disappears. You can see for miles.

When the Tenth Circuit Court of Appeals decided the state of Oklahoma didn't have jurisdiction to execute Patrick, the ruling wasn't about the place where George Jacobs died. It wasn't about the spot on the road or Ms. Smith's allotment or even the community of Vernon.

Their ruling upheld the reservation of Muscogee Nation. All three million acres.

CHAPTER 6

Betrayal

JOHN RIDGE AND ELIAS BOUDINOT WERE STILL ON THEIR SPEAKING tour of the Northeast when the Supreme Court handed down its ruling in *Worcester v. Georgia*. In no uncertain terms, the court ruled Georgia's reign of terror was unconstitutional and must end. But a troubling rumor was already circulating: President Jackson would defy the Supreme Court and ignore the decision. In our democracy, the Supreme Court does not have an army or police; it possesses only the power of the pen. For the court's decision to mean anything, the other branches of government had to carry it out. Jackson, as president, was constitutionally bound to do so. Which led John to believe the rumor would not be realized. "Georgians flatter themselves with the hope that General Jackson will not sustain the court," he wrote. "But in that event what becomes of the Union?" Immediately, he traveled to Washington to meet with the president.

When John Ridge arrived at the White House, the white building fronted by a semicircle of marble pillars was familiar. The seasoned diplomat had been there many times before. Face to face with the president, John argued the Supreme Court decision must be upheld, but Jackson refused. The genius of the Founding Fathers, we are told, was creating a system of checks and balances. Unlike the king of England, if the president stepped out of line, Congress or the Supreme Court would rein them in. But when Jackson defied the Supreme Court, nothing happened. The abuse of power went unchecked. John watched the constitutional crisis unfold. The Cherokee question, he wrote, was the greatest "crisis" that had ever been presented to "the American People." In the end, it would be another time John and his tribe leveraged their mastery of American law, only to learn the law didn't matter.

Cherokees' legal options were limited. They could call on Congress to impeach Jackson or ask the Supreme Court to hold Georgia in contempt, but as John stayed in Washington and met with white allies, none of it felt possible. John McLean, a Supreme Court justice who had fervently sided with Cherokee Nation, told John Ridge there was nothing else the high court could do. Congressional leaders who rallied against the Indian Removal Act advised John that Cherokee Nation was out of options. Even the Christian missionaries who created the school in Cornwall, once the backbone of opposition to removal, advised Chief Ross to sign a treaty. As Elias Boudinot wrote, there was not a "sufficient degree of interest for the welfare of the Aborigines in the United States . . . to save them from oppression."

When rumors spread in Washington papers that John was contemplating removal, he denied it. In his letters home he concealed his true feelings, but privately, the Cherokee leader was going through a painful reversal. From his education and years of diplomacy John could see what was politically possible—arguably more than most of his fellow Cherokees. John began thinking about the previously unthinkable: signing away the land of their ancestors in exchange for land out west. It's a heartbreak many oppressed people have known, but one we don't like to talk about because it shatters our notions of progress—the heartbreak of giving up on justice because you know it's not possible. What had changed was not John's desire for Cherokee Nation to remain in their homeland; it was his hope. In their private meeting, even Andrew Jackson sensed the emotional reversal taking place inside the Cherokee leader. In a letter to an old war buddy, Jackson called it "despair."

Three months after arriving in Washington, John Ridge and Elias Boudinot headed home. In a few short months, the cousins had anxiously awaited the *Worcester v. Georgia* decision, celebrated the legal victory, and came to the crushing realization that it didn't matter. Before departing Washington they met with the secretary of war to discuss possible terms for a removal treaty.

Georgia and the Jackson administration colluded to make life even more unbearable for Cherokees. Five months after John and Elias left Washington, Georgia illegally opened a lottery of all remaining Cherokee land in the state. By August, surveyors sectioned out what was left of Cherokee Nation, and by October, the names of eager settlers were placed in a hopper and the wheels started to spin. The winners descended on Cherokee Nation, driving families from their homes. A lucky lottery winner won Major Ridge's plantation and sold it while Ridge still lived there. Even Principal Chief John Ross came home to find Georgia speculators living in his house. Average Cherokees not insulated by material wealth were worse off; driven from their homes and farms, they were left with no food or shelter. Free and enslaved Black people in Cherokee Nation were kidnapped by white intruders and sold to Southern planters. In a letter to President Jackson, Cherokee leaders complained they were "left at the mercy of the White Robber and assassin." All that Jackson offered to escape the violence was removal. If they didn't move west, Jackson warned that Cherokee Nation's "condition must become worse and worse" until "you will ultimately disappear, as so many tribes have done before you."

SUNK IN THE EARTH AT RED CLAY, TENNESSEE, IS A FRESHWATER spring. The stream it creates runs clear over the rock and leaves of the valley floor, but at its mouth the water is so deep it turns aqua. After Georgia banished their government from its borders, Cherokee Nation moved their capital here. Four months after his meeting with Jackson, John Ridge stood before the National Council at Red Clay and tried to convince his countrymen that removal was their only option. Principal Chief John Ross almost didn't allow John to speak, but the Council wanted to hear him out. His proposal, however, was quickly voted down.

Major Ridge, John Ridge, and Elias Boudinot would spend the next three years writing petitions, making speeches, holding public meetings, and advocating for their fellow citizens to support a removal treaty. They became known as the treaty party. As Elias argued in one letter, what else could the tribe do? If Cherokees took up arms against the United States, they would likely face extermination. If they stayed and became US citizens, the tribe, as a sovereign nation, would cease to exist. Removal, to them, was the only option in which Cherokees, as a people and a nation, would survive. "Did we act in such emergencies as these for our private comfort, we might choose to die here, and bury our bones in the land of our fathers," they wrote in one letter. "Where white people might desecrate our tombs with the ploughshare of the farmer. But when we think of our children," they pleaded, "[we] will, at all hazards, seek freedom in the far regions of the West."

Major Ridge had fought wars, passed laws, and assassinated another Cherokee chief to protect his tribe's homeland. But he also spent those decades building something else: the central government of Cherokee Nation and a new kind of Cherokee nationalism. For years, he fought for both the land and the nation. When that became impossible, he chose Cherokee Nation. The quick reversal of the Ridges and Boudinot confused their fellow citizens and raised suspicion. In addition to treason, they would be accused of corruption, accepting bribes, and being unpatriotic. In a cruel twist of irony, Major Ridge had helped create the stern opposition to removal he now could not overcome.

As the political fault lines in Cherokee Nation deepened, Principal Chief John Ross came to represent the treaty party's opposition. Throughout the conflict, he maintained the support of the majority of the Cherokee people. Ross had once been Major Ridge's political protégé, and Ridge backed Ross's bid for chief. The treaty party accused Ross of lying to the Cherokee people and giving them false hope they could remain—a solution "Mr. Ross himself must've known would not be realized," Elias wrote. If Ross was guilty of anything, it was not deception, but denial. Where the treaty party saw there was no hope, Ross, like most Cherokees, would hold on to hope until the very end.

Ross explored other ideas—dissolving Cherokee Nation and accepting US citizenship, giving up most of their land but retaining a small portion, signing a removal treaty but asking for more money, and simply waiting out the Jackson administration—but he never adopted a clear and public position. For Ross, the role of the principal chief was not to decide for the people but to lead according to their will. If Ross did back a removal treaty, one observer wrote, he would have lost the support of his citizens "and probably his life." The US policy of ethnic cleansing left the leadership of Cherokee Nation in a difficult place; there was no path forward Cherokees would choose for themselves.

The treaty party did not—and never would—represent a majority of their fellow citizens. All they seemed to accomplish was deepening the existing political crisis. After Elias argued for a removal treaty in the *Cherokee Phoenix*, Ross censored him, and Boudinot resigned. Citing the escalating crisis, the National Council suspended upcoming elections, and later impeached John and Major Ridge. On his way home from a tense meeting, one of their supporters was shot and killed.

Meanwhile, Ross was in talks with the Jackson administration. Ross wanted $20 million for Cherokee Nation's homeland. After Jackson scoffed at the amount, Ross proposed letting the Senate—which would ratify any future treaty—decide. The plan backfired: the Senate capped any possible payment for Cherokee homelands at $5 million. John Ridge was also meeting with the Jackson administration. Though unauthorized, he drafted a proposed removal treaty that—according to its own terms— was "utterly invalid" until approved by the Cherokee people. When John Ridge presented his treaty to the National Council, they rejected it. He called a public meeting, but no one came. He colluded with a US agent to coerce better attendance, but the thousands who showed up voted him down. Following in the steps of Georgia, both Tennessee and North Carolina extended their laws over Cherokee Nation and started harassing its citizens; no piece of Cherokee territory was safe. Even the hope Ross had placed in the next presidential election was dashed: Andrew Jackson was elected to a second term.

AS THE JACKSON ADMINISTRATION AND SOUTHERN STATES WORKED TOgether to make life unbearable for Indigenous nations, different tribes sought different solutions. Some chose to stay on their land and become

US citizens, some agreed to move west, others took up arms. Most had factions that did all three. In the telling of our histories, some forms of Indigenous resistance receive more recognition than others. The truth is that no tactic stopped the US policy of ethnic cleansing. But every act of resistance helped us save what we still have—whether it's pieces of our homeland, language, ceremony, or the plain fact that we survived. As Cherokee leaders fought over the best path forward, they watched what happened to their neighbors.

The first treaty negotiated under the Indian Removal Act was the Choctaw Treaty of Dancing Rabbit Creek. Their exodus began in the fall of 1831. For the majority of Choctaw people, the idea of moving west was horrifying. Unlike the Christian belief system where Heaven was above the clouds and Hell was down below, for Choctaws both were on earth, just west. So when the US government told Choctaw people to move west says Choctaw historian Donna Akers, they were telling them to go to the land of the dead.

Overseen by the US government, the first detachments traveled by road. As they walked through the Mississippi swamps, the water was so deep parents had to hold their children over their heads. A large group of people got lost and fell behind. Choctaws traveling ahead begged the US official in charge to send a search party, but he said no. Eventually a group of Choctaw men went themselves. The lost Choctaws had given up on survival and started singing their death songs. Even the men were incoherent and had to be led out of the swamp "by the hand like you would little children," says Akers.

After Chickasaw Nation agreed to removal, they were owed a large sum of money for their homeland. The amount, though, slowly dwindled as the United States charged the tribe for every possible expense related to their expulsion. Chickasaw Nation paid the US government to survey their land, furnish army offices, advertise parcels for sale, and even to supply rations for Chickasaw emigrants who had already died. By financing their own removal, in a small token of grace, Chickasaw Nation traveled under comparatively better conditions than other tribes and saw significantly less death.

The journey to their new home, however, was only the first tribulation. When Chickasaws arrived, they had only what they carried; left behind were their homes, cultivated fields, stored food, and all the infrastructure necessary to survive. Smallpox started circulating through their camps. People arrived too late or were too sick that year to plant much corn and, after a devastating drought, what they managed to get in the ground yielded little. The company contracted to supply food complained that getting to the Chickasaw outpost was too difficult. In desperate letters, Chickasaw leaders pleaded for the promised rations, warning that without them their people would starve.

At the time of removal, Seminoles still made decisions on a community level; while some bands agreed to move west, the majority refused. In response, the army started gathering troops in Florida. During the Second Seminole War, Seminole people clung to their homeland by evading capture. They had to move so often that they could no longer plant corn, and survived by eating coontie roots. To track them down, the army purchased bloodhounds. After an embarrassingly large number of military defeats, the US Army resorted to trickery. Multiple times, when Seminole leaders came under a white flag of truce to negotiate peace they were captured and carted off as prisoners of war. It took seven years for the US Army to deport nearly four thousand Seminoles—several hundred were never captured. While the true number is unknown, historians estimate 20 percent of the population died.

AFTER MUSCOGEE PEOPLE WERE EXILED FROM GEORGIA, THE TRIBE'S land was reduced to five million acres in Alabama. In 1827, Alabama also extended its laws over Muscogee Nation, and white intruders swarmed their land. Driven from their homes, food stores, and crops, Muscogee citizens survived by eating the bark off trees. "Our aged fathers and mothers beseech us to remain upon the land that gave us birth," Muscogee leaders wrote to the Jackson administration. "Where the bones of their kindred are buried, so that when they die they may mingle their ashes together." Jackson in turn only increased the pressure. "I now leave the poor diluted Creeks and Cherokees to their fate," he wrote. "And their annihilation."

While Cherokees were waiting for the decision in *Worcester v. Georgia*,

Muscogee leaders sent a delegation to Washington, led by Opothle Yoholo. They wanted to remain on their homelands, but free from the terror of their Alabama neighbors. Muscogee leaders decided to dissolve their government and become US citizens. Under a treaty signed in March of 1832, the tribe's territory was divided up and each Muscogee family or citizen was assigned a piece of it. Anyone who wanted could sell their land and go west. Though the council still met, it was stripped of its legal power to negotiate with the federal government; they had little say in what happened next.

Private property was supposed to protect Muscogee citizens from white squatters, but land speculators only saw millions of acres in the hands of people with no legal rights. Speculators tricked Creek citizens into signing over their land, used torture and physical assault to coerce sales, and bribed often starving Muscogee citizens to impersonate their neighbors to draw up fraudulent papers. "If they cannot get it in any other way," US agents reported at the time, "they take the indian . . . & [choke] him until he gives it up." "The first thing we knew," Opothle Yoholo would later write, "the land was sold from under us." There was no moral low to which the intruders would not stoop; they robbed Creek graves of silver, and the corpses of their teeth to make dentures.

Opothle Yoholo desperately searched for a solution. He tried striking a bargain with the Jackson administration, which even opened an investigation into the rampant fraud and promised restitution. But then, in the spring of 1836, some 3,000 Muscogee citizens staged an open revolt. They killed white settlers, raided farms, and burned down a mail station, steamboats, and other buildings. The secretary of war demanded his general collect Muscogee citizens and send them immediately west of the Mississippi. The majority of the tribe did not participate in the uprising, but that did not matter. It was pretense enough to remove everyone: 2,495 "hostile Creeks" were marched to Montgomery in chains and loaded onto a steamboat. One group running from US forces killed their own children rather than be captured. When the military transported the prisoners of war west, one steamboat split in half and over 300 people drowned. The army ordered the remaining bulk of the tribe, more than 12,000 people, to collection points for their deportation.

So white invaders would not benefit from their cultivation, Muscogees chopped down their fruit orchards. Alabama sheriffs and constables raided the camps and arrested Muscogee citizens on trumped-up claims to steal what few possessions they had left. Leading the first detachment going west, Opothle Yoholo danced and stayed awake the whole night before they left. Each Muscogee town took care to keep their council fire alive through these acts of cruelty. The fires they carried still burn in Oklahoma today.

The roads leading west were rudimentary and routed through swamps. Unable to move their feet, horses and mules died in the mud. Sickness and death increased. "Old men & women & children dropping off," one army official recorded. To make the tide of death more traumatic, they could not bury their dead; bodies were hastily covered with brush and later eaten by animals. Many people "died absent from their friends" Opothle Yoholo wrote in a letter. "And we are sorry."

During their long journey, the heat and humidity of August turned into the freezing cold of winter. The temperature dropped to zero. The contractors had told Opothle Yoholo and his people to not weigh down the wagons with too many personal items—including winter clothing. Instead the items would be shipped by boat, but the contractors lost the freight. While Muscogee citizens walked through eight inches of snow, their winter clothes were stranded in the Gulf of Mexico.

Of the 12,648 Muscogee citizens forced to march west that year, 3,500 died.

When the US decided it would round up and exile the Indigenous nations living east of the Mississippi, it was 80,000 people. On the scale of today's US population, it would be like forcibly relocating the city of Houston. Expelling our tribes from our homelands was one of the largest—and most expensive—projects the young federal government had ever attempted. As historian Claudio Saunt has tabulated, the federal government spent, in today's currency, one trillion dollars—or $12.5 million per deportee—on removal. Some years, it was nearly half of the entire federal budget. Despite the high cost, the policy actually made money because the government turned around and sold Indigenous lands for profit. The profits claimed by the US Treasury pale in comparison to the money reaped by enterprising US citizens and corporations. Because land speculators acquired the land for almost nothing, the profits they reaped were unimaginable.

The final wave of profiteers were the men who sat atop the slave economy. In the decade following the Indian Removal Act, over three hundred thousand enslaved people were moved from the Eastern Seaboard to the Deep South. For enslaved families, this Second Middle Passage broke apart an estimated one in five marriages and separated a third of children from their parents. With cheap land and free labor, the cotton economy boomed. By the close of the decade, cotton production in Mississippi increased tenfold, and by the time of the Civil War, the Mississippi River Valley had more millionaires per capita than any other place in the US. While the human suffering generated by the Indian Removal Act is too great to ever be calculated, so too are the profits.

WHILE CHEROKEE LEADERS DEBATED THEIR OWN SURVIVAL THEY watched the United States force west Choctaws, Chickasaws, and Muscogees, and the beginning of the Second Seminole War. It seemed that no solution would save their homeland or their lives.

Amid deepening divisions, in the summer of 1835, John Ross reached out. After a closed-door meeting with Elias, John, Major Ridge, and other members of the treaty party, the two factions agreed on a compromise. They would send a joint delegation to Washington to negotiate a final settlement of the difficulties facing Cherokee Nation. The delegation, headed by John Ross, would include John Ridge and Elias Boudinot. For a moment, compromise looked possible.

Though Cherokee Nation had elected representatives, important decisions were still voted on directly by the people. That fall, thousands gathered around the blue spring water of Red Clay to vote on the compromise. But what, exactly, they decided quickly became confused. The crowd gave the delegation authority to enter a treaty with the United States, but voted down selling their homeland for $5 million. The Senate had already capped the value of the Cherokees' land at $5 million, so the vote precluded any treaty. Even the delegation wasn't sure what was decided. Elias accused Ross of creating the confusion on purpose and resigned from the delegation. John Ridge suspected Ross wanted to dissolve Cherokee Nation and make them US citizens, and also threatened to resign. Ross, desperately trying to hold everything together, pleaded with John to continue to Washington and, begrudgingly, he did. Major Ridge and Elias stayed behind.

To negotiate a removal treaty, President Jackson sent the Reverend John Freeman Schermerhorn to Cherokee Nation. Cherokees so despised Schermerhorn they nicknamed him "devil horn." Before the delegation left for Washington, Schermerhorn warned any treaty would have to be negotiated through him. When the delegation ignored his demands, Schermerhorn called his own meeting. He hung paper notices around Cherokee Nation inviting citizens to meet on the third Monday of December in the old capital city New Echota. Whoever did not attend, the paper warned, would "give their ascent and sanction to whatever is done at this council." When the date arrived, Major Ridge and Elias Boudinot were there.

Unlike the official meetings of Cherokee Nation where thousands gathered, the meeting at New Echota was small. Only three hundred people came. Though unelected, the body created their own self-appointed treaty delegation, and began voting on resolutions. On Christmas Eve, Major Ridge addressed the group. "I am one of the native sons of these wild woods. I have hunted the deer and turkey here, more than fifty years," he said, translated into English. "I know the Indians have an older title than theirs. We obtained the land from the living God above. They got their title from the British. Yet they are strong and we are weak. We are few, they are many. We cannot remain here in safety and comfort. I know we love the graves of our fathers. . . . I would willingly die to preserve them, but any forcible effort to keep them will cost us our lands, our lives, and the lives of our children."

On the seventh night, the treaty party met in the home of Elias Boudinot. The once bustling capital square was quiet. By candlelight, the men signed their names to the Treaty of New Echota. Unable to read or write in English, Major Ridge signed his name with an X. He told the others, "I have signed my death warrant."

The Treaty of New Echota opens with a long preamble. In it, the drafters explained that life for Cherokees on the land of their ancestors had become unbearable; to relieve their suffering, removal was necessary. Unlike previous treaties John Ridge had negotiated with the Jackson administration, there was no language requiring approval by the Cherokee people. In exchange for $5 million—plus compensation for property left behind, the cost of removal, and subsistence for one year after—Cherokee Nation would relinquish all of their land east of the Mississippi. The tribe would be granted a delegate in the US House of Representatives, and their new home would never "be included within the territorial limits or jurisdiction of any State" without their consent. To protect the "health" of Cherokees moving west, the treaty stipulated enough physicians, steamboats, and wagons for the journey. While this detail was later removed by the Jackson administration, the original treaty included a provision for those who did not want to go: they would be assigned land and become citizens of the United States.

The most consequential clause of the treaty didn't stand out at first. It set a deadline. Cherokees, the clause read, "shall remove to their new homes within two years from the ratification of this treaty."

When Cherokees found out about the fraudulent treaty, they immediately began organizing against it. They held a meeting at Red Clay and in a month collected 3,352 signatures. In February, they sent a second petition, this time signed by over 14,000 Cherokees—nearly 90 percent of the nation. The petitioners argued that the treaty was fraudulent and could not be legally binding. They warned if Cherokees did leave their ancestral lands under the treaty, it would "be by force."

When the treaty party arrived in Washington, John Ridge left the Cherokee delegation and added his signature to the Treaty of New Echota. For the treaty to be legally binding, it had to be ratified by the Senate. Ross had clear proof the treaty signers were unauthorized to represent the nation, but the Ridges were skilled diplomats and, of course, had the support of the Jackson administration. On May 17, 1836, the Senate ratified the Treaty of New Echota by a margin of one vote.

The accusations of corruption and bribery against Major and John Ridge began immediately and persist today. There is no evidence of bribery. The reason for their betrayal is much sadder: it was the only way they thought Cherokees would survive. "John Ridge may not die tomorrow," John wrote in the third person. "But sooner or later he will have to yield his life as the penalty for signing." It is one thing to choose a death of honor. It is another to choose a death of disgrace. The Ridges forfeited their lives for the Cherokee cause knowing they would be remembered not for their sacrifice, but for their treason.

The treaty was, however, wholly undemocratic and illegal. The Cherokee people had voted down a removal treaty—through public meetings and their elected representatives—multiple times. By circumventing democracy, the treaty denied "Cherokees the right to think for themselves." The treaty party's justification for their illegal act was the immense suffering of the Cherokee people. But shouldn't the Cherokee people—as they argued at the time—decide how best to relieve their own suffering? And under the treaty, their suffering would get immeasurably worse.

A year after the Treaty of New Echota was ratified, the treaty party traveled to Indian Territory in relative comfort. Major Ridge and John Ridge moved to the very northeastern corner of Cherokee Nation's reservation. On a small tributary to the Neosho River called Honey Creek, they built homes, opened a general store, and rebuilt their plantations with enslaved labor. Elias Boudinot moved to Park Hill some fifty miles south, where he worked on translating and printing religious texts. Elias and the Ridges showed no interest in reentering Cherokee politics. Perhaps they knew what would come next. Perhaps they were trying to avoid it by laying low.

Two years after the ratification, only 2,000 Cherokees had emigrated. The majority refused. "Not one man in twenty is willing to . . . submit to the terms of the treaty," one army official wrote. While fighting the treaty in Washington, Ross told his people to stand firm against the treaty, and that the US government would eventually "give up" on enforcing it. Jackson was scheduled to leave the White House in 1837, and Ross was again hopeful a US election might save Cherokee land. Jackson's vice president, Martin Van Buren, was elected, and told Ross the treaty terms would not change. The last petition Cherokees sent to Washington was signed by nearly every Cherokee man, woman, and child—by over 15,000 people in a nation of 16,000. John Ross hand-delivered it to Congress in the spring of 1838. But as Ross and the Cherokee government scrambled for a political solution, the two-year deadline set by the treaty ran out.

HISTORIANS STILL DEBATE WHETHER OR NOT THE UNITED STATES COMmitted genocide against Indigenous peoples. The crime has never been acknowledged by our government. At the time, the term did not exist. The word "genocide," coined in 1944 during the Holocaust, combines the Greek prefix *genos*, which means race or tribe, and the Latin suffix *cide*, meaning killing. In 1948, the crime was defined by the United Nations as the "intent to destroy, in whole or in part, a national, ethnical, racial or religious group" by one or more acts of physical violence including "killing members of the group," "causing serious bodily or mental harm to members of the group" and "deliberately inflicting on the group conditions of life calculated to bring about its physical destruction."

The Cherokee word for our removal is ᏗᏁᏛᏓᏍᏔᏅ. It literally means "when they drove us." It's the same word we use to talk about herding animals.

To prepare, the army split logs, drove them into the ground lengthwise, and built twenty-five open-air stockades. The majority of Cherokee people believed the treaty was still being renegotiated, and that, if successful, they would stay. Earlier that spring they had planted their fields of corn, looking toward the fall harvest. When the deadline set by the treaty arrived, men were out hunting, women were plowing fields, children were visiting friends and relatives. On May 23, 1838, 7,000 US soldiers and militiamen went out into the hills and valleys of Cherokee Nation to round them all up.

Cherokees, startled by bayonets in their gardens or kitchen, were not allowed to collect any possessions for the journey or to find their loved ones. They were forced to cross rivers in their only shoes. When a deaf man did not understand the militiamen's orders, they shot him. At gunpoint, the militia drove a woman in labor from a remote valley town to the main concentration camp. Even after she gave birth, they would not let her rest. Finally, on a riverbank near the stockade, she lay down and died. Over 15,000 people were herded into the camps. The US Army general in charge of the operation had estimated the roundup would take twenty days. It took twenty-five.

The army was woefully unprepared to feed and house their thousands of captives. The open-air stockades provided no shelter or sanitation—there was not even a place to use the bathroom. At night, militiamen roamed the camps, abducting and assaulting Cherokee women. June and July brought one of the hottest summers in people's memory, and with the heat came disease. The deaths of Indigenous people from disease throughout history is treated like an unfortunate act of God, instead of a predictable outcome of extreme violence and deprivation. "We should find little astonishment," a physician at one of the camps wrote, "at finding a high-grade" of illness and death. By fall, Cherokees had buried 2,000 of their fellow citizens. As a newspaper reported at the time, "that is one eighth of the whole number, in less than four months."

Though under unimaginable duress, the Council continued to meet and decided Cherokees would be safer if they could organize the deportation themselves. The army agreed—in large part because Cherokees had deserted the first four detachments by the hundreds. So those that remained in the camps, the majority of the tribe, migrated under their own supervision. The passive resistance of Cherokee citizens saved untold lives.

To try to stem the tide of disease, the leadership of Cherokee Nation decided to wait for colder months to travel. The hottest summer in memory turned into the coldest winter. While the Cherokee-led detachments saw significantly less loss, the trips were still plagued by death. A woman who gave birth on the journey was found dead the next morning with her baby still in her arms. The white landowner nearby would not let her family bury the body so, by wagon, they carried the corpse. People walked over a thousand miles; the footsteps of thousands left a trench in the earth.

Although the exact number is unknown, one missionary estimated 4,000 people died between the camps and removal—a quarter of the total population. Loss of life at this scale compounds with the children who were never born. Cherokee scholar Russell Thornton argues that the total loss of population, including the sharp decline in birth rates, is closer to 10,000—out of a population of 16,000 people.

———

IF THE TREATY OF NEW ECHOTA HAD NOT FORCED CHEROKEES INTO concentration camps, perhaps the removal, though inevitable, would have been less violent. Under that logic, the treaty party was directly responsible for the deaths of thousands. Or maybe, like with the Muscogees, the US government would have found some other pretense to round Cherokees up. It's hard not to ask of history, What if? But laying those questions at the feet of Cherokees, instead of the United States, is asking the victims how best to survive genocide.

During what came to be known as the Trail of Tears, John Ross maintained the confidence and faith of the Cherokee people. The treaty party and the Ridges were blamed for their immense suffering. "They are considered traitors to their country," one missionary wrote. As a young warrior, Major Ridge had witnessed his attack on illegal white settlers result in the retaliatory deaths of eleven people in Pine Log. The weight of it changed him. Now, as an old man, he watched as his decision to sign the Treaty of New Echota resulted in the deaths of thousands. What he felt must have been greater than guilt or remorse. Perhaps it was horror.

Shortly after the last detachment arrived, a public meeting was called between the Western Cherokees and the survivors of the Trail of Tears. Since the late 1700s, generations of traditional Cherokees had moved west to escape white encroachment and lived under their own government. With the addition of the treaty party who arrived a year before the roundup, they numbered about eight thousand. The Western Cherokees wanted the survivors of the Trail of Tears to recognize their government. The survivors, however, argued that they constituted the majority of Cherokee people and wanted their government from the east to continue. To the surprise of many, Major Ridge, John Ridge, and Elias Boudinot came to the meeting. Their presence angered many, and rumors spread that they were influencing the Western Cherokees to hold out against compromise.

After the sun set on the meeting's final day, a group of men gathered in a small cabin. Invoking the very law John and Major Ridge had helped pass—that the punishment for unlawfully ceding Cherokee land was death—the men decided to execute them for treason. Passing around a hat with pieces of paper inside, those who drew an X were chosen as the assassins. John Ross's son was told to guard his father's house and keep him ignorant of their plot. The men split into three groups: one for Major Ridge, one for Elias Boudinot, and one for John Ridge. By morning, the assassins were on their way to find their targets.

As the sun came up that day, John Ridge and his family woke to a loud noise. A group of armed men kicked in their front door. They dragged John from his bed into the front yard, shouting to drown out his pleas; they had been told he was very persuasive, and to not let him speak. Sarah, John's wife, tried to run to him, but she was held back in their doorway. Two men held John's arms, while others held his body. They stabbed him twenty-nine times. They threw John's body up into the air and stomped on his chest until it caved in. Then, as quickly as they had appeared, they left. John was still alive when his wife, Sarah, was finally able to reach him. Laying in their front yard, propped up on an elbow, he tried to speak to her. But all that came out of his mouth was blood.

Boudinot was walking toward his house when a group of Cherokee men approached him, asking for medicine. As he turned to fetch it, they stabbed him in the back and drove a hatchet through his skull. Elias lived long enough for his old friend Samuel Worcester and his wife to find him on the ground, barely breathing. Major Ridge was traveling to Arkansas that morning. Where the road crossed a wide creek, the assassins waited in ambush. When they saw Major Ridge approach, they shot him five times. He slumped in his saddle, then fell off his horse.

Sarah had sent a runner to warn her father-in-law, Major Ridge, of the danger. The runner returned with the news he too was dead.

Two weeks after the assassinations, John Ross called another public meeting. Members of the Western Cherokee attended, but their formal government was not represented. The assembled Cherokees voted to reinstate the government of Cherokee Nation from the east, and granted amnesty to all who had murdered Elias Boudinot, Major Ridge, and John Ridge. In an attempt to prevent retaliatory violence, they extended a pardon to other treaty signers, as long as they did not avenge the recent murders. It did not work. The bloodbath nearly turned into civil war. Family

members of the treaty party avenged the deaths of their loved ones, spur-
ring even more retaliatory violence. "Murders in the country have been
so frequent," one missionary wrote. "Until the people care as little about
hearing these things as they would hear of the death of a common dog."

For years the federal government used the violence as an excuse to
meddle in the tribe's affairs. In response, Ross argued Cherokee Nation
was sovereign, ironically using the language of the Treaty of New Echota.
"The whole treaty of 1835, from beginning to end," he wrote, guaranteed
to Cherokee Nation that they could live and govern themselves forever on
their land "without molestation or interference." Otherwise, Ross argued,
the treaty party never would have signed it.

COUNTY ROAD 340 WINDS THROUGH THE EASTERN EDGE OF DELAWARE
County, hugging the Oklahoma state line. When you near Missouri, a
small family cemetery sits on the left-hand side. Specks of white and gray
tombstones dot the green landscape of old barns and wide cow pastures.
A rusted, painted metal gate marks the cemetery's entrance, upon which
the family name "RIDGE" stretches out in tall letters.

After the murders, John Ridge's family feared more violence, so they
buried him under the darkness of night. His hasty grave was the first
plot in what is now my family cemetery. Next to John lies his father, Major Ridge, and mother, Susanna. Fanning out from there are branches
of family organized in clusters and rows. Today the cemetery holds five
generations of my family. When I am eventually laid to rest, I will be the
seventh.

By my grandmother I was raised to believe the assassinations were
vengeful and wrong. After reading old family letters written by people
alive to witness these violent deaths, I understand where her belief came
from. As an adult, however, I do not agree. For what they did, I think the
Ridges had to die.

According to the very law Major Ridge had helped pass, the punishment for unlawfully ceding Cherokee land was death. And unlike the
republic of the United States at the time, our much older democracy
followed the law. According to an even older law—our traditional blood

law—for the souls of those who died on the Trail of Tears to travel on to the next world, their deaths had to be avenged. Otherwise their blood would forever cry out for justice. From that view, the deaths of my family members allowed the souls of thousands to rest in peace. How could that not be justified?

The Ridges are still considered traitors by a majority of Cherokees, a fate I think they accepted before they died. If what they had been trying to save was their own legacy, they never would have signed the treaty. What I believe they truly cared about, however, did come true. Cherokees, as a nation and a people, are still here.

Part II

CHAPTER 7

The High Court

A LITTLE MORE THAN A YEAR AFTER THE TENTH CIRCUIT COURT OF Appeals upheld the Muscogee reservation, Chief James Floyd found himself in a hotel lobby in downtown Washington, DC. Sparse clouds cast irregular shadows on the downtown glass and concrete. On the other side of the revolving hotel door, the capital city echoed with its usual early morning sounds: car horns, the footsteps of commuters, and the low groans and high screeches of city buses pulling up to a stop. In the lobby, Chief Floyd met the rest of the delegation traveling from Muscogee Nation: the attorney general, Speaker of the Council, and the chief and deputy chief of the tribe's Lighthorse Tribal Police Department. Like generations of tribal leaders before them, they had come to the seat of government to advocate for their treaty rights. From the hotel, the men got in a car and headed to the Supreme Court.

After the Tenth Circuit ruled that the reservation of Muscogee Nation had never been disestablished, Oklahoma appealed. The only court above the Tenth Circuit is the Supreme Court of the United States. "I thought there was a chance we might be able to keep the case out of the [Supreme] Court," Riyaz Kanji, Muscogee Nation's lawyer, told me. After all, the high court had just decided another reservation case—*Parker*—in favor of the tribe, applying the same legal principles and tests raised in *Murphy*. If there was a question of constitutional interpretation or precedent, it had been asked and answered very recently. But then the Trump administration did something unusual: the solicitor general of the United States asked the Supreme Court to overrule the Tenth Circuit decision. It is not uncommon for the Supreme Court to invite the federal government to share its opinion on specific cases, but the Trump administration did so without an invitation. After that, "all the people with Supreme Court chops were like, that's done," Kanji told me. "They're going to take it." Typically, the Supreme Court is asked to hear over seven thousand cases each year. In 2018, they took seventy-two. On May 21 that year, the court announced *Carpenter v. Murphy* would be one of them.

Before entering the courtroom, the Muscogee delegation had to go through security. The guards looked them over carefully. Weeks before, the high court had heard a case involving Yakama Nation. When their tribal council chairman had arrived wearing regalia and a headdress, he was asked to leave. A court official explained that any attire that could be perceived as advocating for one side or the other was not allowed. Under that reasoning—while Western dress was not questioned—traditional Yakama attire was barred. The Muscogee delegation were all in suits and ties, but—much like presidents and senators wear little American flags on their suit jackets—the chief of the Lighthorse had a lapel pin bearing the seal of Muscogee Nation. He was asked to take it off. "Do you have anything that's going to make the justices feel that you're advocating one side or the other?" Chief Floyd remembers one guard asking him. "Well, I'm dark," he replied.

While the official delegation for Muscogee Nation made their way through security, Rosemary McCombs Maxey, lifelong member of the Weogufkee Baptist church, was standing outside "freezing to death." The public can attend Supreme Court hearings, but they cannot reserve a seat. If you want to watch in person, you have to wait in line. Rosemary was planning on arriving at 5:30 a.m. but a friend called at 4 a.m. and said the line was already getting long. The Supreme Court building occupies an entire city block in Washington, DC; by the time Rosemary got there, the line stretched around it.

Rosemary McCombs Maxey

Rosemary had known about the George Jacobs murder; on their way to church on Sunday mornings, Rosemary and her mother would drive through Vernon, and Rosemary would hear the story. She hadn't known George personally, but she knew some of his siblings. It was wild, for Rosemary, to watch that small-town murder make it all the way to the Supreme Court. While she huddled in the cold, she watched the sun rise over the white dome of the Capitol.

By the time *Murphy* reached the Supreme Court, the odds of victory were stacked against the tribe. From the 1950s to 1990, tribes or tribal interests lost the majority of cases brought before the high court, but by a small margin. Starting in the nineties, that margin grew. In the past thirty years, tribal interests have lost two-thirds of all Supreme Court cases. Rather than counting on the Supreme Court to advance or even uphold the sovereignty of Indigenous nations, tribal leaders have watched the high court roll it back.

The legislative and executive branches of the US government have also done immeasurable harm to Indigenous nations, including forcing Indigenous people into concentration camps, systematically removing their children, sterilizing Native women, and outlawing traditional religions and ceremonies. But starting in the 1970s, Indigenous advocates and nations gained more power. At the time, tribes were pulling themselves out of the termination era (during which Congress "terminated" over a hundred tribes by writing them out of legal existence). In response, grassroots activists started the Red Power movement and the American Indian Movement, and tribal leaders lobbied hard in DC. Together they brought about the self-determination era, during which Congress finally recognized that tribal governments know what is best for their citizens and land. In the decades following, Congress passed laws protecting religious freedom, Native families, sacred sites, and tribal self-governance. While far from perfect, the laws coming from Congress started to do more good than harm. At the same time, large setbacks for tribal sovereignty started to come from the Supreme Court.

In 1978—the same year Congress passed laws protecting Native families and restoring religious freedom—the Supreme Court decided *Oliphant v. Suquamish Indian Tribe*. At a large annual celebration that drew thousands of people to the Suquamish reservation, a white man named Mark Oliphant got in a drunk fight. When tribal police tried to place Oliphant under arrest, he fought back. In tribal court, he was charged with disorderly conduct and resisting arrest. Several months later, Oliphant was a passenger in his friend Daniel Belgrade's car when Belgrade also tried to evade arrest—this time in a high-speed car chase. The chase ended when Belgrade crashed into a tribal police car.

Before Mark Oliphant was brought to trial, he filed a federal habeas petition arguing the Suquamish Indian Tribe couldn't prosecute him because he wasn't Native American. He lost twice in federal court, but together with Belgrade appealed his case all the way to the Supreme Court. The Supreme Court ruled in the men's favor, concluding that "while Congress never expressly forbade Indian tribes" from imposing "criminal penalties on non-Indians" it was "the commonly shared presumption" that tribes could not.

Today, other than exceptions carved out by the Violence against Women Act, tribes are prohibited from prosecuting non-Natives who commit crimes on tribal land. This means any non-Native person can enter a reservation and steal a car, murder someone, or just break the speed limit, and the tribe is prohibited from prosecuting them. What followed *Oliphant* was an explosion of violent crime in Indian country, especially against Native women, children, and two spirit relatives.* Native women are more likely than any other racial or ethnic group to experience sexual violence and domestic assault. According to the Department of Justice, four out of five Native women will experience violence in their lifetime. Ninety-seven percent of these women have been the victims of crimes perpetrated by someone who is not Native.

Three years before the Supreme Court issued its decision in *Oliphant*, a federal judge in Montana ruled that tribes didn't have civil jurisdiction over non-Natives, either. Criminal jurisdiction is simply the authority to prosecute crimes, but civil jurisdiction is much broader. It includes the

---

* "Two spirit" is an umbrella term for members of the Native American LGBTQ+ community.

ability to bring forth lawsuits, enact family law, regulate pollution, issue protective orders, and grant business licenses and, in this case, hunting and fishing permits. The case started with a local white resident, James Junior Finch, posing for a photograph while casting his lure into the Bighorn River on the Crow reservation. According to the laws of the Crow Tribe, Finch couldn't fish there, but Finch didn't think the tribe could tell him what to do. The exact place where Finch fished, while within the Crow reservation, was fee land. Fee land lies within a reservation, but because of allotment is no longer owned by the tribe or a tribal member.* The litigation took place against a background of racial hostility: local white residents were mad that they couldn't fish on the Bighorn River. And so, in defiance of tribal law, they fished anyway, leaving their beer cans, threatening tribal police and even calling them racial slurs.

The United States government, the state of Montana, and the Crow Tribe all joined the legal battle over who could regulate fishing on fee land within the Crow reservation. When *Montana v. United States* finally reached the Supreme Court, the justices were divided. They ultimately decided tribes do not have civil jurisdiction over non-Natives on fee land, except for two special circumstances: when a non-Native person or business has entered into a consensual relationship with the tribe—like a contract—or if their conduct threatens "the political integrity, the economic security, or the health or welfare of the tribe." Illegal fishing did not meet the elusive *Montana* exceptions—a bar that has since proven difficult for all tribes to meet. Meaning, if a non-Native business pollutes a reservation, a pharmacy floods tribal communities with opioids, or a domestic violence survivor needs a protective order, there is little the tribe can do. Private property doesn't change civil jurisdiction for cities and states. But for tribes, thanks to the Supreme Court, it does.

Harmful Supreme Court decisions continued into the twenty-first century, and in 2005, one of them came from a justice you might not expect: the late Ruth Bader Ginsburg. After the Oneida Nation bought back

---

* Fee land also includes land that has ever left the ownership of the tribe or tribal member or—using the language of allotment—is no longer restricted.

land that was illegally ceded to the state of New York, the city of Sherrill wanted the tribe to pay property taxes. In *City of Sherrill v. Oneida Indian Nation of New York,* the Supreme Court ruled that the disputed land could not be placed back under tribal jurisdiction because the original theft happened so long ago, and it would cause too much of a disruption to change it now. Writing for the majority, Justice Ginsburg told a distorted history, claiming "it was not until lately that the Oneidas sought to regain ancient sovereignty over land converted from wilderness to become part of cities like Sherrill." Now it was too late, she opined, for the tribe to rekindle the "embers of sovereignty that long ago grew cold."

All three cases began with white people or states breaking the law—Oliphant resisting arrest, Finch fishing, and New York illegally taking Oneida land. Instead of being held accountable—or even restrained—for their illegal behavior, the parties were rewarded. In a move repeated throughout our history, rather than uphold the law to protect Indigenous nations, our government remade the law to fit settlers' needs.

One of the biggest barriers Indigenous nations face in front of the Supreme Court is the sheer ignorance of its justices. During oral arguments in *Sherrill,* Justice Sandra Day O'Connor asked if all white people living on Oneida land would be evicted if the tribe's treaty rights were upheld. In 2013, Chief Justice John Roberts asked a series of questions betraying the fact that he did not understand how tribal citizenship works or what, really, a federally recognized tribe is, including whether tribal membership could be open for "people who want to apply, who think culturally they're a Cherokee." During the same case, about a law protecting the rights of Native parents, liberal justice Stephen Breyer asked if the law would allow Native men to rape non-Native women and keep the baby. "The child would be taken and given to the father," he worried out loud. "Who has never seen it and probably just got out of prison." As recently as 2022, Justice Samuel Alito argued that Indigenous nations do not share a common political interest, because "before the arrival of Europeans, the tribes were at war with each other." What is sad about these statements is that Supreme Court justices are no better or worse than the general public; most people don't know what a federally recognized tribe is, how jurisdiction works on a reservation, or how treaties fit into our Constitution. An entire area of American law—going all the way back to the founding—protects the sovereignty of Indigenous nations. But that law is meaningless if the people in charge of interpreting it—and the citizenry that puts them in power—don't know what it is.

By decree, the role of the Supreme Court is to interpret American law, not write it. Starting in the 1950s, however, the court gave itself more power, shifting the balance away from Congress and the president. Many legal scholars attribute this shift to a backlash against civil rights legislation, large swaths of which (like federal oversight and protections for voters of color) the court has declared unconstitutional. Today in our democracy the Supreme Court, not the president or Congress, has the final word.

In the arena of federal Indian law, that shift produced two competing doctrines: the court sometimes deferring to Congress and other times "usurping the power of the Congress to decide what it wants in federal Indian law," says NYU law professor Maggie Blackhawk, from the Fond du Lac Band Ojibwe. Blackhawk says in the past seventy years these doctrines have existed side by side. Sometimes, like in *Solem* and *Parker*, the court constrained itself to interpreting what Congress said. But in other cases, like *Oliphant, Montana*, and *Sherrill*, it went way offtrack. When the court follows the law as written, tribes usually win. When the Supreme Court makes up or changes the rules, tribes lose.

Title 25 of the United States Code, more commonly called federal Indian law, includes every law passed since the 1790s governing the relationship between the United States and Indigenous nations. Federal Indian law is full of contradictions. Treaties are the supreme law of the land, but Congress can abrogate them at any time for any reason. Indigenous nations are sovereign, but we can't control what happens to our people or on our land. To Blackhawk, these contradictions are unsurprising: "Of course, it's going to have the problems and failures of American colonialism alongside the efforts, advocacy, successes, and sometimes failures and learning lessons of Native people on the other side." Federal Indian law "is deeply flawed," she admits, but "it is not devoid of Native agency." Our ancestors were not able to stop colonialism, but they carved out an important space in American law for tribes to continue to exist. We are left with their wins, their losses, and the unimaginable compromises they were forced to make.

WHEN THE DOORS TO THE SUPREME COURT FINALLY OPENED ON NO-vember 27, 2018, Rosemary McCombs Maxey was guided in. She sat in silence as a trickle of light sneaked through big, flowing red drapes. Tall white pillars symmetrically encircled her chair, four on each side. Before seeing it in person, Rosemary had imagined the courtroom as large and spacious. She was surprised by how small it was. From behind towering crimson velvet curtains, the justices of the Supreme Court emerged. Rosemary was seated toward the front, unbelievably close to the justices. So close she could barely see their faces over the raised bench. "Clarence Thomas, you could only see his forehead," she said. "And then Ginsburg, you could only see just an inch of her."

In the fall of 2018, the court was comprised of four liberal justices, Elena Kagan, Sonia Sotomayor, Stephen Breyer, and Ruth Bader Ginsburg; and five conservative justices, Clarence Thomas, John Roberts, Samuel Alito, Brett Kavanaugh, and Neil Gorsuch. Supreme Court cases are normally heard by all nine justices, but Justice Gorsuch recused himself from *Murphy*, likely because as a judge on the Tenth Circuit he had voted on whether or not the appeals court should rehear the case. Without Gorsuch, the Supreme Court was left with an even eight justices. If the vote ties, that usually means the lower court's decision is affirmed. Meaning that the lawyers for Patrick Murphy and Muscogee Nation only needed four votes to win.

In an antiquated ceremony hearkening back to the town criers of medieval England, the marshal of the US Supreme Court interrupted the silence. "Oyez! Oyez! Oyez! All persons having business before the Honorable, the Supreme Court of the United States, are admonished to draw near and give their attention, for the Court is now sitting," they shouted. "God save the United States and this Honorable Court."

Into his microphone, Chief Justice Roberts announced, "We'll hear argument next in Case 17-1107, *Carpenter versus Murphy*."

"Ms. Blatt," he said, inviting Oklahoma's lawyer to the podium.

———

"THANK YOU, MR. CHIEF JUSTICE, AND MAY IT PLEASE THE COURT," Oklahoma's lawyer began. "Eastern Oklahoma is not an Indian reservation." Lisa Blatt's neatly trimmed bob bounced as she spoke. Her straight hair matched her long face, punctuated by thinly framed glasses. "Congress destroyed all features of a reservation," she went on.

When Lisa Blatt approached the podium on November 27, 2018, she had argued in front of the Supreme Court more times than any other woman in US history. To date, Blatt's win-loss ratio at the high court is impressive: 41–5. To say that she was friendly with the justices is an understatement; when she married her husband, David Blatt, Justice Ruth Bader Ginsburg officiated. Blatt went to law school at the University of Texas before clerking for then appellate judge Ginsburg, and overlapped with Justice Elena Kagan at the US Solicitor General's office. In 2009, she went to work for the corporate law firm Arnold & Porter.

Arnold & Porter was an early defender of civil liberties, including indigent defendants' right to counsel, and the right to plead insanity. But as the firm took on clients like big tobacco it started to shape a different, but equally important, aspect of American law: the role of corporate law firms. The influence of corporate or "big law" at the Supreme Court has dramatically increased since the 1980s as a small cadre of well-paid, elite lawyers represent an oversize portion of the cases the high court even considers. Elite lawyers, like Lisa Blatt, inevitably shape important issues in our democracy, but Blatt says lawyers shouldn't bring their values or personal beliefs to their practice. As Blatt put it on a 2022 Federalist Society panel, "Law firms should be about making money," she said. "What does [the rest of] it matter?"

Murphy was not Blatt's first case opposing Indigenous rights. She had represented the Washington State football team in a legal battle to maintain their trademark and namesake—the dictionary-defined racial slur R—skins. Core to her argument was the fact that companies like porn websites make money off of derogatory names as well. In a 2013 Supreme Court case, Blatt represented a white couple fighting for custody of a Cherokee toddler over the child's biological father. They won.

Blatt was also familiar with Oklahoma. She had worked for the state in a battle with Texas over water rights under then attorney general Scott Pruitt. She won the case and later donated $2,500 to Pruitt's reelection super PAC. To fight the Muscogee reservation, Oklahoma paid Arnold & Porter a total of $643,513.50. According to then attorney general Mike Hunter, the state did not consider other law firms. "When you have a case like this and the implications of it are profound, you have to model the case in sort of a most-negative outcome perspective," he told reporters at the time. "Losing is not an option."

"Congress stripped the former Indian territory of reservation status by terminating all tribal sovereignty over the area to create Oklahoma," Blatt continued in her opening remarks. "Disestablishment occurred—" But then she was quickly interrupted.

"Exactly when did it do this?" Justice Sonia Sotomayor wanted to know. "What's the exact date?"

"I mean," Blatt began. "Our position is it was done by statehood. Our position is more fundamentally that we don't have to—"

But Sotomayor wanted an exact date. If Congress did disestablish the reservation, surely Oklahoma could say when.

"We don't have to give you a date," Blatt curtly replied. "Rome did not fall in a day." As a seasoned Supreme Court advocate, Blatt's strategy was not to win based on a strict reading of the statutes, but rather rhetoric. She had good reason to believe it would carry the day. Normally, to satisfy the *Solem* test—the Supreme Court precedent governing this case— Oklahoma would need to find "hallmark language" in a congressional bill that either got rid of the reservation or made it smaller. That language didn't exist. But Blatt argued she didn't need it, because Oklahoma and the Five Tribes were different. The "birth" of Oklahoma, the state claimed, was a "legislative campaign to dissolve the Five Tribes' communal territories." From 1893 to 1907, Congress passed a raft of legislation that divided up communally held tribal lands, and diminished the power and self-governance of Muscogee Nation. Both sides agreed Congress took a lot of things away from the tribe during this time. They disagreed, however, on whether or not that included the reservation.

During oral arguments, Blatt harped on everything taken during allotment to argue that the reservation was gone too. "All tribal courts are abolished. All tribal taxes are abolished. . . . Tribal law was unenforceable," she listed off. Even tribal property was seized. "Every piece of paper, record, book, dollar bill or coin or property, their buildings, their furniture, their desks, everything was taken away from the tribes." According to the briefs submitted by Oklahoma and the United States, the Muscogee reservation was "destroy[ed]," "dissolv[ed]," "eliminate[d]," "abolish[ed]," "liquidat[ed]," "eviscerat[ed]," "extinguish[ed]," divest[ed]," "overthrow[n]," and "disintegrate[d]" until it was nothing but a "historical artifact." In short, what Congress took away from Muscogee Nation during allotment was *everything*. It was a superficial argument based on circumstantial evidence. But if you didn't know the detailed history of allotment it sounded probable. After all, why would Congress take the buildings, furniture, and even paper away from a tribe, but leave their reservation?

Sitting near the front, Chief Floyd tried not to show what he was thinking on his face. During his administration, the tribe regained ownership of their historic Council House in downtown Okmulgee, one of the buildings, as Blatt pointed out, that was seized during allotment. Floyd remembers local white residents bringing back the desks and chairs their grandparents had looted. It was an awful history to use against them. "You can't unhear what they're saying," he told me.

To Rosemary, Lisa Blatt's version of history felt familiar. As a Native child in Oklahoma schools she had been taught that once Oklahoma became a state the treaty rights of her tribe were destroyed. Her school even had the kids act it out. Every November on the anniversary of statehood the school put on a play where the Native children and the white children acted out a mock wedding. It symbolized how the state of Oklahoma was created through the marriage of her tribe's treaty territory and the white settlers. At the conclusion of the play, the Native students sang a traditional Muscogee hymn and then the entire auditorium sang the musical anthem "Oklahoma."

Over the nearly two decades Patrick Murphy's case was litigated, Oklahoma's reason why it had jurisdiction over the murder of George Jacobs shifted countless times. The state would argue it was a road maintained by the county, Patrick Murphy couldn't raise the issue because of procedural bars, the reservation had been disestablished by Congress according to the *Solem* test, *Solem* didn't apply because Oklahoma was different, and Muscogee Nation never had a reservation to begin with. What the state never did was point to the sentence—or even the law—where Congress got rid of the Muscogee reservation.

Lisa Blatt, a skilled litigator, wanted to have the last word. "Can I reserve the remainder of my time?" she asked the chief justice. "Certainly," he replied. And with that, she left the podium.

After Blatt sat down, the lawyers for the United States (who argued on Oklahoma's side) and for Patrick Murphy took their turns. Riyaz Kanji, Muscogee Nation's lawyer, went last. When Kanji approached the podium on that brisk fall day, it was his first time arguing in front of the Supreme Court. Unbelievably, he wasn't nervous. When Kanji took his place at the podium, Floyd could see only the back of his head and neatly tailored suit. With his papers laid out before him, Kanji raised his eyes to meet the robed justices. A small, white light on the podium turned on. Then he began.

During oral arguments, each lawyer gets an assigned amount of time to speak. Since Muscogee Nation wasn't party to the case, Kanji got only ten minutes. But it wasn't ten minutes to deliver a speech like in a television courtroom drama; the justices could interrupt him at any time. Kanji had a checklist in his mind of ten issues he wanted to address, but knew, realistically, he would get to only a few if he was lucky. The justices seemed stuck in the history of allotment and Blatt's argument that Congress clearly intended to take the reservation away. "So when I got up," Kanji remembers, "I thought that's where I needed to get to somehow."

The historical evidence was complicated but, according to Muscogee Nation, it clearly showed that their reservation still existed. In the 1890s Congress *did* want to get rid of the reservation, but at the time "it was generally believed Congress lacked authority to alter reservations unilaterally," as one brief read. Meaning that Congress needed Muscogee Nation's consent. And the tribe refused. Federal negotiators scrapped their original plan, and "instead settled for an agreement that left Creek land in Creek hands." In legal terms, Congress wanted cession but got allotment.

In lay terms, Congress wanted the tribe to give up their treaty territory, but could only get the tribe to privatize land ownership within it.

During oral arguments, Kanji took it one step further. He argued that if everything else taken from the tribe was used to justify taking their reservation today, no tribe in the United States would be safe. "Congress has told the tribes over time: You—your—your government will be structured in this fashion. Your membership will consist of the following. You will allow this mining and these easements along your land, even if you don't want it. You will allow your children to be taken away and placed in boarding schools, even if no parent would want that," he told the justices. "Even this—the rhetoric about buildings being sold, the Creek Nation is not the only tribe in this country, far from the only one, to have run its government out of churches and house basements for decades." Blatt was asking the court to set a dangerous precedent: to look at one of the darkest chapters in our tribes' history and say that because of those historic wrongs, what we managed to hold on to was no longer ours.

"I had this little spiel in my head and I got to give it," Kanji remembers thinking. The uninterrupted speech to Kanji felt lucky. When his time was up, he stacked his papers and left the podium; in the brief shuffle, the courtroom remained silent. They couldn't applaud, but the Muscogee citizens sitting in the room that day felt proud.

After Kanji sat down, Lisa Blatt returned to the podium for the two minutes she had left—making her the first and last advocate to speak. "There are two thousand prisoners in state court who committed a crime in the former Indian territory who self-identify as Native American," she began. "That's 155 murderers, 113 rapists, and over two hundred felons who committed crimes against children." Furthermore, she argued, the federal government may not be able to "retry any of these cases because the evidence is too stale or the statute of limitations has expired." In other words, affirming the reservation would lead to criminals walking free. "They were hoping to say there's going to be blood in the streets," Floyd remembers thinking.

Oklahoma's first brief to the Supreme Court included a photograph of the skyline of Tulsa, the largest city in the Muscogee Reservation. Blatt warned the court if they upheld the reservation it would create "intoler-able uncertainty" for the 1.8 million people living in eastern Oklahoma. (The petition even argued that before Oklahoma became a state the tribe's treaty territory was lawless.)

Blatt's highly specific numbers of how many inmates, murderers, and rapists could be released from prison hadn't appeared in Oklahoma's briefs at the time. Blatt and the state never provided a publicly verified source for their estimates. When I later asked then attorney general Mike Hunter, the Oklahoma official who had hired Blatt, what the numbers specifically referenced, he did not know. Blatt herself, when asked, pointed us to numbers she cited in a later brief, but not the data.

Over the years, Oklahoma's estimates of how many past convictions would be overturned varied widely from "hundreds" to "thousands" to "over three thousand." By 2021 Oklahoma would claim that up to seventy-six thousand past convictions could be impacted. That number was about three times the entire prison population in the state, and over sixty times the number of Native American inmates from the reservation areas. Despite its gross improbability, the estimate was cited by prominent news outlets and journalists including the Supreme Court correspondent for the *Washington Post*.

If the Supreme Court upheld the Muscogee reservation, and their decision applied to all five tribes in eastern Oklahoma, 19 million acres, or 43 percent of the state, would be Indian country. Oklahoma had been exercising criminal jurisdiction there for well over a century. So it sounded believable that a shift in criminal jurisdiction would be chaotic, but I wanted to double-check the math. In response to an open-records request, the Oklahoma Department of Corrections provided a list that included 1,887 Native Americans incarcerated for crimes that occurred in counties potentially impacted by the decision. That number was a little shy of two thousand, but close. Reservation status would not mean, however, all those people would automatically be released from prison.

In the US criminal justice system, overturning a conviction is difficult. For an inmate to qualify for federal habeas relief—the type of appeal Patrick Murphy used—they have to follow the guidelines outlined in the Antiterrorism and Effective Death Penalty Act. The law places a one-year time limit after a conviction is finalized (when a defendant has either lost their appeal or decided to not appeal). After that, inmates are out of luck.

With Cherokee paralegal Jennifer McAffrey Thiessen, I looked at a sample of about three hundred inmates. While Oklahoma appeared to count all 1,887 inmates—or something close to that—in its warning to the Supreme Court, fewer than 10 percent of the three hundred cases we investigated would actually qualify for a new, federal trial. At the time the Supreme Court was debating all this, lower federal courts had already thrown out habeas petitions from inmates whose one year had run out. And while Oklahoma state courts do not have a statute of limitations for jurisdictional claims, they were telling inmates the reservation issue was waived if they didn't bring it up in their first appeal.

Asking who qualifies for federal habeas relief leaves out the question of who would want it. Winning a federal habeas petition does not get an inmate out of prison; it gets them a new, federal trial. For many crimes, a federal conviction comes with a longer sentence. Also, time served in state prison doesn't necessarily apply to a federal sentence. With help of Cheyenne demographer Desi Small-Rodriguez, we found about a third of inmates of that 1,887 list had already served more than half their sentence (not counting people sentenced to life, death, or those who would be out by the time the court ruled on the case). The appeals process is not swift, and requires multiple stages in multiple courts. Just the paperwork phase in one court alone can take nearly a year. A quarter of the inmates in our data were scheduled to be released within two years—regardless of the outcome in *Murphy*. For many inmates, simply waiting for their release date would be a shorter path to freedom than appealing their conviction. Oklahoma's dire warnings did not hold up to scrutiny.

During oral arguments, however, it appeared Blatt's strategy was working. "Well, suppose an Indian is charged in—with having committed a mugging in Tulsa. What—where would that case end up?" Justice Alito asked. Chief Justice Roberts wanted to know, "Can they say you—you need a license from the tribe to sell alcoholic beverages?"

Even the court's liberal justices had concerns about the practical consequences. "There are 1.8 million people living in this area," Breyer stated, repeating numbers from Oklahoma's brief. "They have built their lives not necessarily on criminal law but on municipal regulations, property law, dog-related law." He asked, "What happens to all those people?" During the entire oral argument Justice Ruth Bader Ginsburg asked one question. It was about whether or not reservation status would affect taxes.

Quickly, Blatt's two minutes were up, and the argument was over. "Thank you, Counsel," Chief Justice Roberts said. "The case is submitted." And then, as quickly and as silently as they came in, the robed justices of the Supreme Court disappeared behind the curtain.

Allowed to speak for the first time in hours, Rosemary turned to the friend she came with, a lawyer. Rosemary wanted to know when the decision would come out. She was surprised to learn it would be summer before they heard anything. The women were escorted through the cavernous bowels of the building and back to the city sidewalk where their day began. The sun now sat high in the sky.

By the time Chief Floyd found himself back on the front steps of the court, the crowd had thinned out. Looking out at the clear blue sky hovering over the meticulously manicured Capitol lawn, Floyd felt hopeful. "My instinct was telling me we've won this case," he remembers. In the back of Floyd's mind, of course, was the possibility that Muscogee Nation could lose. It was hard to think about. The tribe had already lost their homeland once. After the devastation of removal, they rebuilt; reestablished their fires, their tribal towns, their government, and their way of life on land that was promised to them forever. Now that second home was at stake. With the stroke of a pen, the Supreme Court could take it away.

CHAPTER 8

Coercion

AT THE TURN OF THE CENTURY, BOTH OF MY GREAT-GRANDFATHERS got land within what would later become Oklahoma. How they acquired that land, however, was very different. Patrick Sarsfield Nagle was a young lawyer and staunch Democrat whose father emigrated from County Cork, Ireland. On April 22, 1889, he waited on the edge of two million acres with fifty thousand other eager white settlers. Once Congress announced the land run, people came from everywhere. They arrived by train, wagon, horse—even by foot. At noon, guns, trumpets, and cannons fired. And the mob surged forward.

Dust plumed as thousands of settlers raced across the prairie. To claim the allowable 160 acres, they planted little flags in the ground marking out their plots. By nightfall, all two million acres were taken. Towns were planned and tent cities went up overnight. Nagle, driving a wagon hitched to two mules, staked out a smaller town lot in Kingfisher. There he opened a law office, got married, started a family, and helped found the Oklahoma Democratic and then Socialist parties as the land became a state.

The 1889 and subsequent land runs are celebrated today through reenactments at elementary schools; the mascot of the University of

Oklahoma; and by one of the world's largest bronze sculptures, in downtown Oklahoma City. The image of settlers taming the wild frontier is integral not just to Oklahoma, but American identity. Today 46 million Americans—nearly 20 percent of the adult population—descend from white settlers who got free, Indigenous land, myself included.

The two million acres opened for white settlers in the 1889 land run was originally the homelands of the Comanche, Wichita, and Osage tribes, and later the treaty territory of Muscogee Nation. When the Five Tribes (Muscogee, Cherokee, Choctaw, Chickasaw, and Seminole) were expelled west of the Mississippi to what was then called Indian Territory, their new lands were promised to them for "as long as the grass grows or the water runs." At that time, the westernmost US state was Missouri. By the late 1800s, the western boundary of the United States was California. As the US stretched from sea to shining sea, the Five Tribes' treaty territory became an island of Indigenous-controlled land right in the middle. And the political will of the United States to fulfill its treaty obligations buckled.

On September 18, 1900, my great-grandfather William Dudley Polson stepped into a drab federal office in the small town of Vinita, Cherokee Nation. Sixty-one years after the death of John Ridge, his grandson was being interviewed by federal officials. They needed to add William Dudley to a list of every Cherokee citizen so they could begin allotment. Through allotment all land belonging to Cherokee Nation—the land for which John had signed away his life—would be divided up and assigned to individual citizens. In the late 1800s, the US government decided rather than push Native people onto shrinking reservations, it would assimilate Native people to white society by privatizing their land. The policy was called allotment. For William Dudley, the federal officials had a long list of questions: "What is your name?" "What is your age?" "What is your post office address?" "Are you a recognized citizen of the Cherokee Nation?" "What degree of blood do you claim?" "What is the name of your father?" "Is he living?" "Is he an Indian by blood?" "What is your mother's name?" "Is she living?" "Is she an Indian by blood?" "For whom do you apply for enrollment?" "What is the name of your wife?" "Is she living?" "What was the name of your wife before you married her?" "When did you marry

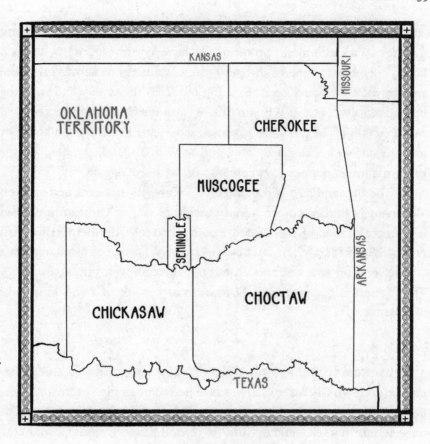

Map of Indian Territory

her?" "Have you a certificate of marriage?" "If you have a certificate of marriage, can you send it to us?" "What is the name of your child?" "How old is he?" "Have you any proof of his birth?" "Is your mother living?" "Is your father dead?" To most of their questions, William Dudley gave two-word answers: "Yes, sir" or "No, sir."

Before allotment, all Cherokee land was owned communally by the tribe. Tribal citizens could build a house, open a store, plant crops, or fence out a farm wherever they wanted. Whatever they built they owned, but the tribe held all the land underneath. The house John Ridge lived in after removal, the farm he started with enslaved labor, and the cemetery where he was buried all stayed in the family. William Dudley lived at the old home place as a child, moved away for school, and came back as an adult. Communal land ownership allowed the farm to pass easily among relatives. With allotment, however, the farm got divided up, with each family member assigned a different piece. William's niece was given the section with the house on it. Fanning out from there, the land smooths into a long, flat prairie. William Dudley and his children were assigned seven rectangles of it—some adjoined, some not. There was no house or place to stay on his assigned land, and so William Dudley rented a place in town a mile up the road, where he worked at a drugstore.

While the land run is remembered today with mascots and statues, allotment is hardly known about outside of Native communities. But it redrew the map of the United States. Through allotment, tribes lost nearly two-thirds of their land base—an area the size of Montana. This chapter of land loss was carried out not through war, but bureaucracy. The mountain of paperwork, however, was capable of a shocking level of violence.

AFTER MAJOR RIDGE, JOHN RIDGE, AND ELIAS BOUDINOT WERE ASSAS-sinated in 1839, Cherokee Nation saw a period of relative peace and prosperity. Unbelievably, the time after removal is called the Golden Age. The tribe rebuilt homes, schools, and its centralized government, and constructed the first college for women west of the Mississippi. The prosperity, however, was made possible by enslaved labor. By the 1840s, Cherokee Nation hardened its slave codes and in Cherokee, Chickasaw, Choctaw, and Muscogee Nations, enslaved people were prohibited from learning to read or write, sing hymns, or even sit at the same table as their owner.

One spring morning in 1842, the plantation community of Webber's Falls in the fertile Arkansas River Valley awoke "to find themselves abandoned by their slaves." Twenty enslaved people had escaped in the darkness of night and were headed to Mexico. Cherokee Nation immediately formed a posse to capture the runaways. As the escapees traveled south, other enslaved people from Muscogee and Choctaw Nations joined them. When the runaways found a slave catcher returning a family to their Choctaw enslavers, they killed the catcher and freed the family. After thirteen days and 280 miles, the Cherokee posse caught them. Five members of the group were sent to jail, but most of them were returned to a punishment materially the same: slavery.

When the US Civil War broke out, the Confederacy courted an alliance with the Five Tribes. Understandably, none of the tribes felt a particular allegiance to the United States, and many of the slaveholding elite sympathized with the South. Federal troops stationed in Indian Territory abandoned their posts, and at the dawn of the Civil War, the promise of federal protection had been withdrawn. At first, Cherokee Nation voted to stay neutral, but after the four other tribes—Chickasaw, Choctaw, Seminole, and Muscogee Nations—signed treaties with the Confederate government, Cherokee Nation formally joined. But Cherokee people were deeply divided.

As Cherokee Nation was pulled into the broader American Civil War, our own civil war broke out. Traditionalists opposed to slavery and the influence of white society fought for the Union. Under the leadership of Stand Watie—Elias Boudinot's brother and a general in the Confederate army—another faction fought for the South. The tribe's conflicting position meant it was invaded by both the Union and Confederacy and offered little protection from either. By the end of the war, Cherokee Nation was devastated. Similar divisions broke out within Muscogee Nation, with Opothle Yoholo and those loyal to the Union fleeing to Kansas—where, in a refugee camp, he died.

Four years after Cherokee Nation signed a treaty of allegiance to the Confederacy, General Robert E. Lee surrendered and the American Civil War was over. Stand Watie waged battles in Indian Territory for another two months—making him the last Confederate general to lay down arms. When leaders from the Five Tribes met with federal officials to negotiate peace, they were startled by the US government's demands. As punishment for siding with the Confederacy, the United States wanted almost half the land set aside in the removal treaties. Tribal leaders tried to protest, but on the losing end of the war there was little they could do. These revised boundaries—as described in the 1866 treaties—are what the Five Tribes consider their reservations today. The treaties also formally ended slavery in all five tribes, and in Cherokee, Seminole, and Muscogee Nations granted full citizenship to formerly enslaved people. But the concession that proved most fatal seemed small at first: at the federal government's insistence, the tribes allowed railroads to pass through their land.

FROM THE PASSENGER WINDOWS OF THE ST. LOUIS, SAN FRANCISCO, and Kansas railroad lines, white people watched fertile farmland, valuable timber, and prime pastures roll by. And like generations of settlers before them, they coveted it. While it was illegal to move there without a permit from the tribes, they came in droves. "We could chase out white men and they [would] be right back the next day," a Euchee man recalled. "Sometimes there are more white people back than we had chased out." First the intruders came by the thousands, then by the tens of thousands, until finally over three hundred thousand white people moved onto the Five Tribes' land—until they outnumbered tribal citizens. In 1890, Muscogee citizens were still the majority of the people on their land. Five years later, they were less than 20 percent. "Whom do you see?" one observer wrote. "*White* men, *white* men everywhere! The scarcest object is an Indian, and this is the *Indian* territory."

Muscogee Nation arrested the squatters and turned them loose in Kansas or Missouri, but they just came back. The federal government, which was obligated to remove the intruders, was no help. When lighthorsemen cut down fences illegally erected by trespassing cattlemen, a federal court indicted them for "malicious mischief." When the lighthorsemen evicted one squatter, US courts awarded the man $100 in damages. Illegal settlers grazed their cattle on Muscogee grass, chopped down Muscogee trees to sell the timber, and erected entire towns on Muscogee land.

By the late 1800s, the squatters started to complain to Congress. They had a piece of land to live on, but they didn't own it. The vast quantities of money they had spent on their illegal fences, farms, homes, and towns would be lost if the United States didn't give them property rights. In Congress, the intruders found a sympathetic ear. In 1893, senators reassured them, "The United States has not forgotten you." As Congress shaped its policies to fit the squatters' demands, one politician emerged as their most powerful ally: Senator Henry L. Dawes.

When the idea of allotment first came to Congress, Senator Dawes—then chair of the Indian Affairs Committee—sponsored it. The Republican and lifelong politician claimed he was helping Indigenous nations by breaking up their treaty territories. Communal land ownership, in Dawes's mind, held tribal citizens back, but allotment would turn them into self-serving capitalists. "They have got as far as they can go," he said of the Cherokees at an annual gathering of East Coast humanitarians, because "there is no selfishness, which is at the bottom of civilization." Tribal leaders told Dawes communal land ownership worked; there were no poor families or "paupers," they said—in contrast to the United States, one Cherokee citizen observed, "where there are so many landless people and so much poverty."

The supposed benefit to tribal citizens was not the only reason allotment was necessary, Dawes argued. The other reason was crime. The land of the Five Tribes had become a refuge for "murderers, train robbers, horse thieves, bank robbers, and the outlaw class in general," one report alleged. In his speech to that gathering of humanitarians, Dawes claimed "something like one thousand men" had been hanged for crimes committed in the Territory. In reality, only a few dozen were executed in twenty-one years. Dawes also argued most tribal citizens actually wanted allotment, but their governments—controlled by "mixed bloods and adopted citizens"—suppressed their voice. Those same "mixed bloods" got rich off communal land ownership by controlling the best farmland, while the average citizen eked out their subsistence in the hills. Some in Congress may have been inclined to uphold the treaty rights of the Five Tribes, but Dawes told them the "wholly corrupt" tribal governments were "unworthy."

After he retired from the Senate, Congress placed Dawes at the head of a three-person commission tasked with bringing allotment to the Five Tribes—whether they wanted it or not. Dawes shared a trait with many white people who have harmed Native nations: the hubris to believe *he* knew what was best for Native people—better than Native people ourselves.

With his plan in tow, Henry Dawes headed to Indian Territory. Everywhere the Dawes Commission went, however, the tribes said no. Cherokee

Nation refused to meet with them. In front of Dawes, the principal chief
of Muscogee Nation asked a crowd of thousands to stand on one side of a
public square if they wanted allotment, and on the other side if they didn't.
In unison, the crowd voted allotment down. The Choctaw general council
made it illegal for any citizen to agree to cede any portion of Choctaw land.
The punishment for the first offense was six to twelve months in jail; for
the second offense, it was death. In joint councils, leaders from the Five
Tribes condemned allotment, printed several thousand copies of their resolutions, and posted the broadsheets around the Territory.

Originally Dawes wanted to assign each tribal citizen some amount of
land, and then open what was left over to white settlers. The land assigned
to tribal citizens would be allotted; the leftover land would be ceded to
the United States. For this plan to work, Congress needed what is called
a land cession. At the time, the body didn't believe it could alter a tribe's
treaty territory without their consent.* The US was happy to coerce that
"consent" through war, torture, starvation, bribes, and trickery, but it still
needed tribal leaders to sign something. To further thwart Congress's
plan, the Five Tribes owned their land outright. On most reservations,
this is not the case: instead the United States owns the land, but holds it
in trust for the benefit and use of the tribe. During removal, negotiators
for the Five Tribes demanded to hold a patent to their land—the same way
a homeowner holds a deed. This worried Congress: if the legal owner of
the land—the tribes—refused to sell, how could anyone else own it? So
Congress gave up on cession. All land within the tribes' treaty territory
would be assigned to tribal citizens; none would be left over for white settlers. While land ownership within it would change, the Five Tribes' treaty
boundaries would remain intact.

Our ancestors were not able to stop allotment or removal, but during
periods of unimaginable loss they fought for every inch they could save.
These smaller victories—holding the patent to the land and preventing
cession—would make all the difference in *Murphy*. Generations of tribal

---

* Congress has since changed its opinion. If Congress wants to get rid of a reservation
today, or every reservation for that matter, it can do so unilaterally.

leaders mitigating colonization allowed their descendants to come back a century later and fight for their reservation.

Allotment, Congress ultimately believed, they could force onto the tribes. And so they did. To bully the tribal governments, Congress took away everything they could—writing the list Lisa Blatt would rattle off twelve decades later. The secretary of the Interior assumed possession of all tribal property, including schools, courts, buildings, and money. Tribal governments were prohibited from meeting except to discuss allotment. Squatters were allowed to incorporate their illegal cities and towns, pass laws, and even start collecting taxes. Finally, Congress scheduled allotment to happen with or without tribal consent. The coercion worked; eventually all five tribes agreed to the allotment of their land.

After the Five Tribes conceded to allotment, resistance to the policy did not stop. It just shifted from the tribes to their citizens. In Muscogee Nation, traditionalists formed their own government,* passed laws forbidding Muscogee citizens from taking an allotment and even whipped the violators. James Floyd's great-grandfather Eufaula Harjo was one of the leaders. He would later tell US senators he wanted the "old treaty" to be upheld. "This land was given to us forever, as long as grass should grow and water run," he told them. But then the government came and "divided the land up without the consent of the Indian people." To put down their resistance, the United States sent in federal marshals and the cavalry.

But still the people protested. Twenty-four thousand tribal citizens refused to enroll for allotment. Some who refused to enroll for allotment were arrested and carted off to jail. But mostly federal agents just changed the rules. Now, the testimony of a family member or neighbor could enroll someone against their will. One day, when he was in town for an errand, the postmaster handed Eufaula Harjo a piece of mail. It was his allotment certificate; he had been assigned land without his knowledge.

---

* The government made their headquarters at Hickory Ground—near the Ryal community where Patrick Murphy and George Jacobs are from. Eufaula Harjo himself was from the Weogufkee tribal town. Even at this time, traditional communities lived in the southern portion of the Muscogee reservation.

Eufaula Harjo

Harjo took the certificate and returned it to the Dawes Commission office. Other traditionalists gave Harjo their certificates, and he returned them in batches. "The Indian people did not know anything about it until the land was cut up," Harjo said of allotment. "We are pushed out of all that we had," he went on. "They are in the houses that we built."

THE FINAL WAVE OF INTRUDERS WERE THE BUREAUCRATS. THE DAWES Commission brought with them an army of office workers—clerks, field inspectors, commissioners, surveyors, and many a man who got his job through a friend in Washington. They opened offices in Wewoka, Atoka, Tishomingo, Muskogee, and Vinita. From behind their desks, they got busy carrying out allotment. The project was massive: 15.7 million acres needed to be divided up and assigned to over a hundred thousand tribal citizens. Each of the Five Tribes' treaty territory was surveyed and sectioned off into perfect little grids, and—no matter how close together or far apart they lived at the time—each citizen had to be assigned an equal portion of it. Muscogee citizens got 160 acres, each Cherokee 110, and each Seminole a different amount depending on the value of the acreage. In Choctaw and Chickasaw Nations—who signed a joint agreement— each citizen got 320 acres, except for formerly enslaved people and their descendants, who received only 40.

Before the Dawes Commission could assign allotments, they needed a list of every tribal citizen who would receive one. Originally the tribes wanted to use their own rolls, but the commission argued that the "corrupt" tribal governments would be unfair. So Congress put the commission in charge. The Dawes Commission segregated the rolls by placing formerly enslaved people and their descendants on a Freedmen roll for each tribe. As tribal citizens, freedpeople were entitled to the same land as everyone else and, as allotment took shape, also experienced the same hardships. At the same time, Indian Territory was the only place in the world, as Choctaw and Chickasaw freedpeople descendant and historian Alaina Roberts writes, "in which land distribution to former slaves was not an unfulfilled promise but a reality."

The commission's hubris quickly turned to frustration. While tens of

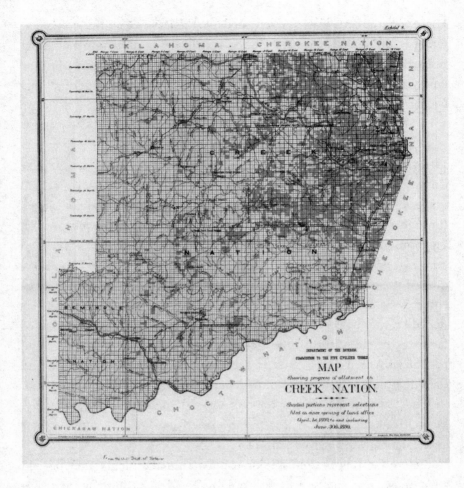

thousands of tribal citizens refused to enroll, over a hundred thousand non-Native people claimed to be citizens of the Five Tribes in order to receive a free piece of land.* The nightmare of finalizing the rolls was characteristic of the time; every task took longer and encountered more obstacles than anticipated. The wheels of bureaucracy were in turn messy, indifferent, cumbersome, violent, and corrupt. But once in motion, they didn't stop.

---

* The Dawes Commission processed the enrollment application of more than 250,000 people but approved only about 101,000.

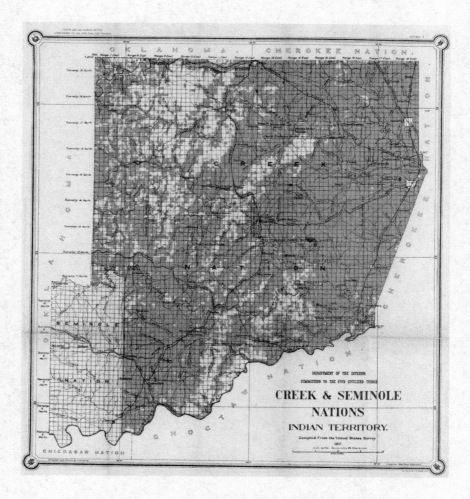

Maps (l and r) showing progress of allotment in Muscogee Nation

AT THE TURN OF THE CENTURY, THE PRINCIPAL CHIEF OF MUSCOGEE Nation warned that "communal land ownership" had been a form of "protective power" for tribal citizens, but that allotment would leave each person to cope "single-handed with the avaricious land sharks of the American continent."

And that is exactly what happened.

CHAPTER 9

The Twist

THE SUPREME COURT, AS AN INSTITUTION, IS SHROUDED IN tradition—most of it arcane. Legally, the court can issue its opinions whenever it wants. By tradition, however, June sees the highest volume of decisions come out—making the long days of summer a time all eyes are on the high court.

The court releases opinions in small batches on prescheduled decision days. On these days—at 10 a.m. Eastern Standard Time—the nine robed justices of the Supreme Court enter their small, ornate courtroom. The chief justice then invites his colleagues who authored a majority opinion to read as much (or as little) of it as they please. There is even a specific order they go in: reverse seniority, with the newest justice going first.

Of the institution's opaque inner workings, the public knows only what it is allowed. Accordingly, no one knows which opinions will be announced on which day until the justices speak. Cameras and phones are not allowed in the courtroom. So a small group of reporters gathers in the court's public information office downstairs, where the audio is piped in. Once the justices start releasing their opinions, the reporters scuttle to yet another room where they are allowed to tweet, blog, and post the day's news. Then, almost instantly, the world knows what happened.

By the middle of June, most decisions from that year's term had been announced, but the leaders of Muscogee Nation were still waiting. It had been seven months since they traveled to Washington, DC, for oral arguments. Every decision day, Chief Floyd would hunch over his computer and hit refresh on the popular *SCOTUSblog*. But day after day, there was no news on *Murphy*.

The morning of Thursday, June 27, 2019, was the last day for the Supreme Court to issue its decisions for that term. There were only a handful of cases left: two about gerrymandering, one about the Fourth Amendment, a census case, and *Murphy*. By process of elimination, Muscogee leaders knew that Thursday would be the day. After years of waiting, finally, they would have an answer; back home, the tribal complex was buzzing. From the bench, the chief justice announced the decision in the gerrymandering cases, then the census, until only *Murphy* was left. "This is it," Floyd remembers thinking. "What are they going to do?"

But, then, no one read an opinion. *Carpenter v. Murphy* will be restored to the calendar for reargument, the chief justice briskly announced from the bench. There was no decision.

Back at the Muscogee Nation tribal complex, the air went out of the room. Muscogee leaders had prayed for a win, even braced themselves for a loss, but what were they supposed to do with this? "So many people had invested so much work into this case," Chief Floyd said in frustration. "And here we are [at] the twelfth hour, and what do we got to show? Nothing."

That one-sentence announcement meant the Supreme Court would likely hear oral arguments in *Murphy* a second time, and Muscogee Nation would have to wait for a decision. Some very famous cases, like *Brown v. Board of Education* and *Roe v. Wade*, have been argued twice, but it is a rare occurrence—typically happening less than once a year. Unlike Congress, where the public hears the debate among lawmakers, when Supreme Court justices meet it is private—not even their law clerks are allowed in the room. So when the court announced it would hear oral arguments in *Murphy* a second time, no one outside the court knew why.

The most experienced Supreme Court litigator on Muscogee Nation's side was Patrick Murphy's pro bono lawyer, Ian Gershengorn. During the Obama administration Ian was the solicitor general of the United States—meaning he represented the federal government in litigation. At the time, Ian had argued in front of the high court fourteen times. Ian and Riyaz Kanji, Muscogee Nation's lawyer, are longtime friends. Before *Murphy* headed to the Supreme Court, the team tapped Ian.

That fall, the team waited for more news. Ian thought they would probably argue *Murphy* again in front of the justices, and maybe submit additional briefs, but wouldn't know until the Supreme Court made an announcement. For months, he heard nothing. When the court published a calendar of all the cases it would hear that October, *Murphy* wasn't listed. Then the court published its calendar for November, and again no *Murphy*. To Ian, that felt "super unusual." Since *Murphy* had already been briefed, it would make sense for it to be one of the first cases on the docket.

Patrick Murphy and Muscogee Nation's team started to come up with a theory: maybe with Gorsuch recused, the Supreme Court was caught in a 4–4 split. A tie vote would have upheld the Tenth Circuit decision, but precluded the justices from writing their own opinion. If the high court could find a different case that raised the same legal question— whether Congress had ever disestablished the Muscogee reservation— but Gorsuch could join, they would be back to an odd number of nine justices. That also meant Gorsuch would cast the deciding vote. As the trees turned bare and fall settled in, Ian became more certain his theory was right, that a different case—not Patrick Murphy's—would settle the reservation status of Muscogee Nation.

After Patrick Murphy had won in the Tenth Circuit, over one hundred inmates in Oklahoma filed appeals claiming their crime happened on a reservation too. Gershengorn and the team kept a running list. The inmates came from all over Oklahoma—not just the Muscogee reservation. "There were lots of cases at that point that were raising a *Murphy* issue," Ian told me. "But we figured that the court would want one that had the Creek reservation, because otherwise the legal questions are not exactly the same." For one of those appeals to reach the Supreme Court, the inmate behind it had to file the correct type of petition, with the right paperwork, at the right time, at every level of appeal all the way up to the

Supreme Court and—for most of them—without a lawyer. By the time Gershengorn started thinking the court might take a different case, only six appeals had made it through that legal gauntlet all the way to the Supreme Court. And only one of those involved the Muscogee reservation.

THE JAMES CRABTREE CORRECTIONAL CENTER SITS ON THE WESTERN edge of the small town of Helena, Oklahoma. The facility, built before Oklahoma became a state, once housed a high school, junior college, and orphanage before becoming a prison in 1982. Today over a thousand men are incarcerated there in medium- and minimum-security dorms.

In the summer of 2017, a group of inmates were watching TV when a local news story caught their attention. A man on Oklahoma's death row had won a stunning victory at the Tenth Circuit Court of Appeals. The federal court had thrown out his state conviction because he was Native American and his crime occurred on the reservation of Muscogee Nation.

"It was all over the networks," one of the inmates, Jimcy McGirt, remembers. Jimcy is also a descendant of Muscogee Nation and enrolled in Seminole Nation of Oklahoma. His crime, for which he had been sentenced to spend the rest of his life in prison, took place on the Muscogee reservation. If the Tenth Circuit was right, Oklahoma didn't have the jurisdiction to prosecute him, either. It was the most hope he had felt in decades.

Inmates at the James Crabtree Correctional Center were allowed six hours each week on a computer in the prison's law library. Over the following months, Jimcy and a group of seven other inmates became a team of jailhouse lawyers. One of them—who had worked as a law clerk—would search Westlaw and pull quotes from relevant cases and statutes. The law librarian let the men share a compact disc on which they saved their work. When one of them typed out a section of an appeal, the others would copy it. To write out his first petition, Jimcy mostly borrowed from the work of fellow inmates, changing the name and other relevant information to reflect his case.

That summer, Jimcy had been incarcerated in Oklahoma for twenty years. In 1997, an Oklahoma jury convicted him of one count of lewd

molestation, one count of rape by instrumentation, and one count of forc-ible sodomy for sexually abusing his wife's three-year-old granddaughter.*
When the sheriff's deputy assigned to the case first heard a recording of the child detailing the assault, he ran into the bathroom to vomit. As an adult, the survivor would testify that the abuse still affected her. It's hard to trust people, she said. Jimcy pleaded not guilty, but an Oklahoma judge sentenced him to one term of life in prison and two terms of five hundred years.

After his 1997 conviction, Jimcy challenged his sentence twenty times, but none of his legal efforts made a dent. One month after the Tenth Circuit ruled in Patrick Murphy's favor, Jimcy filed a writ of habeas corpus in Alfalfa County District Court. But a writ, the district court told him, was the wrong kind of petition. Still without a lawyer, Jimcy appealed that decision four times to appellate courts in Oklahoma, but those appeals were thrown out because he hadn't filed the right kind of paperwork, filed it too late, or filed it in the wrong court. In their dismissal, the district court had told Jimcy he needed to file what's called an application for post-conviction relief. Almost a year later, that's what he did. He was denied relief by the trial and appellate courts in Oklahoma, but still he did not give up.

Two months before the Supreme Court punted its decision in *Murphy*, Jimcy McGirt filed a neatly typed petition for certiorari, with handwritten edits between the lines. Certiorari, or CERT for short, simply means the high court will review the decision of a lower court. For months, Jimcy didn't hear anything. The Supreme Court grants or denies CERT in regularly published lists. Rather than quickly deny Jimcy's petition, the Supreme Court let it hang in limbo. In total, McGirt's petition was relisted eight times.

Gershengorn had been closely watching for what case might replace *Murphy*. He could see that Jimcy McGirt didn't have a lawyer, so Ian reached out. In the fall of 2019, he got Jimcy on the phone. Ian explained he was Patrick Murphy's lawyer, and that he had seen Jimcy's petition. "If

---

* The assaults took place over the course of a week, during which the child turned four.

the court grants," Ian asked, "would you like us to represent you for free?" It was the first offer of legal representation Jimcy had received in twenty years. "You're hired," he replied.

For many tribal citizens following *Murphy*, the *McGirt* case came as a total surprise. For Muscogee leaders, it was hard to think a case involving the sexual abuse of a child would determine the status of their reservation. "In terms of portraying the tribe or the individuals in a positive light? I mean, they're the worst things you could expect," Floyd remembers thinking. "Can they find a more awful case?"

On December 13, 2019—six months after there was no decision in *Murphy*—Jimcy was sitting on his bunk when he heard someone yelling his name. "You're on the news! You're on the news!" his neighboring inmate shouted. The man turned his TV around so Jimcy could watch. And that's how he learned his case was going to the Supreme Court.

CHAPTER 10

Plunder

THE LAND THAT IS NOW OKLAHOMA WAS ONCE SO RICH WITH OIL THAT it seeped out of the ground. The shiny black liquid pooled on the surface of creeks; families digging for water hit crude instead; and natural gas wafting from the earth killed plants. Before allotment came, a few wells were drilled here and there, but not much was produced. Private property—much like Dawes had predicted—brought a wave of new investment, and before the ink was dry on the allotment agreements, oilmen swarmed Indian Territory.

The frenzy with which the oil boom came is hard to overstate. The area produced so much oil so quickly that it didn't have the infrastructure to properly store, transport, or refine the crude. Instead it was held in makeshift open-air pits that ducks and geese would confuse for ponds and die in. When such pits washed out in one oil field, the flood of crude came up to the axles of cars. Oil was more valuable than gas, so drillers would let the natural gas spew hoping it would later release oil. The practice was so common around the town of Ardmore that the city attorney observed that he could see the wasted gas collecting in "bluish-colored" clouds.

But the frenzy paid off. By the time Oklahoma became a state, it was the largest producer of oil and gas in the country. Household names of the

Oil rigs in Glenn Pool Field

industry—like Phillips, Sinclair, and Getty—got their start here. Owner-ship would quickly change, but at the time, the most productive oil fields in the United States were owned by citizens of the Five Tribes.

The first oil field discovered in Indian Territory was in the small Mus-cogee community of Red Fork. After it was declared "the greatest oil well ever found west of the Mississippi river," prospectors flocked there. Moser Naharkey lived in Red Fork. Sometimes called Moses or Mooser, he was a farmer and also served on the Creek council. At the turn of the century, he lived on and cultivated about 80 acres spanning a small tributary to the Arkansas River, now named Moser Creek. Moser received more land than other allottees; after his mother and wife died in quick succession (we don't know how), he inherited their allotments. When it was all said and done, Moser's small family owned 960 acres—nearly the size of the National Mall.

When oil was struck on the Naharkey allotment, papers called it "the best producer ever drilled" in the Cherokee or Muscogee Nations. Under federal regulations, Moser was owed 10 percent in royalties of whatever was drilled there. This was how allotment was supposed to work; private property brought investment and capital to Indian Territory, benefiting tribal citizens and businessmen alike. In a few short years, Moser Naharkey—a humble farmer and councilman—was rich.

One of the oilmen drilling on Moser's land was named Grant C. Stebbins. He would go on to provide the city with its first supply of natural gas, help start the University of Tulsa, and develop the high-end neighborhood of Maple Ridge (where he built his own colonial-style mansion). In 1905, Stebbins purchased an oil and gas lease on Moser's land, but it appears he stopped paying royalties and soon owed Moser a lot of money. So much money that when Stebbins didn't pay, the sheriff seized his stocks and land.

Three days before Christmas in 1905, at the age of forty-seven, Moser died. There is no public explanation for his death. Less than a decade later, federal investigators would uncover land-hungry settlers employed "practically every crime and fraud" to snatch Native land—including murder.

Oil was not the only industry that boomed in the wake of allotment. There was also money to be made from farmland, timber, coal, even urban real estate. Allotment brought a new profession to Indian Territory called grafting. It was simple. Grafters got land from allottees for as little money as possible—by lease, sale, swindle, stealing, deception, fraud, and sometimes violence—and then turned around and sold or rented that land for as much as they could. Sometimes grafters paid bilingual tribal citizens to collect signatures from allottees who didn't read or understand English. Other times, they paid and tricked allottees to leave the grafter the land in a will. Unexplained deaths like Moser's proliferated. If there was no way to trick the allottee into signing the necessary paperwork, the documents were simply forged; one grafter collected the signatures of sixty Choctaws this way. Federal officials in charge of the bureaucratic mess were no help. In 1903, two investigations found court officials, every member of the Dawes Commission, and leaders in the Department of the Interior owned stock in the very land companies profiting from the graft; several served on the company boards.

———

WHEN THE TRIBES AGREED TO ALLOTMENT, A FEDERAL POLICY WAS SUP-posed to protect their citizens from bad business dealings. The policy was called restrictions. At first, when land was allotted, none of it could be sold. Allottees could lease the land or sell the oil underneath, but owner-ship could not change hands. It varied by tribe, but this restricted status was supposed to stay in place for a period of time—ranging from five years to forever.

Restrictions meant that while settlers outnumbered tribal citizens nine to one, tribal citizens still owned most of the land. This the settlers did not like.

Through their churches, commercial clubs, farm bureaus, local mu-nicipalities, bar associations, political clubs, and newspapers, white settlers blasted restrictions, calling them a "burden," a "crime," and "rad-ically wrong." Statehood was supposed to come after allotment and, since restricted land wasn't taxed, the new state wouldn't have enough money for public schools. If white people couldn't own land, hardworking farm-ers and businessmen wouldn't invest in the area, they argued. The only white people who would accept renting from Natives were tenant farmers and the poor, who were called "craven," "inferior," "shiftless," "ignorant," "degraded," and "evil." As one Tulsa attorney put it—representing the bar association of the city—the Territory was "the first land I have ever vis-ited, and perhaps—I trust it will be—the last . . . where the intelligent white man is the renter and the Indian is the landlord."

Like Southern politicians during removal and the Dawes Commission in the preceding decade, leaders of the Territory argued removing restric-tions was actually best for Native people. Tribal citizens didn't need pro-tection because they were "absolutely as competent" as other Americans. Besides, most of them had "only a small percentage of Indian blood" and were basically white.

During the debate a person's "percentage of Indian blood" became a measure of which tribal citizens still needed restrictions and which ones didn't. As if they were recording the pedigree of bred dogs, the Dawes

Commission wrote down the "degree of Indian blood" of most allottees.* When Congress started removing restrictions, one of the first groups was everyone on the segregated Freedmen rolls. J. Coody Johnson, Muscogee Council member and freedperson, estimated two-thirds of Muscogee freedpeople lost their land for "a very inadequate" amount of money. The business community in Indian Territory wanted Congress to get rid of more restrictions—if not for everyone at least people who weren't "full blood."

In 1906, a Senate committee traveled to Indian Territory to hold public hearings about what should be done with restricted land. The senators heard about the grafters' schemes: the forged documents; the illegal sales; the particular way they targeted children, especially orphans. But never in their quest for a policy solution did the senators see the problem as white criminality. Instead the problem was framed as Native ignorance. If only Native people were better at business transactions, they lamented. How can we save these tribal citizens from themselves, they asked with hubris.

With few exceptions, tribal citizens—including traditionalists, Keetoowahs, Crazy Snakes, principal chiefs, Council members, more-assimilated tribal members, and business leaders—told the committee they wanted restrictions to stay in place. "If these restrictions were removed," one Cherokee man warned, "it would not be a year until the white men would have almost everything there is in the whole country and the Indians would have nothing—neither land nor money."

Looking toward statehood, Pleasant Porter, the principal chief of Muscogee Nation, addressed the committee. "I am acting somewhat in the role of a prophet, and I ask you gentlemen to pay attention and see if what I predict will not come to pass," he told the senators. "We will be at the tender mercy of the people and courts of the State, the majority of whom

---

* Blood quantum was codified into US law with the stated goal of "get[ting] rid of the Indian problem"; the idea being once Native children were less than half or a quarter Native they would no longer count and eventually their tribes would no longer exist. Today tribes, not the federal government, set their enrollment criteria. Some tribes kept blood quantum, others didn't.

firmly believe it is true that the only Indian that is worth anything is the one that is dead."

THE FIRST GOVERNOR OF OKLAHOMA WAS INAUGURATED ON NOVEM-
ber 16, 1907. He told the large crowd gathered in downtown Guthrie that Oklahoma was the "first state" where Native people "remained in large numbers," unlike other states which had driven Native Americans from their borders "or buried them beneath the sod." Oklahoma's treatment of Native Americans was so good, he claimed, it was exceptional. (This particular lie was repeated by local district attorneys in a brief they submitted for *Murphy*.) At the ceremony, "Miss Indian Territory" was allegorically married to "Mr. Oklahoma." State officials would swiftly ignore this, but the law Congress passed to create Oklahoma and the state's own constitution carved Native land out of their jurisdiction. The hope Black Americans fleeing the South had placed in the new state was also defeated; Oklahoma's first law segregated railroad cars and waiting rooms.

In Oklahoma's first election, many of the candidates campaigned on "anti-Indian" platforms. And they won. Once Oklahoma's representatives were seated in Congress, they got busy removing remaining federal protections. In 1908, Congress removed all remaining restrictions with two small exceptions: some of the land allotted to people over a half degree of "Indian blood," and everything held by people over three-quarters. Oil and gas leases no longer required federal supervision, all unrestricted land was taxed, and the estates of sixty thousand children came under the jurisdiction of Oklahoma.* Within five years, the majority of unrestricted land was sold for less than it was worth.

WHEN MOSER NAHARKEY DIED, HIS YOUNGEST CHILD WAS A BABY—
only eighteen months old. Millie Naharkey inherited her father's oil-rich

---

* The federal government maintained local probate attorneys who could intervene in specific cases. But the probate attorneys could only file actions in state court.

land, and so her estate was very valuable. Every tribal citizen, including tens of thousands of children, received an allotment. Congress decided that rather than their parents, court-appointed guardians should control the minors' estates. Corruption among the guardians was rampant. Once, Millie's guardian leased her property and pocketed the rent. Another time he charged her estate for a garage bill when she didn't own a car. He loaned his friends money that was never paid back; he loaned himself money that he never paid back. State records showed that guardians typically sold off the minors' land before they turned eighteen and then charged most of the money from the sale for their services. The supervisor of schools for Seminole and Muscogee children observed many of his pupils owned valuable land, but all they ever got from their guardians was "a bunch of bananas, or perhaps that much candy—say something that would cost about 10 cents."

In June 1922, Millie was about to turn eighteen. As an adult, she would be free from her corrupt guardian and in charge of her own land and money. Millie was a shy and soft-spoken teenager. Her quiet demeanor matched her short stature and small frame. Though on the precipice of adulthood, Millie still looked quite young.

Seventeen years after Moser's unexplained death, Grant C. Stebbins was still after the Naharkey allotment. Because other relatives sold off their inheritance, what was left belonged to Millie. A few months before Millie turned eighteen, Grant C. Stebbins tracked down Millie's older brother. At his downtown Tulsa office, Stebbins offered the brother $2,000 if he could get his little sister to sign some papers. Stebbins worried Millie's guardian might try to stop him, and so he didn't want the papers signed in Oklahoma. He told the brother his oil company would pay for the whole family to go on a road trip. While the plan was being hatched, Millie was away at a federally run boarding school designed to assimilate Native children and erase Native culture. By the time she returned home, the plan was already in motion. An agent hired by the oil company visited her brother and then their driver showed up at her house. The whole family—including her brother and mother—left for a nice vacation at a resort nestled deep in the Missouri Ozarks.

A few weeks after her eighteenth birthday, the men took Millie to a law office in southern Missouri. There, they told Millie her guardian

Millie Naharkey

was trying to steal her land, and they were only trying to help her. Millie didn't know what papers she was signing, just that it was a "whole bunch." According to the contract, Stebbins bought her entire inheritance for $25,000, but Millie said he paid only $2,000. At the time, the oil-rich lands were worth an estimated $200,000 to $300,000.

A month into the trip, Millie's mother wanted to go home. Millie wanted to go with her, but the men said no. They lied and said if she went back to Oklahoma she would be arrested. So Millie's mom went home. And Millie stayed with the men—alone.

One day Millie returned to her room at the resort to find her clothes were gone. Her things had been moved to a different room—one that shared a door with the driver Stebbins hired, a man named William McNutt. That is when the assaults started. Millie tried to tell a resort employee, but he was busy. She told a white woman traveling with the group, but she just laughed. William told Millie if she didn't do what he said he would kill her.

By the time Stebbins filed all the paperwork in Tulsa County, her guardian and the Department of the Interior figured out Millie had been abducted for her oil estate. Back in Oklahoma, her mother swore out a warrant for kidnapping, the Interior Department ordered a search, and a special agent headed to Missouri.

The kidnapping likely would have ended sooner, but everyone seemed willing—for a little bit of money—to help Millie's abductors, including local lawyers, local police, the resort owner, his son, and even their employees. To hide her from the police, one taxi driver rolled Millie up in the soft top of his car. To shield William McNutt from rape charges, the men tried to arrange for him and Millie to be married, but the plan fell through. Finally the resort owner's son hid Millie in Kansas City. When Stebbins's agent went to collect her, the son wanted $5,000. When the agent refused to pay, the son told Millie to go to the police. She was not in trouble, he told her, the men had lied. So three months after her abduction began, Millie Naharkey was found when she walked into the Kansas City office of the US Marshals Service.

Millie's abduction was not uncommon for the era. Grafters kept "birthday books" so they knew when minors with valuable estates turned eighteen. A field investigation found the teenagers were "practically kidnapped and carried from place to place." The kidnappings stemmed in part from a race between the grafter and the guardian to control oil estates. In Oklahoma, guardians were not only appointed to children, but also adults declared legally incompetent. "Let oil be discovered on an Indian allotment," a Native rights organization reported. "And one of the profession will promptly file a petition in court to have the individual declared incompetent." Stebbins wanted Millie to sign away her land after she turned eighteen but before she could be declared legally incompetent.

The legal definition for incompetence was malleable. One judge in Okfuskee County declared a Muscogee woman incompetent because she spent her oil royalties on lavish weekend trips with friends. The same judge decided a different Muscogee woman was incompetent because she saved her royalties and didn't spend them. The legal maze was permeated by corruption. Judges doled out guardianships as political plums to people who helped them get elected. The guardians then paid those judges kickbacks with money they embezzled from allottees' estates. When one attorney forced a corrupt judge to resign, someone tried to shoot him—in the courtroom.

For Millie's case federal and tribal officials wanted justice. William McNutt and Stebbins's agent were arrested for kidnapping and their trial was scheduled for December. Disbarment proceedings against the attorney who drew up the fraudulent papers Millie had signed were set for January. The sale of land to Stebbins was declared null and void. Stebbins himself, his company, and the men he hired were sued for $250,000 in damages related to the abduction and assaults.

But Millie was not a party to any of these proceedings. Ten days after her abduction ended, a Tulsa County judge declared her legally incompetent.

Wealth is often seen as a stroke of good fortune. For many allottees the discovery of oil on their land brought tragedy. Muscogee allottee Akey Ulteeskee's guardian took her in when she was only four years old. She later gave birth to his child. Choctaw minor Ledcie Stechi held a valuable oil estate but received so little money from her guardian she was hospitalized for malnutrition. When she died, her grandmother suspected poisoning, but the body was buried without examination. Muscogee freedpeople Stella and Herbert Sells were only ten and fourteen years old when their land became "one of the most valuable pieces of ground in one of the most productive oil fields in the world." They were murdered in their sleep. One of the men who placed dynamite under the floorboards of their house confessed, but no one went to prison, likely because the conspiracy implicated some of the local community's "best people," including a former mayor. The origin story of the great state of Oklahoma contains a vast criminal conspiracy to rob Native people of their land and money.

Allotment teaches us an important lesson about how capitalism has worked in the United States. Namely, who—by any means necessary—was allowed to accumulate wealth. And whose wealth was plundered.

CHAPTER II

The Opposition

ON THE MORNING OF MAY 11, 2020, I WAS IN A HURRY. I WARMED MY cup of coffee, balanced my breakfast plate on the mug, and quickly shuffled to the front bedroom of my house—which, at the time, was serving as a makeshift office. At a desk in the corner, I opened my laptop, found the correct link, and slipped baby-blue headphones over my ears. As I waited for oral arguments in *McGirt v. Oklahoma* to begin, I leaned back in my chair and sipped the coffee. Through the window, I could hear a neighbor mowing their lawn.

Three months after the Supreme Court agreed to hear *McGirt*, COVID-19 shut down life as we knew it. By the second week of March, universities were sending students home and major sports leagues were canceling their games. The Supreme Court followed, announcing their remaining cases would be argued over the phone. Like many institutions that struggled to move their business online, the Supreme Court experienced a few awkward moments, including an infamous toilet flush. But the change also made history. For the first time ever, the public could listen live.

Riyaz Kanji stood in his living room with his notes sprawled out in front of him. His Michigan home was a far cry from the austere court-room in Washington, DC. Sitting and listening were his wife and two children. As the lawyer for Muscogee Nation, arguing the case over the phone came with some benefits and some challenges. He couldn't see the justices' faces or read their body language, but the call came with fewer interruptions—which meant more time for Kanji to speak. The advocates were given a special number to call, which the Supreme Court required they connect to by landline. Ian Gershengorn, Jimcy McGirt's lawyer, had to buy a new phone.

At my house in Oklahoma, I sat up when I heard the marshal's voice. Over a crackling line they read the ceremonial preamble, "The honorable Chief Justice and the Associate Justices of the Supreme Court of the United States. Oyez! Oyez! Oyez!" And then, once again, it began.

Standing in his downtown office in Oklahoma City, the solicitor general of Oklahoma, Mithun Mansinghani—who replaced Lisa Blatt as the state's lawyer—told the court once again Muscogee Nation did not have a reservation. But this time it was for a new and surprising reason. He didn't argue Congress disestablished the reservation. Rather, he claimed, "It never was reservation land." The legal basis on which Oklahoma was hoping to win had changed entirely. In *Murphy*, Oklahoma had argued Congress got rid of the reservation. In *McGirt*, they argued that reservation never existed.

According to Mansinghani, before statehood, Muscogee Nation was a "dependent Indian community," one of the three types of Indian country under federal law, but not a reservation. Oklahoma's switch puzzled more than one of the justices. Two treaties between the United States and Muscogee Nation outlined the boundaries of the "reservation." Even the federal government—which joined the case on Oklahoma's side—did not agree with the state's new theory. Justice Sonia Sotomayor asked the lawyer for the United States, "Are you endorsing that argument?" Stumbling, he replied, "No. No—not—not in terms, we're not." This betrayal of weakness in Oklahoma's argument would seem to pave an easy victory for the tribe, but Oklahoma had another strategy with which it was hoping to win: the practical consequences. "We have currently over seventeen hundred inmates whose crimes were committed in the former Indian territory who identify as Native Americans," Mansinghani told the court.

"So the state presumptively would not have jurisdiction over those people and have to release them."

The implications for old convictions is not where Oklahoma stopped. "On the civil side," Mansinghani continued, "it creates precisely the differential legal treatment between non-Indians and Indians that Congress tried to abolish when it—when it created the state of Oklahoma." Criminal jurisdiction only covers the authority to prosecute crimes. Civil jurisdiction covers basically everything else—from business regulations to taxes and even family law. In their briefs, Oklahoma and its allies painted a bleak picture for the Supreme Court. Reservations, the state claimed, would "upend" everything from private property to liquor sales. Newly affirmed reservations would mean the tribes, not the state, would regulate business on their land. Reservations would also impose federal regulations on those businesses, meaning some would face three levels of rules and red tape: tribal, state, *and* federal. These complicated jurisdictional boundaries would scare off companies from ever investing in Oklahoma. The Five Tribes could even tax non-Natives, meaning in addition to being overregulated, businesses would be double-taxed. On top of all that, a raft of federal regulations that apply on tribal land would kick in, covering everything from environmental regulations, historical preservation, homeland security, and even waste disposal. If Muscogee Nation won, they warned, over a century of laws protecting the "livelihoods and properties of more residents and businesses . . . than are present in any existing Native American reservation" would be totally disrupted.

In a move reminiscent of allotment, the business community—including the farm bureau, the state chamber of commerce, and oil and gas lobbying groups—lined up behind the state and filed a flurry of briefs opposing the Muscogee reservation.* Like they had a century before, they claimed tribal jurisdiction could jeopardize the "substantial sums" they

---

* This included the State Chamber of Oklahoma, the Oklahoma Oil & Gas Association, the Oklahoma Independent Petroleum Association, Oklahoma Farm Bureau Legal Foundation, Mayes County Farm Bureau, Muskogee County Farm Bureau, Oklahoma Cattlemen's Association, and the Environmental Federation of Oklahoma.

invested in Oklahoma. On their face, Supreme Court cases are fought over legal theories and arguments. These high-profile cases are also, of course, about power. In the power struggle over the Muscogee reservation one industry in particular threw its weight behind Oklahoma: oil and gas.

A century after its heyday, Oklahoma is still the sixth largest producer of oil and natural gas in the United States. In the Woodford Shale— Oklahoma's largest and most productive oil basin—there remains an estimated $27 billion worth of oil and gas in the ground. If Muscogee Nation won (and the Supreme Court decision applied to all Five Tribes), 43 percent of the land in Oklahoma (roughly the eastern half of the state) would legally be Indian country. But getting oil out of the ground is expensive. Narrowing the Woodford Shale down to *McGirt*-affected counties and using oil futures and average regional operating costs to calculate profit, the oil and gas reserves on the reservations would generate less than $2 billion in profit—total. If the future price of a barrel of crude doesn't go up much, it would be less than $1 billion.

The first brief the oil and gas industry filed in *Murphy* started in a surprising place: old wells. Of the nearly 200,000 wells dotting Oklahoma, over a third are abandoned—meaning they don't have an operator. Marginal or "stripper" wells still pump oil, but only a trickle—less than fifteen barrels per day. According to the Energy Information Administration, 90 percent of wells in Oklahoma are marginal.

While a significant portion of Oklahoma's oil and gas infrastructure is on the Five Tribes' land (39 percent of pipelines, 80 percent of refineries, and 65 percent of all wells), an even higher portion of *old* oil and gas infrastructure is there: a whopping 81 percent of abandoned wells. In the fight over climate change, plugging old wells (because they leak methane, a greenhouse gas) is often seen as low-hanging fruit. But plugging wells is expensive. Based on cleanup costs provided by the state, plugging just the abandoned wells within the Five Tribes' territory would cost nearly $1 billion. Plugging all wells—many of which are marginal—would cost almost $2 billion. The price tag of cleaning up old wells in eastern Oklahoma is likely higher than the total profits producers could hope to pump there.

A century ago, the state of Oklahoma railroaded tribes to ring in the state's oil boom. Unfettered by environmental regulations and able to ignore basic property laws on allotted land, oilmen made their riches. Today the inheritors of those riches don't want to pay to clean up their mess.

Another reason the oil and gas industry does not want the "mature and stable regulatory regime" in Oklahoma to change is because they control it. Since statehood, the industry has crafted the legislation, staffed the agencies, and worked to ensure they can operate as they please. Oklahoma's first big oil and gas regulation paints this picture. In 1915, the state was in crisis; the oil boom pumped so much crude so quickly that the price crashed. At the industry's behest, the state decided it would control the price of oil by rationing the amount hitting the market—much like OPEC does. The Oklahoma Corporation Commission was chosen to enforce the 1915 law, and is still in charge of regulation today.* In Oklahoma's early years, it was not environmental catastrophes, murdered children, or vast criminal conspiracies that prompted the state to act; it was profit.

In the 1990s, the state was facing another crisis. Hundreds of abandoned wells were draining "directly" into one of the reservoirs that provides the city of Tulsa with its drinking water. The Oklahoma Corporation Commission, tasked with preventing such a crisis, wasn't doing anything about it. One year, the agency failed to plug ten thousand known abandoned wells and collected only 10 percent of the fines it issued. As the crisis escalated, the commission was under investigation by the Oklahoma state legislature and even itself.

In response to the debacle, the Oklahoma state legislature created the Oklahoma Energy Resources Board, which would help plug old and abandoned wells around the state. But the board came with a catch: the oil and gas industry controlled it. Seeing regulation on the horizon, the

---

* Leaders and staff at the Oklahoma Corporation Commission have also worked for Phillips Petroleum, the lobbying group Independent Petroleum Producers of America, Kirkpatrick Oil Company, and fracking giant Chesapeake Energy. As of August 2022, OCC's three elected commissioners have collectively received over $2 million in campaign contributions from oil and gas. A 2021 investigation found that at least half a dozen former OCC staff have gone on to work for public utility companies, "trading in a state government salary for a nice pension and larger private paycheck."

industry got ahead of the problem and lobbied for a board where they held twenty of the twenty-one seats.* When wells are decommissioned under the board's supervision, it's voluntary.

In the early 2000s, the oil and gas industry was scared of potential regulation again. But this time it didn't come from a scandal or possible legislation; it came from tribes. In 1998, Pawnee Nation in central Oklahoma asked the Environmental Protection Agency for authority to set water quality standards on its land. Under the Clean Water, Safe Drinking Water, and Clean Air Acts, state governments must set water and air quality standards. After amendments added in the 1980s, tribes can do the same by applying for what's called "treatment as state." Tribal environmental standards, often more stringent than those of states, can impact what pollutants are allowed in the water upstream and the air upwind of tribal land. In 2003, Cherokee Nation also applied for treatment as state and, a year later, Pawnee Nation's application was approved. Oklahoma's oil and gas leaders were spooked.

At the urging of an industry front group, in 2005, Oklahoma senator Jim Inhofe sneaked some two hundred words into a big, national highway bill making its way through Congress.† The Inhofe rider, as it came to be known, required the EPA get Oklahoma's approval before granting tribes treatment as state. The midnight rider was passed before Oklahoma's tribes issued a single citation or attempted to regulate oil and gas operators on their land. The underhanded legislation wasn't in response to existing tribal regulations; it was to cut off future regulation from ever happening.‡

---

* The leadership and staff of OERB come from oil and gas; board members have included Harold Hamm, the executive chairman of fracking giant Continental Resources, as well as other leaders from Devon Energy, Chesapeake Energy, the Oklahoma Independent Petroleum Association, and the National Stripper Well Association. In a secret memo to Oklahoma's governor, the OERB warned that reservation status could greatly disrupt its work of plugging old wells (of which it has plugged only a fraction).

† The front group—called One Nation—was started with funding from industry groups, and co-founded by the inaugural director of OERB.

‡ Years later, industry briefs in *Murphy*—including from a group that lobbied for the Inhofe rider—claimed that under the Clean Water, Safe Drinking Water, and Clean Air Acts, Muscogee Nation *could* regulate pollution. Their legal team likely knew that Oklahoma would be able to override any such attempt.

Much like Oklahoma did, the oil and gas industry exaggerated *Mc-Girt's* potential impact. Thanks to the *Montana* Supreme Court decision, tribal civil jurisdiction over non-Natives on what's called "fee land" is extremely limited. For the five tribes in eastern Oklahoma, 95 to 99 percent of our reservations is fee land. For the Five Tribes to have real regulatory authority over non-Native businesses on their reservations, Inhofe's midnight rider would have to be repealed and the *Montana* Supreme Court decision would need to be rewritten. The worst-case scenarios peppering the industry's briefs would need more than an affirmed reservation to come true. Exaggerating to win makes sense, but it begs the question: if the potential impact is so small, why care about winning in the first place?

While it seems illogical at first, the strategy in *McGirt* is textbook. The industry is effective at preventing regulation because it is always five steps ahead. Oil and gas producers don't fight regulation as it comes up; the industry lays the groundwork to ensure future regulation is not possible. When local communities started pushing back on fracking, conservative states (including Oklahoma, which saw fracking-induced earthquakes) passed preemption laws forbidding local municipalities from banning fracking. The industry organized similar laws preempting bans on plastic bags—a petroleum product. As of 2020, fifteen states have banned the banning of plastic bags, while only eight limit their use. Nowhere has this forward-looking strategy been more successful than with climate change. In the 1970s, when scientists at Exxon and other major oil companies connected the dots between burning gas and global warming, the industry organized a disinformation campaign that delayed global climate action for decades.

Greed has many forms. In previous generations, land speculators, slave owners, grafters, and oilmen fought for the spoils of removal and allotment. In this generation, the greedy are fighting the possibility that tribes might gain back an inch of what was taken.

BACK AT MY HOUSE IN OKLAHOMA, I WAS STILL SITTING AT MY DESK with headphones over my ears. The phone argument—without the court's usually strict time limits—ran long. After an hour, they were only half-way through. Staring at the blank wall before me, I listened most closely to what the justices had to say, trying to anticipate which way they would vote. With a Supreme Court of nine justices, Muscogee Nation needed five to win. In 2020, the court had four liberal justices and five conservative ones. But the issues of tribal sovereignty often don't follow party lines. The arena of federal Indian law is unique, not mapping easily onto equity, civil rights, or other frameworks progressives use to support marginalized groups. Also, some conservative lawmakers represent rural districts with large tribal constituencies. At the time, four Native Americans served in the US House of Representatives: two Democrats and, from Oklahoma, two Republicans. Guessing how the vote would go in *McGirt* would take more than counting the court's conservative majority.

During oral arguments, some justices clearly supported the reservation of Muscogee Nation. "What do we do with the treaty language here that resulted as—after the Trail of Tears with the Creek Nation?" Justice Sonia Sotomayor asked Oklahoma's solicitor general. "That nation was wrenched from its homeland, marched to Oklahoma, and then given a treaty as recompense which guaranteed its sovereignty." But other justices showed obvious skepticism that such a big area could possibly be a reservation. "Am I correct that more than 90 percent of the people who live in the area directly affected by this case are not members of the Creek tribe?" Justice Samuel Alito asked Muscogee Nation's lawyer. "Won't they be surprised to learn that they are living on a reservation?"

Of the nine justices, I was focused on two: Neil Gorsuch and Ruth Bader Ginsburg. If the prevailing theory was correct—that in *Murphy* the justices were locked in a 4–4 tie—Gorsuch would cast the deciding vote. Before being appointed to the Supreme Court by President Donald Trump in 2017, Gorsuch served on the Tenth Circuit Court of Appeals. That appeals court is home to seventy-eight federally recognized tribes—meaning Gorsuch has a lot of experience in federal Indian law.

On the high court, Gorsuch quickly gained a reputation for upholding treaty rights and tribal sovereignty. As a Republican appointee, this surprised many non-Native commentators. The Supreme Court correspondent for NPR described Gorsuch's jurisprudence on federal Indian law as "loud" and "passionate" and another NPR reporter called him "sympathetic" to tribes. But those characterizations reveal a shallow understanding. Gorsuch is a textualist. Meaning that he believes it is the role of the courts to interpret, not create, law. When the court defers to Congress and follows the law as written, tribes usually win. (Many other so-called textualists throw the letter of the law out the window when it comes to Indigenous nations.) Rather than being "passionate" about Native rights, Justice Gorsuch is consistent about following the law.

During oral arguments, Gorsuch showed little patience for Oklahoma's reasoning. After other justices asked about all the non-Native people living in eastern Oklahoma, Gorsuch declared the demographics were irrelevant. "Especially," he elaborated, "when later demographic evidence sometimes shows nothing more than that states have violated Native American rights." When it came to the practical consequences, Gorsuch mocked Oklahoma's warnings, calling it a "parade of horribles." At the end of the day, Jimcy McGirt's lawyer, Ian Gershengorn, felt sure they had Gorsuch's vote. Gorsuch was "viewing the case the way we viewed it," Ian thought during the teleconference. Which meant—if the Supreme Court *had* been locked in a 4–4 tie—Muscogee Nation would win.

But, listening to the oral arguments, I felt less sure. There was another vote I didn't think the tribe could depend on: Justice Ruth Bader Ginsburg's. "What makes this case hard," Ginsburg told Gershengorn, "is that there have been hundreds, hundreds of prosecutions, some very heinous offenses of the state law . . . for murder, for terrible sexual offenses." Unlike Gorsuch, Ginsburg appeared to believe Oklahoma's dire warnings.

To many who celebrate Ginsburg's liberal legacy, her record on Indigenous rights comes as a surprise. But liberals are no less immune from the prevailing ignorance about tribal sovereignty. During her tenure on the Supreme Court, Ginsburg authored nine cases in the arena of federal Indian law. Of those nine, tribes lost eight. Ginsburg cut her teeth at the ACLU as the director of their Women's Rights Project. Protecting most marginalized groups in the United States looks like fighting for individual liberties and civil rights, but tribal sovereignty is different. Legally, Indigenous rights are held collectively by the tribe—not the individual.

Many liberal groups don't understand the difference. When the citizenship requirements of the Santa Clara Pueblo—which accepted the children of intermarried men but not women—were challenged in federal court, the ACLU weighed in against the tribe. A federal Indian law expert at the time tried to persuade his colleagues not to undermine tribal sovereignty, but Ginsburg wanted to fight for the equality of women.

During her Supreme Court confirmation hearings, Ginsburg was asked how familiar she was with federal Indian law. She replied, "I cannot pretend to [have] any special knowledge in this area of the law." From this ignorance, Ginsburg often skipped over the relevant principles of federal Indian law, to rely on other areas of the law such as taxation, civil rights, or laches—like she did in the 2005 *Sherrill* decision. In the waning years of her tenure on the bench, Ginsburg began to side with tribes more often, and even expressed regret about her earlier decisions. But her track record was not forgotten. In *McGirt v. Oklahoma*, she was arguably the swing vote.

Like Lisa Blatt, Gershengorn reserved two minutes of his time for the very end—giving him the last word. He told the justices not to trust Oklahoma's wild predictions. "The numbers today are mind-boggling [on the] back of the envelope. They don't appear in any of the briefs." But then he was interrupted; his two minutes were up. "Thank you, Counsel," the chief justice interjected. "The case is submitted." And with that, the line piping through my headphones over C-SPAN went silent.

Later that same week, the Supreme Court justices gathered again. This time in private. Then and there, they took a vote. The most senior justice in the majority chose who would write the opinion, and then that justice and their law clerks got busy drafting the final outcome. Months before the public would know anything, the case had been decided.

CHAPTER 12

Slow Bleed

IN THE DECADES FOLLOWING ALLOTMENT, THEFT, CORRUPTION, AND violence descended upon allottees. Policymakers tried to find solutions, but every measure they put in place to protect allottees seemed to cause only more hardship. The obvious solution—stopping theft by holding the thieves accountable—rarely happened. When a Tulsa County judge declared Millie Naharkey legally incompetent, it was to protect her estate from being "squandered and wasted." Something Millie, the court ruled, could not do because she did not understand "business transactions." Millie fought the designation and even hired her own lawyer, but she had little control over what happened next. With the white legal system controlling her life, Millie would see little justice.

By the time her abduction ended, Millie Naharkey was famous. The story of a Native woman flush with oil money and embroiled in scandal fascinated the press. Reporters called Millie an "Indian heiress to fortune" and a "dark-eyed beauty," but the name that stuck was "Poor Little Rich Indian Girl." It was decided Millie Naharkey should no longer live with her family, so she moved into the home of an Indian agent with the Department of the Interior. Millie's land and the royalties from oil drilled there were worth hundreds of thousands of dollars, but the money was tied up in litigation. Millie was destitute. She worked in the home of a doctor as a domestic.

At a preliminary hearing, the kidnapping charges against Stebbins's agent and William McNutt were dismissed. The judge concluded that Millie went to the resort in Missouri "willingly." The men were found guilty of a lesser crime, "giving intoxicants to an Indian"; each paid a $100 fine and served a year in jail. The disbarment case against the lawyer who drew up the fraudulent paperwork was also dropped. While the lawsuit for $250,000 in damages against Stebbins was still pending, he died. Millie's guardian dropped the suit.

With justice for the abduction foreclosed, what was left to recover was Millie's land and royalties owed for what had been drilled there. Barred from doing it herself, Millie's guardians filed about a dozen lawsuits on her behalf. Over the years, Millie's mother and brother had sold sections of the land they had inherited after Moser's death. Those sales were invalid, her guardian argued, because Millie still owned an interest in Moser's land. And that interest was still restricted. In 1936—more than a decade after it started—the Oklahoma Supreme Court settled the dispute. "'Little Millie' Wins" read the headline. At the age of thirty-one, Millie regained her interest in over two hundred acres of land and decades of royalties. Even of this money, Millie saw only a fraction. When her largest debtor offered to settle for less than what they owed, Millie's guardian took the deal. In the end, Millie's estate was awarded $44,000—almost one million dollars in today's money.

As soon as the settlement was announced people started claiming pieces of it. The wife of the Indian agent who housed Millie wanted money after the fact for room and board. The lawyer who worked for Millie's first two guardians (but was fired by the time the case was settled) petitioned for his contingency fee—half of everything. The lawyers working for Millie's new guardian took a 25 percent fee. Over $2,000 was swallowed by guardian's fees, "general services," and "other miscellaneous items." When it was all said and done, Millie's estate was left with less than $27,000.* Ironically,

---

* The Indian agent's wife was not awarded any money, and the first lawyer was eventually paid $2,646.67.

it was only a few thousand more than what Stebbins had tried to swindle her for.

The mountain of litigation that stood between Millie Naharkey and her valuable estate was not unusual for the era. What followed the orgy of speculation, graft, and theft was thousands upon thousands of lawsuits. At one point, a fifth of all land in eastern Oklahoma was tied up in litigation. In a suit brought by Muscogee Nation, the governor was a named defendant. In what came to be known as the "Thirty Thousand Land Suits," the Department of Justice filed a raft of litigation; it covered some 3.8 million acres taken from approximately 16,000 allottees. But even the federal government lacked the appetite to pursue fraud. Within five years, nearly 10,000 cases were dropped. During *Murphy* and *McGirt*, Oklahoma and its business community warned that reservations would create "intolerable uncertainty" and a tide of "time-consuming lawsuits." They forgot that is precisely how our state began.

WHEN THE LITIGATION WAS FINALLY OVER, MILLIE'S GUARDIANSHIP was not. Millie could work and garner wages, but every cent collected from her land went through her guardian. Anytime Millie wanted some of that money, she had to ask for it. Her guardian and a Tulsa County judge decided whether or not the expense was necessary. Millie had to ask permission to buy clothing, pay a hospital bill, for seeds to plant a garden, for lumber to build a garage, for a lawyer to get a divorce, to visit her sick daughter out of state, to tow her car after an accident, to pay her taxes; for dentures, groceries, Christmas presents, home insurance, car insurance, a coat, a roof, a garbage disposal, living-room furniture and curtains, pillowcases, sheets, and towels. When Millie tried to get a divorce, she was told she couldn't. People who have been declared legally incompetent cannot bring any lawsuit on their own behalf. When Millie thought she needed a new refrigerator, her guardian disagreed. Millie took an ice pick, destroyed the refrigerator beyond repair, and asked again. The guardian submitted a one-page request to buy a new Coldspot.

In 1938, at the age of thirty-four, Millie asked the Tulsa County probate judge to restore her competency. Millie Naharkey is "now a sane person," the petition read. "And fully competent and capable of transacting her own business and affairs." The petition was denied.

IN THE LATE 1920S, MEMBERS OF CONGRESS AND FEDERAL OFFICIALS showed interest in how allotment affected Native people, for the first time since the process began. It quickly became clear their policy decisions had been devastating. When the Senate Committee on Indian Affairs traveled to eastern Oklahoma, they found tribal communities threatened by famine and people already dying from starvation. Even the federal advisory board that originally called for allotment admitted they were wrong. An independent Native rights organization reported the corruption, theft, and lawlessness they found in eastern Oklahoma was "almost unbelievable in a civilized country." After three decades, allotment—originally billed as a program that would lift Native people up out of poverty—was deemed an abject failure.

Congress was ready to change course, but Oklahoma voters protested. They were mad that a small percentage of land in their state was still restricted (only 15 percent by 1920). Still, the state legislature called restrictions an "unjust" burden that kept land off their "tax rolls." So Congress struck a compromise. The Oklahoma Indian Welfare Act kept state jurisdiction over guardianship cases like Millie's, but it gave the secretary of the Interior authority to take land into trust for tribes—restoring a tiny fraction of lost land back to tribal jurisdiction. Restrictions stayed in place if allotted land was owned or inherited by someone of one-half blood quantum or more. "Any recognized tribe or band of Indians" could form their own government, but the bill kept a measure suppressing democracy in place: each chief of the five tribes was appointed by the president of the United States, not elected by their people.

WHILE THE INITIAL HEMORRHAGE OF LAND LOSS SLOWED, FOR NATIVE families in Oklahoma the bleeding never stopped. Every Native family in Oklahoma carries the story of how their land was taken. A few hold the story of what they managed to save.

On top of Sue Wind's family land—Seminole and Muscogee—they built a lake. Through the land of Daniel Wind, deputy chief of the Muscogee Lighthorse Tribal Police Department, they built Interstate 40. When Cherokee allottee Louella Kingfisher died in the 1918 flu epidemic, her family didn't speak English. After they didn't file the right kind of paperwork to keep the land restricted, the county seized it for unpaid taxes. When Chickasaw allottee Belzora Allen Thomas died of tuberculosis, her children were at boarding school. They never learned what land she left them, and squatters took it. Squatters took the family land of Sheila Bird (citizen of the United Keetoowah Band of Cherokee Indians) too—in the 1990s. As Choctaw freedpeople, Doris Burris Williamson's great-grandparents lost their restrictions early on. Some of their land was taken for unpaid taxes; other pieces got sold when they needed money. After about a century, the old family cemetery is encircled by land they don't own. The graves—which date back to the 1840s—hold ancestors that traveled the Trail of Tears and family members who were enslaved. Today, Doris can't visit them.

Te'Ata Loper—citizen of Chickasaw Nation and Choctaw descendant—lives on 159 acres of restricted allotment land spanning the clear waters of the Blue River. Because it's spring-fed, the water is always cold. The land across the street is still owned by family, but not restricted, because those cousins' blood quantum wasn't high enough. Until 2018, anytime someone less than one-half blood quantum inherited allotted land, the land was no longer restricted. When Te'Ata was a teenager, her grandmother died, her aunt died, and her father went to prison, in quick succession. So taking care of the land fell to her. Interested buyers approached her, but she said no. For a few years of grad school, she commuted two hours each way. At times it was fragile, but she managed not to lose it. And so, future generations will always have a place to come home. Today, of the over 15 million acres of land that was allotted, less than 400,000 acres are still restricted—just over 2 percent. A victory in *McGirt* would not give back a single acre of land lost. The litigation impacted only reservation boundaries, not private property ownership within it.

William Dudley Polson named his youngest daughter Frances. Unlike her older siblings, Frances was born too late to receive an allotment.

When she was eleven, the family moved to Oklahoma City. She stayed there and came to work as a secretary for Patrick Sarsfield Nagle II—the son of my great-grandfather who made the land run. When his mother found out her firstborn was dating a Cherokee woman, she threatened to disown him. So my grandparents eloped.

William Dudley Polson's family never lived on his allotted land. In 1917, they used it to take out a mortgage and later leased it to an oil and gas company. He held on to it until he died. After his death in 1950, his widow and children inherited the land. The family's blood quantum was too low for it to still be restricted and, within two years, they sold it. A few years later my grandfather Patrick Sarsfield Nagle II died of stomach cancer. In Oklahoma City, Frances worked as a schoolteacher and raised four children. Hanging on her living-room wall were always two framed portraits: one of Major Ridge and one of John. Frances was very proud of her Cherokee family, but lived most of her life away from the tribe and culture. As her granddaughter, I inherited her pride—and her distance.

My grandfather is buried in the Nagle family plot in Kingfisher— next to the generations of our Irish family that settled Oklahoma. But my grandmother had other plans. My direct ancestors did not hold on to their allotment land, but their cousins did. The land where we have lived since removal is still in the family—abutting the Polson cemetery. Down one row and over several yards from the graves of Major and John Ridge is a polished gray headstone engraved with my grandmother's name. Allotment meant there was not an easy place to come back and live. But there is still a place to be buried.

WITH THE OIL MONEY THAT PULSED THROUGH TULSA IN THE EARLY TWEN-tieth century, developers built some of the city's finest neighborhoods— several on top of Naharkey allotments. Since the original sales weren't quite aboveboard, subsequent property owners worried that Naharkey descendants might come back and try to claim the land. If a property owner has such a worry, they can file what's called a quiet title lawsuit. If the property owner wins, the named defendants are barred from ever claiming the land. Because Tulsa was built on the rampant swindle and theft of allotted land, these types of cases are not uncommon in the city's old neighborhoods. Since the 1930s, property owners have filed over 140 lawsuits to quiet the Naharkey family's title to land in Tulsa.

Legally, the named defendants in a quiet title lawsuit have to be notified, but the Tulsa property owners all claimed they couldn't find any Naharkeys. So the family was notified by an ad in the paper—a few paragraphs buried in the back pages of legal notices and real estate sales. Unsurprisingly, the Naharkey family never showed up to court. So, in each suit, the property owners won by default. The lawsuits were brought by corporations like the Salvation Army, Oral Roberts University, and Arvest Bank, and families like the Perrymans, Adairs, Burkharts, Robinsons, Flourneys, Harringtons, and Scotts. The most recent one was filed in 2016.

MILLIE GREW OLD IN A SMALL, ONE-STORY HOUSE IN WEST TULSA. THE family tore down a wall to convert the three-bedroom home into two, and Millie slept in the larger one. Out front there was a big tree and out back a small garage. The house was always full of animals, especially dogs. Little dogs—long and skinny dachshunds—lived inside. The big dogs, like Rottweilers and Dobermans, stayed out. The house sat on a corner lot at the bottom of a small hill. Some family members remember it being white, and others a "God-awful" pink. Today it is painted beige.

Michael Peevey lived in the house when he was about eight or nine. He remembers his great-grandma always sitting in the same chair in the living room. Millie was short her whole life, but in old age she was "tiny," according to Michael. They called her "baby grandma." When they walked through the yard together Millie would teach Michael Muscogee words. It was never simple things—like "dog" or "tree"—but phrases about how Michael should treat people. Darla Yeatman remembers her grandmother always wearing a pink housecoat and little slippers. "She was about as poor as a poor Indian could be," Darla remembers. But Darla never heard Millie complain.

I asked Darla if Millie ever talked about what happened to her. "Never, never, never," she responded. "Grandma never uttered a word." Growing up, Michael knew his great-grandmother had been cheated, but he didn't know how. "I remember hearing stories that she at one time owned a lot of land," he told me. Driving down the highway, older relatives would point to the big Pepsi bottling plant, the YMCA, or Turkey Mountain, and tell Michael it had once all belonged to his grandma. Like most of the family, he didn't find out about the assaults until after Millie died and the once famous story of her kidnapping resurfaced. In a way, the truth helped him understand his grandma; maybe that's why she was so quiet in her old age. Maybe that's why she was so guarded.

Buried in Millie's Tulsa County probate file is an application from her guardian to enroll her in Medicare. Millie Naharkey had a guardian until she died in 1996.

Early in April, when the season was still transitioning from spring to summer, I met Millie's granddaughter Darla Yeatman on a surprisingly warm day. After meeting at a coffee shop, we piled into her car and headed south. The sprawling Memorial Park Cemetery spans 250 acres on the bottom edge of Tulsa. After driving around once, we went to the cemetery's office for help. A man there printed out a little map, and drew a curved line pointing to the piece of ground where she is buried. We drove to the marked section, got out, and started looking. At the corner of every grave, level with the earth, was a small circle of cement the size of my hand. Each circle contained a number. Darla and I fanned out reading the numbers in rows. Where the grass had grown up over the cement circles, I pushed it aside with my foot.

The people who made money from Millie's land founded the city of Sand Springs, the University of Tulsa, and the upscale neighborhoods of Maple Ridge and Stonebraker Heights. Today in their honor stands a library, a boulevard, a historic district, and a bronze statue. After a few minutes, Darla and I found the right number marking an empty space in the grass. After everything that was taken from Millie Naharkey, there was no money for a headstone.

Darla Yeatman at her grandmother Millie's grave

CHAPTER 13

The Victory

JULY 9, 2020, WAS THE LAST DAY OF THE SUPREME COURT'S TERM. THEY had three opinions left to announce. Two about whether or not Donald Trump would reveal his taxes. And then, *McGirt*.

Rosemary McCombs Maxey was at her home near Dustin, Oklahoma, in the southern corner of the Muscogee Reservation. From the large windows in her family room, she could see the pasture, lightly dusted from the dirt road. She had been told by one of her language students, Sarah Deer, that they were expecting the decision any day. When her phone rang—and the caller ID came up with Sarah's name—she knew what it was.

Former principal chief James Floyd was six months out of office and following the news from home. Like many people that day, he was hitting refresh on the popular *SCOTUSblog*. Daniel Wind—acting chief of the Lighthorse Tribal Police Department—was anxiously waiting with recently elected Principal Chief David Hill, and other tribal leaders. Because of COVID the gathering was small, but the room was full of anticipation.

Philip Tinker, the Osage lawyer who had gotten interested in Patrick's appeals in law school, was working remotely from Perú. Riyaz Kanji, who had argued the case in front of the Supreme Court, was sitting at home, the blue glow of his computer screen lighting his face. Ian Gershengorn was on vacation with his family in western Maryland. After feverishly reloading the Supreme Court's opinion page, he saw two links pop up: one to the decision in *Murphy* and one for *McGirt*. He clicked on *Murphy* first. "The judgment of the United States Court of Appeals for the Tenth Circuit is affirmed for the reasons stated in *McGirt v. Oklahoma*," the PDF read. Ian had to think for a moment: "Well, wait." He paused. "Is that good or bad?"

On Oklahoma's death row, Patrick Murphy was handing out lunch when someone saw the verdict on TV. At the James Crabtree Correctional Center, Jimcy McGirt was lying on his bunk when he heard a fellow inmate yell his name.

As the editor in chief of Mvskoke Media, Angel Ellis knew that July 9, 2020, was going to be a busy day. She tried to go to bed early. To her surprise, she fell right asleep, but then, at 4 a.m., she woke up. She got up and made coffee. She went and got donuts. In the dark, she watered her tomato plants. Finally, she just went into work. The newsroom at Mvskoke Media was packed with staff waiting for the Supreme Court's announcement. On decision days, *SCOTUSblog* is almost like Twitter, filled with a river of constant posts—only a few of which actually announce the day's decisions. More than once Angel saw the flash of a new post, thought that was it, but then it wasn't. "I would just catch my breath," she remembers.

MY HOME IN TAHLEQUAH, OKLAHOMA, IS A SMALL, ONE-STORY TWO-bedroom with big windows and a sprawling backyard. At times when I am searching for stillness or peace, I sit in the backyard and watch the trees. On days that are not too windy, their branches move in a quiet unison.

When I woke up that morning, I knew it was the day the case I'd been following for three years would be decided. Praying in the backyard, I felt calm. A victory for Muscogee Nation would ultimately uphold the reservation status of my tribe. And I knew the law was on our side.

But as I stood before my bathroom sink, my confidence failed me. Toothbrush in hand, I started crying. My mind went back to Ruth Bader Ginsburg, and I had this sinking feeling she would vote against the tribe.

But the emotion was something more than worry or even dread. After everything our ancestors sacrificed, our land was in the hands of this one person—who knew a fraction of our history, if that. The feeling was powerlessness.

When I sat down at the desk in my office, the pit of my stomach churned; I was a mess. I watched the time on my phone as the minutes marched forward from 8:55, to 8:58, until finally it struck 9 a.m. Central time. Like everyone else that morning, I started hitting refresh. So many people were on the Supreme Court's website it wouldn't load. I sat waiting through agonizing minutes until finally I saw the link pop up. I clicked on it.

The first thing I wanted to know was who wrote the opinion. In my mind, just that name would indicate if we had won or lost, and by how much. I scrolled past the syllabus, to the bottom of the fourth page. In small, capital letters the PDF read GORSUCH. I started screaming. And then I wept.

"On the far end of the Trail of Tears was a promise," the opinion began. "Forced to leave their ancestral lands in Georgia and Alabama, the Creek Nation received assurances that their new lands in the West would be secure forever. . . . Today, we are asked whether the land these treaties promised remains an Indian reservation for the purposes of federal criminal law. Because Congress has not said otherwise, we hold the government to its word."

THAT FIRST MONTH OF SUMMER IN OKLAHOMA WAS HOT AND DRY. FOR weeks, rain was nowhere in sight. The lush weeds, wildflowers, and grass turned brown and crisp at their edges. Even the trees looked tired. That morning, the sky cracked open and it poured. A hard, pelting rain that pooled in the dirt. It was as if the earth knew. You can deny a people what is rightfully theirs for only so long. Eventually something must give.

That day across eastern Oklahoma, tribal citizens celebrated the victory with joy in abundance. But it was joy that also cut hard and deep. Our blood and our bones knew how much had been lost to reach this one act of justice.

When Angel Ellis saw the sky playing with the idea of rain that morning, she thought maybe it was a bad sign; the clouds felt ominous. But then, timed almost to the second she realized her tribe had won, the sky erupted. And then the rain felt good. It felt like her ancestors were crying with her.

"It's been a century of loss," she told me. "For Indigenous people it's been stomp, trod, move over and just railroading. . . . And finally, finally, some people with power are like we're gonna make the bleeding stop. . . . That never happens."

Rosemary McCombs Maxey is a woman of faith. All along, she believed her tribe would win, but on the phone that morning, she was in shock. "I can't really believe it," she said into the receiver. Before James Floyd could read the decision, his phone was ringing. People called from everywhere. Some were ecstatic; others were sobbing. Most were simply overwhelmed. When the decision came down, Daniel Wind watched the room of tribal leaders explode. To Daniel, it was electric; "there's no other word for it," he said.

At his vacation home in western Maryland, Ian Gershengorn started screaming. "I can't believe we won!" he cried out. To Riyaz Kanji, the victory felt like a dream. For days and even weeks after, he woke up every morning in disbelief. "Did that really just happen?" he would think to himself. Sometime later, when it finally soaked in, he felt like he had been a small part of history. Philip Tinker, like many people, was stunned as he read the first paragraph of the decision. It felt like finally someone in power reflected back to him what he knew all along. That, despite Oklahoma's century of gaslighting tribes, the state was not different. The law applies here just like it does everywhere else.

Even the federal public defenders who worked on the original habeas petition back in 2004 started getting calls—some from each other. When Gary Peterson heard the news, he thought of Lisa. "I wish Lisa was around to savor this victory," he told me. "Because she was the one that got this ball rolling."

After twenty years, nineteen appeals, and two Supreme Court cases, the reservation of Muscogee Nation was affirmed.

"It is important to stop here, in the moment, and to recognize all that it has taken to arrive at this act of justice. There was the resolve, struggle and battle, the food cooked to help those working long hours. There were those who picked up, who took care of the children," wrote Muscogee citizen and US poet laureate Joy Harjo. "Those who kept walking the long distance of heartbreak to arrive, in a reservation, and start all over again. And at last, on the far end of the Trail of Tears, a promise has been kept."

MUSCOGEE NATION WON BY A MARGIN OF ONE VOTE—FOUR OUT OF the nine justices ruled against the tribe. Joining Chief Justice John Roberts's dissent were Alito, Thomas, and Kavanaugh. To them, it was preposterous that such a large area of Oklahoma could be a reservation when it hadn't been recognized in over a century.

"Not only does the Court discover a Creek reservation that spans three million acres and includes most of the city of Tulsa," the chief justice wrote. "But the Court's reasoning portends that there are four more such reservations in Oklahoma." These reservations, the chief justice balked, encompassed half of the entire state and were home to 1.8 million people, "only 10%–15% of whom are Indians."

To get around a strict application of the *Solem* test, Roberts argued that the court shouldn't look at congressional statutes "in a vacuum," but rather employ a "broader inquiry." The dissent admitted there was no act of Congress that divested Muscogee Nation of their reservation. That was no matter, Roberts argued, because if the court factored in all of the "contextual evidence," it was clear that's what Congress intended to do. Like Lisa Blatt, Roberts used the history of everything else taken from the tribe to justify getting rid of the reservation today.

In his dissent, Chief Justice Roberts repeated the lies told about the Five Tribes to justify allotment. The illegal white squatters who poured into Indian Territory, Roberts wrote, "transformed vast stretches of territorial wilderness into farmland and ranches." By virtue of their hard work, he opined, they deserved private property rights. Roberts even argued, as Senator Dawes had, that communal land ownership kept tribal citizens poor and that allotment—unbelievably—helped them out of that poverty. A century later, the excuse for divesting Muscogee Nation of their land had not changed. Some lies about Indigenous people apparently never die.

The dissenting justices were also concerned about the practical consequences. "The State's ability to prosecute serious crimes will be hobbled and decades of past convictions could well be thrown out," they predicted. "Thousands of convictions" including "murder, rape, kidnapping, and maiming" would be called into question. Muscogee Nation's victory "profoundly destabilized" the governance of eastern Oklahoma, Roberts wrote, and would have far-reaching consequences "from zoning and taxation to family and environmental law."

The *McGirt* decision was historic, but it was not groundbreaking. In his opinion, Justice Gorsuch did not create new rules for lower courts to determine whether or not a reservation still exists. He merely followed the existing rules set by earlier decisions. Yet that outcome was still radical. Throughout US history, when laws protecting Indigenous nations are inconvenient for states or a broad base of non-Native constituents, the US government does not follow the law. But this time it did.

Siding with Justice Gorsuch were the four liberal justices at the time: Sonia Sotomayor, Elena Kagan, Stephen Breyer, and, yes, Ruth Bader Ginsburg. The majority opinion started in a familiar place: with the *Solem* test, named after the controlling Supreme Court decision. According to *Solem*, Gorsuch wrote, "there is only one place we may look" to see if the Muscogee reservation was ever disestablished: "the Acts of Congress." During the allotment era, Congress certainly wanted to get rid of the reservation, Gorsuch admitted, but "wishes don't make for laws." Like one would expect in any other area of the law, for Congress to get rid of a reservation, it must do so in writing. Since there was no act of Congress disestablishing the Muscogee reservation, the majority ruled that it must stand. The case was cut-and-dry.

From that swift conclusion, the opinion proceeds for another thirty-four pages. This was necessary because a strict interpretation of *Solem* was never all that Oklahoma (and the dissent) based its reasoning on. As for Oklahoma's argument that Congress took so much from Muscogee Nation that it intended to take the reservation too, Gorsuch had this to say: "It's no matter how many other promises to a tribe the federal government has already broken," he wrote. "If Congress wishes to break the promise of a reservation, it must say so." As for the practical consequences, "dire warnings are just that," the opinion read. "And not a license for us to disregard the law."

In a slippery fashion, Oklahoma argued that since the reservation hadn't been recognized for so long, it would be ridiculous to uphold it now. This logic is not uncommon. Repeated treaty violations have been used as an excuse to ignore treaty rights, or, even worse, evidence that those rights never existed in the first place. But the "magnitude of a legal wrong is no reason to perpetuate it," Gorsuch retorted. Rewarding Oklahoma for the century it spent violating Muscogee sovereignty "would be the rule of the strong, not the rule of law."

In his opinion, Gorsuch called out what had become a dominant trend in US courts—one that has harmed Indigenous nations immensely. "Many of the arguments before us today follow a sadly familiar pattern," he explained. "Yes, promises were made, but the price of keeping them has become too great, so now we should just cast a blind eye."

"We reject that thinking," the opinion concluded. "Unlawful acts, performed long enough and with sufficient vigor, are never enough to amend the law. To hold otherwise would be to elevate the most brazen and longstanding injustices over the law, both rewarding wrong and failing those in the right."

CHIEF JUSTICE ROBERTS THOUGHT IT WAS "IMPROBABLE" THAT "UNBE-knownst to anyone for the past century, a huge swath of Oklahoma is actually a Creek Indian reservation." But for Cheyenne and Muscogee advocate, writer, and elder Suzan Harjo, in that century lies a lesson: tribes have to keep asserting their sovereignty. "There has to be Native people who keep saying, 'this is who we are. This is what we do. This is what we have responsibility for. These are rights that we have,'" she says. "No matter what kind of trickery there's been to try to convince us [otherwise]."

For Harjo, the *McGirt* decision is why Native people cannot be deterred by the losses we face—even when it's a century of loss. "Because we're on a longer timeline anyway," says Harjo. "We're just not on the same timeline that other peoples are in this country. We are on a much longer one, backwards and forwards. And a lot of things are going to be straightened out along the way. Because they're too blatant to stand."

The history of tribal land in the United States has moved, for the most part, unforgivingly in one direction. Prior to July 9, 2020, American Indian reservations made up only 2 percent of all land in the US—or about 56 million acres. For perspective, nearly 200 million acres is reserved for national forests. In the expansion of this great nation, our government set aside more land for trees than for Indigenous people.

The *McGirt* decision resulted in the largest restoration of tribal land in US history.

Taken together, the Five Tribes' reservations cover 19 million acres— about half of the land in Oklahoma and most of the city of Tulsa. It is an area larger than West Virginia and nine other US states.

There is an easy mistake to make in telling the story of this case, which is to say that the reservation was given back to the tribe. This would be incorrect. Despite Oklahoma's position in this case, despite everything that was taken from our tribes, our reservations were never abolished. You can't give back what already belongs to someone.

In one of the darkest chapters of American history, this land was promised to us for "as long as the grass grows or the water runs." In eastern Oklahoma, the grass is still growing, the water is still running, our fires still burn, and we are still here. And, despite the grave injustice of history, our legal right to our land never ended.

Part III

CHAPTER 14

Legacy

FROM COLUMBUS TO PLYMOUTH ROCK, EUROPEANS KNOW THE STORIES of how they discovered this land. As Indigenous peoples we know the stories of how the land was formed, because that is how long we have been here. When Cherokee ancestral homelands were still wet and mud, the buzzard flew for seven days and seven nights looking for dry land. When he got tired, his wings fell and formed valleys. Every time he lifted his wings, he formed the ridges and mountaintops. Cherokee territory once stretched from the highest point of Appalachia east to softer hills, south to the end of the Blue Ridge mountains, west across the steep ridge of the Sequatchie valley to the slopes of the Cumberland plateau and north all the way to the wide waters of the Ohio River. Our land covered parts of present-day North Carolina, South Carolina, Virginia, West Virginia, Georgia, Alabama, Kentucky, and Tennessee. Over 68 million acres.

In thirty-eight land cessions to first the British and then the United States, our territory shrank. It disappeared east of the Mississippi when my family illegally signed the treaty of New Echota. In exchange for the land of our creation, our tribe was promised unencumbered and never-ending sovereignty over a new home west of the Mississippi. But the shrinking followed us there. First by larger cessions and then by thousands of smaller losses that came with allotment, our land got smaller. In 2020, according to the US government, Cherokee Nation had jurisdiction over only 108,000 acres. Sixty-eight million acres to 108,000.

But this story does not end with loss. On March 11, 2021, an Oklahoma appeals court upheld our reservation. All 4.5 million acres.

At first, the Supreme Court's decision in *McGirt v. Oklahoma* applied only to Muscogee Nation. At the time, dozens of other defendants in Oklahoma were already challenging their convictions claiming their crimes, too, occurred on a reservation. One of those defendants, Travis Hogner, was serving fifty years for felony possession of a firearm after he shot a snake in his yard. Hogner argued that his home in Craig County lay within the Cherokee reservation. His case went to Oklahoma's highest court for criminal appeals, which in March of 2021 ruled the Cherokee reservation had never been disestablished. In rulings that spring, the Oklahoma appeals court also upheld the reservations of Seminole, Chickasaw, and Choctaw Nations.

The former Indian territory was also home to eight other tribes with smaller treaty territories in the very northeastern corner. Today four of those reservations—the Quapaw, Miami, Peoria, and Ottawa—have been affirmed. Several others are still under litigation.

The *McGirt* ruling and its aftermath represents the largest restoration of Indigenous land in US history. Taken together, the territories of the Five Tribes encompass over 40 percent of the land in Oklahoma, or 19 million acres. The affirmed reservations significantly increased the total amount of tribal land in the United States—by one-third. For me, the promise of this case was always viscerally connected to the sacrifice of my ancestors. One hundred eighty-two years after the assassination of John and Major Ridge, the treaty territory of Cherokee Nation could no longer be denied.

THE SUPREME COURT'S RULING MEANT OKLAHOMA NO LONGER HAD jurisdiction to detain and execute Patrick Murphy. After twenty years, he left death row. But he was not set free. From the Oklahoma State Penitentiary, federal marshals picked Patrick up and took him to the Pittsburgh

County jail where he awaited trial. A little over a year later, a federal jury found Patrick Murphy guilty of second-degree murder and kidnappings. (He was found not guilty of the most serious charge—murder in the first degree.) The surviving members of George Jacobs's family attended Patrick's sentencing hearing. George's sister wrote in a statement, "it does not matter what the land was called, state or Creek land." For her, it was always about justice for George. She can still remember what her brother's body looked like after it had been mutilated—it's the kind of image you never forget. She tries to replace it in her mind with better memories.

Patrick was sentenced to life in prison. Federal courts can also impose the death penalty, but—because he was convicted of second-degree murder (not first) and is a Native defendant in Indian country—he did not qualify. Eighteen years after Lisa McCalmont found that roadside cross her hope for Patrick's case came true; it saved his life.

Jimcy McGirt also faced a new federal trial—and it got complicated. At first he was found guilty, but that conviction was overturned due to improper jury instructions. Before his second trial got underway, Jimcy pleaded guilty in exchange for a thirty-year prison sentence. Time already served counted toward that sentence, and he was released in May 2024.

The new, federal trials of Patrick Murphy and Jimcy McGirt meant the survivors and victims of their crimes had to relive their trauma decades later. The adult survivor of childhood sexual abuse in Jimcy McGirt's case testified that with everything opened back up she wasn't really able to work. Thinking about it again was really hard on her. On the stand, she was asked if she wanted to relive these memories. She replied, "Not at all." For many tribal citizens in Oklahoma, *McGirt* represented a rare victory—justice at long last. For these families, however, the decision disrupted the justice they had fought so hard for. The full story of the case holds this tension.

AFTER THE VICTORY IN *MCGIRT* CAME THE BACKLASH; TOP OFFICIALS in Oklahoma and industry leaders immediately started trying to undermine the decision. The Supreme Court didn't change the rules that create or take away reservations. It only interpreted laws Congress had already passed. Which meant that if Congress wanted to get rid of the reservation, it still had the power to do so. And fears started circulating that Congress would.

Two weeks after *McGirt* came down, a troubling rumor circulated on social media: Senator Inhofe was going to sneak another rider through Congress—this time getting rid of the reservations entirely. Inhofe denied the allegations, and the rumor was never substantiated. According to congressional staffers at the time, there was "a ton of pressure" on Inhofe to do something, but he was not willing. That same week, the governor of Oklahoma announced a new commission to come up with congressional legislation; the commission was populated by oil and gas industry leaders. Using very coded language, the commission recommended getting rid of the reservations. At a press conference, commission chairman Larry Nichols said that while the business leaders "worship" tribal sovereignty and respect the rights of tribes to have things like "cultural centers," they didn't want reservations in Oklahoma.

One last threat of congressional legislation came from a surprising place: the Five Tribes. In the same frenzied weeks following the decision, Oklahoma's attorney general released an outline for potential congressional legislation. It wasn't a draft bill; nothing had been introduced to Congress. Rather it was an agreement between the tribes and Oklahoma about what Congress should pass. Congress, the outline read, should codify the reservation boundaries in law, but give Oklahoma back most of the criminal and civil jurisdiction it lost—including the authority to prosecute and tax tribal citizens on reservation lands. Basically, the Five Tribes would have reservations in name, but most of the practical consequences would be erased. Lawyers representing each of the five tribes had been meeting with the attorney general's office for over two years (for the last several months of correspondence the lawyer for Seminole Nation was no longer included). "I think that we were both conscious of the fact that the case could go either way," then Attorney General Mike Hunter said of the negotiations. If the tribes lost *McGirt*, the proposed legislation wasn't a bad deal; it saved the reservations. Tribal citizens did not, at any point, know these negotiations were taking place. Worried public knowledge would impact the Supreme Court decision, the entire working group signed nondisclosure agreements.

The response from tribal citizens was powerful and immediate. They protested on Facebook, called their elected officials, organized open letters, and rallied outside a tribal council meeting. Within forty-eight hours the agreement fell apart. First Seminole and Muscogee Nations, and later Choctaw Nation, publicly backed out. Oklahoma's multiple attempts at congressional legislation were easily defeated—a testament to the political power of our tribes. And when tribal leaders went astray, the quick defeat of the ill-fated agreement was a testament to the power of tribal citizens—who organized what, according to scholars, was probably the biggest moment of citizen advocacy in the Five Tribes since allotment.

For most of the 1.9 million people living in eastern Oklahoma, life continued like normal after *McGirt*. Oklahoma residents still dropped their kids off at the same public schools, paid the same taxes, followed the same liquor and tobacco laws, and owned the same house or farm just like they did before. According to one opinion poll, most Oklahomans (roughly four out of five) thought tribes were good for the state and wanted to see tribes and Oklahoma work together to implement the decision.

Despite the industry's panicked response and attempts to roll *McGirt* back, little changed in its aftermath. As my reporting predicted, the regulatory sea change the industry warned of never came. Some leaders now admit that. Joe Robson, business leader and member of the governor's commission, agreed a lot of "assertions and speculation" never came true. People "talk about worst-case scenarios and they get scared," he said. Even Larry Nichols, prominent oil and gas leader and the commission chairman, agreed the regulatory impact of *McGirt* was a "non-issue" for his industry. "For most of the industry, it's not a problem," he said.

Reservations come with less power than most people think. The decision's impact on civil jurisdiction (which affects things like taxes, environmental regulations, and lawsuits) was limited by the *Montana* Supreme Court decision which left tribes with almost no regulatory say over the conduct of non-Natives on what's called fee land. For tribes in eastern Oklahoma, that's over 95 percent of our reservations. While some federal laws give tribes authority to regulate pollution, those laws don't apply in

Oklahoma thanks to Senator Inhofe's 2005 midnight rider. Less than two weeks after *McGirt* came down, Oklahoma's governor asked the EPA to invoke the dormant rider and the agency granted his request. There was one small area where Oklahoma *did* lose regulatory authority. A 1977 law puts the Department of the Interior in charge of all coal mining on Indian land. Additionally, tribal citizens who live and work on their reservation have challenged Oklahoma's authority to tax them. That issue is still under litigation.

TO MANY, THE *MCGIRT* DECISION CAME AS A SURPRISE. AFTER ALL, THE Muscogee reservation hadn't been recognized in over a century. If it existed all that time, some asked, why didn't Muscogee Nation fight for it sooner? History, however, reveals the ruling was a long time in the making. Oklahoma spent more than one hundred years ignoring the law. And the Five Tribes spent that same century clawing their way out of allotment.

The biggest barrier to the Five Tribes reclaiming their sovereignty in the twentieth century was the US government not allowing us to practice democracy. Starting with allotment, the principal chiefs of each tribe were appointed by the US president—not elected. Congress did not rescind this measure until 1970. One year later, Muscogee Nation elected their first chief since allotment. The tribe also adopted a new constitution in 1979, and elected a new national council in 1980. The four other tribes reconstituted their democracies too with new constitutions and elections.

In the wake of allotment, Oklahoma exercised jurisdiction on tribal land it did not have. *McGirt* was not the first time a federal court told the state to stop. In 1986, an Oklahoma deputy sheriff shot a Cherokee man in the leg, which later had to be amputated. The victim sued. Among other things, he argued Oklahoma didn't have jurisdiction to arrest him, because he was on tribal land. Oklahoma argued there was no more tribal land in the state, but the Tenth Circuit Court of Appeals disagreed. Unless Congress has said otherwise, the court reasoned, the land was still Indian country.

That decision left a checkerboard of jurisdiction—like the sheet cake of scattered pieces Patrick Murphy's lawyers first investigated. Where allotted land was still restricted or where land was held in trust, Oklahoma lost jurisdiction. In response, the Five Tribes rebuilt police forces and court systems that had been shuttered since allotment. By the time *McGirt* came around, the Five Tribes had been exercising criminal jurisdiction for decades.

The Tenth Circuit Court of Appeals also had to tell Oklahoma it did not have civil jurisdiction on tribal land. After Muscogee Nation opened a bingo hall, the state tried to impose taxes and regulations. In 1987, the Tenth Circuit told Oklahoma to back off, carving out basically the same landscape of civil jurisdiction as what we have today (in which the state mostly has civil jurisdiction on fee land and the tribes mostly have it on restricted and trust land). In other words, the regulatory sea change industry leaders warned about had already happened.

Before *McGirt*, tribes were not sitting idly by; their governments and citizens were challenging the state's overreach. Rather than some dramatic upset, *McGirt* is just the latest in a long string of cases.

THE LAST TREATY MUSCOGEE NATION SIGNED WITH THE UNITED STATES of America was in 1866 at the close of the Civil War. That treaty defined the reservation boundaries that—154 years later—were upheld by the Supreme Court. The treaty also guaranteed tribal citizenship to the people Muscogee Nation had enslaved and their descendants. A year before the *McGirt* decision came out, Rhonda Grayson got a letter in the mail. It was from the citizenship board of Muscogee Nation. The letter informed Rhonda she was not eligible for citizenship in the tribe because she was not Muscogee "by blood." Her application was rejected. At the time of allotment, Rhonda's great-grandmother was placed on the Creek Freedmen roll—a separate, segregated list for formerly enslaved people and their descendants. When Muscogee Nation ratified its new constitution in 1979, it excluded descendants of freedpeople. If the Dawes Commission hadn't placed their ancestor on the "by blood" roll, people like Rhonda couldn't enroll.

To Rhonda, the timing betrayed a gross hypocrisy; how could Mus-

Rhonda Grayson

cogee Nation demand the United States uphold its end of the treaty, but not uphold theirs? "Creek freedmen were part of the tribe before there was even a Creek Nation," Rhonda told me. "They traveled on the Trail of Tears." With a fellow freedpeople descendant, Rhonda sued the citizenship board in Muscogee Nation court, arguing the board's decision violated the treaty of 1866.

Muscogee Nation was not alone. Under our modern governments, all five tribes have excluded or disenfranchised the descendants of freedpeople. In September of 2001, Marilyn Vann applied for citizenship in Cherokee Nation. Her father, an original allottee, was placed on the Cherokee Freedmen roll. Marilyn had always known her family was Cherokee—both by adoption and blood—so she assumed she would be able to enroll without a problem. "I was very shocked to get back this rejection letter," she told me. At first under Cherokee Nation's 1976 constitution, anyone who descended from an original allottee could enroll, but starting in the 1980s, the tribe disenrolled freedpeople descendants, also claiming tribal citizenship was reserved for Cherokees "by blood."

Marilyn sat with her rejection letter and thought about it. "I'm looking around and I see historical[ly] anybody that has gotten anything done they have had to be organized," she remembers thinking. "And generally they have had to use the courts." Marilyn founded an advocacy organization called the Descendants of Freedmen of the Five Tribes. And, she filed a lawsuit. Suing first the tribe and then officials of Cherokee Nation, Marilyn alleged they illegally disenfranchised her.

In 2017, a federal court ruled on Marilyn's case. Marilyn had no idea when the ruling would come out and was sitting in the beauty salon when her phone started blowing up. "I said well we must have won the case," she remembers. The federal court ruled—based on the treaty of 1866—descendants of Cherokee freedpeople were guaranteed citizenship in the tribe. After decades of legal battles, Cherokee Nation dropped the fight and started enrolling descendants of freedpeople. Marilyn was already planning to travel to the Cherokee capital for the tribe's annual holiday weekend. Before her trip she gathered up all the paperwork she needed to enroll her grandchildren. "They won't remember a time when they're not members of the tribe," she thought. "All nations that have enslaved people have had to take some responsibility for them," Marilyn reflected. "The Cherokee Nation has to do that just like the United States."

Over four years after she got that rejection letter, the District Court of Muscogee Nation ruled on Rhonda Grayson's case. She won. "For more than 100 years," the decision read, Muscogee Nation followed the 1866 treaty and extended citizenship to freedpeople and their descendants. On the heels of *McGirt*, it would be "disingenuous," the judge wrote, for the tribe to fight for the United States to follow the treaty of 1866, but not follow it themselves. Two weeks before the district court ruling, Principal Chief David Hill was elected to a second term. Publicly, he has stated the case presents a complicated issue, but his administration has to follow the constitution. His attorney general vowed to appeal the district court decision, stating under their constitution "non-Creek individuals" cannot be citizens. As of this writing, the case is still pending. Today descendants of freedpeople have full citizenship rights in Cherokee Nation, can enroll in Seminole Nation with limited access to services, and are still denied citizenship in Chickasaw, Choctaw, and Muscogee Nations.

If Indigenous nations are truly sovereign, then we are responsible for our mistakes. Like any other government, we are responsible for the harm we have caused. We cannot hold the United States accountable for the wrongs of history committed against us, but not take account for the wrong of chattel slavery. The people we enslaved did not choose to become Cherokee or Muscogee—we made that choice for them. They and their families endured the hardships of the Trail of Tears *and* slavery, allotment *and* segregation. On the long path of repair, citizenship is only the first step.

WHEN I STEPPED INTO ROSEMARY MCCOMBS MAXEY'S LIVING ROOM three years after the *McGirt* ruling, it was already full. In a circle made by a couch, two recliners, and chairs pulled from the kitchen, a group of Muscogee language students sat. They were all spending a week at Rosemary's house to learn from her. Pinned to red fabric on the wall little cards displayed Muscogee words. *Cate* for red. *Palen-hokkolohkaken* for twelve. Rosemary sat in front of her television with a pile of papers at her feet. After the circle introduced themselves, she prayed.

Rosemary learned Muscogee the way most people learn a language—as a kid. For Indigenous languages in the United States this type of natural language acquisition has mostly stopped. Few Indigenous children grow up speaking their language. Today most fluent Muscogee speakers are like Rosemary—older. If a new generation doesn't learn the language, Muscogee will no longer be spoken. The language contains more than just a vocabulary; it holds the Muscogee worldview.

Most often when people think of what Native Americans lost, they think of land, but that's just what white people gained. What Native people lost is so much more. When the tribes refused to concede to allotment, Congress punished them by seizing control of tribal schools. At the turn of the twentieth century, the secretary of the Interior complained the Five Tribes' schools did not prioritize the "necessity for learning the English language." To make things worse, boys were not taught farming, and instead of the "domestic arts," girls were learning Latin and mathematics. So the United States started sending the Five Tribes' children to government-run boarding schools. Created to eradicate Indigenous cultures by assimilating Native children to white society, the schools punished Native kids for speaking their language. The schools were also sites of widespread physical, emotional, and sexual abuse. Today, on the historic grounds of the largest boarding school in Oklahoma are the unmarked graves of sixty-seven children who died there.

By 1934, the majority of school-age children in the Five Tribes attended state-run public schools. When John Ross entered kindergarten, he didn't speak English. On the eastern edge of Cherokee Nation where he lived, everyone spoke Cherokee. In elementary school, if John made a mistake in English, his teacher paddled him. "Depending on how many you missed," he told me of learning how to spell. "That's how many licks you got."

When Sheila Bird's older brothers started school, they didn't speak English, either. If they spoke Cherokee, their teacher slapped their hands with a ruler. Sheila's family didn't want their daughter to be hit too, so before she started kindergarten in 1973, they made sure she could speak English. That meant she didn't speak Cherokee. "I used to get mad at my mom," she told me. "How come you didn't make me learn Cherokee too?"

For Sheila's generation, not speaking Cherokee to children was a form of protection. Today there are fewer than two thousand Cherokee fluent speakers in Oklahoma—most over the age of sixty. If we don't want to lose our language, we have one generation to reverse the cumulative effect of centuries of US policy. Our language holds our medicine and our ceremonies. John Ross and many other speakers say when we lose our language we will lose what it means to be Cherokee.

There were many bureaucratic traps set up to ensnare allotted land, so Rosemary's mother stayed vigilant. Her parents feared the county would say they owed taxes, or someone would file something against them, and—whether or not it was legal—they would lose their land. So every year, the family took a daylong trip to Holdenville, the county seat. There, they would go to the county courthouse and check: did they still own their land? "They survived the allotment era, I guess," Rosemary says. Today Rosemary lives on her grandmother's allotment. It is still restricted.

When Rosemary's sons went to Oklahoma State University, they took a Muscogee language class. "They would call home to say, how do you say this? And what does this mean?" Rosemary remembers. When the Muscogee language teacher at OSU could no longer teach, Rosemary was asked to step in. After the older teacher passed, one of her students wanted to keep learning in her memory. He asked Rosemary if maybe she could teach a class in the summer. Maybe on her land, he suggested.

On the day I visit, Rosemary's language class is performing a play. Before passing out the script, Rosemary thought for a moment about how to say "script" in Muscogee. She translated it as a paper that has been written on. As they passed around animal masks, the group practiced saying *culv, nokose,* and *cufe* for fox, bear, and rabbit. On the couch, a small dog lay curled on a blanket. For most of the day, the dog slept. But when a visitor popped by to say hello, she growled—creating an opportunity for Rosemary to teach *efv hekes*—the dog growls.

Generations of Rosemary's family protected the allotted land where Rosemary now lives. She now uses that land to protect the Muscogee language. Indigenous land, sovereignty, language, and culture are all connected. Whenever we lost land, our languages and culture also suffered.

Conversely, where we held on to land is often the place where culture is still practiced and Indigenous languages are still spoken.

The victory in *McGirt* corrects a very specific wrong—Oklahoma's denial of the Muscogee reservation. It doesn't fix everything else. It doesn't return stolen and swindled allotted land. It doesn't reverse centuries of language loss. It does not relieve us from the burden of fighting for every inch of our sovereignty. *McGirt* is one step in the long process of pulling ourselves out of allotment. It does not return all that was lost. It just helps us stop the bleeding.

CHAPTER 15

The Backlash

A LITTLE MORE THAN A YEAR AFTER THE DECISION CAME OUT, THE governor of Oklahoma hosted a forum to talk about *McGirt*. The convention center hall of patterned carpet and blank walls was full. The governor leaned slightly over to speak into the microphone, his hands gripping the edge of a pale, wooden podium. "There's a problem brewing," he told the crowd. "With crimes being prosecuted." But the governor was unable to complete his statement; the crowd was shouting at him—drowning out his words. The forum was meant to highlight how *McGirt* upended the criminal justice system in Oklahoma and made the state less safe. The panel of Oklahoma prosecutors and police did not include any tribal leaders. Over one hundred tribal citizens and protesters, however, did not let them speak. "For it to be so one-sided," Muscogee citizen and organizer Brenda Golden told me, "it needed to be shut down." The governor ended the forum an hour early. Over his closing remarks, the crowd booed. As he left the stage, they chanted "Shame on you" to his back. In the fallout from *McGirt*, the relationship between tribes and the state had soured. And—as the forum highlighted—the rancor swirled mostly around one man: Governor Kevin Stitt.

During his election campaign, Stitt claimed he had "firsthand" knowledge of Oklahoma's tribal nations because he is a citizen of my tribe, Cherokee Nation. Citizenship in our tribe is open to anyone who descends from an original allottee. When Stitt's ancestors—the Dawsons—went to enroll for allotment, Cherokee Nation protested. At the time, the Dawson family were already citizens of Cherokee Nation, but the tribe alleged that they obtained that citizenship by fraud.

A lawyer who helped the Dawsons enroll (and later spent time in jail for mail fraud) admitted he bribed a Cherokee Nation court clerk to push their case through. Friends and neighbors testified the Dawsons bragged about how they bought their citizenship. The only evidence of Cherokee ancestry the family provided was the testimony of an old doctor; he said he knew their Cherokee grandmother. According to the doctor, this grandmother was a teenager in the 1820s, but at the time the woman was married with seven children. When asked under oath how he was Cherokee, one Dawson brother replied, "I don't know, I couldn't answer the question."

The Dawes Commission had the final say. They ruled it wasn't relevant the family may have no Cherokee ancestry because "the only question" was if they had committed fraud. Evidence of bribery was not enough; Cherokee Nation had to prove the bribe "tainted the judgment itself." And so, over one hundred members of the Dawson family were placed on the Cherokee roll. For several hundred dollars they received over 10,000 acres of land. History repeats itself in incredible ways. Generations later, tribes would again find themselves in a battle over truth with a member of the Dawson family. And again, the tribes would lose.

At first, tribal leaders noticed small things. Under the preceding governor, Muscogee Nation was negotiating the purchase of a state park. Under Stitt, the deal fell through. After the state legislature passed a law protecting the right of Native students to wear eagle feathers and regalia at their graduation, Stitt vetoed it. When the state's 2004 gaming compacts were about to sunset, Stitt wanted the tribes to pay Oklahoma 15 to 20 percent more of their profits. During the ensuing and unsuccessful legal battle, Stitt spent $1.4 million of Oklahoma's money and lost the support of the Republican leaders of the state House and Senate, his secretary of Native Affairs, and the attorney general. To tribal leaders it felt like wherever they had cooperative agreements with the state—including tobacco sales, hunting and fishing rights, even the operation of highway welcome centers—Stitt broke them.

While other Oklahoma officials adjusted to life after *McGirt*, Governor Stitt refused. To news stations, to law enforcement, to the business community, to anyone who would listen, Stitt preached that *McGirt* was the worst thing that could have ever happened to Oklahoma. The ruling, he claimed, was the "biggest issue that's ever hit" an American state since the Civil War.

Almost a year after the *McGirt* verdict, Oklahoma's Attorney General Mike Hunter made a surprise announcement: he was resigning. At the time, he had raised over $150,000 for his reelection campaign. Oklahoma outlets reported the attorney general was having an affair, and he publicly stated that "certain personal matters" had become a "distraction" from his office. According to an employee at the time, that was not the full story. The relationship between Attorney General Hunter and Governor Stitt had soured after the gaming compact controversy. Hunter wanted to work with the tribes to implement *McGirt*, but Stitt wanted to fight it. By the time the decision came down, they rarely spoke. Hunter's differences with the governor over *McGirt* were a significant factor in his decision to leave office.

Two months after Hunter resigned, Governor Stitt picked a new attorney general. When Tulsa attorney John O'Connor was previously nominated to be a federal judge, the American Bar Association rated him "unqualified." When it came to *McGirt*, Stitt and O'Connor were on the same page. "Personally, I have very high regard for friends who are Oklahomans with Native American ancestry," O'Connor said at the time. "But I'm not about to let half of our state be essentially divided from the United States and belong to the Indian nations."

Ten months before O'Connor took office, Justice Ruth Bader Ginsburg died; she was replaced on the bench by Justice Amy Coney Barrett. In the 5–4 *McGirt* split, Ginsburg had voted for Muscogee Nation. The changing makeup of the court, in Stitt's mind, opened the "possibility" the justices would "reverse their decision." In a private email, an oil and gas lobbyist told the governor and a close group of allies, "Wouldn't be surprised if things change when *McGirt* is revisited." So Governor Stitt and Attorney General O'Connor took the extraordinary step of asking the Supreme Court to overturn *McGirt v. Oklahoma*—over fifty times.

THE LATIN TERM *STARE DECISIS* LITERALLY MEANS "LET THE DECISION stand." In the American legal system, stare decisis means courts are bound to follow what's already been decided. Unlike Congress or the presidency, which change their positions with the tides of politics, courts are supposed to be consistent and predictable. For the Supreme Court to overturn a decision just because the makeup of the court had changed would be a blatant violation of this bedrock legal principle. What Oklahoma wanted was extreme.

To ask the Supreme Court to take such a drastic measure, Oklahoma needed a reason. That reason was crime. According to Oklahoma, *McGirt* had created a "calamitous" and "unprecedented disruption" that was "worsening by the day" and "affecting every corner of daily life in Oklahoma." The decision, Oklahoma and their allies told the court, resulted in "a complete dismantling of the criminal justice system" and was basically a "get-out-of-jail-free card" for "hundreds, or even thousands, of criminals." In short, "no recent decision has spurred such instant and sweeping turmoil in an American state."

Oklahoma backed up this characterization of chaos with some wild claims. On reservation land, Oklahoma lost jurisdiction to prosecute crimes where either the defendant or victim was Native American. Depending on the crime, that jurisdiction passed to the tribe, the federal government, and in some instances both. In May of 2021, ten months after the decision, Oklahoma's old warning about convicted criminals walking free came back. But this time it was different. That month, Governor Stitt told a local Fox News reporter that "potentially seventy-six thousand cases" could be overturned. "There's people being released from prison," he said. Oklahoma repeated this estimate in its petition to the Supreme Court, claiming "at least seventy-six thousand" old criminal cases could be impacted. At face value, the estimate was improbable; it was over 60 times the number of Native people then incarcerated from the reservation area, 25 times the state's previous estimate, and about 3 times the *total* prison population in Oklahoma. But if state officials presented it as fact to the Supreme Court, surely they had something to back it up.

Oklahoma told the Supreme Court their estimate came from a survey of district attorneys. Together with reporter Allison Herrera, I asked the governor's office to show us the math. Their communications director replied, "You'd need to ask the district attorneys. Our office was presented with the estimate, we did not help to compile it." So we asked every district attorney in eastern Oklahoma to pass along the number they provided the governor. Most didn't get back to us, but the ones who did had a surprising answer. They didn't know what we were talking about. "To my knowledge, we have made no such communication to the governor's office, nor has one been requested," Tim Webster, the district attorney for Atoka, Bryan, and Coal Counties, wrote in an email. Even Stephen Kunzweiler, the district attorney for Tulsa—eastern Oklahoma's most populous county—said he didn't provide data specific to the governor's estimate. A spokesperson for the attorney general was unable to confirm the estimate. A private lawyer on contract with the governor said the estimate was "conservative" and "extrapolated" from information provided by the district attorneys.

At the time, the number of past convictions that got overturned was not a mystery. The Oklahoma Department of Corrections tracked every inmate who was released in the wake of *McGirt*. According to the list they provided, in the nearly eighteen months following the Supreme Court's decision, 68 people were released from prison; their crimes ranged from drug possession to murder. An additional 123 people were released to tribal or federal custody, 13 people successfully overturned one conviction but were still incarcerated on other charges, and 4 defendants were already on probation at the time they won their appeal. Rather than hundreds or thousands or tens of thousands of old convictions getting thrown out, it was dozens.

It is easy to assume that every past conviction would be overturned, but appeals are complicated. Overturning a conviction in our criminal justice system is extremely difficult—and rare. A lot of issues—like ineffective assistance of counsel, or improper jury instructions—are waived if not brought up at the right time. On the other hand, Oklahoma courts had long held that jurisdiction cannot be waived. It was possible the tide of defendants raising reservation arguments would prevail, but it was up to Oklahoma's highest court for criminal appeals to decide.

Finally, in August of 2021, the Oklahoma Court of Criminal Appeals ruled *McGirt* did *not* apply to old convictions. Meaning that anyone who was sentenced before July 9, 2020, and didn't immediately appeal raising a reservation claim, was out of luck. There was a window of time when Oklahoma courts did apply *McGirt* to old cases, but it was short. That is why only sixty-eight people got out.

One other thing helped some Oklahoma inmates get released: Oklahoma prosecutors didn't file their own appeals on time. In several high-profile cases, including a manslaughter conviction for a drunk-driving accident that killed five people, district attorneys didn't fight the overturned conviction until months after it was too late. The day after that drunk driver got out of prison, Oklahoma's highest court for criminal appeals recalled its own mandate applying *McGirt* to old convictions, and the presiding Tulsa County judge started staying her orders in similar cases. The prosecutor in charge—Tulsa County District Attorney Stephen Kunzweiler—did not respond to our request for comment.

TWO WEEKS BEFORE OKLAHOMA FIRST ASKED THE SUPREME COURT TO overturn *McGirt*, the *Washington Post* published an article headlined, "'Complete, Dysfunctional Chaos': Oklahoma Reels after Supreme Court Ruling on Indian Tribes." In an email, the governor's special counsel praised the article as "our best coverage yet." Attributing the estimate to Oklahoma, the *Post* article reported that seventy-six thousand convictions could be overturned, though it noted that tribal leaders believed that number was "massively exaggerated." *After* printing that number, *Post* reporter Annie Gowen asked Tulsa District Attorney Kunzweiler why it was so high—even noting the figure was many times larger than Oklahoma's previous estimates and the state's total prison population. The *Post* did not include that context in its article, which was coauthored by the paper's Supreme Court correspondent, Robert Barnes. When contacted, a spokesperson from the *Washington Post* said that they do not discuss their reporting, but they "did meet with representatives from the Native American community."

In a normal trial, there are rules of evidence. Hearsay is inadmissible. If an expert witness makes unsubstantiated claims, they get cross-examined. As you move up the ladder of appellate law, the rules of evidence get murky. In recent years, this problem has been exacerbated by the Internet. Now attorneys can cite news articles or any link in their briefs, creating a perverse system where litigants work to place media and then use that media as evidence. In a petition to the Supreme Court, Oklahoma cited their "best coverage yet" from the *Washington Post*.

Media was not Oklahoma's only trick. Another strategy greatly increases the odds the Supreme Court will hear your case: hiring a Supreme Court insider. On average, the Supreme Court is asked to hear over seven thousand cases each year, but takes only a tiny fraction—sixty-six for its 2021 term. Between 2004 and 2012, a small group of elite lawyers worked on only 1 percent of those petitions, but represented almost half of the cases the court decided to hear.

The elite lawyer Oklahoma retained for their Hail Mary strategy was a man named Kannon K. Shanmugam. When it comes to getting the Supreme Court to take a client's case, Shanmugam is one of the best lawyers in the country—one year his team worked on almost 10 percent of all cases the high court argued. Paul, Weiss, where Shanmugam works, was the fifth-most-profitable law firm globally in 2021, and is best known for representing big oil, big banks, big tobacco, the NFL's cover-up of concussions, and the opioids industry. Shanmugam once told a crowded room at the Federalist Society that the purpose of law firms like his is not fighting for social justice, but rather "corporate interests" and "well-off individuals." To secure Shanmugam's services, Oklahoma inked a contract for up to $1.4 million.

AFTER THE OKLAHOMA APPEALS COURT RULED *MCGIRT* WOULD NOT APply to old convictions, Oklahoma didn't stop claiming the decision created chaos. They just changed their story. "Hundreds of criminal cases," Governor Stitt claimed, "are going unprosecuted." Oklahoma's story went like this: federal prosecutors were so overwhelmed that they were filing charges only for the most serious crimes. All other cases—including attacks on Tulsa police officers, child sexual abuse, burglaries, strangulation, and stabbings—got dropped. Like Senator Henry Dawes a century earlier, Oklahoma painted tribal land as a lawless dystopia.

Oklahoma again provided the Supreme Court with shocking numbers.* The state claimed it had lost jurisdiction to prosecute eighteen thousand cases each year. Federal and tribal prosecutors were not picking all those cases up because they didn't have the capacity. As a result, the state suggested about ten thousand cases a year were going unprosecuted. Again, Oklahoma did not provide a citation for its estimate. Many of the anecdotes peppering the briefs were attributed to unnamed Oklahoma officials. When asked where that number came from, Shanmugam did not respond.

Again, Allison Herrera and I wanted to check the state's math. According to data provided by the Tulsa district attorney and the Oklahoma District Attorneys Council, the total number of criminal cases filed in eastern Oklahoma did fall in the year after *McGirt*. But by 13,131—not 18,000. According to an Oklahoma prosecutor some of that decline was due to COVID, which decreased arrests and prosecutions nationwide. By the spring of 2022, the Five Tribes had filed 11,400 criminal cases, and federal prosecutors filed nearly 1,000 cases in 2021. Taken together, that leaves a gap of fewer than 1,000 cases—some of which were because of COVID, not *McGirt*.

Oklahoma's briefs, some of the press coverage, and even a bizarre academic report used a sleight of hand to create the appearance of thousands of cases falling through the cracks: they didn't count tribal prosecutions.

---

* After trying to get solid numbers from Oklahoma prosecutors on how many cases were impacted by *McGirt*, I eventually learned those numbers did not exist. "While the impact to our office has been significant," a staffer in one DA's offices told us, "we have not tracked cases or case numbers." We got a smattering of data from districts that represent 64 percent of the Native population in eastern Oklahoma. Collectively, those districts tracked 4,617 cases impacted in the fifteen to twenty months after *McGirt*— including old convictions and new prosecutions.

Sometimes tribal data was not included at all; other times Oklahoma compared a few months of tribal prosecutions to a year of state data. Federal prosecutors don't have jurisdiction over many low-level crimes in Indian country (which are more common than things like murder in the US). The story that federal prosecutors weren't trying thousands of low-level crimes was true, but those cases didn't get dropped. Because the tribes picked them up.

ON A SWELTERING DAY IN JUNE OF 2023, I STEPPED INTO A CHOCTAW Nation Lighthorse patrol car. After all the stories of lawlessness on reservations, I wanted to see it for myself. While we chatted, Officer Robert Rocha pulled out of the police station parking lot and began his patrol of Bryan County. Heading east out of Durant, cattle ranches and hayfields quickly surrounded us. When we drove through the small town of Bennington, residents waved at Rocha's car. Outside town, the pavement turned to gravel, buttressed by the early summer bloom of wildflowers.

Policing did not change much after *McGirt*. Cross-deputization agreements—which allow Oklahoma police to arrest tribal citizens under the authority of the tribe, and vice versa—had been in place for decades. On the back roads, Rocha got a call from back in Durant. An angry casino employee had thrown his cell phone at a supervisor and now wouldn't leave the property. It was hot outside—over 90 degrees—and he didn't want to walk home. Without placing him under arrest, Rocha gave the man a ride. After all of the warnings about crime and violence, that was the extent that I saw.

While Oklahoma police officers could still arrest tribal citizens, Oklahoma district attorneys could not prosecute them. When Kara Bacon went to work for Choctaw Nation in 2019, she was the only full-time prosecutor in her office. After *McGirt*, the tribe hired 133 new people—including court clerks, police, a victim advocate, and prosecutors. To Kara, who is also a citizen of Choctaw Nation, the transition wasn't "chaos," but it was hectic. In just a few months, the tribe updated their criminal code, changed their statutes of limitations, set up a hotline to verify tribal citizenship, and went from handling about a hundred cases a year to thousands. Before the Choctaw reservation was affirmed, Oklahoma DAs handed Kara a list of cases they had to drop and she indicted 125 people. "You hear a lot from Governor Stitt about how there's no cooperation," she said. "And that just wasn't what we were seeing on the ground."

Behind the raised bench of Choctaw Nation's district courtroom stand three flags—one for the United States, one for Oklahoma, and one for Choctaw Nation. I sat through court on a day it processed its misdemeanor docket. A crowd of mostly defendants sat in pewlike wooden benches covered in gray fabric. Some people looked nervous—most looked bored. Almost everyone pleaded out, and only two people were sentenced to prison time. While sentencing a nineteen-year-old charged with public intoxication, the judge recommended places he might volunteer to fulfill his court-ordered community service hours. As a former state prosecutor, Kara saw how courts can create cycles people can't get out of. As a Choctaw prosecutor, Kara tries to keep incarceration and court fines to a minimum. One of the most frequent sentences I heard was mandatory drug and alcohol counseling.

The shift in criminal jurisdiction was not perfect, but it was successful. The Five Tribes built new court buildings and established agreements with local jails and the Bureau of Prisons, and expanded their police and court staff. The federal system, too, added new prosecutors, court staff, and even judges. The problems that did surface were more nuanced than headlines about criminals walking free. In the federal system, once a complaint is filed, the case goes to the next grand jury. If the federal prosecutor isn't ready, the defendant might not be arrested for a while. To help, tribes would hold defendants on their own charges. Inmates in the federal system can be sent to prison anywhere in the United States—often far away from the family and community bonds that help people through and after incarceration. Another challenge is the problem of incarceration itself. Many tribal citizens don't want to recreate a criminal justice system that has historically harmed our communities. Conversations about alternatives are much harder to have when the *Washington Post* is calling your reservation "complete, dysfunctional chaos."

While Oklahoma complained the transition wasn't working, state officials added to the hiccups. In some counties "the elected district attorneys

were so hostile to tribal jurisdiction that there was essentially zero communication," Sara Hill, then attorney general of Cherokee Nation, told
me. Some district attorneys wouldn't give Cherokee Nation a list of which
cases they had to drop. So Hill's staff would sit through open court to
catch cases as they got dismissed. When Choctaw Nation asked to subcon-
tract out beds in the state's juvenile and mental health facilities, they were
told no. "When I hear agencies talk," Kara Bacon told me, "they'll say, oh,
my boss said we can't formally do this because they don't want retaliation
from Governor Stitt."

The *Wall Street Journal*'s editorial board ran a dozen articles claiming *McGirt* "upended the legal system in Oklahoma," creating "mayhem"
and "criminal anarchy." One article repeated Oklahoma's claim that federal prosecutors were so overwhelmed that they weren't filing charges
for most crimes—suggesting ten thousand cases a year were getting
dropped. Before the article ran, a member of the editorial board wanted
to corroborate Oklahoma's story. Kyle Peterson emailed multiple district
attorneys asking for "conclusive numbers," written correspondence with
federal prosecutors, examples of specific cases that got dropped, or "another way to substantiate" Oklahoma's overall claims. From the emails
I obtained, the district attorneys provided none of this. The *Wall Street
Journal* wanted to get the story out "in the next few days" because the
Supreme Court was scheduled to review another round of CERT petitions
that Friday. And so Peterson decided to use on-the-record interviews with
Oklahoma prosecutors. When asked if he ever did independently verify
those numbers, Peterson didn't respond.

Angel Ellis, editor in chief of Mvskoke Media, watched the news coverage roll in. As a journalist, she was shocked. "It was like a fable," she told
me. "They never tell a full story. They never tell the context." Local papers
ran headlines about vacated murder charges for defendants that had already been charged in federal court. Outlets published sensationalized
and misleading statements from Governor Stitt without context. After
DNA testing identified an alleged serial rapist from the 1990s, local TV
reporter Lori Fullbright claimed he got off because of *McGirt*. (The *Wall
Street Journal* also reported on the case.) The federal statute of limitations
for the original crimes had run out, but it was also likely too late under

Oklahoma law—which their reporting didn't mention. Angel watched the media turn people against her tribe. "It was devastating," she told me. "I felt like I was watching a hate crime play out."*

Journalism is often thought of as the first draft of history. Instead of having an accurate record of what happened after *McGirt*, we have a mess. A lot of the coverage was fair, a lot was misleading, some was demonstrably wrong. For over a hundred years, crime has been used as an excuse to chip away at tribal sovereignty. The aftermath of *McGirt* could have taught us that this age-old lie is false. Instead, the people who want to use the lie of lawlessness can easily do so. They have plenty of headlines to choose from.

NEARLY TWO WEEKS AFTER THE PUBLICATION OF KYLE PETERSON'S rushed *Wall Street Journal* article, the Supreme Court granted CERT to *Oklahoma v. Castro-Huerta*. The justices would later say they took the case because of the sudden significant questions about "public safety" and "the criminal justice system in Oklahoma." It appears that Oklahoma's campaign worked. The court rejected the state's bid to overturn *McGirt* completely, but agreed to hear a narrower question. In a handful of its dozens of petitions, Oklahoma also asked the court to reconsider what kind of jurisdiction states have on reservations. At the time, states could not prosecute crimes if either the victim or perpetrator were Native. Oklahoma wanted a slice of that back: jurisdiction over cases where the perpetrator is non-Native, but the victim is Native. Oklahoma claimed this was necessary because many crimes against Native Americans were going unpunished.

In the spring of 2022, the Supreme Court gathered again for oral arguments. The justices were back in the courtroom but, two years into the COVID-19 pandemic, access to the public was limited. The rows of stern wooden chairs sat mostly empty. I listened from home. The day

---

*   In partnership with the Indigenous Journalist Association, Oklahoma outlets received training on *McGirt*, and bias in local reporting got better.

before, Allison Herrera and I had published our findings about the errors in Oklahoma's numbers in the *Atlantic*. As I sat with headphones over my ears, staring at the blank wall in my office, I waited to see if Oklahoma's lawyer would repeat the state's bogus claims. Almost immediately, he did.

"Whole categories of crimes are going unprosecuted in the aftermath of *McGirt*," Shanmugam told the justices. But a few minutes later, Justice Sotomayor interrupted him. "I want you to address where you get your figures from," she said. "There's an article in the *Atlantic* that suggests that your figures are grossly exaggerated." I screamed. As a journalist, I always hope my reporting has an impact. Very rarely do I get to see it.

Shanmugam was ready for the question. "If we're going to litigate what's been said in the press," he responded, "I would refer the Court to the *Wall Street Journal* article earlier this week." He was right. The public record told both tales: one where Oklahoma's claims were demonstrably false and the other where they were true.

The central question presented by *Castro-Huerta*—whether or not states have jurisdiction to prosecute crimes committed by non-Natives against Natives in Indian country—is not answered by hysterics. It has to be answered using legal principles. To get there, Oklahoma came up with a novel theory. "The state has inherent sovereign authority to punish crimes committed within its borders," Shanmugam told the justices. Normally, states don't have authority on tribal land, unless that authority has been granted by Congress. Shanmugam wanted to turn that rule on its head; he argued states *do* have authority unless Congress has taken it away.

Several of the justices mocked Shanmugam's approach. "I'm sorry, but this Court has—has indicated six times that you're wrong. Congress has indicated that you're wrong," Justice Kagan told him. "The executive branch has said that you're wrong in all but one decade." Even Chief Justice Roberts—who authored the dissent in *McGirt*—accused Oklahoma of "waving a bloody shirt." How the state would garner five votes, I couldn't see. But then the decision came out.

In a 5–4 opinion authored by Justice Kavanaugh, Oklahoma won. Now all states in our country—not just Oklahoma—can prosecute crimes committed by non-Natives against Natives on tribal lands. This was necessary, Kavanaugh reasoned, because in the wake of *McGirt* some criminals had "simply gone free." Without a citation, Kavanaugh wrote that "the State estimates that it will have to transfer prosecutorial responsibility for more than 18,000 cases per year." Oklahoma's lies prevailed.

In his opinion, Kavanaugh argued that *Worcester v. Georgia*—the 1830s decision in which the Supreme Court said Georgia didn't have jurisdiction on Cherokee land—was no longer the law. *Worcester* is still taught as part of the foundation of federal Indian law, but Kavanaugh argued that it had long been overturned. And thus, states have long had the inherent authority to prosecute all crimes committed by non-Natives on tribal land. Several other recent Supreme Court decisions contradict this, but Kavanaugh didn't claim to overrule those decisions. Instead he just ignored them. In his dissent, Gorsuch mocked the opinion as coming "as if by oracle"—detached from history and the court's legal authority. "Truly, a more ahistorical and mistaken statement of Indian law would be hard to fathom." Instead of following the law, the majority just made it up.

After Muscogee Nation won *McGirt*, Oklahoma threw a tantrum. Led by Governor Stitt, Oklahoma launched a disinformation campaign to paint the reservations as descending into lawless chaos. Rather than investigate those claims, prominent media outlets repeated them. After efforts at congressional legislation failed, and courts in Oklahoma resoundingly rejected the state's novel legal theories, Governor Stitt, his handpicked attorney general, and their high-dollar corporate lawyer took their effort to roll *McGirt* back all the way to the Supreme Court. What should have been the hardest institution to move was the only one to crumble.

What happened in *Castro-Huerta* is not isolated. The case is emblematic of several disturbing trends at our nation's highest court. *Castro-Huerta* is not the only case where the high court played fast and loose with the facts. In cases about constitutional limits to police searches, detaining immigrants, employee privacy in the workplace, same-sex marriage, and voting rights, the Supreme Court's majority opinion contained factual errors. Oklahoma is far from the only state to ask the court to do something unprecedented. As the federal judiciary has shifted further to the right, Republican state attorneys general are launching more and more radical lawsuits—including one to overturn the results of a democratic election. Litigators like Shanmugam—who by his own admission is focused on protecting "corporate interests" and "well-off individuals"—have become the norm before the high court, not the exception. And the corporate law firms behind them are shaping important aspects of American law—from campaign finance to consumer protections. Finally, when it comes to stare decisis—that bedrock legal principle that courts should follow previous decisions—*Castro-Huerta* is not the only case where the high court left precedent in the dust. Five days before *Castro-Huerta* came out, the Supreme Court overturned *Roe v. Wade* and the constitutional right to an abortion.

Following the fall of *Roe*, public faith in the Supreme Court reached its lowest point in fifty years. Three-quarters of Americans say the court has become "too politicized," and less than half feel "trust and confidence" in the institution. Some research shows people's faith in the Supreme Court may be tied to their faith in law itself. If half our citizens don't believe the Supreme Court is legitimate, how will our democracy function?

"Like the Miner's Canary," an early scholar of federal Indian law wrote, "the Indian marks the shift from fresh air to poison gas in our political atmosphere." How our government treats Indigenous peoples, he argued, "reflects the rise and fall of our democratic faith." The concern growing among many Americans about the Supreme Court is a reality Indigenous nations have been living with for a long time. Sometimes when the law is on our side we win. But more often, we watch the institution depart from law and precedent at will. Our experience has long reflected the strengths and weaknesses of the Supreme Court, the chaos of its decision-making, and the power it has given itself outside of constitutional bounds. If only more people had been paying attention.

Epilogue

UNLIKE THE WROUGHT-IRON FENCE THAT ENCIRCLES THE GRAVE OF Andrew Jackson, the cornfield is open. When I am there, it has already been harvested. In swarms, blackbirds eat the broken pieces left on the ground. A spring-fed creek carves out the lowest place. From there, the ground rises east to a grassy knoll and then again east to a distant ridge lined with trees. There is little color in the hard dirt and faded stalks before my feet. It looks mournful, as if the earth knows what history it holds. When Cherokees were rounded up and forced into concentration camps, this was the largest one. They stayed close to the spring for water. There is no marker.

Visiting the public parks that were clearly labeled and dedicated to the history of our removal was no less jarring. The visitors seemed most interested in the architecture of the early-1800s buildings. They walked their dogs. It is a heavy history to truly hold—a weight our public and our government has never lifted.

The *McGirt* Supreme Court decision resulted in the largest restoration of Indigenous land in US history. After it was denied for over a century, the court ruled Muscogee Nation still had a reservation. Subsequently, eight other reservations, covering nearly half the land in Oklahoma, were upheld. Including my own.

The historic status of the *McGirt* decision is ironic when you understand what happened legally. The Supreme Court didn't overturn anything, strike anything down, or change their own precedent. All the court did was follow the law. But still, that was radical.

When it comes to tribal sovereignty, the US government is spineless. Most often when states or non-Native people want something that belongs to a tribe—whether it's gold, oil, land, or power—they get it. Even when the law clearly protects the tribe. Sometimes our government simply looked the other way. Other times settlers wanted so much that our government remade the law to fit their demands. Greed—not justice—has governed more of our history than we are willing to admit. Oklahoma's greed in *McGirt* was refusing to give up an ounce of power—even when exercising that power was illegal.

To avoid calling it greed, lies are told. The land belonged to Georgia. Illegal squatters in Indian Territory deserved property rights. There were never reservations in Oklahoma. *McGirt* caused chaos and crime. Often, the lies are about Indigenous peoples ourselves: we are backward, corrupt, lawless, unworthy. The most persistent lie by far is that policies which obviously harm us are somehow for our benefit.

Indigenous nations have been governing ourselves since before this country was founded—since before it was even an idea. As the United States was built around us, we shaped it. Since the founding, tribal leaders, Indigenous intellectuals, Native diplomats, warriors, lawyers, and advocates carved out a space in American law through which our inherent sovereignty was recognized. Over the generations, we continue to leverage the legal foothold our ancestors created.

Federal Indian law today is not all good or all bad—rather it is the totality of our history. Embedded in American law are the victories and defeats of our ancestors, and the unimaginable compromises they were forced to make. The legal terrain with which we are left is tricky: the protections Indigenous nations have under US law are not enough, yet we have to constantly fight for those protections to remain and be followed. We demand the US government fulfill its legal obligations to us, knowing it often will not. Native nations don't have a constitutional amendment or Supreme Court decision that ended our legal subordination. What we are left with is a government that still contains both impulses: The impulse to uphold the inherent and legally recognized sovereignty of Indigenous nations. And the impulse to railroad tribes because it can.

The lesson of *McGirt* is not that when the law is on our side and we fight hard, justice prevails. The lesson is that although justice for Indigenous nations is rare, in our democracy, it is possible.

In our self-conception, America is a beacon of democracy for the rest of the world. Even when our founding sins are recognized, we like to believe things have gotten better. The story we tell ourselves is one of progress. In reality, our government committed genocide. It has never reformed itself or changed its laws to prevent such atrocities from happening again.

So now, when our government wants to ban Muslims from entering our country, suspend the international rules of war to fight terror, detain enemy combatants indefinitely, put migrants in detention camps, and separate families at the border, it uses principles of federal Indian law to do so. As scholar Maggie Blackhawk has pointed out, the legal doctrines the US created to take Indigenous land still govern how the US treats those living at the margins of our empire. Native history is often treated like a tragic, distant chapter of the American story, and the legal terrain it created like a siloed backwater of American law. But it is foundational.

The Founding Fathers wanted a democracy that, unlike the king of England, would derive its power from "the consent of the governed." But they also wanted an empire. And so they built both: a democracy that at its center gave every citizen a voice and a vote, and an empire that, as it constantly expanded, controlled the lives and the lands of people who had no say. While over the centuries who was included in that center of democracy changed, the edge of empire never went away. From Indigenous nations, to Guam and Puerto Rico, to migrants detained at our border, there have always been people who lived under the raw power of our government but without the liberties and privileges of our Constitution. Our inheritance as American citizens is a democracy that is often wildly antidemocratic—a government that rules by both consent and by conquest.

When I left the cornfield, I drove north. The side of the road was punctuated with signs letting me know it had once been a route on the Trail of Tears. The small town a few miles north of the internment camp was the army's base of operations. I got out there and walked a small circle of residential blocks. One of the streets was named after the secretary of war who oversaw the deportation—another after the army general in charge. For a moment, I watched a family decorate their home for Christmas. They pulled green garlands and red and silver balls out of plastic bins. I felt overwhelmed by the weight of it all. And so alone in that feeling.

Acknowledgments

OFTEN, BOOKS ARE PRESENTED AS SOLO ENDEAVORS. THIS BOOK WAS not. Without a lot of help from a lot of people, it would have never happened.

Before there was a book, there were people who gave me a platform to tell this story and find my voice as a writer. First, there was Mark Trahant (Shoshone-Bannock), the trailblazing Native journalist who hired me to write my first article about *Murphy* for *ICT* and gave me some of my earliest work as a journalist. At the Poynter Institute's Power of Diverse Voices in 2019, I wrote a draft opinion piece about *Murphy* that was later published in the *Washington Post*. My peers there told me I was a writer before I believed those words myself—a confidence boost that has truly changed my life. Tanya Somanader at Crooked Media read that opinion piece and had the wild idea to turn it into a podcast. An amazing team helped create the first season of the podcast *This Land* including Gabrielle Lewis, Mukta Mohan, Catherine St. Louis, and Vikram Patel. Thank you, Crooked Media, for giving this story such a big platform. For the podcast, I got a journalism award from the Heising-Simons Foundation. After hearing I was maybe interested in writing a book, their program officer Brian Eule connected me to Samuel G. Freedman (who teaches book writing at Columbia), and Freedman connected me to a book agent. And that agent, Kristine Dahl, secured the deal that made this book.

At HarperCollins, this project was shepherded by editors Jennifer Barth, Jenny Xu, and Sarah Haugen—who really helped pull it all together. Thank you to the rest of the HarperCollins team who worked to bring this book into the world, including Tina Andreadis, Jonathan Burnham, Doug Jones, John Jusino, Ezra Kupor, Joanne O'Neill, and Leah Wasielewski.

So many hands went into the research. Maddie Stone and Steve Horn researched the oil and gas industry in Oklahoma, corporate lawyers, and helped me track down a lot of data. Amber Morning Star Byars (Choctaw Nation of Oklahoma) wrangled court documents. Kathryn E. Gardner and the Reporters Committee for Freedom of the Press filed a lawsuit on my behalf when the governor and attorney general of Oklahoma did not comply with multiple Open Records Requests. Arthur Berman crunched the numbers on the value of eastern Oklahoma's oil and gas reserves. Allison Herrera (Xolon Salinan), Jennifer McAffrey Thiessen (Cherokee Nation), Desi Small-Rodriguez (Northern Cheyenne and Chicana), and Joey Stipek helped me tackle the huge task of crunching Oklahoma's criminal justice data. Joseph Cloud (Cherokee Nation) and Leslie Bigaouette-Serrano (Cherokee Nation) organized and digitized primary sources. Genealogist Regina Pickard (Cherokee Nation) helped me find Millie Naharkey's living descendants. Alyssa Wind (Ak-Chin Indian Community and Mvskoke, Sac and Fox, and Tohono O'odham descendant), Aimee Harjo (Chahta and Mvskoke), and Nick Haddox (Cherokee Nation) helped collect stories from tribal citizens. Thank you to the College of the Muscogee Nation for connecting me with some of your talented students. Thank you, Joy Harjo, for your inspiring words, and Jennifer Foerster for coordinating.

Thank you to all the historians who offered their expertise, pointed our research in the right direction, and tracked down particularly hard-to-find primary sources including Donna L. Akers (Choctaw Nation of Oklahoma), Jack D. Baker (Cherokee Nation), Russell Cobb, Peter Hoffer, Paul Kelton, Daniel Littlefield, Troy Wayne Poteete (Cherokee Nation), Julie Reed (Cherokee Nation), Brett Riggs, Alaina E. Roberts (Chickasaw and Choctaw freedpeople descendant), and Claudio Saunt. Thank you, Nancy Brown (Seneca-Cayuga Nation and Cherokee descendant), for being the custodian of so much of our family's history, especially our cemetery.

Thank you to all the records keepers who gave generously of their time to put primary sources in my hands, especially Rose Buchanan at the US National Archives and Records Administration, Lina Ortega at the Western History Collections at University of Oklahoma Libraries, Emily Walhout at Houghton Library at Harvard University, Chris W. Dial at the Tulsa County Court clerk's office, and Terri Rogers at the Tulsa County Warehouse. Court reporters Shelley Ottwell and Trixi Ingram provided the transcripts for the *Murphy* and *McGirt* trials.

Huge thanks to my ride-or-die research partner James Anthony Owen, who gathered hundreds of primary source documents for this book. I seriously would not have been able to do it without you. Thank you for sticking with me these past few years.

The indomitable Wudan Yan fact-checked this book. Cody Hammer (Cherokee Nation) and Brittany Bendabout (Cherokee Nation and Otoe-Missouria) did the photography. Keli Gonzales (Cherokee Nation) illustrated the maps. Thank you, Sarah Deer (Muscogee (Creek) Nation), Catherine Foreman Gray (Cherokee Nation), and Rebecca Landsberry-Baker (Muscogee Nation), for reading the very rough first drafts and giving your feedback. Maureen Sun helped get the manuscript in shape.

To all the people who spoke to me, trusted me with their story, and graciously gave me their time, thank you, including Janelle Adair (United Keetoowah Band of Cherokee Indians), Mike Andrews, Barbara Armstrong, Kara Bacon (Choctaw Nation of Oklahoma), Adam Barnett, Gary Batton (Choctaw Nation of Oklahoma), Norma Ballenger, Roger Ballenger, Sheila Bird (United Keetoowah Band of Cherokee Indians and descendant of the Keetoowah Nighthawks), Maggie Blackhawk (Fond du Lac Band Ojibwe), M. Sharon Blackwell (Omaha Tribe of Nebraska and Muscogee matrilineal descendant), Scott Braden (Osage Nation), Miko Brandon (Chickasaw Nation), Tim Brown (Cherokee Nation), Elizabeth Butler (Muscogee Nation), Jason Chennault, Kristi Christopher, Iris Dalley, Kevin Dellinger (Muscogee Nation), Desiree, Margaret Quennie Wilson Dietrich (Choctaw

Nation of Oklahoma), Lindsay Dowell (Cherokee, Pawnee, and Quapaw), John Echohawk (Pawnee), Angel Ellis (Muscogee Nation), Lewis Ervin (Choctaw freedpeople descendant), Roxanne Evans (Muscogee Nation), Abi Fain (Choctaw Nation), Anderson Fields Jr., Anderson Fields Sr., Matthew Fletcher (Grand Traverse Band of Ottawa and Chippewa Indians), James Floyd (Muscogee Nation), Amelia Gambler (Muscogee Nation), Julie Gardner, Ian Gershengorn, Patti Ghezzi, David Giampetroni, Brenda S. Golden (Muscogee Nation), Bobby Gray, Rhonda Grayson (Muscogee freedpeople descendant), Stephen Greetham, Effie Cato Guyton, Jeannine Hale (Cherokee Nation), Suzan Shown Harjo (Cheyenne and Hodulgee Muscogee), Victoria Holland (United Keetoowah Band of Cherokee Indians), Kendra Horn, Chuck Hoskin Jr. (Cherokee Nation), Mike Hunter, Lewis Johnson (Seminole Nation of Oklahoma), John Jones, Irvin Judd, Riyaz Kanji, Eldon Kelough (Muscogee Nation), Patrick Kincaid (Cheyenne and Lakota), Pamela Kingfisher (Cherokee Nation), Stephen Kunzweiler, Larry Lane, Stacy Leeds (Cherokee Nation), Ryan Leonard, Te'Ata Loper (citizen of Chickasaw Nation and Choctaw descendant), Melody McCoy (Cherokee Nation), Mike McBride III, Rosemary McCombs Maxey (Muscogee (Creek) Nation of Oklahoma), Jimcy McGirt (Seminole Nation of Oklahoma and Muscogee descendant), Melody McPerryman (Muscogee Nation), Rachel Anne Miller (Choctaw Nation of Oklahoma), Patrick Murphy (Muscogee Nation), J. Larry Nichols, Richard O'Carroll, Russell Overton, Terry Park, M. Alexander Pearl (Chickasaw Nation), Michael Peevey (Muscogee Nation), Gary Peterson, Georgia (Judy) Proctor (Muscogee Nation), Keli Proctor (Muscogee Nation), Liza Proctor (Muscogee Nation), Tim Ramsey (Cherokee Nation), Joe Robson, Robert Rocha, John Ross (Cherokee Nation), Mark Taylor (Muscogee Nation), Shawn Terry (Muscogee Nation), J. Miko Thomas (Chickasaw Nation), Philip Tinker (Osage Nation), Tim Turner, Marilyn Vann (Cherokee Nation), Tonya Wapskineh (Cherokee Nation), Kevin Washburn (Chickasaw Nation), Stephen Wermiel, Yvette Wiley (Muscogee Nation), Doris Burris Williamson (Choctaw freedpeople descendant), Ty Wilson (Cherokee Nation), Daniel Wind III (Muscogee Nation and Cherokee descendant), Sue Wind (Muscogee and Seminole), Darla Yeatman (Muscogee Nation), and all the people who talked to me on background or off the record. Tracking down people to interview is a huge task; special thanks to those who helped me, including Galen Cloud (Muscogee Nation), Tabatha Keton, and Morgan Taylor (Muscogee Nation).

This book would not have been possible without the institutional support of Blue Mountain Center, which gave me the space to reconnect with myself as a writer, and to think about this project in a big way; MacDowell, which took care of me while I limped over the finish line and handed the book in; and the NYU-Yale American Indian Sovereignty Project, which supported this book's research and completion. Thank you, Ned and Maggie, for being continuously generous with the resources you have access to.

The highs and lows of this project were shouldered by a community of support I feel so lucky to have. Thank you to my family, especially my parents. Your faith in me has buoyed my faith in myself. Thank you to Frances, for raising me to know this history. Matt and Olive, you supported me more than you know. May and Carina, thank you for reading. I am forever indebted to the friends who listened to me complain about the overwhelm, helped me puzzle through difficult parts, and celebrated milestones, especially Alexa, Allison, Aura, Becca, Candessa, Carina, Joseph, Junauda, Karl, Kate, Liz, Marx, May, and Peter.

This book stands within a long tradition of Indigenous intellectual thought, histories, and resistance. Thank you to the ancestors who made our survival and struggle possible.

All mistakes are my own.

Further Reading

THIS BOOK IS SITUATED WITHIN A LONG TRADITION OF NATIVE AMERI-can writing, reporting, and scholarship. For other Indigenous perspectives on the law, history, and the *McGirt* case, here is a list of suggested reading.

From Muscogee Writers

- For an overview of tribal nations in Oklahoma, read legal scholar Blue Clark's *Indian Tribes of Oklahoma: A Guide*.

- For more on the maze of criminal jurisdiction in Indian country, how it perpetuates violence against Native women, and what can be done about it, read Sarah Deer's *The Beginning and End of Rape*.

- For a poetic portrayal of the pull and heartbreak of ancestral homelands, read US poet laureate Joy Harjo's "An American Sunrise."

- For an overview of the treaty relationship between Indigenous nations and the United States, read *Nation to Nation*, edited by Suzan Shown Harjo.

- For in-depth coverage of *McGirt* and its implementation, and breaking news in Muscogee Nation, read Mvskoke Media at https://mvskokemedia.com.

From Cherokee Writers

- For a classic history of the Cherokee people, read Emmet Starr's *History of the Cherokee Indians and Their Legends and Folk Lore*.

- For a legal perspective on the legacy of *McGirt*, read scholars Dylan R. Hedden-Nicely and Stacy L. Leeds's article "A Familiar Crossroads: *McGirt v. Oklahoma* and the Future of Federal Indian Law Canon" in the *New Mexico Law Review*.

- For more history and translations of the *Cherokee Phoenix*, read Constance Owl's master's thesis, "*Tsalagi Tsulehisanvhi*: Uncovering Cherokee Language Articles from the *Cherokee Phoenix* Newspaper, 1828–1834."

- For a history of Cherokee Nation in the nineteenth century, read scholar Julie Reed's *Serving the Nation*.

- For a collection of personal and academic perspectives on allotment, read *Allotment Stories*, edited by Daniel Heath Justice (Cherokee Nation) and Jean M. O'Brien (White Earth Ojibwe).

From Other Writers from the Five Tribes

- For a history of removal from an Indigenous perspective, read historian Donna Akers's article "Removing the Heart of the Choctaw People" in the *American Indian Culture and Research Journal*.

- For a history of eastern Oklahoma and the Five Tribes that centers Chickasaw and Choctaw freedpeople from Reconstruction to allotment, read Alaina Roberts's book *I've Been Here All the While*.

From Other Native American and Indigenous Writers

- For a compelling overview of how colonization has shaped the Constitution and laws of the United States, read scholar Maggie Blackhawk's *Harvard Law Review* article "The Constitution of American Colonialism."

- For a sweeping and overdue retelling of US history that centers the colonization and resistance of Indigenous peoples, read historian Ned Blackhawk's award-winning book *The Rediscovery of America*.

- For an overview of federal Indian law, read legal scholar Matthew Fletcher's book *Principles of Federal Indian Law*. For breaking news and helpful links to court cases affecting tribal sovereignty, read the blog he runs at turtletalk.blog.

- For in-depth reporting on *McGirt*, its aftermath, and tribal politics in Oklahoma, read Allison Herrera's coverage for KOSU at https://kosu.org/people/allison-herrera.

- For a history of slavery in Cherokee Nation through the story of one enslaved family, read historian Tiya Miles's book *Ties That Bind*.

- For a book that puts the *McGirt* decision in its legal and historical context, read Robert Miller and Robbie Ethridge's *A Promise Kept*.

- For a compelling argument about why tribal law is a fundamental part of American law, read Elizabeth Hidalgo Reese's *Stanford Law Review* article "The Other American Law."

- For a concise history of how the Supreme Court has impacted the land rights of Indigenous nations, read Angela Riley's article "The History of Native American Lands and the Supreme Court."

- For an insider's perspective on the legal battle over the Muscogee reservation, read Philip Tinker, Riyaz Kanji, and David Giampetroni's *Tulsa Law Review* article "Reflections on *McGirt v. Oklahoma*: A Case Team Perspective."

Appendix: Sensitive or Triggering Subject Matter

THE STORY OF THIS SUPREME COURT CASE AND ITS CONNECTED HIS-tory includes accounts of murder, suicide, racial violence, and sexual violence. Where that content is described or mentioned in the book is outlined below. If content is only "mentioned," it doesn't include details. Please take care of yourself while you read.

- Murder is described on these pages: 15–18, 65, 109–10, 162.
- Death by suicide is mentioned on page 55.
- A suicide attempt is mentioned on page 66.
- Domestic violence is described on page 13.
- Sexual violence is mentioned on the following pages: 59, 60, 150–51, 162, 195, 203.
- Kidnapping and assault are described on pages 159–62.
- Systemic violence against Indigenous people and racial violence is described on the following pages: 25–26, 32–34, 59, 70–71, 95, 98–101, 106–7, 155–62.

Notes

PROLOGUE

1   to west of the Mississippi: Andrew Jackson, "December 8, 1829: First Annual Message to Congress," transcript, Presidential Speeches, Miller Center, University of Virginia, https://millercenter.org/the-presidency/presidential-speeches/december-8-1829-first-annual-message-congress.

2   are mostly wrong: EchoHawk Consulting and First Nations Development Institute, "Reclaiming Native Truth," June 2018, https://illuminative.org/wp-content/uploads/2022/06/FullFindingsReport-screen-spreads.pdf.

2   legal scholar Sarah Deer: Sarah Deer, "I just have to remark one more time that this is a BIG F DEAL," Facebook, August 9, 2017, screenshot in possession of author.

2   "in peace and plenty": Andrew Jackson, "Letter to the Creek Indians," March 23, 1829, Gerhard Peters and John T. Woolley, the American Presidency Project, https://www.presidency.ucsb.edu/node/342176.

2   the Tenth Circuit Court of Appeals . . . upheld: *Murphy v. Royal*, 07-7068 (Tenth Circuit), August 8, 2017.

2   "a recognized reservation again!": Sarah Deer, "I just have to remark . . ."

2   then a podcast: Rebecca Nagle, "Half the Land in Oklahoma Could Be Returned to Native Americans. It Should Be," *Washington Post*, November 28, 2018; Rebecca Nagle, *This Land* (podcast), Crooked Media, May 2019, https://crooked.com/podcast/this-land-episode-1-the-case/.

3   and Elizabeth Hidalgo Reese: Alaina E. Roberts, *I've Been Here All the While: Black Freedom on Native Land* (Philadelphia: University of Pennsylvania Press, 2021); Joy Harjo, *An American Sunrise* (New York: W. W. Norton & Co., 2019); Elizabeth A. Reese, "The Other American Law," *Stanford Law Review* 73 (2021): 555.

4   the wrongs of history: *McGirt v. Oklahoma*, 18–9526 (US Supreme
      Court), July 9, 2020, Roberts Dissenting, 4–6; *Royal v. Murphy*, 17-1107 (US
      Supreme Court), Petition for a Writ of Certiorari, February 6, 2018; *Carpenter
      v. Murphy*, 17-1107 (US Supreme Court), Oral Argument Transcript, Novem-
      ber 27, 2018.

CHAPTER 1 | The Crime

9   "like an oil stain": Anderson Fields Jr. (community member and wit-
      ness) in discussion with the author, December 2021.

10   porch was trees: *Oklahoma v. Murphy*, CF-1999-164A (McIntosh County
      District Court), trial transcript, vol. 4, April 13, 2000, 945–47.

10   had been fighting: *USA v. Murphy*, trial transcript, vol. 3, 707–18; *USA v.
      Murphy*, 20-CR-078-RAW (US District Court, Eastern District of Oklahoma),
      trial transcript, vol. 2, August 4, 2021, 299–300; *USA v. Murphy*, trial tran-
      script, vol. 2, 949.

10   "It was all cousins [that] stayed down there": Amelia Gambler (family
      member) in discussion with the author, February 2022.

10   were buried in the yard: Roxanne Evans (family member) in discussion
      with the author, February 2022; Mark Taylor (family member and witness)
      in discussion with the author, December 2021; Amelia Gambler in discus-
      sion with the author, February 2022; *Murphy v. Mullin*, CIV-03-443-WH (US
      District Court, Eastern District of Oklahoma), Exhibit K of Petition for Writ of
      Habeas Corpus, Affidavit of Eldon Kelough, January 7, 2004.

11   did they return home: Roxanne Evans in discussion with the author,
      February 2022.

11   Patrick moved back to Ryal: *Murphy v. Mullin*, CIV-03-443-WH (US
      District Court, Eastern District of Oklahoma), Exhibit M of Petition for Writ
      of Habeas Corpus, Affidavit of Elizabeth Jane Gambler Murphy, January
      22, 2004; *Oklahoma v. Murphy*, trial transcript, vol. 5, 1316–19; *Murphy v.
      Oklahoma*, PCD-2001-1197 (Oklahoma Court of Criminal Appeals), Exhibit
      4 of Original Application for Post-Conviction Relief, Affidavit of Elizabeth
      Murphy, January 16, 2002; *Murphy v. Mullin*, CIV-03-443-WH (US District
      Court, Eastern District of Oklahoma), Exhibit A of Petition for Writ of Habeas
      Corpus, Affidavit of George Rawlings, February 26, 2004; Patrick Kincaid
      (Patrick Murphy's college classmate) in discussion with the author, January
      2022; Mark Taylor in discussion with the author, December 2021; Roxanne
      Evans in discussion with the author, February 2022.

11   back roads of McIntosh County by truck: *Oklahoma v. Murphy*, trial
      transcript, vol. 4, 945–63; *Oklahoma v. Murphy*, trial transcript, vol. 3, 656–70,
      680; Mark Taylor in discussion with the author, December 2021.

11   cousins in a way: Amelia Gambler in discussion with the author, February 2022.

11   she would later say: *USA v. Murphy*, trial transcript, vol. 2, 188–90; *Oklahoma v. Murphy*, trial transcript, vol. 5, 1219–25.

12   the braided curves of the North Canadian River: *USA v. Murphy*, trial transcript, vol. 2, 77–78, 189–90; *Oklahoma v. Murphy*, trial transcript, vol. 3, 583–84.

12   fix the place up: "Betty Elouise Jacobs," obituary, Integrity Funeral Service, https://www.integrityfuneralservice.com/obituary/Betty-Jacobs; *Oklahoma v. Murphy*, trial transcript, vol. 3, 587–88.

12   left in Vernon are churches: Papers and records of Vernon Charitable Foundation, private collection of Effie Cato Guyton; Effie Cato Guyton (president, Vernon Charitable Foundation) in discussion with the author, March 2022; Larry O'Dell, "All-Black Towns," *The Encyclopedia of Oklahoma History and Culture*, Oklahoma Historical Society, https://www.okhistory.org/publications/enc/entry.php?entry=AL009.

12   only road out of town: Vernon Road: *Oklahoma v. Murphy*, trial transcript, vol. 3, 589–91, 652.

13   Patrick would beat her mother: *USA v. Murphy*, trial transcript, vol. 1, 45–47; *USA v. Murphy*, 20-CR-078-RAW (US District Court, Eastern District of Oklahoma), Sentencing Hearing Proceedings, May 10, 2022, 14.

13   to see George: *USA v. Murphy*, trial transcript, vol. 1, 48.

13   "get them one by one": *Oklahoma v. Murphy*, trial transcript, vol. 3, 735.

13   the baby of all the cousins: Amelia Gambler in discussion with the author, February 2022; Mark Taylor in discussion with the author, December 2021.

13   "drug him down that road": Mark Taylor in discussion with the author, December 2021.

14   save money on beer: *Oklahoma v. Murphy*, trial transcript, vol. 3, 789–99; *Oklahoma v. Murphy*, trial transcript, vol. 4, 958; *USA v. Murphy*, trial transcript, vol. 2, 140, 159.

14   left on Vernon Road: *Oklahoma v. Murphy*, trial transcript, vol. 4, 958–61.

15   coming toward him: *Oklahoma v. Murphy*, trial transcript, vol. 2, 260–66; *Oklahoma v. Murphy*, trial transcript, vol. 3, 591.

15   jumped out of Patrick Murphy's truck: *Oklahoma v. Murphy*, trial transcript, vol. 2, 592–95.

15   George lying in the ditch: *Oklahoma v. Murphy*, trial transcript, vol. 2, 596–601.

16   called the sheriff: Anderson Fields Jr. in discussion with the author, December 2021; *Oklahoma v. Murphy*, trial transcript, vol. 2, 309–15.

16   "gushing out just about from everywhere": Anderson Fields Jr. in discussion with the author, December 2021.

16   the location of the crime scene: Iris Dalley (former OSBI crime-scene investigator) in discussion with the author, November 2021; *Oklahoma v. Murphy*, trial transcript, vol. 2, 420–26.

16   a body lying in the ditch: Iris Dalley in discussion with the author, November 2021; *Oklahoma v. Murphy*, trial transcript, vol. 2, 427–32.

17   he bled to death: *Oklahoma v. Murphy*, trial transcript, vol. 2, 428, 445–50, 762.

17   the Indian Nation Turnpike below them: *Oklahoma v. Murphy*, trial transcript, vol. 2, 474; *Oklahoma v. Murphy*, trial transcript, vol. 3, 602–4.

17   "I killed George Jacobs": Mark Taylor in discussion with the author, December 2021; *Oklahoma v. Murphy*, trial transcript, vol. 3, 664–70.

17   "He looked so pale": Mark Taylor in discussion with the author, December 2021.

17   listened to his mom and came back inside: *Oklahoma v. Murphy*, trial transcript, vol. 3, 613–14, 796–97; *USA v. Murphy*, trial transcript, vol. 2, 159.

18   a flare in the dark night: *Oklahoma v. Murphy*, trial transcript, vol. 3, 616–17, 709–13.

18   and got into bed: *USA v. Murphy*, trial transcript, vol. 2, 128–31.

18   the truck out on Vernon Road: *Oklahoma v. Murphy*, trial transcript, vol. 2, 260–66, 371–72.

18   Patrick Murphy was still asleep: *USA v. Murphy*, trial transcript, vol. 2, 293–99, 328–31.

18   surrounding Patrick's trailer: *USA v. Murphy*, Sentencing Hearing Proceedings, 15.

18   before she hit the earth: *USA v. Murphy*, Sentencing Hearing Proceedings, 15–16.

19   just like he said: *USA v. Murphy*, Sentencing Hearing Proceedings, 16–17.

19   Oklahoma's death penalty alone: *Oklahoma v. Murphy*, CF-1999-164A (McIntosh County District Court), Docket entry, December 17, 1999; *Oklahoma v. King*, CF-2000-182 (McIntosh County District Court), Judgment and Sentence, February 7, 2002; *Oklahoma v. Long*, CF-1999-164B (McIntosh County District Court), Judgment and Sentence, September 21, 2000; Mark Sherman, "Justices to Review Oklahoma's Indian Territory Murder Appeal," *Muskogee Phoenix* (Muskogee, OK), May 22, 2018.

20   the district attorney told the jury: *Oklahoma v. Murphy*, trial tran-
      script, vol. 3, 581–652, 656–96; *Oklahoma v. Murphy*, trial transcript, vol. 4a,
      1087–108.

20   someone was wrong: *Oklahoma v. Murphy*, trial transcript, vol. 2, 310,
      386, 422–25.

20   he kept contradicting himself: *Murphy v. Mullin*, CIV-03-443-WH (US
      District Court, Eastern District of Oklahoma), Petition for Writ of Habeas
      Corpus, March 4, 2004; *Oklahoma v. Murphy*, trial transcript, vol. 4, 868–69;
      Murphy v. Oklahoma, PCD-2001-1197 (Oklahoma Court of Criminal Appeals),
      Original Application for Post-Conviction Relief, February 7, 2002; *Oklahoma
      v. Murphy*, trial transcript, vol. 4, 945–1059.

21   "fix his punishment at death": *Oklahoma v. Murphy*, trial transcript, vol.
      5, 1219–25, 1401.

21   below the cold water: Irvin Judd (pastor who baptized Patrick Murphy)
      in discussion with the author, 2022.

CHAPTER 2 | Beginning

24   and brought it with her: Janelle Adair (traditional storyteller and citizen of
      United Keetoowah Band of Cherokee Indians) in discussion with the author,
      October 2020.

25   owned it all: Theda Perdue, *Cherokee Women: Gender and Culture
      Change, 1700–1835* (Lincoln and London: University of Nebraska Press, 1998).

25   it was Cherokee women they purchased it from: Julie Reed (Cherokee
      historian) in discussion with the author, October 2020.

25   for the corn to be replanted: Jessica Choppin Roney, "1776, Viewed
      from the West," *Journal of the Early Republic* 37, no. 4 (2017), 655–700; J. G.
      M. Ramsey, "Description by J. G. M. Ramsey of an Attack by the North Car-
      olina Militia on the Cherokee Nation," in *Annals of Tennessee* (Philadelphia:
      Lippincott, Grambo & Co., 1853), vol. 10, 881–85, vol. 2, 165–68, vol. 1, 161–64,
      167–69; *The State Records of North Carolina*, ed. Walter Clark, North Caro-
      lina Records of the American Revolution, vol. 22, James Martin statement,
      145–47.

25   ᏐᎵ became a refugee: Thomas L. McKenney and James Hall,
      *History of the Indian Tribes of North America with Biographical Sketches and An-
      ecdotes of the Principal Chiefs*, vol. 1 (Philadelphia: E. C. Biddle, 1836), 368–73.

25   burned everything they could find: Ramsey, *Annals of Tennessee*, vol. 1,
      264–68.

25   now came to the Indian Agent: Julie Reed in discussion with the author,
      October 2020.

25   Peace was reached in 1785: Treaty of Hopewell, November 28, 1785.

26   execute the women and children with an ax: Ramsey, "A Minute Account of Sevier's Further Services Is Given by Haywood," in *Annals of Tennessee*, vol. 3, 419–21, 576–78.

26   "but their total extinction": Ramsey, *Annals of Tennessee*, vol. 3, 419.

26   barely escaped death himself: McKenney and Hall, *Indian Tribes of North America*, vol. 1, 371, 373–74; Thurman Wilkins, *Cherokee Tragedy: The Ridge Family and the Decimation of a People* (Norman: University of Oklahoma Press, 1989), 12–13 (map), 18–21; Ramsey, *Annals of Tennessee*, 421–22. *Cherokee Tragedy* says Major Ridge was seventeen; McKenney and Hall's Major Ridge chapter says he was fourteen at this time.

26   In retaliation: McKenney and Hall, *Indian Tribes of North America*, vol. 1, 374–75; Wilkins, *Cherokee Tragedy*, 24.

26   the size of a US state: C. C. Royce. Map of the former territorial limits of the Cherokee "Nation of" Indians; Map showing the territory originally assigned Cherokee "Nation of" Indians. [S.l, 1884] Map. https://www.loc.gov/item/99446145/.

28   "become industrious like the white people": Return J. Meigs, handwritten copy of his Address to the Cherokee Council at Broom Town, August 29, 1808, *Record Group 75 Records of the Bureau of Indian Affairs*, microfilm M208, University of Georgia Main Library, reel 4.

28   ᏍᎣᎵᎵ chose to stay: "To Thomas Jefferson from Cherokee Nation, 21 December 1808," *Founders Online*, National Archives, https://founders.archives.gov/documents/Jefferson/99-01-02-9361, accessed February 14, 2023; Return J. Meigs to Secretary of War, June 3, 1808, *Record Group 75 Records of the Bureau of Indian Affairs*, microfilm M208, University of Georgia Main Library, reel 4.

28   Cherokee Nation's emerging National Council: Rennard Strickland, *Fire and the Spirits: Cherokee Law from Clan to Court* (Norman: University of Oklahoma Press, 1975), 24–26, 47–62.

28   the punishment was fixed at death: Strickland, *Fire and the Spirits*, 76–79. McKenney and Hall, *Indian Tribes of North America*, vol. 1, 382–83.

28   who walks along the top of the mountain: McKenney and Hall, *Indian Tribes of North America*, vol. 1, 368–69.

29   the foundation of Muscogee society: Jean Chaudhuri and Joyotpaul Chaudhuri, *A Sacred Path: The Way of the Muscogee Creeks* (Los Angeles: UCLA American Indian Studies Center, 2001), 14–22; Mvskoke Youth, "Mvskoke Creation Story," April 27, 2020, https://www.youtube.com/watch?v=4a8GQkWESoc.

29 the most prominent feature of their homeland: Creeks: Michael D. Green, *The Politics of Indian Removal: Creek Government and Society in Crisis* (New York: Bedford/St. Martin's Press, 1985), 4.

30 in guns and ammunition: Robert J. Miller and Robbie Ethridge, *A Promise Kept: The Muscogee (Creek) Nation and McGirt v. Oklahoma* (Norman: University of Oklahoma Press, 2023), 13–41; Green, *Politics of Indian Removal*, 37–38; Theodore Isham and Blue Clark, "Creek (Mvskoke)," The Encyclopedia of Oklahoma History and Culture, Oklahoma Historical Society, https://www.okhistory.org/publications/enc/entry.php?entry=CR006.

30 was to fight America together: Thomas L. McKenney and James Hall, *History of the Indian Tribes of North America*, vol. 2, "Opthole Yoholo Biography" (Philadelphia: D. Rice & Co., 1872), 7–12; Green, *Politics of Indian Removal*, 40; Benjamin Hawkins to Secretary of War William Eustis, Sep. 21, 1811, *Letters of Benjamin Hawkins*, vol. 2 (Savannah: Georgia Historical Society, 1916), 591–92; G. W. Campbell to Lyman Draper, March 31, 1884, "Tecumseh & Cherokee Chiefs," Draper MSS vols. 7–13 YY. Tecumseh's campaign was not the first time Indigenous nations had come together to resist colonization. In the 1730s, an intertribal alliance that included the Muscogee Confederacy nearly toppled the colony of South Carolina, and in 1791 the Western Confederacy—which included the Shawnee, Miami, Lenape, and Potawatomi—defeated the entire standing US Army.

31 the Mississippi River flowed backward: Draper, "Tecumseh's Visit to the Cherokees," 1811, Draper MSS vol. 4, 26–31.

31 war between the Red Sticks and the United States: Tiya Miles, *Ties That Bind: The Story of an Afro-Cherokee Family in Slavery and Freedom* (Oakland: University of California Press, 2005), 75–84, 78, 79; Green, *Politics of Indian Removal*, 38–43; Records of BIA, Georgia Commissioners to Secretary of War: May 8, 1812, microfilm, RG75.

32 fight with the United States: Georgia Commissioners to Secretary of War: May 8, 1812, *RG75 Records of the BIA*, microfilm M208, UGA Main Library, reel 4; McKenney and Hall, *Indian Tribes of North America*, vol. 1, 391.

32 a force of about two thousand men: Green, *Politics of Indian Removal*, 43. Steve Inskeep, "How Jackson Made a Killing in Real Estate," *Politico Magazine*, July 4, 2015, https://www.politico.com/magazine/story/2015/07/ontot-jackson-made-a-killing-in-real-estate-119727/; Miles, *Ties That Bind*, 79.

32 "supply the wants of millions": Roger L. Nichols, *Massacring Indians: From Horseshoe Bend to Wounded Knee* (Norman: University of Oklahoma Press, 2021), 12–25.

32 would later write: Nichols, *Massacring Indians*, 12.

32 They ate the potatoes: David Crockett, *Davy Crockett's Own Story As*

Written by Himself: The Autobiography of America's Great Folk Hero (New York: Citadel Press, 1955), 70–71.

32   survived by eating acorns: Wilkins, *Cherokee Tragedy*, 72.

32   allied Muscogee, Choctaws, and Cherokee soldiers joined Jackson's forces: Miles, *Ties That Bind*, 80.

32   waited on the far side of the river: Wilkins, *Cherokee Tragedy*, 76–77; Andrew Jackson to Thomas Pickney, March 28, 1814, Andrew Jackson Papers (AJC): Series 1, General Correspondence and Related items 1775–1885.

32   "if management could effect it": Andrew Jackson to Thomas Pickney, March 28, 1814, Andrew Jackson Papers: Series 1, General Correspondence and Related Items, 1775–1885.

33   By some accounts, it was ᏍᎤᏟ: Emmet Starr, *History of the Cherokee Indians and Their Legends and Folk Lore* (Baltimore: Genealogical Publishing Co., 2008), 98; Wilkins, *Cherokee Tragedy*, 76. Starr credits "private Charles Reese," 42; Wilkins, *Cherokee Tragedy* says it was Major Ridge, 76.

33   cut off each person's nose as they made their tally: "Counting the Dead at Horseshoe Bend," Draper MSS vols. 7–13 YY, Tecumseh Papers, vol. 8, doc 94.

33   From their skin, they cut long strips: Justin Scott Weiss, "The Ghosts of Horseshoe Bend: Myth, Memory, and the Making of a National Battlefield" (master's thesis, Arizona State University, 2014).

34   a result of total war: Treaty of Fort Jackson, August 9, 1814; Green, *Politics of Indian Removal*, 42–44.

34   same pensions as their white counterparts: December 1813 entry, *The Moravian Springplace Mission to the Cherokees, vol. 1: 1805–1813*, trans. Rowena McClinton (Lincoln and London: University of Nebraska Press, 2007); Cherokee Delegation to Madison, Feb. 10, 1816, *RG75 Records of the BIA*, microfilm M208, UGA Main Library, reel 4; Nanohetahee [Pathkiller] to John Lowrey, John Walker, Major Ridge et al., January 10–11, 1816, The *Papers of Chief John Ross*, Vol. 1, ed. Gary E. Moulton (Norman: University of Oklahoma Press, 1985), 22–24; Second Principal Chief Charles Hicks to Return J. Meigs, April 30, 1816, *RG75 Records of the BIA*, microfilm M208, UGA Main Library, reel 4.

34   bury their dead: Robert Henry Dyer to John Coffee, Jan. 2, 1815.

34   a supper in Greenville: Treaty of Ghent, December 24, 1814; Jackson to Coffee, April 24, 1815, *Correspondence of Andrew Jackson*, vol. 2, ed. John Spencer Bassett, vol. 2 (Washington, DC: Carnegie Institute of Washington, 1926), 312.

35   "circumstances have entirely changed": Andrew Jackson to James Monroe, March 18, 1817, *Correspondence of Andrew Jackson*, vol. 2, 369.

35 what my great-great-great-great-grandfather is called: Major Ridge: McKenney and Hall, *Indian Tribes of North America*, 369–402.

CHAPTER 3 | The Argument

37 that could save her client's life: Henry Weinstein, "Lisa McCalmont, 49; Lawyer Challenged Execution by Injection," *Los Angeles Times*, November 14, 2007; *Murphy v. Oklahoma*, PCD-2004-321 (Oklahoma Court of Criminal Appeals), Exhibit M of Second Application for Post-Conviction Relief, Affidavit of Mike Evett, March 24, 2004.

38 the star was in the wrong place: *Oklahoma v. Murphy*, CF-1999-164A (McIntosh County District Court), trial transcript, vol. 2, April 11, 2000; *Murphy v. Oklahoma*, Exhibit M of Second App. for PCR.

38 got in his patrol car and headed south: *Oklahoma v. Murphy*, trial transcript, vol. 2, 385–97; *USA v. Murphy*, 20-CR-078-RAW (US District Court, Eastern District of Oklahoma), trial transcript, vol. 1, August 3, 2021, 101.

38 The distance was about 150 feet: *Oklahoma v. Murphy*, trial transcript, vol. 2, 385–97.

38 at his feet: *Oklahoma v. Murphy*, trial transcript, vol. 2, 385–97; Eldon Kelough (former officer, Muscogee Nation Lighthorse Tribal Police Department) in discussion with the author, November 2021.

39 a mile and a half away: *Murphy v. Oklahoma*, Exhibit M of Second App. for PCR.

39 one of her biggest cases: Kristi Christopher (former federal public defender and counsel for Patrick Murphy) in discussion with the author, March 2022; Weinstein, "Lisa McCalmont."

40 whatever it took to save their lives: Sean Murphy, "OK Death Penalty Foe Commits Suicide," Associated Press, November 7, 2007; Weinstein, "Lisa McCalmont"; Kristi Christopher in discussion with the author, November 2021.

40 He lost both: *Murphy v. Oklahoma*, D-2000-705 (Oklahoma Court of Criminal Appeals), Opinion, May 22, 2002; *Murphy v. Oklahoma*, PCD-2001-1197 (Oklahoma Court of Criminal Appeals), Opinion Denying Application for Post-Conviction Relief and Granting Evidentiary Hearing, September 2, 2002; *Murphy v. Oklahoma*, PCD-2001-1197 (Oklahoma Court of Criminal Appeals), Opinion Denying Application for Post-Conviction Relief Regarding Mental Retardation after Remand for Evidentiary Hearing, March 21, 2003.

40 pending execution were unconstitutional: *Murphy v. Mullin*, CIV-03-443-WH (US District Court, Eastern District of Oklahoma), Petition for Writ of Habeas Corpus, March 4, 2004.

40   "like the four musketeers": Gary Peterson (former counsel for Patrick
     Murphy) in discussion with the author, March 2019 and October 2021.

40   "they mess it up": Gary Peterson in discussion with the author, March 2019.

41   "The rich don't get executed": Scott Braden (former federal public
     defender and counsel for Patrick Murphy) in discussion with the author,
     October 2021.

41   twenty-three to twenty-four hours a day: Bobby Gray (former sheriff of
     McIntosh County) in discussion with the author, 2022; Tom Kuntz, "A Grim
     Glimpse at Oklahoma's Thoroughly Modern Death Row," *New York Times*,
     January 15, 1995, https://www.nytimes.com/1995/01/15/weekinreview
     /word-for-word-amnesty-international-grim-glimpse-oklahoma-s-thoroughly
     -modern.html; Roy D. King, "Conditions for Death Row Prisoners in H-Unit,
     Oklahoma State Penitentiary," Amnesty International, March 1994, https://
     www.amnesty.org/en/wp-content/uploads/2021/06/amr510351994en.pdf.

41   did nothing but sleep: Deborah Fins, "Death Row U.S.A.: Summer
     2000," NAACP Legal Defense and Educational Fund, 2000, https://www
     .naacpldf.org/wp-content/uploads/DRUSA_Summer_2000.pdf; Patti Ghezzi
     (former federal public defender and counsel for Patrick Murphy) in discussion
     with the author, October 2021; Patrick Murphy in discussion with the author,
     April 2023.

41   the country's leading executioner: *Furman v. Georgia*, Oyez, https://
     www.oyez.org/cases/1971/69-5030; "State Execution Rates," Death Penalty
     Information Center, https://deathpenaltyinfo.org/stories/state-execution-rates.

42   "the eeriest thing": Scott Braden in discussion with the author, October
     2021.

42   a way to say goodbye: Patrick Murphy in discussion with the author, April
     2023.

42   to examine the photos: *Murphy v. Oklahoma*, PCD-2004-321 (McIntosh
     County District Court), Evidentiary Hearing Transcript, vol. 1, November 18,
     2004, 128–131.

42   jurisdiction to prosecute Patrick: Scott Braden in discussion with the
     author, October 2021.

42   her background in geology and oil: Weinstein, "Lisa McCalmont."

43   the land was still Indian country: *Murphy v. Oklahoma*, PCD-2004-321
     (Oklahoma Court of Criminal Appeals), Exhibit F of Second Application for
     Post-Conviction Relief, Affidavit of Jeff O'Dell, January 30, 2004; *Murphy v.
     Oklahoma*, PCD-2004-321 (McIntosh County District Court), Evidentiary Hear-
     ing Transcript, vol. 1, November 18, 2004, 157–74.

43   a broader sense of community: "NCAI Response to Usage of the Term

'Indian Country,'" National Congress of American Indians, December 27, 2019, https://archive.ncai.org/news/articles/2019/12/27/ncai-response-to-usage-of-the-term-indian-country.

43   land reserved for tribes and Native people: "Indian Country Defined," United States Department of Justice, May 2001, https://www.justice.gov/archives/jm/criminal-resource-manual-677-indian-country-defined.

43   Muscogee Nation does not: *Murphy v. Oklahoma*, PCD-2004-321 (Oklahoma Court of Criminal Appeals), Exhibit F of Second Application for Post-Conviction Relief, Affidavit of Jeff O'Dell, January 30, 2004; Ken Murray and Jon M. Sands, "Race and Reservations: The Federal Death Penalty and Indian Jurisdiction," *Federal Sentencing Reporter* 14, no. 1 (2001): 28–31, https://doi.org/10.1525/fsr.2001.14.1.28.

44   climb the economic ladder: Angie Debo, *And Still the Waters Run: The Betrayal of the Five Civilized Tribes* (Princeton, NJ: Princeton University Press, 1940), 21–22; S. Misc. Doc. No. 24, 53rd Congress, 3rd Session, 1894; S. Doc. No. 12, 54th Congress, 1st Session, 1895.

44   only a few scattered pieces were left: Rebecca Nagle, "Q&A: Lauren King on What the Five Tribes' Agreement-in-Principle Means for Oklahoma," *Native News Online*, July 20, 2020, https://nativenewsonline.net/sovereignty/q-a-lauren-king-on-what-the-five-tribes-agreement-in-principle-means-for-oklahoma.

44   by her son and another descendant: *Murphy v. Oklahoma*, Exhibit F of Second App. for PCR; *Murphy v. Oklahoma*, Evidentiary Hearing Transcript, vol. 1, 157–74.

44   "to which title has not been extinguished": "Indian Country Defined," United States Department of Justice.

45   legal terrain of tribal land: Résumé of M. Sharon Blackwell, courtesy of M. Sharon Blackwell, in possession of author; M. Sharon Blackwell (legal expert in service to Patrick Murphy's legal team) in discussion with the author, November 2021.

45   "Yes. I guess so": M. Sharon Blackwell in discussion with the author, November 2021.

45   where the murder occurred fit all three: *Murphy v. Oklahoma*, PCD-2004-321 (Oklahoma Court of Criminal Appeals), Second Application for Post-Conviction Relief, March 29, 2004.

46   Muscogee churches and ceremonial grounds: Scott Braden in discussion with the author, October 2021.

47   "got along much better back then": Elizabeth Butler, Melody McPerryman, Georgia (Judy) Proctor, and Keli Proctor (Weogufkee Ceremonial Grounds members) in discussion with the author, February 2023.

47   the tribe outlawed it: Angie Debo, *The Road to Disappearance: A History of the Creek Indians* (Norman: University of Oklahoma Press, 1979), 116–20.

47   the congregation used as a baptismal font: Weogufkee Indian Baptist Church records, private collection of Liza Proctor; Rosemary McCombs Maxey and Liza Proctor (Weogufkee Indian Baptist Church members and Muscogee language teacher) in discussion with the author, February 2023.

47   she kept doing it: Rosemary McCombs Maxey and Liza Proctor in discussion with the author, February 2023; Rosemary McCombs Maxey in discussion with the author, July 2022.

50   was still Indian country: *Murphy v. Oklahoma*, Second App. for PCR.

50   "disestablishment of a reservation": M. Sharon Blackwell in discussion with the author, November 2021.

50   Only Congress can: US Constitution, Article 2, §2, c2.1.

50   gotten rid of the Muscogee reservation: M. Sharon Blackwell in discussion with the author, November 2021.

50   was still a reservation: *Murphy v. Oklahoma*, Second App. for PCR.

50   "treaty lands are tantamount to reservations": M. Sharon Blackwell in discussion with the author, November 2021.

51   constituted cruel and unusual punishment: *Murphy v. Mullin*, CIV-03-443-WH (US District Court, Eastern District of Oklahoma), Petition for Writ of Habeas Corpus, March 4, 2004.

51   "You can't do anything": Gary Peterson in discussion with the author, March 2019.

51   "the happiest man on death row": Kristi Christopher in discussion with the author, November 2021; Patti Ghezzi in discussion with the author, October 2021.

51   he almost won: Kristi Christopher in discussion with the author, November 2021.

51   before she died: Photo of Patrick and Elizabeth Murphy, courtesy of Scott Braden, in possession of author; Kristi Christopher in discussion with the author, November 2021; Scott Braden in discussion with the author, October 2021.

52   for an evidentiary hearing: *Murphy v. Oklahoma*, Second App. for PCR; *Murphy v. Mullin*, Pet. for Writ of Habeas Corpus; *Murphy v. Oklahoma*, PCD-2004-321 (Oklahoma Court of Criminal Appeals), Order Remanding for Evidentiary Hearing, October 5, 2004.

52   to testify: *Murphy v. Oklahoma*, PCD-2004-321 (District Court of McIntosh County), Evidentiary Hearing Transcript, vol. 1, November 18, 2004, 73–93, 128–31.

52   "No, sir": *Murphy v. Oklahoma*, Evidentiary Hearing Transcript, vol. 1, 30.

53   maintained the gravel: *Murphy v. Oklahoma*, Evidentiary Hearing Transcript, vol. 1, 21–24.

53   the DA objected: *Murphy v. Oklahoma*, Evidentiary Hearing Transcript, vol. 1, 194–98.

53   "has not been disestablished": *Murphy v. Oklahoma*, PCD-2004-321 (Oklahoma Court of Criminal Appeals), Affidavit of M. Sharon Blackwell in Defendant's Offer of Proof, December 2, 2004.

53   had an intellectual disability: *Murphy v. Oklahoma*, PCD-2004-321 (Oklahoma Court of Criminal Appeals), Opinion Granting in Part Petitioner's Application for Post-Conviction Relief, December 7, 2005.

54   execute people with intellectual disabilities: *Atkins v. Virginia*, Oyez, https://www.oyez.org/cases/2001/00-8452.

54   read and write letters: *Murphy v. Oklahoma*, PCD-2001-1197 (Oklahoma Court of Criminal Appeals), Exhibit 4 of Original Application for Post-Conviction Relief, Affidavit of Elizabeth Murphy, January 16, 2002; *Murphy v. Oklahoma*, PCD-2001-1197 (Oklahoma Court of Criminal Appeals), Exhibit 5 of Original Application for Post-Conviction Relief, Affidavit of Amelia Gambler, January 16, 2002; *Murphy v. Oklahoma*, PCD-2001-1197 (Oklahoma Court of Criminal Appeals), Exhibit 16 of Original Application for Post-Conviction Relief, Affidavit of John R. Smith, MD, February 4, 2002; *Murphy v. Oklahoma*, PCD-2001-1197 (Oklahoma Court of Criminal Appeals), Respondent's Post-Evidentiary Hearing Response, November 26, 2002; *Murphy v. Workman*, CIV-12-191-RAW (US District Court, Eastern District of Oklahoma), Exhibit 22 of Petition for Writ of Habeas Corpus, Declaration of Patrick Kincaid, May 16, 2012; *Murphy v. Workman*, CIV-12-191-RAW (US District Court, Eastern District of Oklahoma), Exhibit 19 of Petition for Writ of Habeas Corpus, Affidavit of Sterling Williams, April 19, 2012; *Murphy v. Workman*, CIV-12-191-RAW (US District Court, Eastern District of Oklahoma), Exhibit 15 of Petition for Writ of Habeas Corpus, Affidavit of Dale Anderson, April 24, 2012; *Murphy v. Workman*, CIV-12-191-RAW (US District Court, Eastern District of Oklahoma), Exhibit 18 of Petition for Writ of Habeas Corpus, Affidavit of Alfred Mitchell, April 19, 2012; Kristi Christopher in discussion with the author, March 2022.

54   could, in fact, be executed: An Act Relating to Criminal Procedure, Oklahoma Statute §701.10b (2006); *Murphy v. Oklahoma*, PCD-2004-321 (Oklahoma Court of Criminal Appeals), Opinion Affirming Order of Trial Court on Claim of Mental Retardation and Denying Post-Conviction Relief, April 5, 2012.

55   Lisa had died by suicide: Kristi Christopher in discussion with the author, March 2022; Scott Braden in discussion with the author, October 2021; Weinstein, "Lisa McCalmont."

55   "most vulnerable to mental illness": Murphy, "OK Death Penalty Foe Commits Suicide."

55   "forever and forever and forever": "Lisa S. McCalmont," Find a Grave, July 23, 2017, https://www.findagrave.com/memorial/181688611/lisa-s-mccalmont.

55   "We'd never seen anything like her before": Gary Peterson in discussion with the author, March 2019.

55   habeas relief on all grounds: *Murphy v. Mullin*, CIV-03-443-RAW-KEW (US District Court, Eastern District of Oklahoma), Civil Docket, August 11, 2003–August 26, 2020; *Murphy v. Mullin*, CIV-03-443-RAW-KEW (US District Court, Eastern District of Oklahoma), Opinion and Order, August 1, 2007.

CHAPTER 4 | Promise

57   treaty territory of Indigenous nations: Claudio Saunt, *Unworthy Republic: The Dispossession of Native Americans and the Road to Indian Territory* (New York: W. W. Norton & Co., 2020), 36–40, 188–96.

57   entered into a public lottery: Green, *Politics of Indian Removal*, 93.

57   "sick with the expectation of Indian land": "Augusta Georgia 10th Dec. 1831," *Cherokee Phoenix* (New Echota, CN), December 24, 1831.

57   *way up yonder in the Cherokee Nation*: Anchor: A North Carolina History Online Resource, "The Cherokee and the Trail of Tears," NCpedia, https://www.ncpedia.org/anchor/cherokee-and-trail-of-tears, accessed January 23, 2024.

57   treaty territory of Cherokee and Muscogee Nations: Saunt, *Unworthy Republic*, 38; Green, *Politics of Indian Removal*, 89.

59   the entire school felt less "pious": Herman Daggett to Samuel Worcester, December 18, 1818, ABCFM 12.I II (2nd Series): 101, American Board of Commissioners for Foreign Missions Papers (ABCFM), Houghton Library, Harvard University.

59   "very useful to his Nation": November 1, 1820, entry, *The Brainerd Journal: A Mission to the Cherokees, 1817–1823*, ed. Joyce B. Phillips and Paul Gary Phillips (Lincoln and London: University of Nebraska Press, 1998), 194–95.

59   found out about the abuse and stopped it: December 25, 1814, entry, August 12–13, 1811, entry, April 29, 1811, entry, *Moravian Springplace Mission to the Cherokees*, vol. 1, 427, 445–46, vol. 2, 48; Report of Springplace Mission Conference, May 1, 1811, *Records of the Moravians Among the Cherokees: The Anna Rosina Years, Part 2: Warfare on the Horizon*, vol. 4, ed. C. Daniel Crews and Richard W. Starbuck (Norman: University of Oklahoma Press, 2012), 1577–78.

59   The missionaries doted on him: Daggett to Worcester, February 6, 1820, *ABCFM*, ABCFM 12.I II (2nd Series): 114; *MSMC*, vol. 1, 66.

60   the teenager stayed for two years: Robert Sparks Walker, *Torchlights to the Cherokees: The Brainerd Mission* (New York: Macmillan Co., 1931), 156–57, 160–61.

60   her brother set it on fire: "Marriage at Cornwall," *Religious Intellligencer* (New Haven, CT), April 10, 1824; Wilkins, *Cherokee Tragedy*, 151–52; Jedidiah Morse, *A Report to the Secretary of War of the United States, on Indian Affairs* (New Haven: Davis & Force, 1822), 275–76.

60   "an Indian": *Christian Herald*, Dec. 20, 1823, 468, quoted in Wilkins, *Cherokee Tragedy*, 147.

60   pressure to assimilate was also practical: Elias Boudinot, "Address to the Whites Delivered in the First Presbyterian Church, on the 26th of May, 1826 (Philadelphia: William F. Geddes, 1826), in *Cherokee Editor: The Writings of Elias Boudinot*, ed. Theda Perdue (Athens: University of Georgia Press, 1996), 66–79.

62   land could be opened for white settlers: Thomas Jefferson to Congress, January 18, 1803, "A Confidential Letter: Jefferson's Message to Congress on the Expedition West," Thomas Jefferson Foundation, https://www.monticello.org /ontot-jefferson/louisiana-lewis-clark/origins-of-the-expedition/a-confidential -letter/.

62   "difficult to defraud us of the possession": "Coosa River, in Turkey Town," *Cherokee Phoenix* (New Echota, CN), March 4, 1829, quoted in Wilkins, *Cherokee Tragedy*, 206–7.

62   "rest by the side of our fathers": US Congress, House of Representatives Select Committee, *Report of the Select Committee of the House of Representatives, to Which Were Referred the Messages of the President U.S., of the 5th and 8th February, and 2d March, 1827, with Accompanying Documents: and a Report and Resolutions of the Legislature of Georgia*, 19th Congress, 2nd Session, 1827, H.R. Doc. 98, 100–101, 106–7, 111–12.

62   John would become close friends: *HR 98*, 111–12; McKenney and Hall in Green, *Politics of Indian Removal*, 108. Opothle Yoholo's name is also spelled "Opothleyahola" and "Opothleyoholo."

62   "in general council": *HR 98*, 86–91, 112, quote on 129; Green, *Politics of Indian Removal*, 81–84.

62   "I now warn you of your danger": Christopher D. Haveman, *Rivers of Sand: Creek Indian Emigration, Relocation, and Ethnic Cleansing in the American South* (Lincoln: University of Nebraska Press, 2016), 11–12.

65   Muscogee leaders were stunned: Green, *Politics of Indian Removal*, 89.

65   for another eighteen months: Treaty of Indian Springs, February 12, 1825, Ratified Indian Treaty 125 Article VIII, https://digitreaties.org/treaties /treaty/121182953/, accessed January 20, 2024.

65   gunned down in his front doorway: *HR 98*, 455, 129, 151.

65   David Vann and John Ridge: *HR 98*, 259, 578, 582, 712.

65   signed the Treaty: Green, *Politics of Indian Removal*, 93.

66   the nation "could not live upon it": *HR 98*, 713–17.

66   could easily be exterminated: *HR 98*, 718, 722, 760.

66   Opothle Yoholo attempted suicide: Green, *Politics of Indian Removal*, 118.

66   the Treaty of Washington was ratified: *HR 98*, 764–65; Treaty of Washington, April 22, 1826, Telamon Cuyler, Hargrett Rare Books and Manuscript Library, box 01, folder 19, document 2, University of Georgia Libraries.

66   "all remaining lands" in Georgia: Green, *Politics of Indian Removal*, 132, quote 138.

67   Congress called for an inquiry: "Under the Head, Congress, Will Appear . . . ," *Cherokee Phoenix* (New Echota, CN), April 3, 1828; "For the *Cherokee Phoenix*," *Cherokee Phoenix* (New Echota, CN), June 25, 1828; "Communications," *Cherokee Phoenix* (New Echota, CN), July 2, 1828; Elias Boudinot, "Indian Emigration," *Cherokee Phoenix* (New Echota, CN), February 21, 1828.

67   five million acres in Alabama: Green, *Politics of Indian Removal*, 141–42.

67   shot and killed by white Georgians: Green, *Politics of Indian Removal*, 141–42; Haveman, *Rivers of Sand*, 73–74.

67   edit the tribe's new newspaper: Perdue, *Cherokee Editor*, 15; Ellen Cushman, *The Cherokee Syllabary: Writing the People's Perseverance* (Norman: University of Oklahoma Press, 2011), 89–11.

69   "just like white people do": Constance Owl, "*Tsalagi Tsulehisanvhi*: Uncovering Cherokee Language Articles from the *Cherokee Phoenix* Newspaper, 1828–1834" (master's thesis, Western Carolina University, 2019), http://libres.uncg.edu/ir/wcu/f/Owl2020.pdf.

69   enslaved by the Spanish and British: Constitution of Cherokee Nation, in Theda Perdue and Michael D. Green, eds., *The Cherokee Removal: A Brief History with Documents* (New York: Bedford/St. Martin's, 2005), 62; Perdue, *Cherokee Women*, 67–69.

69   "to be human meant being free": Miles, *Ties That Bind*, 142.

69   The Council obliged: Miles, *Ties That Bind*, 33–34, 56–57; Rebecca Nagle, "Cherokee Nation Adopted Racism from Europeans. It's Time to Reject It," *High Country News*, July 10, 2020.

69   supported anti-Black policies within Cherokee Nation: Miles, *Ties That Bind*, 136–37, 164, 179–80.

70   "misfortune & disgrace": John Ridge to Albert Gallatin, Mar. 10, 1826,

in "John Ridge on Cherokee Civilization in 1826," ed. William Sturtevant, *Journal of Cherokee Studies* 6, no. 2 (Fall 1981): 79–91.

70   "by the Treaties concluded with the United States": "Constitution of the Cherokee Nation: Formed by a Convention of Delegates from the Several Districts, at New Echota, July 1827," in Perdue and Green, *The Cherokee Removal*, 60–70.

71   the side of the road to die: John Ross to Hugh Montgomery, Feb. 6, 1830, and John Ross to Elias Boudinot, February 13, 1830, in *The Papers of Chief John Ross*, Vol. 1, 182–87.

71   some were tortured: Strickland, *Fire and the Spirits*, 66; "New Echota, May 22, 1830," *Cherokee Phoenix* (New Echota, CN), May 23, 1830; "Ross to Boudinot, 25th December, 1830," *Cherokee Phoenix* (New Echota, CN), February 12, 1831.

71   "they are poor and wish to be rich": "Augusta Georgia 10th Dec. 1831," *Cherokee Phoenix* (New Echota, CN), December 24, 1831.

71   he won the vote by 97 percent: Theda Perdue and Michael D. Green, *The Cherokee Nation and the Trail of Tears* (New York: Penguin Books, 2007), 59; Saunt, *Unworthy Republic*, 48–49.

72   "quiet submission to the state laws": US Congress, Senate, *Message from the President of the United States*, S. Doc. No. 65, 21st Cong., 2nd Sess. (1831), 5.

72   a policy of ethnic cleansing: Andrew Jackson, "December 8, 1829: First Annual Message to Congress," transcript, Presidential Speeches, Miller Center, University of Virginia, https://millercenter.org/the-presidency /presidential-speeches/ontotoc-8-1829-first-annual-message-congress.

72   petition drives a decade earlier: Tiya Miles, "'Circular Reasoning': Recentering Cherokee Women in the Antiremoval Campaigns," *American Quarterly* 61, no. 2 (June 2009): 221–43; Perdue and Green, *The Cherokee Removal*, Cherokee women petitions, 129–34; Alisse Theodore Portnoy, "'Female Petitioners Can Lawfully Be Heard': Negotiating Female Decorum, United States Politics, and Political Agency, 1829–1831," *Journal of the Early Republic* 23, no. 4 (2003): 573–610; US Congress, House of Reps., "Memorials of the Cherokee Nation, Signed by Their Representatives, and by 3,085 Individuals of the Nation," 21st Congress, 1st Sess., Rep. No. 311, February 15, 1830, 7–9; John Ridge to Mr Elliott Cresson, February 6, 1831; "From Poulsons American Daily Advertisers," *Cherokee Phoenix* (New Echota, CN), April 16, 1831; Elias Boudinot, "New Echota," *Cherokee Phoenix (New Echota, CN)*, March 27, 1828.

73   the will of the people: Chester County, Pennsylvania, Citizens Memorial of Protest, Dec. 31, 1830, Petitions and Memorials, Protection of Indians, Records of the US Senate, SEN21A-G8, NARA; US Congress, House of Reps., "Memorials of the Cherokee Nation, Signed by Their Representatives, and by 3,085 Individuals of the Nation," 21st Congress, 1st Sess., Rep. No.

311, February 15, 1830, 1–9; Jasper Cope, Elliston Perot et al. [Citizens of Pennsylvania] to Congress, "The Memorial of the Subscriber's Citizens of the United States," March 26, 1832, Record Group 46 Records of the US Senate, Petitions & Memorials, Sen. 22A-G7, Box 59, NARA; Citizens of Augusta, Maine Petition to Congress, February 2, 1832, Record Group 46 Records of the US Senate, Sen. 22A-G7, Box 59, NARA; Cherokee Nation Citizens to the Commissioner of Indian Affairs, Nov. 1834, Record Group 46 Records of the US Senate, Sen. 23A-G6, Box 59, NARA. Signed by over 300 Cherokees in syllabary; Citizens of Sand Lake, Rensselaer Co. NY to Congress, December 5, 1837, Record Group 46 Records of the US Senate, HR 25A-G7.2.

73   "the United States in their favor": "Washington City, 25th Dec. 1830," [John Ridge to Major Ridge] Cherokee Phoenix (New Echota, CN), Feb. 12, 1831.

73   could not coexist: Saunt, Unworthy Republic, 7; Annals of Congress, Gales and Seaton, Senate, 21st Congress, 1st Session (1830), 326.

73   "who makes the difficulties?": Elias Boudinot, "New Echota, February 24, 1830," Cherokee Phoenix (New Echota, CN), February 24, 1830.

73   "praying for a redress of grievances": Wilson Lumpkin, "Speech of the Hon. Wilson Lumpkin, of GA. in Committee of the Whole House, on the State of the Union, on the Bill Providing for the Removal of the Indians," in The Removal of the Cherokee Indians from Georgia, vol. 1 (New York: Dood, Mead & Co., 1907), 67.

74   the bill would have never passed: Saunt, Unworthy Republic, 77.

74   punish our country for our sins: "New York Observer Letters from Washington No. XIV," Cherokee Phoenix (New Echota, CN), March 26, 1831.

74   "for bathing Warsaw in blood?": "Extract of a Letter, Dated Washington City, January 9," Cherokee Phoenix, (New Echota, CN), February 18, 1832.

74   "which can never be washed away": "The National Intelligencer of Thursday Morning," Religious Intelligencer (New Haven, CT), June 5, 1830.

74   a man named John Ross: "Ridge's Ferry, June 24, 1828," Cherokee Phoenix (New Echota, CN), July 2, 1828.

74   could win in the Supreme Court: Tim Alan Garrison, The Legal Ideology of Removal: The Southern Judiciary and the Sovereignty of Native American Nations (Athens: University of Georgia Press, 2002), 108–111.

75   "and Georgia nothing": John Ross to William Wirt, Oct. 30, 4026.83, John Ross Papers, Tulsa, Gilcrease Museum.

75   owned it by right of "discovery": Johnson v. M'Intosh, 21 U.S. 543 (1823), 567–71, 573–85.

75   Cherokee Nation was a "domestic dependent nation": Garrison, Legal Ideology of Removal, 130–47.

75   without a permit from the state: Georgia State Legislature, "An Act to
prevent the exercise of assumed and arbitrary power by all persons under
pretext of authority from the Cherokee Indians," December 22, 1830, in *Red
Clay, 1835: Cherokee Removal and the Meaning of Sovereignty,* Reacting to the
Past, Jace Weaver, Laura Adams Weaver (Chapel Hill: University of North
Carolina Press, 2017), 73; Georgia State Legislature, "An Act, To lay out the
Gold region in the lands at present in the occupancy of the Cherokee Indians
into small lots," January 1829, reprinted in "Georgia Laws," *Cherokee Phoenix*
(New Echota, CN), January 21, 1832.

76   "Here and in Hell": Vicki Rozema, ed., *Voices from the Trail of Tears,* Real
Voices, Real History (Winston-Salem, NC:J. F. Blair, 2003): 53–61, excerpts
from the Reverend Samuel Worcester's account of his second arrest by the
Georgia Guard.

76   to prosecute crimes on Cherokee land: Garrison, *Legal Ideology of Removal,* 169–74; Wilkins, *Cherokee Tragedy,* 225–27.

76   referendum on the Cherokee cause: Garrison, *Legal Ideology of Removal,* 176.

76   reportedly so moved he cried: Garrison, *Legal Ideology of Removal,*
176–77.

76   acquired "the lands from sea to sea": *Worcester v. Georgia,* 31 U.S. (6 Pet.)
515 (1832).

77   the Constitution of the United States: Garrison, *Legal Ideology of
Removal,* 134–147, 185; *Johnson v. McIntosh,* 21 U.S. 543 (1823), 569–70, 585,
593–94.

77   declared null and void: *Worcester v. Georgia,* 31 U.S. (6 Pet.) 515 (1832), 520.

77   has even called it "schizophrenic": Zack Smith, "How Clear Is Clear
Enough: A Mix of Textualism, Tribal Sovereignty, and Bankruptcy at the
Supreme Court," Heritage Foundation, https://www.heritage.org/courts
/commentary/how-clear-clear-enough-mix-textualism-tribal-sovereignty-and
-bankruptcy-the.

77   "It's a battlefield": Maggie Blackhawk (law professor) in discussion with
the author, January 2023.

77   huge crowds of white allies: "From the New-Haven Religious Intelli-
gencer: Cherokee Meeting in New Haven," *Cherokee Phoenix* (New Echota,
CN), March 24, 1832; "Cherokee Meeting. New York, February 3," *Cherokee
Phoenix* (New Echota, CN), March 3, 1832.

77   no longer face Georgia's terror alone: Elias Boudinot to Stand Watie,
March 7, 1832, in *Cherokee Cavaliers: Forty Years of Cherokee History as Told in the
Correspondence of the Ridge-Watie-Boudinot Family,* ed. Edward Everett Dale and
Gaston Litton (Norman: University of Oklahoma Press, 1939), 4–7.

CHAPTER 5 | The Appeal

79   they still had a reservation: James Floyd (former principal chief of Muscogee Nation) in discussion with the author, March 2022.

79   Patrick Murphy's lead counsel: Patti Ghezzi in discussion with the author, October 2021; Darla Shelden, "Federal Public Defender Patti Ghezzi Retires after Highly Regarded Career," *City Sentinel*, Oct. 18, 2020.

79   Tenth Circuit Court of Appeals announced: *Murphy v. Warrior*, 07-7068 and 15-7041 (Tenth Circuit), Order, January 6, 2016.

80   "still dealing with the trauma of this case": James Floyd in discussion with the author, March 2022.

80   which legal vehicle will settle important issues: Riyaz Kanji (counsel for Muscogee Nation) in discussion with the author, November 2021.

82   "do something about it": James Floyd in discussion with the author, March 2022.

82   "The law was on our side": James Floyd in discussion with the author, March 2022.

82   could change the tide: Philip Tinker (counsel for Muscogee Nation) in discussion with the author, November 2021 and October 2021; *Osage Nation v. Irby*, 09-5050 (Tenth Circuit), March 5, 2010.

82   "No way in hell are we taking this case": Riyaz Kanji in discussion with the author, November 2021.

83   every week to bend his ear: Riyaz Kanji in discussion with the author, November 2021.

83   Patrick's public defender: Philip Tinker in discussion with the author, February 2022.

83   a separate reservation case: *Nebraska v. Parker*, 14-1406 (US Supreme Court), March 22, 2016.

83   "We should talk to the Nation": Riyaz Kanji in discussion with the author, November 2021.

83   still had a reservation: *Murphy v. Warrior*, 07-7068 and 15-7041 (Tenth Circuit), Order, January 6, 2016; *Murphy v. Duckworth*, 07-7068 and 15-7041 (Tenth Circuit), Order, July 18, 2016; *Murphy v. Royal*, 07-7068 and 15-7041 (Tenth Circuit), Order, August 3, 2016.

84   read over weekends: Muscogee Nation, https://www.muscogeenation .com; Constitution of Muscogee (Creek) Nation, Oct. 9, 1979, articles 5–7; James Floyd in discussion with the author, March 2022.

84   43 percent of the land in Oklahoma: *Royal v. Murphy*, 17-1107 (US

Supreme Court), Petition for a Writ of Certiorari, February 6, 2018; Matthew Fletcher, "News Media Writers: Please Stop Saying 'Half' of Oklahoma Is 'Indian Lands' or 'Indian Territory'—It's Not (Yet)," Turtle Talk (blog), August 5, 2020, https://turtletalk.blog/2020/08/05/news-media-writers-please-stop -saying-half-of-oklahoma-is-indian-lands-or-indian-territory-its-not-yet/.

84   worked closely together: James Floyd in discussion with the author, March 2022.

84   "had ever been disestablished": Kevin Dellinger (former attorney general of Muscogee Nation) in discussion with the author, March 2019.

84   got rid of the reservation: *Murphy v. Royal*, 07-7068 and 15-7041 (Tenth Circuit), Brief of Respondent-Appellee, November 4, 2016.

84   "divest a reservation of its land": *Solem v. Barlett*, 82-1253 (US Supreme Court), February 22, 1984.

85   "absolute miracle": Philip Tinker in discussion with the author, October 2021.

85   whether or not they could win: Riyaz Kanji in discussion with the author, November 2021.

85   "we begin with the text": *Nebraska v. Parker*, 14-1406 (US Supreme Court), March 22, 2016.

86   vast oil and gas infrastructure: Email correspondence with US Department of Transportation, in possession of author; presentation obtained under FOIA from the US Department of Interior, Office of Surface Mining Reclamation, in possession of author; data provided by the Oklahoma Corporation Commission, in possession of author.

86   didn't *intend* to get rid of the reservation: *Murphy v. Royal*, 07-7068 and 15-7041 (Tenth Circuit), Brief Amicus Curiae of the Muscogee (Creek) Nation and the Seminole Nation of Oklahoma, August 12, 2016, 15–17, 30.

86   made it into the brief: *Murphy v. Royal*, 07-7068 and 15-7041 (Tenth Circuit), Brief Amicus Curiae of the Muscogee (Creek) Nation and the Seminole Nation of Oklahoma, August 12, 2016; Philip Tinker in discussion with the author, October 2021.

86   But the tribe did: Silas Allen, "University of Oklahoma Sells Okmulgee Rehabilitation Center to Muscogee (Creek) Nation," *Oklahoman*, August 13, 2013; Shawn Terry (Secretary of Health for Muscogee Nation) in discussion with the author, March 2019; Roger Ballenger (former Oklahoma state senator) in discussion with the author, March 2019; Norma Ballenger (patient at Muscogee Nation health facility) in discussion with the author, March 2019; Desiree (mom of patient at Muscogee Nation health facility) in discussion with the author, March 2019; Amanda Rutland, "New Report Shows Muscogee (Creek) Nation Had $866 Million Economic Impact on Oklahoma Economy," Muscogee

Nation, June 26, 2019, https://www.muscogeenation.com/2019/06/26/new -report-shows-muscogee-creek-nation-had-866-million-economic-impact-on -oklahoma-economy; Allison Herrera, "Oklahoma Tribes Boast Billions in Economic Impact in New Report," KOSU, March 23, 2022.

87 "no matter what the consequences": Kevin Dellinger in discussion with the author, March 2019.

87 "State efforts to assert jurisdiction": *Murphy v. Royal*, 07-7068 and 15-7041 (Tenth Circuit), Brief Amicus Curiae of the Muscogee (Creek) Nation and the Seminole Nation of Oklahoma, August 12, 2016.

88 over half of which are in Oklahoma: "Architectural Style," Tenth Circuit Court of Appeals, https://www.ca10.uscourts.gov/architectural-style; Miller and Ethridge, *A Promise Kept*, 180; *Murphy v. Royal*, 07-7068 and 15-7041 (Tenth Circuit), Motion for Permission to Participate in Oral Argument as Amicus Curiae, February 2, 2017.

88 went over everything one last time: Philip Tinker in discussion with the author, February 2022.

88 to the podium: *Murphy v. Royal*, 07-7068 and 15-7041 (Tenth Circuit), Audio Recording of Oral Arguments, March 22, 2017, in possession of author.

88 She won: Shelden, "Federal Public Defender Patti Ghezzi Retires."

89 she began: *Murphy v. Royal*, audio recording.

89 "the lands of the tribe": *Murphy v. Royal*, audio recording.

89 "no sense": *Murphy v. Royal*, audio recording.

89 "I cannot": *Murphy v. Royal*, audio recording.

89 "Difficult issue": *Murphy v. Royal*, audio recording.

90 none of that happens on a set schedule: "Practitioner's Guide to the United States Court of Appeals for the Tenth Circuit, 13th Edition," Office of the Clerk, United States Court of Appeals for the Tenth Circuit, January 2023, https://www.ca10.uscourts.gov/sites/ca10/files/documents /downloads/2024PracGuideUpdate-13thEdition.pdf.

90 "We won the whole thing": David Giampetroni (counsel for Muscogee Nation) in discussion with the author, November 2021.

90 "live up to the promises that were made": Philip Tinker in discussion with the author, October 2021.

90 Oklahoma would appeal to the Supreme Court: James Floyd in discussion with the author, March 2022; James Floyd in discussion with the author, March 2019; Kevin Dellinger in discussion with the author, March 2019.

91 "doesn't happen very often": Kevin Dellinger in discussion with the author, March 2019.

91   "fails to reveal disestablishment at step one": *Murphy v. Royal*, 07-7068 (Tenth Circuit), August 8, 2017, 70.

91   "remain with Congress": *Murphy v. Royal*, 126.

CHAPTER 6 | Betrayal

93   was constitutionally bound to do so: Garrison, *Legal Ideology of Removal*, 169–97; Wilkins, *Cherokee Tragedy*, 235; *Worcester v. Georgia*, 31 U.S. (6 Pet.), 515 (1832).

93   "But in that event what becomes of the Union?": "one of the Delegation [John Ridge] to Editor of the *Cherokee Phoenix* [Elias Boudinot] 10th Dec. 1831," *Cherokee Phoenix* (New Echota, CN), December 24, 1831.

94   The abuse of power went unchecked: Wilkins, *Cherokee Tragedy*, 236.

94   "the American People": Ridge to Watie, April 6, 1832.

94   advised Chief Ross to sign a treaty: Wilkins, *Cherokee Tragedy*, 236–39; Garrison, *Legal Ideology of Removal*, 169–97, 190–98.

94   not a "sufficient degree of interest": Elias Boudinot to Reverend E. Cornelius, New Echota, March 11, 1829, in *Cherokee Editor*, 47–48.

94   Jackson called it "despair": Wilkins, *Cherokee Tragedy*, 236.

95   Free and enslaved Black people: Georgia Laws Timeline, compiled by James Owen from Lindsay Robertson, *Conquest by Law: How the Discovery of America Dispossessed Indigenous Peoples of Their Lands* (Oxford and New York: Oxford University Press, 2005); *Laws of the Cherokee Nations, Adopted by the Council at Various Periods* (Knoxville, TN: n.p., 1826); US Congress, House of Representatives, "Memorial and Protest of the Cherokee Nation," H.R. Doc. 286, 24th Congress, 1st Session (1836), 5–6; Miles, *Ties That Bind*, 132–35; State of Georgia Land Lottery Certificate, Drawn by Harbard Hills Orphans, Decatur 15th District, 2d Section, Cherokee County, 40 Acres (Rome, Georgia: Chieftans Museum and Major Ridge Home, May 24, 1832), Georgia Land Lottery Exhibit, image Fall 2022; "Chieftans after Cherokee Removal" (Rome, Georgia: Chieftans Museum and Major Ridge Home, n.d.) Cherokee Removal and Georgia Land Lotteries; State of Georgia Plat Map for Lot 196 Major Ridge Home, Floyd Co., GA, 100 acres (Rome, Georgia: Chieftans Museum and Major Ridge Home, May 1837) Cherokee Removal and Georgia Land Lotteries; US Congress, Senate, John Ridge & Cherokee Chiefs to Lewis Cass, April 5, 1833, 23rd Congress, 1st sess., S. Doc. 512, IV (serial 247), 168–70, 200; Elbert Herring to John Ridge & Cherokee Chiefs, May 1, 1833, 23rd Congress, 1st sess., S. Doc. 512, III (serial 246), 681; Wilson Lumpkin to Lewis Cass, November 18, 1833, 23rd Congress, 1st sess., S. Doc. 512, IV (serial 247), 717–18; "Indians," published correspondence includes Lewis Cass to Cherokees East of the Mississippi, April 17, 1832, John Ross to Cass, January 8, 1833, Cass to

Ross, January 9, 1833, Ross et al. to Cass, January 28, 1833, *Cherokee Phoenix* (New Echota, CN), August 17, 1833.

95   "White Robber and assassin": Records of the Bureau of Indian Affairs, Cherokee Delegation at Brown Hotel, Washington City, to Andrew Jackson: Mar. 12–13, 1834, microfilm, RG75, entry 329–30.

95   "as so many tribes have done before you": "Memorial and Protest of the Cherokee Nation," H.R. Doc. 286 (1836), 5–6.

95   was quickly voted down: John Ridge to Major Ridge et al., March 10, 1835, in *Cherokee Cavaliers*, 12–14.

96   as a people and a nation, would survive: "Letter from Elias Boudinot to Elijah Hicks, Oct. 2, 1832," "Resolutions of the 'Friends of Free Discussion' 1834," S. Doc. 121 (1838), 7–10; "Memorial and Protest of the Cherokee Nation," H.R. Doc. 286 (1836), 5–6; George Magruder Battey Jr., *A History of Rome and Floyd County, State of Georgia, United States of America, Including Numerous Incidents of More Than Local Interest, 1540–1922* (Atlanta: Cherokee Publishing Co., 1969), 43–45; John Ridge to John Ross, February 2, 1833, *Papers of Chief John Ross (PCJR)*, Vol. 1, 259–60.

96   "seek freedom in the far regions of the West": "Memorial of a Council Held at Running Waters," H.R. Doc. 91 (1835).

96   and being unpatriotic: US Congress, Senate, "John Ridge to John Ross, November 25, 1836," "Elias Boudinot to Editor of Cherokee Phoenix, October 2, 1832" S. Doc. 121, 25th Cong. 2nd Sess. (1838), 28, 9.

96   support of the majority of the Cherokee people: Treaty of New Echota, December 29, 1835; Wilkins, *Cherokee Tragedy*, 87, 142.

96   backed Ross's bid for chief: Wilkins, *Cherokee Tragedy*, 142.

96   "known would not be realized": "Elias Boudinot to Elijah Hicks, October 2, 1832," S. Doc. 121 (1838), 7–10.

97   lead according to their will: "John Ross to John Ridge, December 4, 1835," H.R. Doc. 286 (1836), 102.

97   "and probably his life": US Congress, Senate, "J. Mason to the Secretary of War, Sept. 25, 1837," S. Doc.120, 25th Congress, 2nd Session (1838), 985.

97   one of their supporters was shot and killed: "Elias Boudinot to the Readers of the *Cherokee Phoenix*, Red Hill, Cherokee Nation, August 1, 1832," S. Doc 121 (1838), 3–4; Rec. of the BIA, Cherokee Council Meeting, Aug. 24, 1834, microfilm, RG75, frames 404–5; "Memorial of a Delegation from the Cherokees, June 25, 1834," in S. Doc. 486, 23rd Cong., 1st Sess. (1834), 1–2.

97   payment for Cherokee homelands at $5 million: "Lewis Cass to John Ross and Others, February 27," S. Doc. 120 (1838), 96–97; US Congress,

House, "Memorial of the Cherokee Representatives, December 1835," H.R. Doc. 286, 24th Cong., 1st Sess. (1836), 19.

97   was "utterly invalid": "Memorial and Protest of the Cherokee Nation," H.R. Doc. 286 (1836), 33.

97   next presidential election was dashed: "Benjamin Currey to Elbert Herring, May 23, 1835," "Benjamin Currey to Elbert Herring, July 27, 1835," "Schermerhorn to Elbert Herring, Aug. 5, 1835," S. Doc. 120 (1838), 463, 369–71, 390–92; Rec. of the BIA, Ross to Cherokee Agency, Montgomery, Nov. 3, 1834, RG 75, frames 303–4; US Congress, Senate, "Memorial of a Delegation from the Cherokees," June 25, 1834, S. Doc 486, 23rd Cong., 1st Sess. (1834), 10; US Congress, Senate, "Documents in Relation to the Validity of the Cherokee Treaty of 1835, January 22, 1838," S. Doc. 121, 25th Cong., 2nd Sess., 1838; John Ross to William Carroll, July 24, 1835, PCJR, Vol. 1, 346–47.

98   Their exodus began: Treaty of Dancing Rabbit Creek, Sept. 27, 1830.

98   So when the US government told Choctaw: Donna L. Akers, "Removing the Heart of the Choctaw People: Indian Removal from a Native Perspective," American Indian Culture and Research Journal 23, no. 3 (1999): 63–76; Donna Akers (Choctaw historian) in discussion with the author, October 2020.

98   The lost Choctaws had given up on survival: Akers, "Removing the Heart of the Choctaw People," 71.

98   Even the men were incoherent: Donna Akers in discussion with the author, October 2020.

98   By financing their own removal: Saunt, Unworthy Republic, 210–18, 268–70.

99   without them their people would starve: Grant Foreman, Indian Removal: The Emigration of the Five Civilized Tribes of Indians (Norman: University of Oklahoma Press, 1974), 56–57, 218–26.

99   20 percent of the population died: Foreman, Indian Removal, 326, 343, 350–55, 384–85; Saunt, Unworthy Republic, 300–301.

99   Alabama also extended its laws: Green, Politics of Indian Removal, 141.

99   survived by eating the bark off trees: Green, Politics of Indian Removal, 141; Haveman, Rivers of Sand, 91.

99   "I now leave the poor diluted Creeks and Cherokees to their fate": Haveman, Rivers of Sand, 89–90, 93.

100   had little say in what happened next: Green, Politics of Indian Removal, 169, 170–72.

100   in the hands of people with no legal rights: Saunt, Unworthy Republic, 219.

100 "If they cannot get it in any other way": Haveman, *Rivers of Sand*, 107.

100 "the land was sold from under us": Hopoethleyoholo to Major General Jesup, August 26, 1836, in Christopher D. Haveman, *Bending Their Way Onward: Creek Indian Removal in Documents* (Lincoln: University of Nebraska Press, 2018), 255–57.

100 teeth to make dentures: Green, *Politics of Indian Removal*, 179.

100 to collection points for their deportation: McKenney and Hall, *Indian Tribes of North America*, vol. 1, 7–14; Haveman, *Rivers of Sand*, 131, 180–85; Haveman, *Bending Their Way Onward*, 181–88, 231–32, 258–60.

101 what few possessions they had left: Journal of Detachment 1, SIAC Agent (Reynolds), Account (1687) Year (1838), NARA in Haveman, *Bending Their Way Onward*, 237–39; Haveman, *Rivers of Sand*, 202–3.

101 "Old men & women & children dropping off": Haveman, *Bending Their Way Onward*, 237–48; Journal of detachment 1, SIAC Agent (Reynolds), Account (1687) Year (1838), NARA.

101 To make the tide of death more traumatic: Haveman, *Rivers of Sand*, 231.

101 "And we are sorry": Tuckabatchee Headmen to Warriors, Oct. 9, 1836, Records of the Adjutant General's Office, 1780s-1917, Entry 159-Q, Records of Major General Thomas S. Jesup, Container 19, Folder: "Letters Received Relating to Creek and Seminole Affairs, September–December 1836, NARA, reprinted in Haveman, *Bending Their Way Onward*, 263–65.

101 While Muscogee citizens walked through eight inches of snow: Haveman, *Rivers of Sand*, 231; C.A. Harris to Capt. John Page, February 6, 1837, SIAC, Agent (Reynolds), Account (1687), Year (1838), NARA, reprinted in Haveman, *Bending Their Way Onward*, 284; General M. Arbuckle to C.A. Harris, December 18, 1836, Letters received by the Office of Indian Affairs, Creek Agency Emigration, microfilm Roll 238, 9–10, reprinted in Haveman, *Bending Their Way Onward*, 279–80.

101 3,500 died: Haveman, *Rivers of Sand*, 297–99.

102 speculators acquired the land for almost nothing: Saunt, *Unworthy Republic*, 307–9.

102 more millionaires per capita: Ira Berlin, *The Making of African America: The Four Great Migrations* (New York: Penguin Books, 2010), 91–92, 95; Saunt, *Unworthy Republic*, 307–9.

102 compromise looked possible: "Major Ridge and John Ridge to Ross, July 31, 1835," "Memorial and Protest of the Cherokee Nation, March 11, 1836," H.R. Doc. 286 (1836), 60–61, 16–32; John Ross to John Ridge and Major Ridge, July 30, 1835, John Ross to D. Irwin, August 17, 1835, *PCJR*, Vol. 1, 349, 351–52.

103 Major Ridge and Elias stayed behind: "Resolution of the Cherokee Nation Council, Oct. 23, 1835," "John Ridge to John Ross, Dec. 4, 1835," H.R. Doc. 286 (1836), 79–80, 102; "Letter Addressed to a 'Friend,'" May 16, 1836, Sen. Doc. 121 (1838), 15–26; "Documents in Relation to the Validity of the Cherokee Treaty of 1835, January 22, 1838," S. Doc. 121, 25th Cong., 2nd Sess. (1838), 18; John Ross to the General [Cherokee] Council, October 22, 1835, Ross to Boudinot, November 23, 1835, Ross to Ridge, December 4, 1835, *PCJR*, Vol. 1, 360–62, 375, 378.

103 hung paper notices: "Schermerhorn and Ross correspondence, Oct., 1835," H.R. Doc. 286 (1836), 32–45; Nos. 4–5, 45; Nos. 8–9, 46–47; No. 11, 47–48; Nos. 13–17, 48–52; Nos. 42–51, 83–88; Nos. 55–57, 92–93; John Ross, *The Papers of Chief John Ross*, Vol. 1, 6–17.

103 Whoever did not attend, the paper warned: "J. F. Schermerhorn Notice to the Chiefs and Headmen, and people of the Cherokee Nation of Indians," S. Doc. 120 (1838); *The Papers of Chief John Ross*, Vol. 1, 518.

103 began voting on resolutions: US Congress, House, "Memorial of the Cherokee Representatives, December 1835," H.R. Doc. 286, 24th Cong., 1st Sess., (1836), 112; James Trott to Ross, January 6, 1836, William Adair to Ross, January 8, 1836, *PCJR*, Vol. 1, 379–80, 382–83.

103 "I know we love the graves of our fathers": Wilkins, *Cherokee Tragedy*, 286–87.

103 "I have signed my death warrant": Wilkins, *Cherokee Tragedy*, 286–87.

104 become citizens of the United States: Treaty of New Echota, Dec. 29, 1835.

104 "within two years from the ratification of this treaty": Treaty of New Echota, Dec. 29, 1835.

104 in a month collected 3,352 signatures: "Petition from the Citizens of Aquohee and Taquohee in Cherokee Nation," H.R. Doc. 286 (1836), 107–8.

104 nearly 90 percent of the nation: US Congress, House, "Petition from the Citizens of Aquohee and Taquohee in Cherokee Nation," "Resolved by the Committee and Council, Samuel Bunter et al., February 3, 1836," "Edward Gunter to John Ross, February 11, 1836," "George Lowrey to Ross, February 11, 1836," H.R. Doc. 286 (1836), 107–8, 114–15, 118–19; Ross to a Friend, July 2, 1836, *PCJR*, Vol. 1, 444–50. A timeline of Cherokee protests against the Treaty of New Echota begins on page 29 of the March 11, 1836, Memorial.

104 They warned if Cherokees did leave: "Memorial and Protest of the Cherokee Nation," H.R. Doc. 286 (1836), 1–5.

104 the Senate ratified: Wilkins, *Cherokee Tragedy*, 291–93.

105 There is no evidence of bribery: Wilkins, *Cherokee Tragedy*, 295–300, 304, 308–310; US Congress, Senate "A List of the names of Cherokee emigrants . . .

taken from the register of payments," "Abstract of disbursements by Dr. Philip Minis . . . in fulfilment of Cherokee Treaty of 29th December," "Abstract of Disbursements on account Cherokee Treaty of December, 1835," Sen. Doc 120, 873–75, 1019, 1027, 1030–32, 1049, 1055.

105 "sooner or later he will have to yield his life": Wilkins, *Cherokee Tragedy*, 292.

105 the immense suffering of the Cherokee people: "Documents in Relation to the Validity of the Cherokee Treaty of 1835, January 22, 1838," S. Doc. 121, 25th Cong., 2nd Sess. (1838), 25.

105 decide how best to relieve their own suffering: "Memorial and Protest of the Cherokee Nation," H.R. Doc. 286 (1836), 16–32.

105 Perhaps they were trying to avoid: Wilkins, *Cherokee Tragedy*, 300–13.

105 "Not one man in twenty is willing": "John. E. Wool to C. A. Harris, Aug. 8, 1836," S. Doc. 120 (1838), 631–32.

106 the two-year deadline set by the treaty ran out: "John Ross to George Lowrey, May 26, 1836," S. Doc. 120 (1838), 680–81; Perdue and Green, *Cherokee Nation*, 112–15.

106 7,000 US soldiers: Wilkins, *Cherokee Tragedy*, 319–22.

107 It took twenty-five: John Howard Payne, *John Howard Payne to His Countrymen* (Athens: University of Georgia Press, 1961); Daniel S. Butrick, *Cherokee Removal: The Journal of Rev. Daniel S. Butrick: May 19, 1838–Apr. 1, 1839* (Park Hill, OK: Trail of Tears Association, Oklahoma Chapter [1998]), Thursday, Dec. 13; Wilkins, *Cherokee Tragedy*, 319–22.

107 The army was woefully unprepared: "John E. Wool to B. F. Butler, Nov. 14, 1836," S. Doc. 120 (1838), 61.

107 "We should find little astonishment": Butrick, *Cherokee Removal*; Quote from J.W. Lide to Capt. John Page, July 30, 1838, in Rozema, *Voices from the Trail of Tears*, 129. Butrick makes frequent mention of Cherokee illness and the deaths that occurred almost every day.

107 "one eighth of the whole number": Rozema, *Voices from the Trail of Tears*, 29; "Report from Dr. Butler," *Missionary Herald*, October 1838, 29.

107 under their own supervision: John Ross and Cherokee Council to Major General Winfield Scott, July 23, 1838, in Rozema, *Voices from the Trail of Tears*, 118.

107 The white landowner nearby: John Howard Payne, Thursday, December 13, *The Payne-Butrick Papers*, ed. William L. Anderson, Jane L. Brown, and Anne F. Rogers (Lincoln and London: University of Nebraska Press, 2010); Butrick, *Cherokee Removal*.

107 Although the exact number is unknown: "Butler to Greene, January 25, 1839," Transcription: ABCFM 18.3.1, X-73.

107   out of a population of 16,000 people: Russell Thornton, "Cherokee Population Losses during the Trail of Tears: A New Perspective and a New Estimate," *Ethnohistory* 31 (Autumn, 1984): 289–300.

108   "considered traitors to their country": "Butler to Greene, August 2, 1838," Transcription: ABCFM 18.3.1, X-70a.

108   The survivors, however, argued that they constituted: John Ross et al. to the Senate and House of Representatives, February 28, 1840, in *PCJR*, Vol. 2, 6–17; US Congress, House, "Memorial of the Delegates and Representatives of the Cherokee Nation, West," April 1, 1840, H. R. Doc. 162, 25th Cong., 1st Sess., 8.

109   all that came out of his mouth was blood: John R. Ridge, *Poems* (San Francisco: Henry Payot & Co., 1868).

109   Elias lived long enough: "Worcester to Greene, June 26, 1839," transcription: ABCFM 18.3.1, X-136.

109   formal government was not represented: "Memorial of the Delegates and Representatives of the Cherokee Nation, West," April 1, 1840, 5–8.

110   "Until the people care as little about hearing": John Candy to Stand Watie, April 10, 1846, in *Cherokee Cavaliers*, 32–33.

110   to meddle in the tribe's affairs: Ross to US Senate, February 28, 1840, Ross to Joseph Vann, March 22, 1840, Ross to US Congress, *PCJR*, Vol. 2, 6–17, 20–22, 285–95.

110   "The whole treaty of 1835": John Ross et al to the Senate and House of Representatives, April 30, 1846, in *PCJR*, Vol. 2, 296.

CHAPTER 7 | The High Court

115   headed to the Supreme Court: James Floyd in discussion with the author, March 2022.

115   Oklahoma appealed: *Royal v. Murphy*, 17-1107 (US Supreme Court), Petition for a Writ of Certiorari, February 6, 2018.

115   "I thought there was a chance": Riyaz Kanji in discussion with the author, November 2021.

116   without an invitation: *Royal v. Murphy*, 17-1107 (US Supreme Court), Petition for a Writ of Certiorari, Brief for the United States as Amicus Curiae; Matthew Fletcher (law professor) in discussion with the author, April 2019.

116   "They're going to take it": Riyaz Kanji in discussion with the author, November 2021.

116   He was asked to take it off: Aris Folley, "Washington Tribal Leader Barred from Entering Supreme Court Hearing for Wearing Traditional Headdress," *The Hill*, November 1, 2018.

116   "Well, I'm dark": James Floyd in discussion with the author, March 2022.

116   the line stretched around it: Amy Howe, "Courtroom Access: The Nuts
and Bolts of Courtroom Seating—and the Lines for Public Access," *SCOTUS-
blog*, Apr. 1, 2020, https://www.scotusblog.com/2020/04/courtroom
-access-the-nuts-and-bolts-of-courtroom-seating-and-the-lines-to-gain-access
-to-the-courtroom/; Rosemary McCombs Maxey in discussion with the author,
July 2022.

118   the white dome of the Capitol: Rosemary McCombs Maxey in discussion with the author, July 2022;

118   two-thirds of all Supreme Court cases: Grant Christensen, "Predicting
Supreme Court Behavior in Indian Law Cases," *Michigan Journal of Race and
Law* 26, no. 12 (2021).

118   and tribal self-governance: US Congress, Senate, 92 Stat. 469 Vol.
92, *Joint Resolution American Indians Religious Freedom*, 95th Congress, 2nd
Session, 1978, 469-470; US Congress, Senate, 92 Stat. 3069 Vol. 92, *Indian
Child Welfare Act*, 95th Congress, 2nd Session, 1978, 3069-3078; US Con-
gress, House, 104 Stat. 3048 Vol. 104, *Native American Graves Protection and
Repatriation Act*, 101st Congress, 2nd Session, 1990, 3048-3058; US Congress,
House, Public Law 93-638 *Indian Self-Determination and Education Assis-
tance Act*, 118th Congress, 1996, US Code Chapter 46, Sections 5321-5332,
Amended Through Public Law 118-15, September 30, 2023.

119   into a tribal police car: Sarah Krakoff, "Mark the Plumber v. Tribal
Empire, or Non-Indian Anxiety v. Tribal Sovereignty? The Story of *Oliphant v.
Suquamish Indian Tribe*," in *Indian Law Stories*, ed. Carole E. Goldberg, Kevin
Washburn, and Philip P. Frickey (New York: Foundation Press [St. Paul, MN]:
Thomson Reuters, 2011), 264, 270; *Oliphant v. Suquamish Indian Tribe*, 76-
5729 (US Supreme Court), March 6, 1978.

119   lost twice in federal court: Krakoff, "Mark the Plumber v. Tribal Empire," 273.

119   that tribes could not: *Oliphant v. Suquamish Indian Tribe*.

119   by someone who is not Native: "2013 and 2022 Reauthorizations of the
Violence against Women Act (VAWA)," US Department of Justice Office of
Tribal Justice, https://www.justice.gov/tribal/2013-and-2022-reauthorizations
-violence-against-women-act-vawa; André B. Rosay, "Violence against Amer-
ican Indian and Alaska Native Women and Men," *National Institute of Justice
Journal* 277 (2016): 38–45; Marie Quasius, "Native American Rape Victims:
Desperately Seeking an *Oliphant*-Fix," *Minnesota Law Review* 93 (2009): 1902.

120   even calling them racial slurs: John P. LaVelle, "Beating a Path of
Retreat from Treaty Rights and Tribal Sovereignty: The Story of *Montana
v. United States*," in Goldberg, Washburn, and Frickey, *Indian Law Stories*,
535–56.

120   "health or welfare of the tribe": *Montana v. United States*, 79-1128 (US Supreme Court), March 24, 1981.

120   difficult for all tribes to meet: LaVelle, "Beating a Path of Retreat," 572–79.

121   "that long ago grew cold": *City of Sherrill v. Oneida Indian Nation of New York*, 03–855 (US Supreme Court), March 29, 2005.

121   sheer ignorance of its justices: Matthew Fletcher in discussion with the author, April 2019; John Echohawk (executive director of the Native American Rights Fund) in discussion with the author, January 2023.

121   if the tribe's treaty rights were upheld: *City of Sherrill v. Oneida Indian Nation of New York*, 03-855 (US Supreme Court), Oral Argument Transcript, January 11, 2005, 28.

121   "who think culturally they're a Cherokee": *Adoptive Couple v. Baby Girl*, 12-399 (US Supreme Court), Oral Argument Transcript, April 16, 2013, 39.

121   "probably just got out of prison": *Adoptive Couple v. Baby Girl*, 12-399 (US Supreme Court), Oral Argument Transcript, April 16, 2013, 41.

121   "at war with each other": *Haaland v. Brackeen*, 21-376 (US Supreme Court), Oral Argument Transcript, November 9, 2022, 172.

122   has the final word: Christensen, "Predicting Supreme Court Behavior in Indian Law Cases"; Maggie Blackhawk in discussion with the author, January 2023; *Shelby County v. Holder*, Oyez, https://www.oyez.org/cases/2012/12-96; Nikolas Bowie and Daphna Renan, "The Supreme Court Is Not Supposed to Have This Much Power," *Atlantic*, June 8, 2022; Matthew Fletcher in discussion with the author, April 2019.

122   "what it wants in federal Indian law": Maggie Blackhawk in discussion with the author, January 2023.

122   full of contradictions: Kevin Washburn (law professor) in discussion with the author, February 2021.

122   "not devoid of Native agency": Maggie Blackhawk in discussion with the author, January 2023.

123   "just an inch of her": Rosemary McCombs Maxey in discussion with the author, July 2022.

123   "and this Honorable Court": "The Court and Its Procedures," US Supreme Court, https://www.supremecourt.gov/about/procedures.aspx.

124   "all features of a reservation": *Carpenter v. Murphy*, 17-1107 (US Supreme Court), Oral Argument Transcript, November 27, 2018, 4.

124   for the corporate law firm Arnold & Porter: Jessica Gresko, "Female Lawyers Are Still Rare at US Supreme Court," Associated Press, January 20, 2011;

"Weddings; Lisa Schiavo, David Blatt," *New York Times*, October 22, 1995; Lisa Blatt, "Reflections of a Lady Lawyer," *Texas Law Review* 59 (2020): 60.

124   role of corporate law firms: "Arnold & Porter," SourceWatch, https://www.sourcewatch.org/index.php/Arnold_%26_Porter; Adrian Kinnane, *Arnold & Porter: The Early Years, 1946–1980* (Adrian Kinnane, 2016), 133.

124   the high court even considers: Joan Biskupic, Janet Roberts, and John Shiffman, "At America's Court of Last Resort, a Handful of Lawyers Now Dominates the Docket," *Reuters*, December 8, 2014.

124   "What does [the rest of] it matter?": Federalist Society, "Showcase Panel III: Lawyers, the Adversarial System, and Social Justice," 2022 National Lawyers Convention, December 1, 2022, video, 1:01:59, https://www.youtube.com/watch?v=JuuPCRBxz8g.

124   They won: Ian Shapira, "Lisa Blatt: The Legal Mind Behind the Redskins 'Take Yo Panties Off' Trademark Defense," *Washington Post*, November 5, 2015; *Adoptive Couple v. Baby Girl*, 12-399 (US Supreme Court), June 25, 2013.

125   did not consider other law firms: *Tarrant Regional Water District v. Herrmann*, Oyez, https://www.oyez.org/cases/2012/11-889; "PAC Profile: Oklahoma Strong Leadership PAC," Open Secrets, https://www.opensecrets.org/political-action-committees-pacs/oklahoma-strong-leadership-pac/C00572198/summary/2016; "Page by Page Report Display (Page 39 of 90)," Federal Election Commission, https://docquery.fec.gov/cgi-bin/fecimg/?201507309000458386; "Annual Report of Private Attorney Contracts, Fiscal Year 2019," Oklahoma Office of the Attorney General, https://www.oag.ok.gov/sites/g/files/gmc766/f/fy_19_20i_report.pdf; "Annual Report of Private Attorney Contracts, Fiscal Year 2020," Oklahoma Office of the Attorney General, https://www.oag.ok.gov/sites/g/files/gmc766/f/fy_20_20i_report.pdf; Mike Hunter (former attorney general of Oklahoma) in discussion with the author, June 2022.

125   "Losing is not an option": Molly M. Fleming, "State Paid Nearly $500K to Defend Murphy Case," *Journal Record*, February 27, 2019.

125   "Rome did not fall in a day": *Carpenter v. Murphy*, Oral Argument Transcript, 6.

125   "dissolve the Five Tribes' communal territories": *Royal v. Murphy*, 17-1107 (US Supreme Court), Petition for a Writ of Certiorari, February 6, 2018, 3.

125   whether or not that included the reservation: *Carpenter v. Murphy*, Oral Argument Transcript, 11, 68–69; *Royal v. Murphy*, 17-1107 (US Supreme Court), Petition for a Writ of Certiorari, February 6, 2018, 15; *Carpenter v. Murphy*, 17-1107 (US Supreme Court), Brief for Amicus Curiae, Muscogee (Creek) Nation, September 26, 2018, 19.

126 "Tribal law was unenforceable": *Carpenter v. Murphy*, Oral Argument Transcript, 11.

126 "taken away from the tribes": *Carpenter v. Murphy*, Oral Argument Transcript, 19–20.

126 nothing but a "historical artifact": *Royal v. Murphy*, 17-1107 (US Supreme Court), Petition for a Writ of Certiorari, February 6, 2018; *Royal v. Murphy*, 17-1107 (US Supreme Court), Brief for the United States as Amicus Curiae, March 9, 2018.

126 seized during allotment: "The Council House," Creek Nation Council House, https://www.creekcouncilhouse.net/history.

126 "unhear what they're saying": James Floyd in discussion with the author, April 2023.

126 sang the musical anthem "Oklahoma": Sarah Deer, "Reclaiming Our Reservation: *Mvskoke Tvstvnvke Hoktvke Tuccenet (Etem) Opunayakes*," *Tulsa Law Review* 56 (2021): 519.

127 never had a reservation to begin with: *Murphy v. Oklahoma*, PCD-2004-321 (Oklahoma Court of Criminal Appeals), Respondent's Response to Order Regarding Second Application for Post-Conviction Relief, August 3, 2004; *Murphy v. Mullin*, CIV-03-443-WH (US District Court, Eastern District of Oklahoma), Response to Petition for Writ of Habeas Corpus, June 14, 2004; *Murphy v. Royal*, 07-7068 and 15-7041 (Tenth Circuit), Brief of Respondent-Appellee, November 4, 2016; *Royal v. Murphy*, 17-1107 (US Supreme Court), Petition for a Writ of Certiorari, February 6, 2018; *McGirt v. Oklahoma*, 18-9526 (US Supreme Court), Brief for Respondent, March 13, 2020.

127 he wasn't nervous: Riyaz Kanji in discussion with the author, November 2021.

127 "where I needed to get to somehow": Riyaz Kanji in discussion with the author, November 2021.

127 "alter reservations unilaterally": *Royal v. Murphy*, 17-1107 (US Supreme Court), Brief in Opposition, April 9, 2018.

127 "Creek land in Creek hands": *Royal v. Murphy*, 17-1107 (US Supreme Court), Brief in Opposition, April 9, 2018.

128 "house basements for decades": *Carpenter v. Murphy*, Oral Argument Transcript, 70–71.

128 "and I got to give it": Riyaz Kanji in discussion with the author, November 2021.

128 "the statute of limitations has expired": *Carpenter v. Murphy*, Oral Argument Transcript, 75–76.

128   "there's going to be blood in the streets": James Floyd in discussion with
      the author, March 2022.

128   a photograph of the skyline of Tulsa: *Carpenter v. Murphy*, 17-1107 (US
      Supreme Court), Brief for Petitioner, July 23, 2018, 3.

129   "intolerable uncertainty": *Royal v. Murphy*, 17-1107 (US Supreme Court),
      Petition for a Writ of Certiorari, February 6, 2018.

129   he did not know: Mike Hunter in discussion with the author, June
      2022.

129   up to seventy-six thousand past convictions could be impacted: *Royal
      v. Murphy*, 17-1107 (US Supreme Court), Reply of Petitioner, April 23, 2018;
      Royal v. Murphy, 17-1107 (US Supreme Court), Petition for a Writ of Certiorari,
      Brief for the United States as Amicus Curiae, March 9, 2018; *Carpenter v.
      Murphy*, 17-1107 (US Supreme Court), Reply Brief for Petitioner, October 19,
      2018; *Carpenter v. Murphy*, Oral Argument Transcript, November 27, 2018;
      Carpenter v. Murphy, 17-1107 (US Supreme Court), Supplemental Brief for
      Petitioner, December 28, 2018; *McGirt v. Oklahoma*, 18-9526 (US Supreme
      Court), Brief for Respondent, March 13, 2020; *McGirt v. Oklahoma*, 18-9526
      (US Supreme Court), Oral Argument Transcript, May 11, 2020; *Oklahoma v.
      Castro-Huerta*, 21-429 (US Supreme Court), Petition for a Writ of Certiorari,
      September 17, 2021; Dan Snyder, "Gov. Stitt: 'Don't Think There's Ever Been a
      Bigger Issue' for Oklahoma Than *McGirt* Ruling," KOKH, May 17, 2021.

129   the Supreme Court correspondent for the *Washington Post*: "Incarcer-
      ated Inmates and Community Supervision Offenders Daily Count Sheet,"
      Oklahoma Department of Corrections, July 19, 2021, https://ontotoc.gov/
      content/dam/ok/en/doc/documents/population/count-sheet/2021/OMS-
      Count-7-19-21.pdf; "Native American Inmate Count by Controlling Offense
      County," data provided by the Oklahoma Department of Corrections, in
      possession of author; Annie Gowen and Robert Barnes, "'Complete, Dysfunc-
      tional Chaos': Oklahoma Reels after Supreme Court Ruling on Indian Tribes,"
      Washington Post, July 24, 2021.

129   in counties potentially impacted by the decision: Data provided by the
      Oklahoma Department of Corrections, in possession of author.

130   after a conviction is finalized: US Congress, House, Public Law 104-132,
      *An Act to Deter Terrorism, Provide Justice for Victims, Provide for an Effective
      Death Penalty, and for Other Purposes*, April 24, 1996, H Rept. 104-518, H
      Rept. 104-383.

130   didn't bring it up in their first appeal: Data analysis performed by
      Jennifer McAffrey Thiessen, Desi Small-Rodriguez, and author, data provided
      by the Oklahoma Department of Corrections, in possession of author; *Barbre
      v. Whitten*, CIV 18-259-RAW-KEW (US District Court, Eastern District of
      Oklahoma), Aug. 22, 2019; *Tanner v. Oklahoma*, PC-2018-1075 (Oklahoma

Court of Criminal Appeals), Opinion Affirming Denial of Application for Post-Conviction Relief, April 9, 2019.

130   did not hold up to scrutiny: Henry J. Sadowski, "Interaction of Federal and State Sentences When the Federal Defendant Is under State Primary Jurisdiction," US Bureau of Prisons, July 7, 2011, https://www.bop.gov/re-sources/pdfs/ifss.pdf; data analysis performed by Desi Small-Rodriguez, data provided by the Oklahoma Department of Corrections, in possession of au-thor; Rebecca Nagle, "Oklahoma's Suspect Argument in Front of the Supreme Court," *Atlantic*, May 8, 2020.

130   "where would that case end up?": *Carpenter v. Murphy*, Oral Argument Transcript, 64.

130   "to sell alcoholic beverages?": *Carpenter v. Murphy*, Oral Argument Transcript, 50.

131   "all those people?": *Carpenter v. Murphy*, Oral Argument Transcript, 44.

131   reservation status would affect taxes: *Carpenter v. Murphy*, Oral Argu-ment Transcript, 35.

131   "The case is submitted": *Carpenter v. Murphy*, Oral Argument Tran-script, 78.

131   before they heard anything: Rosemary McCombs Maxey in discussion with the author, July 2022.

131   "we've won this case": James Floyd in discussion with the author, March 2022.

CHAPTER 8 | Coercion

133   from County Cork, Ireland: Joseph B. Thoburn and Muriel H. Wright, *Oklahoma: A History of the State and Its People*, vol. 2 (New York: Lewis Histor-ical Publishing Co., 1929), 916–17.

133   fifty thousand other eager white settlers: Stan Hoig, "Land Run of 1889," *The Encyclopedia of Oklahoma History and Culture*, Oklahoma Historical Society, https://www.okhistory.org/publications/enc/entry.php?entry=LA014.

133   tent cities went up overnight: Thoburn and Wright, *Oklahoma*, vol. 2, 916–17; Hoig, "Land Run of 1889"; John Alley, "Patrick Nagle: A Party Leader" (unpublished paper, n.d.), WHC M-7, Series 2, 2–3, Western History Collection, University of Oklahoma, Norman, OK; Patrick Sarsfield Nagle, *The Man on the Section Line: An Argument; Extracts of a Speech of P. S. Nagle; Delivered before an Audience of Farmers in a Country School House in Kingfisher County, Oklahoma* (Kingfisher, OK: n.p., n.d.); R. O. Joe Cassity Jr., "The Political Career of Patrick S. Nagle, 'Champion of the Underdog,'" *Chronicles of Oklahoma* 64, no. 4 (Winter 1986–87), 49.

133   the land became a state: Alley, "Patrick Nagle," 4–7; Nagle, *Man on the Section Line*; Cassity, "The Political Career of Patrick S. Nagle," 49–51.

134   white settlers who got free, Indigenous land: Alisa Trager, "The Relationship Between Race and Place: UCSB Professor Talks Discrimination and Residential Segregation in New Book," April 30, 2011, https://www.independent.com/2011/04/30/relationship-between-race-and-place/; Fourth Economy: A Steer Company, "The Inequitable Roots of Home Ownership: Systemic Racism & the Wealth Gap," April 16, 2019, https://www.fourtheconomy.com/post/the-inequitable-roots-of-home-ownership-systemic-racism-the-wealth-gap.

134   "as long as the grass grows or the water runs": Andrew Jackson, "Jackson to the Creek Indians, March 23, 1829," The American Presidency Project, https://www.presidency.ucsb.edu/documents/letter-the-creek-indians.

135   "Yes, sir" or "No, sir": DOI Commission of the Five Civilized Tribes, "Matter of the Application of William D. Polson for the Enrollment of Himself and Child as Cherokee Citizens, Sep. 18, 1900"; "Applicant Appears in Person Jan. 19, 1903," William Dudley Polson enrollment jacket Cherokee card 2925, Oklahoma Historical Society, 1–3, 5–7.

135   came back as an adult: William Dudley Polson enrollment jacket Cherokee card 2925, OHS, 1–3, 5–7.

136   some adjoined, some not: Indian Territory Map Co., *Cherokee Nation Township 24 North, Range 25 East* (Muskogee, OK: Indian Territory Map Co., 1909), Library of Congress County Landownership Maps, https://www.loc.gov/item/2011585467/.

136   where he worked at a drugstore: William Dudley Polson enrollment jacket Cher 2925, OHS, 7.

136   an area the size of Montana: US Department of the Interior, Indian Affairs, "History of Indian Land Consolidation: Roots for Fractionation: The Allotment Policy (1887–1934)," https://www.bia.gov/guide/history-indian-land-consolidation; National Congress of American Indians, "Policy Issues: Land & Natural Resources, Trust Lands," from House Resolution 375 "Protect the Land Into Trust Process and Existing Indian Trust Lands," https://www.ncai.org/policy-issues/land-natural-resources/trust-land.

136   west of the Mississippi: Roderick C. Essery, "The Cherokee Nation in the Nineteenth Century: Racial Tensions and the Loss of Tribal Sovereignty" (PhD diss., Flinders University of South Australia, April 2015), 109–21.

136   the same table as their owner: Roberts, *I've Been Here All the While*, 23–25.

136   "to find themselves abandoned by their slaves": *Fort Smith Elevator* (Fort Smith, AR), February 5, 1897, from C. T. Forman, "Webbers Falls," 458–59, quoted in Miles, *Ties That Bind*, 170.

137   materially the same: slavery: Miles, *Ties That Bind*, 171–73.

137   Cherokee people were deeply divided: *Cherokee Cavaliers*, 98–102; Confederate States of America Treaty with the Cherokees, October 7, 1861, "Gallery: Native Americans in the War," Special Collections and University Archives, University of Tulsa, Oklahoma, https://www.civilwarvirtualmuseum.org/1861 -1862/native-americans-in-the-war/csa-cherokee-1863-treaty.php.

137   in a refugee camp, he died: Miles, *Ties That Bind*, 186–88; Christopher Haveman, "Opothle Yoholo" (July 25, 2008), *Encyclopedia of Alabama*, https:// encyclopediaofalabama.org/article/opothle-yoholo/.

138   tribes allowed railroads: *Cherokee Cavaliers*, 98–102; William D. Pennington, "Reconstruction Treaties," *The Encyclopedia of Oklahoma History and Culture*, Oklahoma Historical Society, https://www.okhistory.org/publications /enc/entry.php?entry=RE001, accessed December 12, 2023.

138   they came in droves: Debo, *Road to Disappearance*, 197–99, 286–87.

138   "than we had chased out": Clark Wilson, a Euchee quoted in Debo, *Road to Disappearance*, 330–31.

138   they were less than 20 percent: US Congress, Senate, the Dawes Commission, *Report of the Commission Appointed to Negotiate with the Five Civilized Tribes of Indians, Known as the Dawes Commission*, 54th Congress, 1st Session, 1895, S. Doc. 12, 9–15.

138   "and this is the *Indian* territory": Charles F. Meserve, *The Dawes Commission and the Five Civilized Tribes of Indian Territory* (Philadelphia: Office of the Indian Rights Association, 1896), 11–12.

138   they just came back: US Congress, Senate, Select Committee to Investigate Matters Connected with Affairs in the Indian Territory, *Report of the Select Committee to Investigate Matters Connected with Affairs in the Indian Territory, with Hearings, November 11, 1906–January 9, 1907*, "Testimony of Pleasant Porter," 59th Congress, 2nd Session, 1907, S. Rep. No. 5013, Part 1, 624–25.

138   entire towns on Muscogee land: Debo, *Road to Disappearance*, 368, 331.

138   "The United States has not forgotten you": Debo, *Road to Disappearance*, 347.

139   Senator Dawes . . . sponsored it: US Congress, *An Act to Provide for the Allotment of Lands in Severalty to Indians on the Various Reservations, and to Extend the Protection of the Laws of the United States and the Territories over the Indians, and for Other Purposes* (Dawes Act), Dec. 6, 1886, 49th Congress, 2nd Session.

139   "which is at the bottom of civilization": Debo, *And Still the Waters Run*, 21–22.

139   no poor families or "paupers": US Congress, Senate, Select Committee, *Report*, 1907, "Testimony of Pleasant Porter," 624–25.

139   "and so much poverty": Meserve, *Dawes Commission and the Five Civilized Tribes*, 22–23.

139   The other reason was crime: Dawes Commission, *Report* 1894, 8–12.

139   "the outlaw class in general": Meserve, *Dawes Commission and the Five Civilized Tribes*, 15.

139   only a few dozen were executed in twenty-one years: Debo, *And Still the Waters Run*, 26; *Proceedings of the Fourteenth Annual Meeting of the Lake Mohonk Conference of Friends of the Indian, 1896* (Lake Mohonk Conference 1897), "The Indian Territory," Speech by Hon. H. L. Dawes, October 14–16, 1896, 50–55, quote on 54; Meserve, *Dawes Commission and the Five Civilized Tribes*, 42. The primary source documents here contradict each other; one of the reports of the speech claims that Dawes said about one hundred men had been hanged.

139   tribal governments were "unworthy": Dawes Commission, *Report*, 1895, 11, 19–20.

140   posted the broadsheets around the Territory: Debo, *Road to Disappearance*, 346–48; Dawes Commission *Report*, 1895, 3–12, 20–21.

140   Congress gave up on cession: US Congress, Senate, the Dawes Commission, *Report of the Commission Appointed to Negotiate with the Five Civilized Tribes of Indians, Known as the Dawes Commission*, 53rd Congress, 3rd Session, 1894, S. Mis. Doc. 24, 1–5.

141   fight for their reservation: Dawes Commission, *Report* 1894, 1; *Carpenter v. Murphy*, Oral Argument Transcript, 16.

141   agreed to the allotment of their land: US Congress, Senate, *An Act for the Protection of the People of the Indian Territory, and for Other Purposes* (Curtis Act), June 28, 1898, Sec. 3, Sec. 11; Debo, *Road to Disappearance*, 373; Debo, *And Still the Waters Run*, 32–33; US Congress, Senate, *An Act to Provide for the Allotment of the Lands of the Cherokee Nation, for the Disposition of Town Sites Therein, and for Other Purposes* (Cherokee Allotment Agreement), July 1, 1902, 57th Congress; US Congress, Senate, *Choctaw and Chickasaw Atoka Allotment Agreement* (Atoka Agreement), June 28, 1908, 60th Congress; US Congress, Senate, *An Act to Ratify and Confirm an Agreement with the Muscogee or Creek Tribe of Indians, and for Other Purposes* (Creek Allotment Agreement), Mar. 3, 1901, Senate, 57th Congress; *An Act to Ratify the Agreement Between the Dawes Commission and the Seminole Nation of Indians* (Seminole Allotment Agreement), Dec. 16, 1897, 55th Congress.

141   sent in federal marshals and the cavalry: Donald L. Fixico, "The Crazy Snake Movement and the Four Mothers Society," *Chronicles of Oklahoma* 100, no. 4 (Winter 2022–2023), 395–96; "Interview with William Bruner" and

"Interview with Laurel Pitman," Doris Duke American Indian Oral History Collection, Western History Collection, University of Oklahoma; US Department of the Interior, *Annual Report: Report of Agencies in Indian Territory,* 1901, "Snake Uprising," 235–37; Debo, *And Still the Waters Run,* 55–56.

143 he returned them in batches: Select Committee, *Report,* "Statement of Eufaula Harjo and Others," 89–100; DOI, *Annual Report: Report of Agencies in Indian Territory,* 1901, "Citizens by Blood and Intermarriage," 201.

143 "They are in the houses that we built": Select Committee, *Report,* "Statement of Eufaula Harjo and Others," 89–100.

143 who received only 40: Debo, *And Still the Waters Run,* 51; Kent Carter, "Dawes Commission," The Encyclopedia of Oklahoma History and Culture, Oklahoma Historical Society, https://www.okhistory.org, accessed Oct. 29, 2023; *Cherokee Allotment Agreement,* July 1, 1902, Sec. 11, 2; *Choctaw & Chickasaw Atoka Allotment Agreement,* June 28 1908; *Creek Allotment Agreement,* Mar. 3, 1901; *Seminole Allotment Agreement,* Dec. 16, 1897.

143 tribal governments would be unfair: US Congress, Senate, Dawes Commission *Report,* 1895, 16–19.

143 "an unfulfilled promise but a reality": Roberts, *I've Been Here All the While,* 45.

144 claimed to be citizens of the Five Tribes: *Encyclopedia of Oklahoma History and Culture,* "Dawes Commission."

145 "the avaricious land sharks of the American continent": Isparhecher, Principal Chief, Muscogee Nation to the National Council of the Muscogee Nation, October 8, 1897, in US Congress, Senate, *Agreement with the Five Civilized Tribes. Letter from the Secretary of the Interior, Submitting to Congress, for Its Consideration and Ratification, an Agreement between the Commissioners of the United States to Negotiate with the Five Civilized Tribes and the Commission on the Part of the Muscogee or Creek Nation, Concluded on the 27th day of September, 1897,* 55th Congress, 2nd Session, S. Doc 34, 11.

CHAPTER 9 | The Twist

147 all eyes are on the high court: "Final Stat Pack for October Term 2019," *SCOTUSblog,* July 20, 2020, https://www.scotusblog.com/wp-content/uploads/2020/07/Final-Statpack-7.20.2020.pdf.

147 the world knows what happened: "FAQs: Announcements of Orders and Opinions," *SCOTUSblog,* https://www.scotusblog.com/faqs-announcements-of-orders-and-opinions/.

148 no news on *Murphy:* James Floyd in discussion with the author, March 2022.

148   a census case, and *Murphy*: "Live Blog of Opinions," *SCOTUSblog*, June 27, 2019, http://live.scotusblog.com/Event/Live_blog_of_opinions __June_27_2019?Page=0. Accessed August 2022.

148   "What are they going to do?": James Floyd in discussion with the author, March 2022.

148   "what do we got to show? Nothing": James Floyd in discussion with the author, March 2022.

148   less than once a year: Stephen Wermiel (law professor and author at *SCOTUSblog*) in discussion with the author, June 2019.

148   allowed in the room: "Supreme Court Procedures," United States Courts, https://www.uscourts.gov/about-federal-courts/educational-resources /about-educational-outreach/activity-resources/supreme-1.

149   the team tapped Ian: "Ian Heath Gershengorn," Jenner & Block, https:// www.jenner.com/en/people/ian-heath-gershengorn; "Ian H. Gershengorn," Oyez, https://www.oyez.org/advocates/ian_h_gershengorn; Ian Gershengorn (counsel for Patrick Murphy and Jimcy McGirt) in discussion with the author, April 2022.

149   one of the first cases on the docket: "Supreme Court of the United States, October Term 2019," US Supreme Court, September 11, 2019, https://www.supremecourt.gov/Oral_arguments/Argument_calendars /Monthlyargumentcaloctober2019.Pdf; Ian Gershengorn in discussion with the author, April 2022.

149   the reservation status of Muscogee Nation: Ian Gershengorn in discussion with the author, April 2022.

149   "the legal questions are not exactly the same": Ian Gershengorn in discussion with the author, April 2022.

150   involved the Muscogee reservation: List of cases appealed to Supreme Court in 2019, in possession of author.

150   in medium- and minimum-security dorms: "JCCC Fact Sheet," Oklahoma Department of Corrections, March 2023, https://ontotoc.gov/content /dam/ok/en/doc/documents/agency-information/fact-sheets/2023.03 %20JCCC%20Fact%20Sheet.pdf, accessed August 2022.

150   "It was all over the networks": Jimcy McGirt (defendant) in discussion with the author, August 2022.

150   took place on the Muscogee reservation: *McGirt v. Oklahoma*, 18-9526 (US Supreme Court), Petition for a Writ of Certiorari, April 17, 2019, 6; *McGirt v. Oklahoma*, 18-9526 (US Supreme Court), July 9, 2020, 5.

150   other relevant information to reflect his case: Jimcy McGirt in discussion with the author, August 2022.

151   three-year-old granddaughter: See *USA v. McGirt*, 20-CR-50-JFH (US District Court, Eastern District of Oklahoma), trial transcript, vol. 2, November 5, 2020, 139.

151   he ran into the bathroom to vomit: *USA v. McGirt*, 20-CR-50-JFH (US District Court, Eastern District of Oklahoma), trial transcript, vol. 2, November 5, 2020, 291.

151   he did not give up: *Oklahoma v. McGirt*, CF-1996-00355 (Wagoner County District Court) Docket; *McGirt v. Bryant*, WH-17-22 (Alfalfa County District Court), Pro Se Petition for Writ of Habeas Corpus, September 29, 2017; *McGirt v. Bryant*, WH-17-22 (Alfalfa County District Court), Order Dismissing Petition for Writ of Habeas Corpus, November 6, 2007; *McGirt v. Bryant*, HC-2017-1169 (Oklahoma Court of Criminal Appeals), Order Declining Jurisdiction, November 29, 2017; *McGirt v. Bryant*, HC-2018-131 (Oklahoma Court of Criminal Appeals), Order Declining Jurisdiction, March 2, 2018; *McGirt v. Bryant*, HC-2017-1169 (Oklahoma Court of Criminal Appeals), Order Declining Jurisdiction, November 29, 2017; *McGirt v. Bryant*, HC-2018-131 (Oklahoma Court of Criminal Appeals), Order Declining Jurisdiction, March 2, 2018; *McGirt v. Bryant*, 116,873 (Oklahoma Supreme Court), Order, March 21, 2018; *McGirt v. Oklahoma*, PC-2018-1057 (Oklahoma Court of Criminal Appeals), Pro Se Petitioner's Post-Conviction Petition in Error with Incorporated Brief, October 15, 2018; *McGirt v. Oklahoma*, CF-1996-00355 (Wagoner County District Court), Order, August 21, 2018; *McGirt v. Oklahoma*, PC-2018-1057 (Oklahoma Court of Criminal Appeals), Order Affirming Denial of Application for Post-Conviction Relief, February 25, 2019.

151   relisted eight times: *McGirt v. Oklahoma*, 18-9526 (US Supreme Court), Petition for a Writ of Certiorari, April 17, 2019, 6; "*McGirt v. Oklahoma*," SCOTUSblog, https://www.scotusblog.com/case-files/cases/mcgirt-v-oklahoma/.

152   "You're hired," he replied: Ian Gershengorn in discussion with the author, April 2022; Jimcy McGirt in discussion with the author, August 2022.

152   "Can they find a more awful case?": James Floyd in discussion with the author, March 2022.

152   going to the Supreme Court: Jimcy McGirt in discussion with the author, August 2022; "*McGirt v. Oklahoma*," SCOTUSblog.

CHAPTER 10: Plunder

153   "bluish-colored" clouds: Joseph Stanley Clark, *The Oil Century: From the Drake Well to the Conservation Era* (Norman: University of Oklahoma Press, 1958), 90, 151; Kenny A. Franks, "Petroleum Industry," *The Encyclopedia of Oklahoma History and Culture*, https://www.okhistory.org/publications/enc/entry?entry=PE023

153   producer of oil and gas in the country: Gib Knight, "A Look Back at One
of the Biggest Oil Fields," Oklahoma Minerals, https://www.oklahomaminerals
.com/look-back-one-biggest-oil-gas-fields.

154   "greatest oil well ever found west of the Mississippi river": "Gusher at
Red Fork Shot Four Hundred Feet High," *The Daily Ardmoreite* (Artdmore,
IT), June 26, 1901; "Greatest Oil Gusher Yet," *El Paso Herald* (El Paso, TX),
June 25, 1901; "Biggest Gusher Yet Reported," *Daily Arkansas Gazette* (Little
Rock, AR), June 28, 1901.

154   nearly the size of the National Mall: DOI, Commission of the Five Civi-
lized Tribes, "In the Matter of the Application of Moses Naharkey,
October 28, 1901," "In the Matter of the Application of Moses Naharkey,
Jan. 12, 1900," Naharkey Family land jacket, Creek BB 4363, 4364, 4365,
4366, Oklahoma Historical Society; "Homestead Deed to Heirs, Creek Indian
Roll No. 4364," "Allotment Deed to Heirs, Creek Indian Roll No. 4364,"
"Township 19 North, Range 12 East [allotment maps]"; agent notes on deaths of
Naharkey family members, Naharkey Family land jacket, Creek BB 4363, 4364,
4365, 4366, OHS. Allotment maps in this file label all allotments with individual Creek names and roll numbers; John D. Flanagan, "Mooser Creek Green-
way: Restoration and Preservation of a Historic Pristine Stream," I-1, II-1.

155   oil was struck on the Naharkey allotment: "The Creek Payment," *Wagoner
Weekly Sayings* (Wagoner, IT), Oct. 6, 1904; "One Full-Blood Secured $2295,"
The Weekly Examiner (Tulsa, IT), Oct. 22, 1904; "Notes of the Oil Field," *The
Red Fork Derrick* (Red Fork, IT), June 3, 1905; "Notes of the Oil Field," *The Red
Fork Derrick* (Red Fork, IT), Apr. 8, 1905; "Notes of the Oil Field," *The Red Fork
Derrick* (Red Fork, IT), May 20, 1905; "Trouble Over Naharkey Land," *The Tulsa
Weekly Democrat* (Tulsa, IT), June 16, 1905; "Notes of the Oil Field," *The Red
Fork Derrick* (Red Fork, IT), July 8, 1905; "Notes of the Oil Field," *The Red Fork
Derrick* (Red Fork, IT), July 29, 1905; "Notes of the Oil Field," *The Red Fork Der-
rick* (Red Fork, IT), Sep. 23, 1905; "Notes of the Oil Field," *The Red Fork Derrick*
(Red Fork, IT), Sep. 30, 1905; "Notes of the Oil Field," *The Red Fork Derrick* (Red
Fork, IT), Nov. 18, 1905; "The Stockton Oil Company Has . . . ," *Coffeyville Daily
Record* (Coffeyville, IT), Dec. 5, 1905; "Real Estate Transfers," *The Tulsa Tribune*
(Tulsa, IT), May 30, 1905; "Valuable Lease," *The Tulsa Democrat* (Tulsa, IT),
July 7, 1905; "Notes of the Oil Field," *The Red Fork Derrick* (Red Fork, IT),
May 13, 1905; "No Claim against Stansbery Addition," *The Tulsa Tribune* (Tulsa,
IT), Sep. 21, 1905; "Notes of the Oil Field," *The Red Fork Derrick* (Red Fork, IT),
Jan. 27, 1906; "Notes of the Oil Field," *The Red Fork Derrick* (Red Fork, IT),
Mar. 24, 1906; "Notes of the Oil Field," *The Red Fork Derrick* (Red Fork, IT),
Apr. 7, 1906; "To Administer Estate," *The Tulsa Tribune* (Tulsa, IT), Aug. 9,
1906; "Administrator's Notice," *The Tulsa Chief* (Tulsa, IT), Sep. 4, 1906; "Notes
of the Oil Field," *The Red Fork Derrick* (Red Fork, IT), Mar. 3, 1906; "Admin-
istrator's Notice," *The Oklahoma Critic* (Tulsa, IT), Sep. 4 1906; No Title, *The
Gove County Record* (Grinnell, KA), Sep. 27, 1907; "Case No. 4019—Sammie

Naharkey," *Muskogee Daily Phoenix and Times-Democrat* (Muskogee, OK), Mar. 2, 1910; "Title Settled on Some Valuable Land in Tulsa," *Muskogee Times-Democrat* (Muskogee, OK), June 11, 1910; "Real Estate Transfers," *Tulsa Tribune* (Tulsa, OK), June 14, 1910.

155   papers called it "the best producer ever drilled": "The Stockton Oil Company Has . . . ," *Coffeyville Daily Record* (Coffeyville, IT), December 5, 1906.

155   Under federal regulations: Select Committee, *Report*, "Statement of US Indian Agent Dana H. Kelsey for the Union Agency at Muscogee," 59th Congress, 2nd Session, 1907, S. Rep. No. 5013, Part 1, 561–98.

155   his own colonial-style mansion: "10. Stebbins/Talbot house (1030 East 19th Street) 1915," Maple Ridge Properties: Maple Ridge Historic District Representative Sample of Properties, Tulsa Preservation Commission, 2019, https://tulsapreservationcommission.org/neighborhoods-districts/nrhp /districts-listed/mapleridge/, accessed January 23, 2024; Larry O'Dell, "Stebbins, Grant Case (1862–1925)," *The Encyclopedia of Oklahoma History and Culture*, Oklahoma Historical Society, https://www.okhistory.org/publications /enc/entry?entry=ST027, accessed January 23, 2024.

155   the sheriff seized his stocks and land: *Moses Naharkey and D.A. McDougal v. Grant C. Stebbins*, 1 (Tulsa County District Court), document title illegible (July 8, 1907), Journal entry (Nov. 16, 1912), Journal Entry (Nov. 21, 1912), document title illegible (Nov. 21, 1914), Journal entry (December 4, 1912), Journal entry (December 5, 1912), Journal entry (December 6, 1912), Journal entry (date illegible); Moses Naharkey, Tulsa County Probate Records, vol. 1, 28–30, vol. 4, 1565–566.

155   Moser died: "Administrators Notice,"*The Tulsa Chief* (Tulsa, IT), September 4, 1906; Decree (March 16, 1907), 247 (Western District of IT, Tulsa), *Naharkey v. Naharkey*.

155   "practically every crime and fraud": US Department of the Interior, *Annual Report*: Report of the Commissioner of Indian Affairs, 1913 (Washington, DC: Government Printing Office), "Field Work," 476.

155   several served on the company boards: Select Committee, *Report*, 650–72; Debo, *And Still the Waters Run*, 75, 81–83, 102, 118, 120–25, 200, 218, 260–62; Select Committee, *Report*, "Statement of Dana H. Kelsey Agent, Muskogee, Ind. T.," 561–98.

156   tribal citizens still owned most of the land: Debo, *And Still the Waters Run*, 90–91.

156   a "burden," a "crime," and "radically wrong": US Congress, Senate, *Removal of Restrictions Upon the Sale of Surplus Allotments, Etc. (Removal of Restrictions)*, "Memorial from Citizens of Indian Territory," 58th Congress, 2nd Session, 1905, S. Doc 169, 1–6; Select Committee, *Report*, 1383, 1866–67, 1890, 1073.

156   enough money for public schools: *Removal of Restrictions*, 5.

156   "craven," "inferior," "shiftless," "ignorant," "degraded," and "evil": Select Committee, Vol. 1, 1125; *Removal of Restrictions*, 23, 30.

156   "and the Indian is the landlord": Select Committee, Vol. 2, 1327, 1336.

156   actually best for Native people: Select Committee, Vol. 1, 392–424.

156   "only a small percentage of Indian blood": *Removal of Restrictions*, 8–9.

157   "inadequate" amount of money: Select Committee, Vol. 1, "Statement of J. Coody Johnson, A Creek Freedman, Member of the National Council of the Creek Nations," 441; Debo, *And Still the Waters Run*, 89–90.

157   who weren't "full blood": Doug Keil, "Bleeding Out: Histories and Legacies of Indian Blood," in *The Great Vanishing Act: Blood Quantum and the Future of Native Nations*, ed. Kathleen Ratteree and Norbert S. Hill (Golden, CO: Fulcrum Publishing, 2017), 89.

157   they targeted children, especially orphans: Select Committee, *Report*, 868, 1099, 1072–73.

157   they asked with hubris: Select Committee, *Report*, 62–63, 1111–25, 1025–26.

157   they wanted restrictions to stay in place: Select Committee, *Report*, 89–100, 97, 640–41, 974–79, 292–307, 240–46, 243–46, 429–30, 440. Exceptions: "Statement of Mr. D. W. C. Duncan, a Cherokee Indian, on behalf of the Commercial Club of Vanita," 180–90, and "Statement of Mr. Robert L. Owen," 392–424.

157   "neither land nor money": Select Committee, *Report*, 1907, p. 303.

158   "is the one that is dead": Select Committee, *Report*, 1907, p. 639.

158   "buried them beneath the sod": Charles Evans and Clinton Orrin Bunn, *Oklahoma Civil Government* (Ardmore, OK: Bunn Brothers Publishers, 1908), 63–64.

158   in a brief they submitted for *Murphy*: *McGirt v. Oklahoma*, No. 18-9526 (US Supreme Court), Brief of Amici Curiae, Seventeen Oklahoma District Attorneys and the Oklahoma District Attorneys Association in Support of Respondent, March 9, 2020, 1–5.

158   was allegorically married to: Evans and Bunn, *Oklahoma Civil Government*, 63.

158   out of their jurisdiction: *Constitution and Enabling Act of the State of Oklahoma*, compiled by Clinton O. Bunn and William C. Bunn (Ardmore, OK: Bunn Brothers Publishers, 1907), Article 1, Section 4, 9–10.

158   "anti-Indian" platforms: Gertrude Bonnin, Charles H. Fabens, and Matthew K. Sniffen, *Oklahoma's Poor Rich Indians: An Orgy of Graft and Exploita-*

tion of the Five Civilized Tribes—Legalized Robbery (Philadelphia: Office of the Indian Rights Association, 1924), 10.

158   all unrestricted land was taxed: *Indian Affairs: Laws and Treaties*, compiled, annotated, and edited by Charles J. Kappler (Washington, DC: Government Printing Office, 1913), vol. 3, 351–54.

158   under the jurisdiction of Oklahoma: US Department of the Interior, *Annual Report*, "Indian Affairs," 1912 (Washington, DC: Government Printing Office), 467.

158   sold for less than what it was worth: DOI, *Annual Report*, vol. 2: *Report of the Commissioner of Indian Affairs* (Washington, DC, 1913), 476–77.

158   only eighteen months old: Testimony of Millie Naharkey, *Millie Naharkey Classified File (MNCF)* 29257-1923-175.2-Creek (Central Classified Files, 1907-1939), Entry PI-163 121A, RG 75, National Archives and Records Administration, Washington, DC, 102.

159   that was never paid back: US Probate Attorney Peter Deichman to Hon. R.B. Drake, October 15, 1923, *MNCF*.

159   the money from the sale for their services: US Congress, Senate, *An Act to Ratify and Confirm an Agreement with the Muscogee or Creek Tribe of Indians, and for Other Purposes* (Creek Allotment Agreement), Mar. 3, 1901, 57th Cong., Section 727; *Select Committee*, "Statement of Nelson H. McCoy," Vol. 1, 1052–1073, Vol. 2, 1188; Kate Barnard, "Legal Work in the County Courts Throughout the State," in *Fourth Report of the Commissioner of Charities and Corrections, Oct. 1, 1911–Oct. 1, 1912* (Oklahoma City: Oklahoma Engraving & Printing Co, 1912), 135–40.

159   "that would cost about 10 cents": Select Committee, Vol. 1, "Statement of Mr. Walter Falwell, Supervisor of Schools for the Creek and Seminole Nations," 240.

159   about to turn eighteen: Millie Naharkey Testimony, *MNCF*, 102–114.

159   Millie still looked quite young: Bonnin, Fabens, and Sniffen, *Oklahoma's Poor Little Rich Indians*, 26.

159   for the whole family to go on a road trip: Interview with A.B. Reese, *MNCF*, vol. 2, 112–33; Petition Cause of Action, (n.d.) 19374 (Tulsa County, OK), *Naharkay v. Page*.

159   in the Missouri Ozarks: Millie Naharkey Timeline 60972, *MNCF*, vol. 3, 163–72; Statement of Millie Naharkey, *MNCF*, vol. 2, 99.

160   her guardian was trying to steal her land: A.B. Reese Interview, Deposition of Martha James, *MNCF*, vol. 2, 115–33, 180–81.

160   what papers she was signing: Statement of Millie Naharkey, *MNCF*, 102–14.

160   paid only $2,000: Grant C. Stebbins Vendor Contract No. 203984 (July 3, 1922), 19387 (Tulsa County, OK) Tulsa Probate Records; Journal Entry (n.d.) 19387 (Tulsa County, OK), *Naharkey v. Naharkey*.

160   an estimated $200,000 to $300,000: Motion to Set Aside Dismissal and Reinstate Case (n.d.), 19374 (Tulsa County, OK), *Naharkey v. Page*; Petition to Set Aside Dismissal, and Reinstate Cause (n.d.), 19395 (Tulsa County, OK), *Naharkey v. Hardesty*; Motion to Set Aside Dismissal and Reinstate Case (n.d.), 19388 (Tulsa County, OK), *Naharkey v. Charley*.

160   Oklahoma she would be arrested: A.B. Reese Interview, *MNCF,* vol. 2, 102–114, 117; *Millie Naharkey vs. Charles Page et al.,* 19374 (District Court of Tulsa County, OK), Motion to Set Aside Dismissal and Reinstate Case, n.d.; Deposition of Martha James, Statement of Robert F. Blair 41564, *MNCF,* vol. 2, 180–81, 140–45.

160   stayed with the men—alone: Millie Naharkey Timeline 60972, A.B. Reese Interview, Statement of Millie Naharkey, *MNCF,* vol. 2, 117, 104.

160   named William McNutt: Interview with A.B. Reese, *MNCF,* vol. 2, 112–33; Petition Cause of Action, (n.d.) 19374 (Tulsa County, OK), *Naharkay v. Page.*

161   but she just laughed: Statement of William G. Hip, Statement of Millie Naharkey, *MNCF,* 225–30, 102–14.

161   he said he would kill her: Statement of Millie Naharkey, Interview with AB Reese, Statement of R.E. Bruner, *MNCF,* vol. 2, 105–6,115–33, 218–22; *Millie Naharkey vs. Gladys Bell Oil Company, A Corporation of G.C. Stebbins, A.B. Reese and Wm. R. McNutt,* 24917 (District Court of Tulsa County, OK), petition, n.d.; *Millie Naharkey vs. the Gladys Bell Oil Company et al.,* 23231 (District Court of Tulsa County, OK), Protest and Deposition, subscribed and sworn, September 28, 1923.

161   a special agent headed to Missouri: Thomas P. Roach, US Special Officer, to Chas. H. Burke, Commissioner of Indian Affairs, May 19, 1923, *MNCF,* 65–80.

161   up in the soft top of his car: A.B. Reese Interview, Statement of Leo Hutchins, Millie Naharkey timeline, *MNCF,* vol. 2, 119, 120, 122, 96, vol. 3, 171.

161   but the plan fell through: A.B. Reese Interview, Statement of R. E. Bruner, Statement of William G. Hip, Statement of W. R. McNutt, Millie Naharkey Deposition, Millie Naharkey Timeline 60972, *MNCF,* vol. 2, 115–33, 218–22, 225–30, 146–50, 102–114, vol. 3, 169–72.

161   she walked into the Kansas City office of the US Marshals Service: Interview with A. B. Reese, Statement of W. R. McNutt, Statement of R. E. Bruner Jr., Second Interview with RE Bruner Jr., November 15, 1922, Statement of Millie Naharkey, *MNCF,* 115–33, 146–50, 218–23, 102–14.

161 "carried from place to place": Bonnin, Fabens, and Sniffen, *Oklahoma's Poor Little Rich Indians*, 14; DOI, *Annual Report*, "Indian Affairs," 1912, 476.

161 "the individual declared incompetent": Bonnin, Fabens, and Sniffen, *Oklahoma's Poor Little Rich Indians*, 14.

162 saved her royalties and didn't spend them: Bonnin, Fabens, and Sniffen, *Oklahoma's Poor Little Rich Indians*, 18.

162 When one attorney forced: Bonnin, Fabens, and Sniffen, *Oklahoma's Poor Rich Indians*, 5–7; US Department of the Interior, *Annual Report: Report of the Commissioner of Indian Affairs* (Washington, DC: Government Printing Office, 1920), 38–42; DOI, *Annual Report: Report of the Commissioner of Indian Affairs* (Washington, DC: Government Printing Office, 1919), 312, 382–83, 384–85; DOI, *Annual Report: Indian Affairs* (Washington, DC, 1913), 475–81; Kate Barnard, "The Crisis in Oklahoma Indian Affairs: A Challenge to Our National Honor," *Report of the Thirty-Second Annual Lake Mohonk Conference on the Indian and Other Dependent Peoples* (NY: Lake Mohonk Conference on the Indian and Other Dependent Peoples, 1914), 16–26.

162 to the abduction and assaults: *The Tulsa Tribune*, "Brother and Sister Dispute Title to Naharkey Estate," Dec. 9, 1922; *The Morning Tulsa Daily World*, "Judge Kennamer Bars Himself in Wiley Lynn Case," Dec. 30, 1924; Statement of Robert F. Blair, 41564 (May 22, 1923), Decision, Robert F. Blair Disbarment (January 10, 1925), No. 4128 Law (Eastern District of OK), Creek National Attorney A.J. Ward to Commissioner of Indian Affairs Chas Burke (July 6, 1923), Chas Burke to A.J. Ward (July 16, 1923), *MNCF*, vol. 1, 5–6, 7, vol. 3, 19, 13–28, vol. 2, 130–35; Petition (n.d.) 24917 (Tulsa Co. District Court, OK), *Naharkey v. Gladys Belle Oil Co.*

162 declared her legally incompetent: Motion to Substitute Party Plaintiff, (n.d.) 19374 (District Court of Tulsa County, OK), *Millie Naharkey v. Charles Page & Sand Springs Home*; Millie Naharkey timeline 60972, Thomas P. Roach to Chas Burke 41564, May 22, 1923, *MNCF*, vol. 3, 172, vol. 2, 17–27.

162 She later gave birth to his child: Bonnin, Fabens, and Sniffen, *Oklahoma's Poor Little Rich Indians*, 37.

162 the body was buried without examination: Bonnin, Fabens, and Sniffen, *Oklahoma's Poor Little Rich Indians*, 26–28.

162 "most productive oil fields in the world": "United States Indian Office Takes a Hand," *Muskogee Daily Phoenix* (Muskogee, OK), March 24, 1911.

162 including a former mayor: Creek Nation Freedmen Roll entry, DOI Commission of the Five Civilized Tribes Creek Nation Newborn No. 250 Certificate, *Sells Family Land Jacket*, Oklahoma Historical Society, 1, 18; "United States Indian Office takes a Hand," *Muskogee Daily Phoenix* (Muskogee,

OK), March 24, 1911; "Negro Confesses in the Dynamite Case," *The Hooker Advance* (Hooker, OK) January 5, 1912; "State to Drop Murder Charge Against Coombs," *Muckogee Daily Phoenix* (Muskogee, OK), January 7, 1912; "Wrecked Home in Which They Slept Officers Declare," *Muskogee Daily Phoenix* (Muskogee, OK), April 4, 1911; "Arrest Martin; Murder," *Muskogee Daily Phoenix* (Muskogee, OK), April 18, 1911; "Release Martin Under Fifteen Thousand bond," *Muskogee Daily Phoenix* (Muskogee, OK), April 19, 1911.

CHAPTER 11 | The Opposition

163 argued over the phone: Amy Howe, "Courtroom Access: Faced with a Pandemic, the Supreme Court Pivots," *SCOTUSblog*, Apr. 16, 2020, https://www.scotusblog.com/2020/04/courtroom-access-faced-with-a-pandemic-the-supreme-court-pivots/.

163 infamous toilet flush: Ashley Feinberg, "Investigation: I Think I Know Which Justice Flushed," *Slate*, May 8, 2020, https://slate.com/news-and-politics/2020/05/toilet-flush-supreme-court-livestream.html.

164 for Kanji to speak: Riyaz Kanji in discussion with the author, November 2021.

164 had to buy a new phone: Ian Gershengorn in discussion with the author, April 2022.

164 it began: "Supreme Court Oral Argument: *McGirt v. Oklahoma*," C-SPAN video, May 11, 2020, https://www.c-span.org/video/?471673-1/mcgirt-v-oklahoma-oral-argument.

164 "never was reservation land": *McGirt v. Oklahoma*, 18-9526 (US Supreme Court), Oral Argument Transcript, May 11, 2020, 47.

164 but not a reservation: *McGirt v. Oklahoma*, 18-9526 (US Supreme Court), Brief for Respondent, March 13, 2020.

164 "we're not": *McGirt v. Oklahoma*, Oral Argument Transcript, 79.

165 "have to release them": *McGirt v. Oklahoma*, Oral Argument Transcript, 54.

165 "when it created the state of Oklahoma": *McGirt v. Oklahoma*, Oral Argument Transcript, 55.

165 would be totally disrupted: *McGirt v. Oklahoma*, 18-9526 (US Supreme Court), Brief of Amici Curiae, Environmental Federation of Oklahoma, Inc., et al., March 20, 2020; *Carpenter v. Murphy*, 17-1107 (US Supreme Court), Brief of Amici Curiae, Environmental Federation of Oklahoma, Inc., et al., July 30, 2018; *McGirt v. Oklahoma*, 18-9526 (US Supreme Court), Brief for Respondent, March 13, 2020; *Royal v. Murphy*, 17-1107 (US Supreme Court), Brief of Amici Curiae, Oklahoma Independent Petroleum Association on Writ of Certiorari, March 9, 2018.

165 opposing the Muscogee reservation: See *Murphy v. Royal*, 07-7068 and 15-7041 (Tenth Circuit), Motion for Leave to File Brief Amici Curiae in Support of Respondent-Appellee Terry Royal, Warden's, Petition for Panel Rehearing or Rehearing En Banc of Environmental Federation of Oklahoma, et al., November 11, 2017; *Murphy v. Royal*, 07-7068 and 15-7041 (Tenth Circuit), Motion for Leave to File Brief of Amicus Curiae, Oklahoma Independent Petroleum Association in Support of Appellee's Petition for Panel Rehearing or Rehearing En Banc, September 27, 2017; *McGirt v. Oklahoma*, 18-9526 (US Supreme Court), Brief of Amici Curiae, Environmental Federation of Oklahoma, Inc., et al., March 20, 2020; *Royal v. Murphy*, 17-1107 (US Supreme Court), Brief of Amici Curiae, Oklahoma Independent Petroleum Association on Writ of Certiorari, March 9, 2018.

165 "substantial sums": *Murphy v. Royal*, 07-7068 and 15-7041 (Tenth Circuit), Brief Amici Curiae in Support of Respondent-Appellee Terry Royal, Warden's, Petition for Panel Rehearing or Rehearing En Banc of the Oklahoma Oil & Gas Association, et al., November 9, 2017.

166 threw its weight behind Oklahoma: oil and gas: *Royal v. Murphy*, 17-1107 (US Supreme Court), Brief of Amici Curiae, Oklahoma Independent Petroleum Association on Writ of Certiorari, March 9, 2018.

166 oil and natural gas in the United States: "Crude Oil Production," US Energy Information Administration, https://www.eia.gov/dnav/pet/pet_crd_crpdn_adc_mbbl_a.htm.

166 old wells: *Murphy v. Royal*, 07-7068 and 15-7041 (Tenth Circuit), Motion for Leave to File Brief of Amicus Curiae Oklahoma Independent Petroleum Association in Support of Appellee's Petition for Panel Rehearing or Rehearing En Banc, September 27, 2017.

166 90 percent of wells: Data provided by the Oklahoma Corporation Commission, in possession of author; Adam Wilmoth, "Older, Marginal Wells Increase Nationwide," *Oklahoman*, December 15, 2017.

166 81 percent of abandoned wells: Data provided by the Oklahoma Corporation Commission, in possession of author.

166 $2 billion: Data analysis by Maddie Stone, data provided by the Oklahoma Corporation Commission, in possession of author.

167 "mature and stable regulatory regime": *Royal v. Murphy*, 17-1107 (US Supreme Court), Brief of Oklahoma Independent Petroleum Association as Amicus Curiae in Support of Petitioner, March 9, 2018.

167 they control it: See: Journal News Services, "Oil's the Life for Watts," *The Ottawa Citizen*, June 1, 1981; "Director, Oil and Gas Conservation Division State of Oklahoma Corporation Commission," *Daily Oklahoman*, September 5, 1993; "Mike McGinnis, Deputy Director of the Oil and Gas Conservation Division at Oklahoma Corporation Commission," LinkedIn,

https://www.linkedin.com/in/mike-mcginnis-8a517190/; Janelle Stecklein, "Questions Raised about Conflicts of Interest Involving Oklahoma Corporation Commission," *CNHI News*, Dec. 26, 2021; "Bob Anthony," FollowTheMoney.org, https://www.followthemoney.org/show-me?dt=1&c -t-eid=6668808&d-ccg=5#%5B%7B1%7Cgr0=d-eid; "Todd Hiett," FollowTheMoney.org, https://www.followthemoney.org/show-me?dt=1&c -t-eid=6569712&d-ccg=5#%5B%7B1%7Cgr0=d-eid; "Dana Murphy," FollowTheMoney.org, https://www.followthemoney.org/show-me?dt=1&c-t -eid=6583648&d-ccg=5#%5B%7B1%7Cgr0=d-eid.

167   the price crashed: Bob Burke and Eric Dabney, *Prospects to Prosperity: The Story of Oklahoma's Oil and Gas Industry* (San Antonio, TX: Historical Publishing Network, 2012), 12–14.

167   the Oklahoma state legislature and even itself: Roberto Bernier, "Region VI Pollution Report," United States Environmental Protection Agency, 2007, https://response.epa.gov/sites/3334/files/north%20oologah%20polrep.pdf; Bob Vandewater, "Commission Extends Anti-Pollution Unit," *Oklahoman*, January 5, 1991; Bob Vandewater, "Panel Continuing Commission Probe," *Oklahoman*, October 5, 1985; Associated Press, "Fines Not Collected," *Sapulpa Daily Herald*, December 15, 1985; "Lake Oologah Oil Well P&A and Clean Up Project," US EPA, Oklahoma Corporation Commission, and Oklahoma Energy Resources Board, November 15, 2004, https://trainex.org/osc_readiness/2004materials /OologahMeeting111504.pdf; Roberto Bernier, "Region VI Pollution Report; "Oologah Lake Management Plan," Oklahoma Department of Wildlife Conservation, 2008, https://www.wildlifedepartment.com/sites/default/files/2021-08 /Oologah2008.pdf.

168   of the twenty-one seats: See "Oklahoma Energy Education Foundation, Form 990 for Period ending December 2006," *ProPublica*, https://projects .propublica.org/nonprofits/display_990/204707442/2007_04_EO%2F20 -4707442_990_200612; "Continental Resources Announces Addition of Longtime Energy Industry Leader to Executive Team," PRNewswire, April 11, 2012, https://www.prnewswire.com/news-releases/continental-resources -announces-addition-of-longtime-energy-industry-leader-to-executive-team -146954975.html; "NSWA Board & Staff," National Stripper Well Association, http://nswa.us/board-staff/.

168   it's voluntary: Bob Vandewater, "Expansion of Energy Fee OK'd," *Daily Oklahoman*, May 20, 1993; Russell Ray, "Thompson Leaves OIPA Presidency," *Tulsa World*, October 13, 2005; Bob Vandewater, "Energy Board Gears Up for Expansion," *Daily Oklahoman*, August 17, 1993; Bob Vandewater, "Bill Aimed at Oil Producers Clears Senate Committee," *Daily Oklahoman*, April 3, 1992; Bob Vandewater, "Senate Passes Oil Industry Check-Off Bill," *Daily Oklahoman*, April 8, 1992; Ray Tuttle, "Ad Urges Energy Producers to Fund Program," *Daily Oklahoman*, February 16, 1994; Bob Vandewater, "Board Delays Oil Fee Start," *Daily Oklahoman*, October 14, 1992.

168 oil and gas leaders were spooked: "Decision Document: Partial Approval of Pawnee Nation of Oklahoma Application for Program Authorization
Under §303© and §401 of the Clean Water Act," US EPA Region 6, October
2004, https://www.epa.gov/sites/default/files/2015-07/documents/pawnee
_nation_approval_and_maps.pdf; National Environmental Justice Advisory
Council, Indigenous Peoples Subcommittee, "Meaningful Involvement and
Fair Treatment by Tribal Environmental Regulatory Programs," Environmental Protection Agency, November 15, 2004, https://www.epa.gov/sites/default
/files/2015-02/documents/ips-final-report.pdf; timeline provided by Jeannine
Hale, then Administrator, Environmental Programs for Cherokee Nation, in
possession of author.

169 "fee land" is extremely limited: *Montana v. United States* (United States
Supreme Court) 544 (1981).

169 delayed global climate action for decades: Joe Wertz, "Gov. Fallin Signs
Bill to Prevent Towns, Cities and Counties from Banning Fracking," *State
Impact Oklahoma*, June 1, 2015, https://stateimpact.npr.org/oklahoma
/2015/06/01/gov-fallin-signs-bill-to-prevent-towns-cities-and-counties-from
-banning-fracking/; Samantha Maldonado, Bruce Ritchie, and Debra Kahn,
"Plastic Bags Have Lobbyists. They're Winning," *Politico*, January 20, 2020,
https://www.politico.com/news/2020/01/20/plastic-bags-have-lobbyists
-winning-100587; Neela Banerjee, John Cushman, David Hasemyer, and Lisa
Song, "Exxon: The Road Not Taken," *Inside Climate News*, October 28, 2015;
Diego Rojas, "The Climate Denial Machine: How the Fossil Fuel Industry
Blocks Climate Action," Climate Reality Project (blog), September 5, 2019,
https://www.climaterealityproject.org/blog/climate-denial-machine-how
-fossil-fuel-industry-blocks-climate-action.

170 "which guaranteed its sovereignty": *McGirt v. Oklahoma*, Oral Argument Transcript, 56.

170 "they are living on a reservation?": *McGirt v. Oklahoma*, Oral Argument
Transcript, 38.

170 seventy-eight federally recognized tribes: Miller and Ethridge, *A Promise
Kept*, 180.

171 "sympathetic" to tribes: Nina Totenberg, "Supreme Court Hands Defeat
to Native American Tribes in Oklahoma," *All Things Considered*, NPR, June 29,
2022, https://www.npr.org/2022/06/29/1108717407/supreme-court-narrows
-native-americans-oklahoma.

171 when it comes to Indigenous nations: *Adoptive Couple v. Baby Girl*,
12-399 (US Supreme Court), June 25, 2013, Thomas Concurring; *Haaland v.
Brackeen*, 21-376 (US Supreme Court), June 15, 2023, Thomas
Dissenting; *Haaland v. Brackeen*, 21-376 (US Supreme Court), June 15, 2023,
Alito Dissenting; *Adoptive Couple v. Baby Girl*, 12-399 (US Supreme Court),

June 25, 2013; *Nevada v. Hicks*, 99-1994 (US Supreme Court), June 25, 2001.

171   "the way we viewed it": Ian Gershengorn in discussion with the author, April 2022.

171   "for terrible sexual offenses": *McGirt v. Oklahoma*, Oral Argument Transcript, 12.

172   the equality of women: Carole Goldberg, "Finding the Way to Indian Country: Justice Ruth Bader Ginsburg's Decisions in Indian Law Cases," *Ohio State Law Journal* 70, no. 4 (2009): 1003.

172   "this area of the law": Meredith Alberta Palmer, "Ruth Bader Ginsburg's Notoriety in Indian Country and Cornell's Campus Landscape," Cornell University and Indigenous Dispossession Project (blog), January 4, 2021, https://blogs.cornell.edu/cornelluniversityindigenousdispossession/2021/01/04/ruth-bader-ginsburgs-notoriety-in-indian-country-and-cornells-campus-landscape/.

172   often skipped over the relevant principles: *City of Sherrill v. Oneida Indian Nation of New York*, 03-855 (US Supreme Court), March 29, 2005.

172   "They don't appear in any of the briefs": *McGirt v. Oklahoma*, Oral Argument Transcript, 91.

172   "The case is submitted": *McGirt v. Oklahoma*, Oral Argument Transcript, 91.

CHAPTER 12 | Slow Bleed

173   "squandered and wasted": Petition to Declare Millie Naharkey Incompetent and for Appointment of Guardian (June 14, 1922): 500 (Tulsa County, OK), Millie Naharkey Probate Records (MNPR), vol. 2, Ancestry.com, 953–54.

173   "business transactions": Motion to Set Aside Dismissal and Reinstate Cause (n.d.), 19374 (Tulsa County, OK) *Naharkey v. Page*.

173   Millie fought the designation: Answer and Response to Petition and Motion (n.d.), Order and Journal Entry (n.d.), Response to Objection of Guardian to Allowance for Attorney Fees (n.d.), Objection to the Allowance of the Claim of C.E. Baldwin (n.d.), Order (n.d.): 500 (Tulsa Co, OK), MNPR, vol. 2, 1003–7, 870–71, 887, 915–16, 891–92.

173   Reporters called Millie: "Boxer's Love of Indian Maiden Is All in Vain," *The Tulsa Tribune* (Tulsa, OK), Nov. 12, 1922; International News Service, "Indian Heiress to Fortune Is Object of Hunt," *The Cushing Citizen* (Cushing, OK), Apr. 7, 1927; "Millie Naharkey, Missing Indian Heiress," *McAlester News-Capital* (McAlester, OK), Oct. 3, 1922; "Indian Heiress Missing from Home," *Daily Ardmoreite* (Ardmore, OK), Mar. 28, 1927.

173   An Indian agent with the Department of the Interior: Thomas P. Roach
      to Charles Burke, May 19, 1923: 500 (Tulsa County, OK), *MNCF*.

174   She worked in the home: Petition (n.d.), Petition for Order Authorizing
      Guardian to Pay for Support (n.d.): 500 (Tulsa County, OK), MNPR, vol. 2,
      846, 843–44; Deposition of Thomas P. Roach and John B. Reynolds (Sept. 28,
      1923): 23231 (Muscogee County, OK), Muscogee County Courthouse Records;
      (Tulsa County, OK), *Naharkey v. Gladys Bell Oil*; Motion to Advance (n.d.)
      19374 (Tulsa Co. District Court, OK), *Naharkey v. Page*.

174   At a preliminary hearing, the kidnapping charges: "M'Nutt's Trial Date
      Unknown," *Tulsa Daily World*, June 27, 1925; Thomas P. Roach to Charles
      Burke, May 19, 1923, *MNCF*, 18–19.

174   The judge concluded that Millie went to the resort in Missouri "will-
      ingly": "Oil Men Sued by Indian Girl for $250,000," unknown newspaper
      clipping cataloged by investigating agent, *MNCF*, 148.

174   Millie's guardian dropped the suit: Associated Press, "Oil Man Sen-
      tenced," *Morning Examiner* (Bartlesville, OK), July 14, 1926; Associated
      Press, "Tulsan Guilty in Booze Case," *Tulsa World*, June 18, 1926; "Judge Blair
      Acquitted," *Tulsa World*, Jan. 11, 1925; Suggestion of Death of G. C. Stebbins
      and Application for Order of Revival (May 1925): 24917 (Tulsa County, OK),
      Naharkey v. Gladys Bell Oil; Dismissal (n.d.): 23231 (Tulsa Co, OK), *Naharkey
      v. Gladys Bell Oil*; "M'Nutt's Trial Date Unknown," *Tulsa Daily World*, June 27,
      1935; Petition (n.d.) 23231 (Muskogee Co. District Court) *Naharkey v. Gladys
      Belle Oil Company*.

174   almost one million dollars in today's money: Summary and Timeline of
      Naharkey allotment litigation, compiled by author; Tulsa County Courthouse
      Record Book, 1922 case log, 1922 court dockets, photographs, and spreadsheet
      in possession of author; Petition (n.d.), Journal Entry (August 7, 1925), Journal
      Entry of Judgment (February 25, 1930): 19374 (Tulsa County, OK), *Naharkey v.
      Page*; Petition (n.d.), Judgment (June 15, 1933): 19388 (Tulsa County), *Naharkey
      v. Charley*; Journal Entry (n.d.), 19387 (Tulsa County), *Naharkey v. Naharkey*;
      Petition (n.d.), 24917 (Tulsa County), *Naharkey v. Gladys Bell Oil*; Journal en-
      try (n.d.), Journal Entry (April 29, 1926), Order Vacating Judgment Rendered
      on April 7, 1926 (April 15, 1926): 19395 (Tulsa County), *Naharkey v. Hardesty*;
      "Little Millie Wins . . . ," *Oklahoma News* (Oklahoma City, OK), Mar. 10, 1936;
      Answer and Response to Petition and Motion (n.d.), Application for Order
      Authorizing Disbursements (n.d.), Application of Guardian (n.d.): 500 (Tulsa
      County), MNPR, vol. 2, 1003–5, 1067, 1052–54, 1072–73, 1076, 1296–97.

174   Millie's estate was left with less than $27,000: Petition of Shell S. Bas-
      sett for the Allowance of an Attorney Fee (n.d.), Release and Satisfaction of the
      Claim of Shell S. Bassett (May 27, 1937), Order (April 7, 1937), Order (second,
      April 7, 1937), Receipts and Disbursements July 1, 1936 to May 31, 1937 (n.d.),
      Order Allowing Annual Account Compensation for Special Services . . .

(July 19, 1937): 500, MNPR, vol. 2, 1048–51, 866–67, 1132–33, 10–84, 1069–73, 1076–77.

175   Within five years, nearly 10,000 cases: Debo, *And Still the Waters Run*, 203, 205–8.

175   "intolerable uncertainty": Petition for a Writ of Certiorari, Nov. 16, 2017, Capital Case 17 (US Supreme Court), *Royal v. Murphy*.

175   "time-consuming lawsuits": On the Writ of Certiorari to the Oklahoma Court of Criminal Appeals, March 20, 2020, 18-9526 (US Supreme Court), *McGirt v. Oklahoma*.

175   Millie had to ask permission: Order Authorizing Sale of Government Bonds (June 3, 1938), In the matter of the estate of Millie Naharkey, Incompetent, First Trust & Savings Bank, Guardian (June 11, 1928), Order (Oct. 29, 1926), Order Authorizing Disbursements (April 9, 1937), Order Authorizing Purchase of Automobile and Insurance (April 9, 1937), Order Authorizing Disbursement (April 19, 1937), Order Authorizing Payment for Insurance (Oct. 20, 1937), Application for Order Authorizing Payment for Insurance (Oct. 20, 1937), Application for Order Authorizing Disbursement (n.d.), Order Authorizing Special Allowance (Mar. 14, 1938), Application for Order Authorizing Special Allowance (n.d.), Application for Order Authorizing Dental Work (n.d.), Order Authorizing Dental Work (May 3, 1938), Application for Order Authorizing Disbursement of Funds to Improve Real Estate (Oct. 28, 1938), Order Authorizing Disbursement of Funds to Improve Real Estate (Oct. 31, 1938), Application for Order Authorizing Purchase of Refrigerator (July 23, 1937), Application for Order Authorizing Special Allowance (n.d.): 500 (Tulsa County, OK), MNPR, vol. 2, 1064, 1037, 920, 1138, 1124–25, 1137, 1085, 1136, 874, 878, 913, 862, 865, 872, 882, 1062–63, 864; Application for Expenses (Nov. 4, 1943), Application and Order Authorizing Special Disbursement (Mar. 21, 1962), Application and Order Authorizing Special Disbursement (second, Mar. 21, 1962), Application for Order Authorizing Expenditure for Support of Ward (May 3, 1954), Application for Order Approving Purchase of Furniture (Oct. 31, 1963), Application and Order for Authority to Purchase Refrigerator for Ward (July 26, 1962): 500 (Tulsa County, OK), MNPR, vol. 1, 10–11, 4, 5, 12, 6, 7; Order Authorizing Settlement of Taxes (June 29, 1940), Petition for Order Authorizing Compromise of [1937] Taxes (n.d.), Application for Order Authorizing Special Allowance (n.d.), Order Authorizing Special Allowance (Dec. 9, 1940), Application for Order to Sell Personal Property at Private Sale (n.d.): 500 (Tulsa County, OK), MNPR, vol. 3, 1322, 1442, 1317, 1328, 1410–11; Order Authorizing Expenditures (Dec. 18, 1952), Application for Authority to Expend Funds for the Benefit of Ward (n.d.), Application for Order Authorizing Increase of Expense Allowance and Authorizing Christmas Allowance for Ward (Dec. 7, 1955), Application for Authorizing Disbursement for Property of the Ward (Jan. 14, 1959), Application for and Order Approving Purchase of Garbage Disposal (Aug. 19, 1969), Creditor's Claim

(May 8, 1959): 500 (Tulsa County, OK), MNPR, vol. 4, 1578, 1589, 1611, 1614, 1489, 1477–79.

175   A one-page request to buy a new Coldspot: Petition for Order Authorizing Guardian to Pay for Support (n.d.), Order (Feb. 12, 1928), Order Approving Sale of Personal Property (Dec. 1, 1938), Objection to the Claim of C. E. Baldwin (n.d.), Order and Journal Entry (Aug. 4, 1938): 500 (Tulsa County, OK), MNPR, vol. 2, 1026–27, 1023, 915, 916, 870–71; Application for Order to Pay Attorney's Fees (n.d.), synopsis of Services Performed on Behalf of Millie Yeatman, nee Naharkey (Dec. 4, 1943), Legal Service Performed for and on Behalf of Millie Yeatman, nee Naharkey in Second Action for Divorce (Dec. 4, 1943): 500 (Tulsa County, OK), Application and Order for Authority to Purchase Refrigerator for Ward, MNPR, vol. 3, 1416–17, 1418, 1419–20, vol. 1, 7; Darla Yeatman (Millie Naharkey's granddaughter) in discussion with the author, April 2023.

176   "capable of transacting her own business and affairs": 500 (Tulsa County, OK), MNPR, vol. 2, 952, 955.

176   Even the federal advisory board: Debo, *And Still the Waters Run*, 349, 353, 355–56.

176   the corruption, theft: Bonnin, Fabens, and Sniffen, *Oklahoma's Poor Rich Indians*, 3.

176   only 15 percent by 1920: Debo, *And Still the Waters Run*, 349; DOI Annual Report, *Report of Commissioner of Indian Affairs*, "Town Sites" (1920), 38–42, 256–64.

176   kept land off their "tax rolls": Debo, *And Still the Waters Run*, 357–59, *Oklahoma Session Laws* (Oklahoma City: Press of the State Capital Company, 1931), 395–96.

176   "Any recognized tribe or band of Indians": US Congress, Senate, An Act to Promote the General Welfare of the Indians of the State of Oklahoma (the Oklahoma Indian Welfare Act or Thomas-Rogers Act), June 26, 1936, 74th Congress, 2nd Session, Section 3.

177   Doris can't visit them: Sue Wind (Muscogee Nation citizen and Seminole descendant) in conversation with the author, July 2023; Daniel Wind (deputy chief of the Muscogee Lighthorse Tribal Police Department) in conversation with the author, July 2023; J. Miko Thomas (citizen of Chickasaw Nation) in conversation with the author, October 2023; Pam Kingfisher (citizen of Cherokee Nation) in conversation with the author, April 2019; Sheila Bird (citizen of the United Keetoowah Band of Cherokee Indians, consultant and historian) in conversation with the author, April 2019; Doris Burris Williamson (Choctaw freedpeople descendant) in conversation with the author, November 2023.

177   always have a place to come home: Te'Ata Loper and Miko Brandon (citizens of Chickasaw Nation) in conversation with the author, October 2023.

177   just over 2 percent: Danielle A. Atkinson (Seminole Nation of Okla-
       homa Program Manager, Land Research Program) email exchange with
       author, October 2023; Randy Sachs (Choctaw Nation Director of Public Rela-
       tions) email exchange with author, October 2023; Rachel Langley (Muscogee
       Nation TAAMS Coordinator) in discussion with the author, October 2023;
       "Real Estate Services," Cherokee Nation, accessed November 2023, https://
       www.cherokee.org/all-services/real-estate-services/.

178   my grandparents eloped: Frances Pauline Polson, State of Missouri
       Certificate of Birth, 45994 (July 29, 1912); Patrick S. Nagle and Frances Ver-
       million Polson marriage certificate, 6446, Worth County Iowa (June 12, 1935);
       Cherokee Nation Cherokee Roll tribal enrollment card, W. D. Polson, roll no.
       29456 (Enrollment Cards of the Five Civilized Tribes, 1898–1914, National
       Archives and Records Administration), Field No. 2925; DOI Cherokee Land
       Office, Newborn Minor Citizen enrollment card, Marjorie Polson, July 25,
       1907; "Frances Pauline Polson Nagle," obituary, Oklahoman, July 26, 2002,
       https://www.oklahoman.com/story/news/2002/07/26/frances-pauline-polson
       -nagle/62086447007/; Mama to Hoolie, Aug. 3, 1934, letter in possession of
       author.

178   and raised four children: Peoples Bank, Southwest City, MO, Mort-
       gage on Real Estate Certification, Oct. 23, 1917, Book 217, 377; Oklahoma
       Corporation Commission Oil and Gas Conservation division, Certificate of
       Non-Development (Delaware County, OK), Apr. 3, 1975, Oklahoma County
       Records, book 334, 61; Order Allowing Final Account of Administrator,
       determining Heirs and Final Decree of Distribution and Discharge (Oct. 14,
       1952), 1981 (Delaware County, OK), William D. Polson Estate; Marie Alameda
       Polson Scott General Warranty Deed (Feb. 11, 1952), Ridge Polson General
       Warranty Deed (Feb. 9, 1952), 59085, 59086 (Delaware County, OK), Okla.
       County Records, Book 218, 156–57.

179   With the oil money that pulsed: Rebecca Nagle, "Naharkey Litigation
       and Quiet Title Lawsuits," spreadsheet compiled from case logs, court journal
       entries, and court dockets in Tulsa County Courthouse Record Books and
       Oklahoma State Courts Network database, unpublished 2023.

179   notified by an ad in the paper: "No. 107732 Notice by Publication," Tulsa
       Daily (Tulsa, OK), n.d.; Decree Determining Heirship and Quieting Title
       (June 9, 1964), 107732 (Tulsa County), Hughes v. The Heirs, Tulsa County re-
       cords, Book 414, 582; Petition to Determine Heirship and Quiet Title (March
       12, 1951), Decree (April 2, 1951) 81921 (Tulsa Co. District Court) Owen, Mansur
       and Steele v. Unknown Heirs.

179   lawsuits were brought by corporations: Civil Misc.: Quiet title (July 28,
       2011), CV-2011-756 (Tulsa County), Salvation Army v. Naharkey, Deceased;
       Notice by Publication (April 22, 1980) C-80-962 (Tulsa County), Oral Roberts
       University v. Naharkey; Civil Misc.: Quiet Title (Dec. 28, 2016), CV-2016-982

(Tulsa County), *Arvest Bank v. Callinan & Naharkey Heirs*; Civil Relief: Quiet Title (July 23, 2004), CJ-2004-3071 (Tulsa County), *Perryman v. Naharkey*; Judgment (Mar. 11, 1955), C-55-88884 (Tulsa County), *Adair v. The Heirs of W. Naharkey*; Case Log Entry (1983 n.d.), C-83-987 (Tulsa County), *Burkhart v. Naharkey Heirs*. Tulsa County no longer has records of this case, but it is listed in the 1983 case log, photograph in possession of author; Civil Relief: Quiet Title (Feb. 21, 2006), CJ-2005-7559 (Tulsa County), *Robinson v. Naharkey*; Journal Entry (Nov. 3, 1955), 90144 (Tulsa County), *Flourney v. Heirs of Wehiley Naharkey*, Book 134, 353; Election Not to Remove (Dec. 10, 1952), 84789 (Tulsa County), *Harrington v. Naharkey Heirs*; Petition (Feb. 2, 1953), 85889 (Tulsa County), *Lulu Scott v. Heirs of Naharkey Heirs*; Civil Misc.: Quiet Title (Dec. 28, 2016), CV-2016-982 (Tulsa County), *Arvest Bank v. Callinan*.

179   others a "God-awful" pink: Darla Yeatman in discussion with the author, April 2023; Michael Peevey (Millie Naharkey's great-grandson) in discussion with the author, March 2023.

180   until she died in 1996: Order Authorizing Sale of Personal Property and Investment in First Mortgage Upon Real Property (April 10, 1961) 500 (Tulsa County District Court) Book, 347, 362.

180   The sprawling Memorial Park Cemetery: *Memorial Park Cemetery: Caring for Tulsa's Memories Since 1927*, 5111 S. Memorial Drive, Tulsa, OK, 74145, Park Tour Pamphlet (n.d.), 7; marked pamphlet map in possession of author.

CHAPTER 13 | The Victory

183   And then, *McGirt*: Kalvis Golde, "Live Blog of Opinions," *SCOTUSblog*, July 9, 2020, https://www.scotusblog.com/2020/07/live-blog-of-opinions-59/, accessed August 2022.

183   she knew what it was: Rosemary McCombs Maxey in discussion with the author, July 2022.

183   on the popular *SCOTUSblog*: James Floyd in discussion with the author, March 2022.

183   anxiously waiting: Daniel Wind in discussion with the author, July 2022.

183   working remotely from Perú: Philip Tinker in discussion with the author, February 2022.

184   computer screen lighting his face: Riyaz Kanji in discussion with the author, November 2021.

184   "the reasons stated in *McGirt v. Oklahoma*": *Sharp v. Murphy*, 17-1107 (US Supreme Court), Per Curiam Opinion, July 9, 2020.

184   "Is that good or bad?": Ian Gershengorn in discussion with the author,
       April 2022.

184   saw the verdict on TV: Patrick Murphy in discussion with the author,
       April 2023.

184   heard a fellow inmate yell his name: Jimcy McGirt in discussion with
       the author, August 2022.

184   "I would just catch my breath": Angel Ellis (Director of Mvskoke Media)
       in discussion with the author, July 2020.

185   "we hold the government to its word": *McGirt v. Oklahoma*, 18–9526
       (US Supreme Court), July 9, 2020, 1.

186   "That never happens": Angel Ellis in discussion with the author, July 2020.

186   she said into the receiver: Rosemary McCombs Maxey in discussion
       with the author, July 2022.

186   Most were simply overwhelmed: James Floyd in discussion with the
       author, March 2022.

186   "there's no other word for it": Daniel Wind in discussion with the au-
       thor, July 2022.

186   a small part of history: Riyaz Kanji in discussion with the author, No-
       vember 2021.

186   just like it does everywhere else: Philip Tinker in discussion with the
       author, February 2022.

186   "this ball rolling": Gary Peterson in discussion with the author, March
       2019.

186   nineteen appeals: Patrick Murphy first filed a Direct Appeal (D-2000-
       705), which was appealed to the US Supreme Court. He then filed his first
       Application for Post-Conviction Relief (PCD 2001-1197), which was appealed
       to the Oklahoma Court of Criminal Appeals. Murphy then filed a second ap-
       plication for post-conviction relief (PCD-2004-321); the reservation issue was
       remanded to trial court, then appealed to the Oklahoma Court of Criminal
       Appeals, and finally appealed to the US Supreme Court. The intellectual dis-
       ability claim was also remanded to trial court and appealed to the Oklahoma
       Court of Criminal Appeals. Patrick Murphy filed his federal habeas petition
       (CIV-03-443-WH) in the US District Court, Eastern District of Oklahoma,
       which was appealed to the Tenth Circuit (07-7068 and 15-7041) and finally
       appealed to the US Supreme Court (17-1107). Jimcy McGirt first filed a Writ
       of Habeas Corpus (WH-2017-00022), which was appealed to the Oklahoma
       Court of Criminal Appeals (HC-2017-1169), the Oklahoma Supreme Court
       (116,661), again to the Oklahoma Court of Criminal Appeals (HC-2018-131),
       and again to the Oklahoma Supreme Court (116,873). Jimcy McGirt then filed

an application for post-conviction relief (PC-2018-1057), which was appealed to the Oklahoma Court of Criminal Appeals, and finally appealed to the US Supreme Court in the case that became *McGirt v. Oklahoma*.

187   "a promise has been kept": Joy Harjo, "After a Trail of Tears, Justice for 'Indian Country,'" *New York Times*, July 14, 2020.

187   "only 10%–15% of whom are Indians": *McGirt v. Oklahoma*, Roberts Dissenting, 1.

187   "in a vacuum": *McGirt v. Oklahoma*, Roberts Dissenting, 6.

187   "broader inquiry": *McGirt v. Oklahoma*, Roberts Dissenting, 2.

187   "contextual evidence": *McGirt v. Oklahoma*, Roberts Dissenting, 10.

187   "farmland and ranches": *McGirt v. Oklahoma*, Roberts Dissenting, 4.

188   "could well be thrown out": *McGirt v. Oklahoma*, Roberts Dissenting, 1.

188   "murder, rape, kidnapping, and maiming": *McGirt v. Oklahoma*, Roberts Dissenting, 34.

188   "family and environmental law": *McGirt v. Oklahoma*, Roberts Dissenting, 2.

188   "the Acts of Congress": *McGirt v. Oklahoma*, 7.

189   "it must say so": *McGirt v. Oklahoma*, 8.

189   "disregard the law": *McGirt v. Oklahoma*, 41.

189   "no reason to perpetuate it": *McGirt v. Oklahoma*, 38.

189   "not the rule of law": *McGirt v. Oklahoma*, 28.

189   "just cast a blind eye": *McGirt v. Oklahoma*, 42.

189   "failing those in the right": *McGirt v. Oklahoma*, 42.

189   "actually a Creek Indian reservation": *McGirt v. Oklahoma*, Roberts Dissenting, 1.

189   "to convince us [otherwise]": Suzan Harjo (Cheyenne and Muscogee policy advocate and writer) in discussion with the author, March 2022.

190   "too blatant to stand": Suzan Harjo in discussion with the author, March 2022.

190   about 56 million acres: "Frequently Asked Questions," US Department of the Interior, Bureau of Indian Affairs, https://www.bia.gov/frequently-asked-questions.

190   nearly 200 million acres: "By the Numbers," US Department of Agriculture, Forest Service, https://www.fs.usda.gov/about-agency/newsroom/by-the-numbers.

CHAPTER 14 | Legacy

193   Over 68 million acres: Buncombe County Register of Deeds, Eastern
Band of Cherokee Indians, Museum of the Cherokee Indian, "As Long As the
Grass Shall Grow: A History of Cherokee Land Cessions and the Formation of
Buncombe County," Buncombe County Register of Deeds (NC), https://
storymaps.arcgis.com/stories/e9913eb717dc4e68aebe7a7c7d3f42c3, accessed
January 9, 2024; C. C. Royce, "Map of the Former Territorial Limits of the
Cherokee Nation of Indians; Map Showing Territory Originally Assigned
Cherokee Nation of Indians." Plate VIII, Library of Congress Geography
and Map Division, Washington, DC, 20540-4650, 1884; "Introduction: The
Cherokees and US Indian Policy," and "Constitution of the Cherokee Nation,"
Article 1, July 1827, in Perdue and Green, *The Cherokee Removal*, 5–19, 60–61;
"Map of the Cherokee Country," in John P. Brown, *Old Frontiers: The Story
of the Cherokee Indians From Earliest Times to the Date of Their Removal to
the West, 1838* (Kingsport, TN: Southern Publishers, Inc, 1938), 1–2; "Map 1,
Cherokee Nation, 1819–1838," in John R. Finger, *The Eastern Band of Cherokees, 1819–1900* (Knoxville: University of Tennessee Press, 1984), 12; Appalachian Regional Commission, "About the Appalachian Region," "Subregions in
Appalachia, 2021 (Data)," https://www.arc.gov/about-the-appalachian-region/,
accessed January 9, 2024.

194   jurisdiction over only 108,000 acres: "Real Estate Services," Cherokee
Nation, https://www.cherokee.org/all-services/real-estate-services/, accessed
November 2023.

194   Cherokee reservation had never been disestablished: *Hogner v. Okla-
homa*, CF- 2015-263 (Oklahoma Court of Criminal Appeals), Brief of the
Appellant, August 29, 2018; *Hogner v. Oklahoma*, CF- 2015-263 (Oklahoma
Court of Criminal Appeals), Opinion, March 11, 2021.

194   reservations of Seminole, Chickasaw, and Choctaw Nations: *Grayson v.
State*, F-2018-1229 (Oklahoma Court of Criminal Appeals), Opinion Remand-
ing with Instructions to Dismiss, April 1, 2021; *Sizemore v. Oklahoma*, F-2018-
1140 (Oklahoma Court of Criminal Appeals), Opinion, April 1, 2021; *Bosse v.
Oklahoma*, PCD-2019-124 (Oklahoma Court of Criminal Appeals), Opinion
Granting Post-Conviction Relief, March 11, 2021.

194   are still under litigation: Allison Herrera, "Three Tribal Nations in
Northeast Oklahoma Have Reservation Statuses Recognized," KOSU, May 17,
2023; "Indian Country," United States Attorney's Office Northern District of
Oklahoma, July 19, 2022, https://www.justice.gov/usao-ndok/indian-country;
Curtis Killman, "Three Ottawa County Tribes Sue State of Oklahoma over
Reservation Status," *Tulsa World*, Mar. 22, 2023; Louise Red Corn, "Four
Tribes Sue Drummond over Prosecution Disparities of 'Reservation Indians'
and Undermining Supreme Court," *Osage News*, March 24, 2023; Matthew
L. M. Fletcher, "Seneca-Cayuga Sues Oklahoma Officials over Reservation

Boundaries Post-*McGirt*," Turtle Talk (blog), March 27, 2023, https://turtletalk.blog/2023/03/27/ontot-cayuga-sues-oklahoma-officials-over-reservation-boundaries-post-mcgirt/; Herrera, "Three Tribal Nations."

194   largest restoration of Indigenous land in US history: Matthew Fletcher in discussion with the author, October 2023.

195   murder in the first degree: *USA v. Murphy*, 20-CR-078-RAW (US District Court, Eastern District of Oklahoma), trial transcript, vol. 3, August 5, 2021, 466.

195   in her mind with better memories: *USA v. Murphy*, 20-CR-078-RAW (US District Court, Eastern District of Oklahoma), Sentencing Hearing Proceedings, May 10, 2022, 13–14.

195   it saved his life: Grant Christensen, "The Wrongful Death of an Indian: A Tribe's Right to Object to the Death Penalty," *UCLA Law Review*, December 2, 2020, https://www.uclalawreview.org/the-wrongful-death-of-an-indian-a-tribes-right-to-object-to-the-death-penalty/; *Title 18 of the United States Code*, Chapter 51: Homicide, Section 1111, Murder.

195   Time already served counted: Jordan Tidwell, "Jimcy McGirt Released from Prison After Plea Deal Gave Him Credit for Time Served," News 9, May 23, 2024, https://www.news9.com/story/664f47d4a035046c96086675/jimcy-mcgirt-released-from-prison-after-plea-deal-gave-him-credit-for-time-served#:~:text=The%20United%20States%20Attorney's%20Office,1997%2C%20he%20has%20been%20released.

195   "Not at all": *USA v. McGirt*, 20-CR-50-JFH (US District Court, Eastern District of Oklahoma), trial transcript, vol. 2, November 5, 2020, 128.

196   getting rid of the reservations entirely: National Congress of American Indians (@NCAI1944) 2020, "NCAI's mission is to fully protect and support the sovereignty of every tribal government across the country. Read our statement on legislative efforts to diminish tribal sovereignty in #Oklahoma: https://bit.ly/tribalsovereigntyok," July 23, 2020, 5:43 p.m., https://twitter.com/NCAI1944/status/1286416610954293254; "Re: Concerns about the establishment of a congressional working group undermining Tribal sovereignty and jurisdiction," National Congress of American Indians, August 13, 2020, https://web.archive.org/web/20221205212419/https://www.indianz.com/News/2020/08/13/mcgirt081320.pdf.

196   Inhofe denied the allegations: Chris Casteel, "As Questions Mount, Prospects Dim for Federal Bill on Oklahoma Reservations," *Oklahoman*, August 16, 2020.

196   they didn't want reservations in Oklahoma: Commission on Cooperative Sovereignty, "One Oklahoma," Office of the Governor of Oklahoma, October 22, 2022, https://oklahoma.gov/content/dam/ok/en/governor/documents/commission-on-cooperative-sovereignty-report.pdf; Response to Open

Records Request, Office of the Governor of Oklahoma, in possession of author; "Governor Stitt Gives Update on *McGirt v. Oklahoma* Ruling and Its Effects on Oklahoma," Governor Kevin Stitt, October 22, 2020, video, https://www.youtube.com/watch?v=0SCKKILEUek; "Governor Stitt Forms Commission to Advise State of Oklahoma Following US Supreme Court Ruling," Office of Governor J. Kevin Stitt, August 13, 2021, https://oklahoma.gov/governor/newsroom/newsroom/2020/july/governor-stitt-forms-commission-to-advise-state-of-oklahoma-foll.html.

196   lawyer for Seminole Nation was no longer included: Rebecca Nagle, "Q&A: Lauren King on What the Five Tribes' Agreement-in-Principle Means for Oklahoma"; "Murphy/McGirt Agreement-in-Principle," Office of the Attorney General of Oklahoma, July 15, 2020, https://www.oag.ok.gov/sites/g/files/gmc766/f/documents/2020/doc_-_2020-07-15_-_murphy_final_-_agreement-in-principle.pdf; Breanna Mitchell and Wendy Weitzel, "Plan of Action Remains Unsettled after *McGirt* Decision," *NonDoc*, July 28, 2020; Response to Open Records Request, Office of the Attorney General of Oklahoma, in possession of author.

196   "the case could go either way": Mike Hunter in discussion with the author, June 2022.

197   signed nondisclosure agreements: "Rules Committee Meeting—7/20/2020," Cherokee Nation, July 20, 2020, video, https://www.youtube.com/watch?v=ZwxXyiDTb-c; Response to Open Records Request, Office of the Attorney General of Oklahoma, in possession of author.

197   rallied outside a tribal council meeting: Suzan Harjo, "Open Letter to Muscogee (Creek) Nation Chief and National Council: Please do not undercut this great victory!," Facebook, July 17, 2020, https://www.facebook.com/suzan.harjo/posts/3139773212776585; "Rules Committee Meeting—7/20/2020," Cherokee Nation, July 20, 2020, video, https://www.youtube.com/watch?v=ZwxXyiDTb-c; Grant D. Crawford, "Tribal Controversy: CN Chief, Councilor Butt Heads during Committee Meeting," *Tahlequah Daily Press*, July 20, 2020.

197   publicly backed out: Seminole Nation of Oklahoma, "Seminole Nation Chief Releases Statement Regarding Principles of Jurisdiction Announcement from Tribes Impacted by *McGirt v. Oklahoma*," *ICT*, July 17, 2020; Principal Chief David Hill, "To my fellow Muscogee (Creek) Nation citizens," Facebook, July 17, 2020, https://www.facebook.com/ChiefDavidHill/photos/a.102967257936230/173241494242139/; Derrick James, "Batton: 'More questions than answers' after McGirt ruling," *McAlester News-Capital*, July 31, 2020, https://www.mcalesternews.com/news/local_news/batton-more-questions-than-answers-after-mcgirt-ruling/article_72653fe8-15c8-56b3-8804-74810f496435.html.

197   citizen advocacy: Stacy Leeds (Cherokee legal scholar) in discussion with the author, June 2023.

197   work together to implement the decision: Pat McFerron, "Voters Over-
      whelmingly Support Cooperation with Tribes," Sooner Survey: vol. 35, no. 6,
      September 25, 2023, https://chs-inc.com/sooner-survey-tribal-cooperation-2/.

197   "and they get scared": Joe Robson (Tulsa area developer) in conversation
      with reporter Maddie Stone, June 2022.

197   "it's not a problem": Larry Nichols (previous chairman, Devon Energy)
      in discussion with reporter Maddie Stone, August 2023.

197   over 95 percent of our reservations: Danielle A. Atkinson (Seminole
      Nation of Oklahoma Program Manager, Land Research Program) email ex-
      change with author, October 2023; Randy Sachs (Choctaw Nation Director of
      Public Relations) email exchange with author, October 2023; Rachel Langley
      (Muscogee Nation TAAMS Coordinator) in discussion with the author, Octo-
      ber 2023; "Real Estate Services," Cherokee Nation, https://www.cherokee.org
      /all-services/real-estate-services/, accessed November 2023.

198   the agency granted his request: "Petroleum Alliance Praises Stitt's
      Move to Ensure State Regulatory Primacy," the Petroleum Alliance of Okla-
      homa, https://www.thepetroleumalliance.com/petroleum-alliance-praises
      -stitts-move-to-ensure-state-regulatory-primacy/; "The State of Oklahoma's
      Request to Administer EPA Approved Environmental Programs in Areas of
      the State that Are in Indian Country," Kevin Stitt, Governor of the State of
      Oklahoma, July 22, 2020, https://www.epa.gov/system/files
      /documents/2021-12/oklahoma-july-2020-request_0.pdf.

198   in charge of all coal mining on Indian land: https://www.federalregister
      .gov/documents/2021/05/18/2021-10400/loss-of-state-jurisdiction-to
      -administer-the-surface-mining-control-and-reclamation-act-of-1977; the Sur-
      face Mining Control and Reclamation Act of 1977; we also got correspondence
      about this in a FOIA summarized here: https://docs.google.com
      /document/d/1rpkrG9-WyzlnBW2CnpkNWqnTdtluRKe_zCIepGQNohc/edit.

198   still under litigation: Molly Young, "Do Tribal Citizens Owe State
      Taxes after McGirt? Oklahoma Supreme Court Will Hear Case," Oklahoman,
      October 19, 2023.

198   new constitutions and elections: Miller and Ethridge, A Promise Kept,
      121; "Mvskoke History: A Short Course for Muscogee Nation Employees,"
      Muscogee Nation, https://sde.ok.gov/sites/ok.gov.sde/files/Mvskoke_History
      _Powerpoint.pdf.

198   the land was still Indian country: Ross v. Neff, 88-1404 (10th Circuit)
      July 19, 1990.

199   Tenth Circuit told Oklahoma to back off: Indian Country, U.S.A. v. Okla-
      homa Tax Com'n, 86-1819, 86-1832 and 86-1887 (10th Circuit), September 22,
      1987.

199   people Muscogee Nation had enslaved and their descendants: US Treaty
      with the Creeks, July 19, 1866, Article 2.

199   it excluded descendants of freedpeople: Constitution of Muscogee
      (Creek) Nation, Oct. 9, 1979, articles 5–7.

201   "They traveled on the Trail of Tears": Rhonda Grayson (board chair-
      woman, Muscogee Creek Indian Freedmen Band) in discussion with the
      author, November 2020.

201   Rhonda sued the citizenship board: Allison Herrera, "Two Descendants
      of Muscogee Freedmen Are Fighting for Tribal Citizenship in Court. Here's
      What You Need to Know," KOSU, April 4, 2023.

201   "to get back this rejection letter": Marilyn Vann (president of the
      Descendants of Freedmen of the Five Civilized Tribes) in discussion with the
      author, March 2019.

201   reserved for Cherokees "by blood": Constitution of Cherokee Nation, June
      26, 1976, article 3; S. A. Ray, "A Race or a Nation? Cherokee National Identity
      and the Status of Freedmen's Descendants," *Michigan Journal of Race & Law* 12
      (2007): 387.

201   they illegally disenfranchised her: "Judge Rules Freedmen Can Sue
      Cherokee Nation," https://indianz.com/News/2006/017461.asp, December 20,
      2006.

201   "we must have won the case": Marilyn Vann in discussion with the au-
      thor, March 2019; Will Chavez, "Federal Court Rules in Cherokee Freedmen
      Case," *Cherokee Phoenix*, August 31, 2017.

201   freedpeople were guaranteed citizenship in the tribe: *Cherokee Na-
      tion v. Nash*, 13–01313 (US District Court, District of Columbia), Aug. 30,
      2017.

202   "just like the United States": Marilyn Vann in discussion with the au-
      thor, March 2019.

202   the case is still pending: Allison Herrera, "Muscogee Freedmen Take
      Step toward Citizenship Following Tribal Court Ruling," KOSU, Septem-
      ber 28, 2023; Allison Herrera, "'My Citizenship Is on the Line': Muscogee
      Freedmen Descendants Get Their Day in Court," KOSU, April 6, 2023; "The
      questions and the issues brought on by the citizenship status of Freedmen
      descendants," Principal Chief David Hill, Facebook, May 27, 2021, https://
      www.facebook.com/ChiefDavidHill/photos/a
      .103154854584137/329890001910620/?type=3.

202   still denied citizenship in Chickasaw, Choctaw, and Muscogee Nations:
      Joseph Lee, "A Native American Tribe in Oklahoma Denied Black Citizens
      COVID-19 Vaccines and Financial Relief," *Buzzfeed News*, March 19, 2021; "Choc-
      taw & Chickasaw Freedmen Establish New Advocacy Group," the Choctaw Chick-

asaw Freedmen Association, September 30, 2021, https://static1.squarespace.com
/static/61046b9e78a7fc61dcc861c3/t/61566f3ca961224c3e3341b0/1633054593368
/PRESS+RELEASE-+9-30-2021.pdf.

203   it holds the Muscogee worldview: Rosemary McCombs Maxey in discussion with the author, July 2022; Craig Womack and Steve Bransford, "Hearing the Call: The Cultural and Spiritual Journey of Rosemary McCombs Maxey, Steve Bransford and Anandi Silva Knuppel," *Southern Spaces*, April 30, 2018, video, 45:11, https://southernspaces.org/2018/hearing-call-cultural-and-spiritual-journey-rosemary-mccombs-maxey/.

203   "necessity for learning the English language": US Department of the Interior, *Annual Report* (Washington, DC: Government Printing Office, 1898), 32.

203   sixty-seven children who died there: Allison Herrera, "Chilocco Indian Agricultural School Should Remain 'a Site of Conscience,'" KOSU, December 21, 2021.

203   attended state-run public schools: A. M. Landman, *Superintendent's Annual Narrative and Statistical Reports from Field Jurisdictions of the Bureau of Indian Affairs, 1907–1938*, Superintendent of Five Civilized Tribes Office Files, microfilm, RG75, M1011, 1935.

203   "That's how many licks you got": John Ross (Cherokee first language speaker and translator) in discussion with the author, April 2019.

203   "How come you didn't make me learn Cherokee too?": Sheila Bird in discussion with the author, April 2019.

204   fewer than two thousand Cherokee fluent speakers in Oklahoma: Lindsey Bark, "Speaker Services Improves Longevity of Cherokee Speakers," *Cherokee Phoenix*, October 6, 2022; Rebecca Nagle, "The U.S. Has Spent More Money Erasing Native Languages Than Saving Them," *High Country News*, November 5, 2019.

204   what it means to be Cherokee: John Ross in discussion with the author, April 2019.

204   It is still restricted: Rosemary McCombs Maxey in discussion with the author, July 2022.

204   "And what does this mean?": Rosemary McCombs Maxey in discussion with the author, July 2022.

CHAPTER 15 | The Backlash

207   "it needed to be shut down": Brenda Golden (Muscogee lawyer and protest organizer) in discussion with the author, June 2023.

207   chanted "Shame on you" to his back: Chris Polansky, "Stitt Leaves

Tribal Sovereignty Forum Early as Crowd Jeers Lack of Native Representation on Panel," *Public Radio Tulsa*, July 14, 2021; Molly Young, "Oklahoma Gov. Kevin Stitt's Forum on *McGirt* Ruling Turns Contentious in Tulsa," *Oklahoman*, July 13, 2021; "McGirt forum: Crowd boos and turns backs on Oklahoma Gov. Stitt after he threatens to end forum," *TulsaWorld*, video, 2021, https://www.youtube.com/watch?v=TIwSsudYbNg; "McGirt forum: Oklahoma Gov. Stitt's closing statement draws crowd's ire," *TulsaWorld*, video, 2021, https://www.youtube.com/watch?app=desktop&v=DmKB1W4FchE.

208 obtained that citizenship by fraud: Graham Lee Brewer and Simon Romero, "Oklahoma's Tribes Unite Against a Common Foe: Their Cherokee Governor," *High Country News*, February 20, 2020.

208 was married with seven children: "In the Matter of the Application of Frances Marion Dawson, September 17, 1900," Dawson Family enrollment jacket, Fold3.com, Flora Harmon, Cherokee 10756 Trans. From D475, 31, 33, 38, 40.

208 "I couldn't answer the question": "In the Matter of the Application of Frances Marion Dawson, September 17, 1900," Dawson Family enrollment jacket, Fold3.com, Flora Harmon, Cherokee 10756 Trans. From D475, 118.

208 were placed on the Cherokee roll: "In the Matter of the Application of Frances Marion Dawson, September 17, 1900," Dawson Family enrollment jacket, Fold3.com, Flora Harmon, Cherokee 10756 Trans. From D475, 73, 169, 171, 180, 187.

209 Stitt broke them: James Floyd in discussion with the author, April 2023; Associated Press, "Oklahoma Legislature Overrides Governor's Veto of Tribal Regalia Bill," *ICT*, May 25, 2023; Connor Hansen, "Lawsuit and Response Lay Out Timeline of Oklahoma Gaming Compact Debate," KOKH, December 31, 2019; Kevin Stitt, "Gov. Kevin Stitt: New Gaming Compacts Must Protect the Interests of the Tribes and the State," *Tulsa World*, July 8, 2019; Allison Herrera, "Oklahoma Gov. Stitt Resurrects Gaming Compact Fight with Tribes, Hires New Outside Legal Counsel," KOSU, October 24, 2022; Tres Savage, "Lisa Billy Resigns as Gov. Stitt's Secretary of Native American Affairs," *NonDoc*, December 23, 2019; Herrera, "Oklahoma Gov. Stitt Resurrects Gaming Compact Fight"; Sean Murphy, "Native American Tribes in Oklahoma Will Keep Tobacco Deals, as Lawmakers Override Governor's Veto," Associated Press, July 31, 2023; Allison Herrera, "Oklahoma Gov. Stitt Won't Renew Hunting, Fishing Compacts between Cherokee, Choctaw Nations," KOSU, December 13, 2021; Tres Savage, "State Reclaiming Welcome Centers It Once Leased for Free," *NonDoc*, January 6, 2022.

209 since the Civil War: Snyder, "Gov. Stitt: 'Don't Think There's Ever Been a Bigger Issue' for Oklahoma Than *McGirt* Ruling"; Chris Casteel, "*McGirt* Decision Not Most Pressing Issue in Oklahoma, Voters Say," *Oklahoman*, October 9, 2021; Response to Open Records Request, Office of the Governor of Oklahoma, in possession of author.

209 a "distraction" from his office: Nolan Clay and Chris Casteel, "Oklahoma Attorney General Mike Hunter Announces Resignation," *Oklahoman*,
May 26, 2021.

209 rated him "unqualified": Associated Press, "Stitt Taps Tulsa Lawyer for
AG Despite 'Not Qualified' Rating," *Public Radio Tulsa*, July 23, 2021.

209 "and belong to the Indian nations": Carmen Forman, "New Oklahoma
AG John O'Connor Talks *McGirt*, ABA Rating and State's Top Legal Issues,"
Oklahoman, September 2, 2021.

209 "reverse their decision": Dick Pryor, "Capitol Insider: Governor Kevin
Stitt on State-Tribal Relations," *KGOU*, February 5, 2021.

210 "if things change when *McGirt* is revisited": Don Nickles email message
to Commission on Cooperative Sovereignty members, obtained by Open
Records Request, October 19, 2020, in possession of author.

210 over fifty times: List of SCOTUS CERT petitions, in possession of author.

210 "affecting every corner of daily life in Oklahoma": *Oklahoma v. Castro-
Huerta*, 21-429 (US Supreme Court of the U.S.) Petition for a Writ of Certiorari,
September 17, 2021.

210 "get-out-of-jail-free card": *Oklahoma v. Castro-Huerta*, 21-429 (US Supreme Court of the U.S.) Brief of Amici Curiae, Oklahoma District Attorneys
Association, et al., October 21, 2021.

210 "hundreds, or even thousands, of criminals": *Oklahoma v. Castro-
Huerta*, 21-429 (US Supreme Court of the U.S.) Brief of the Cities of Tulsa
and Owasso, Oklahoma, October 21, 2021.

210 "sweeping turmoil in an American state": *Oklahoma v. Castro-Huerta*,
21-429 (US Supreme Court), Petition for a Writ of Certiorari, September 17,
2021.

210 "people being released from prison": Snyder, "Gov. Stitt: 'Don't Think
There's Ever Been a Bigger Issue' for Oklahoma Than *McGirt* Ruling."

210 "at least seventy-six thousand": *Oklahoma v. Castro-Huerta*, 21-429 (US
Supreme Court), Petition for a Writ of Certiorari, September 17, 2021.

211 60 times the number of Native people: "Native American Inmate Count
by Controlling Offense County," data provided by Oklahoma Department of
Corrections, possession of author.

211 25 times the state's previous estimate: *McGirt v. Oklahoma*, 18-9526 (US
Supreme Court), Oral Argument Transcript, May 11, 2020.

211 3 times the *total* prison population: "Incarcerated Inmates and Community Supervision Offenders Daily Count Sheet," Oklahoma Department of
Corrections, July 19, 2021, https://oklahoma.gov/content/dam/ok/en/doc
/documents/population/count-sheet/2021/OMS-Count-7-19-21.pdf.

211   from a survey of district attorneys: *Oklahoma v. Castro-Huerta*, 21-429
      (US Supreme Court), Petition for a Writ of Certiorari, September 17, 2021, 20.

211   the list they provided: "*McGirt v. Oklahoma* Releases," data provided by
      Oklahoma Department of Corrections, data analysis by author, in possession
      of author.

212   jurisdiction cannot be waived: *Matloff v. Wallace*, PR-2021-366 (Okla-
      homa Court of Criminal Appeals), Amicus Brief of the Oklahoma Criminal
      Defense Lawyers Association, July 29, 2021.

212   *McGirt* did *not* apply to old convictions: *Matloff v. Wallace*, PR-2021-366
      (Oklahoma Court of Criminal Appeals), Opinion, August 12, 2021.

212   In several high-profile cases: *Oklahoma v. Shaw*, CF-2014-00096
      (Pontotoc County District Court) Docket, https://www.oscn.net/dockets
      /GetCaseInformation.aspx?db=pontotoc&number=CF-2014-96; Oklahoma
      v. Graham, CF-2007-5987 (Tulsa County District Court) Docket, https://
      www.oscn.net/dockets/GetCaseInformation.aspx?db=tulsa&number=CF
      -2007-5987; *Graham v. White*, 23-CV-0164-CVE-SH (US District Court,
      Northern District of Oklahoma), Opinion and Order, June 20, 2023; *Oklahoma
      v Mars*, CF-2014-00419 (District Court of Garvin Co.) Docket, https://oscn.net
      /dockets/GetCaseInformation.aspx?db=garvin&number=CF-2014-419.

212   staying her orders in similar cases: *Oklahoma v. Elton*, CF-2002-5476
      (District Court of Tulsa Co.) Docket, https://www.oscn.net/dockets/GetCa-
      seInformation.aspx?db=Tulsa&cmid=1312780; *Oklahoma v. Fire*, CM-2018-
      4216 (District Court of Tulsa Co.) Docket, https://www.oscn.net/dockets
      /GetCaseInformation.aspx?db=Tulsa&cmid=3186838; *Oklahoma v. Bradford*,
      CF-2016-2502 (District Court of Tulsa Co.) Docket, https://oscn.net
      /dockets/GetCaseInformation.aspx?db=tulsa&number=cf-2016-2502.

212   Supreme Court correspondent, Robert Barnes: Annie Gowen and Rob-
      ert Barnes, "Complete, Dysfunctional Chaos": Oklahoma Reels after Supreme
      Court Ruling on Indian Tribes," *Washington Post*, July 24, 2021; Response
      to Open Records Request, Office of the Attorney General of Oklahoma, in
      possession of author; Annie Gowen email message to Tulsa DA Stephen
      Kunzweiler, obtained by Open Records Request, July 30, 2021, in possession
      of author.

213   exacerbated by the Internet: Riyaz Kanji in discussion with the author, May
      2023.

213   their "best coverage yet" from the *Washington Post*: Oklahoma v.
      Castro-Huerta, 21-429 (US Supreme Court), Petition for a Writ of Certiorari,
      September 17, 2021.

213   almost half of the cases the court decided to hear: Richard J. Lazarus,
      "Docket Capture at the High Court," *Yale Law Journal* 119, no. 89 (2009): 89;
      Huchen Liu and Jonathan P. Kastellec, "The Revolving Door in Judicial Politics:

Former Clerks and Agenda Setting on the U.S. Supreme Court," *American Politics Research* 51 (2022): 3–22.

213   "well-off individuals": Federalist Society, "Showcase Panel III: Lawyers, the Adversarial System, and Social Justice."

213   To secure Shanmugam's services: Derek Seidman, "Not Just Exxon: Paul Weiss's Addiction to Defending Rogue Corporate Actors," *Eyes on the Ties*, February 20, 2020; Michael Janofsky, "Big Tobacco, in Court Again. But the Stock Is Still Up," *New York Times*, August 8, 2014; Mike Scarcella, "Paul, Weiss Inked $700K Contract with Oklahoma to Undo Tribal Rights Ruling," *Reuters*, August 16, 2021; ALM Staff, "The 2022 Am Law 100: Ranked by Profits per Equity Partner," *American Lawyer*, April 26, 2022; Allison Herrera, "Oklahoma Paid Outside Counsel Double the Fees for Arguing SCOTUS Case," KOSU, May 18, 2022.

213   "are going unprosecuted": Chris Casteel, "Chickasaw Nation Says Gov. Kevin Stitt Exaggerating Impacts of *McGirt v. Oklahoma*," *Oklahoman*, April 14, 2021.

214   got dropped: *Oklahoma v. Castro-Huerta*, 21-429 (US Supreme Court), Brief of Amici Curiae, Oklahoma District Attorneys Association, et al., October 21, 2021; *Oklahoma v. Castro-Huerta*, 21-429 (US Supreme Court), Brief of the City of Tulsa, March 7, 2022; *Oklahoma v. Castro-Huerta*, 21-429 (US Supreme Court), Brief for Amicus Curiae, Muscogee (Creek) Nation, November 16, 2021.

214   ten thousand cases a year were going unprosecuted: *Oklahoma v. Castro-Huerta*, 21-429 (US Supreme Court), Reply Brief for the Petitioner, December 8, 2021.

214   a gap of fewer than 1,000 cases: Keli Blanchett, executive assistant to Tulsa County DA, email message to author, March 21, 2022; Cases Filed CY 2019, 2020, 2021 by county, data provided by the Oklahoma District Attorneys Council, possession of author; "US District Courts–Criminal Cases Commenced, Terminated, and Pending (Including Transfers), During the 12-Month Periods Ending December 31, 2020 and 2021," United States Courts, possession of author; Stephen Kunzweiler (Tulsa County district attorney) in discussion with the author, March 2022; *Oklahoma v. Castro-Huerta*, 21-429 (Supreme Court of the U.S.) Brief of Amici Curiae, the Cherokee Nation, et al., April 4, 2022.

214   used a sleight of hand: *Oklahoma v. Castro-Huerta*, 21-429 (US Supreme Court), Reply Brief for the Petitioner, December 8, 2021; Editorial Board, "The Native American Victims of *McGirt*," *Wall Street Journal*, January 9, 2022; Dr. Jason Pudlo and Dr. William Curtis Ellis, "*McGirt v. Oklahoma* Victim Impact Report," Tulsa District Attorney's Office, August 20, 2021, https://da.tulsacounty.org/docs/08.22.21-McGirt-Final-Report%20-%20Disclaimer%20Added.pdf.

215   low-level crimes in Indian country: Arvo Q. Mikkanen, "Indian Country
       Criminal Jurisdictional Chart," US Attorney's Office, Western District of
       Oklahoma, August 2020, https://www.justice.gov/usao-wdok/page
       /file/1300046/download.

215   than things like murder in the US: John Gramlich, "What the Data Says
       (and Doesn't Say) about Crime in the United States," Pew Research Center,
       November 20, 2020, https://www.pewresearch.org/short-reads/2020/11/20
       /facts-about-crime-in-the-u-s/.

215   did not change much after McGirt: "Re: Guidance for Oklahoma law en-
       forcement following McGirt v. Oklahoma, No. 18-9526 (U.S.)," Oklahoma Office
       of the Attorney General, July 2020, https://static1.squarespace.com/static
       /5cddbbaa2f4d890001005c42/t/5f209bba935d726bc7c2260e/1595972539308
       /AG+-+Memo+to+Law+Enforcement+Following+McGirt+%282020.07.10%29
       +%28002%29.pdf.

216   she indicted 125 people: Kara Bacon (Choctaw Nation tribal prosecutor)
       in discussion with the author, May 2022; Kara Bacon in discussion with the au-
       thor, June 2023; Oklahoma v. Castro-Huerta, 21-429 (US Supreme Court), Brief
       of Amici Curiae, the Cherokee Nation, et al., April 4, 2022; "McGirt Impact as
       of May, 2023," Choctaw Nation, May 2023, https://www.choctawnation.com
       /wp-content/uploads/2023/06/1640809-mcgirt-graphic.pdf.

216   "what we were seeing on the ground": Kara Bacon in discussion with
       the author, June 2023.

216   keep incarceration and court fines to a minimum: Kara Bacon in discus-
       sion with the author, June 2023.

216   and expanded their police and court staff: See: Oklahoma v. Castro-
       Huerta, 21-429 (US Supreme Court), Brief of Amici Curiae, the Cherokee
       Nation, et al., April 4, 2022.

216   hold defendants on their own charges: Kara Bacon in discussion with
       the author, June 2023.

217   "there was essentially zero communication": Chrissi Nimmo, deputy
       attorney general of Cherokee Nation, email message to author, March 17,
       2022.

217   "they don't want retaliation from Governor Stitt": Kara Bacon in discus-
       sion with the author, June 2023.

217   "upended the legal system in Oklahoma": Sadie Gurman, "Supreme
       Court Upended the Legal System in Oklahoma and Could Do It Again," Wall
       Street Journal, March 12, 2022.

217   "mayhem" and "criminal anarchy": Editorial Board, "More McGirt May-
       hem in Oklahoma," Wall Street Journal, February 21, 2022.

217 ten thousand cases a year were getting dropped: Editorial Board, "The Native American Victims of McGirt," *Wall Street Journal*, January 9, 2022.

217 "another way to substantiate" Oklahoma's overall claims: Response to Open Record Request, Office of Tulsa County District Attorney, in possession of author; Response to Open Record Request, Office of District Attorney, District 12, in possession of author.

217 "They never tell the context": Angel Ellis in discussion with the author, May 2023.

217 already been charged in federal court: Curtis Killman, "Appellate Court Tosses Murder Conviction, Life Sentence for Man Convicted of Tulsa Murder," *Tulsa World*, December 4, 2021; Public Affairs, "Tulsa Man Convicted of Carjacking Resulting in Death," United States Attorney's Office Northern District of Oklahoma, Friday, March 10, 2023, https://www.justice.gov/usao-ndok/pr/tulsa-man-convicted-carjacking-resulting-death.

217 statements from Governor Stitt without context: Houston Keene, "Oklahoma Gov. Stitt Says Dangerous Criminals Walking Free Thanks to 'Horribly Wrong' Supreme Court Ruling," Fox News, April 7, 2021; Clifton Adcock, "From a Convicted Murderer's Release to Contested Taxes, We Fact Checked Gov. Stitt's Claims about the *McGirt* Ruling," *The Frontier*, April 23, 2021.

217 claimed he got off because of *McGirt*: Lori Fullbright / News on 6, "A suspected rapist is now a free man," Facebook, August 27, 2020, screenshot in possession of author; Chinh Doan, "Federal Judge Dismisses Charges Against Suspected Muskogee Co. Serial Rapist," News on 6, August 27, 2020, video, https://www.newson6.com/story/5f4868d388bebf6bdb49e635/federal-judge-dismisses-charges-against-suspected-muskogee-co-serial-rapist.

217 *Wall Street Journal* also reported on the case: Gurman, "Supreme Court Upended the Legal System in Oklahoma and Could Do It Again."

218 which their reporting didn't mention: 22 Oklahoma Statute §152 (2022); "Bill Eliminating Statu[t]e of Limitation for Sex Crimes Wins Final Senate Passage," Oklahoma Senate, May 16, 2002, https://oksenate.gov/press-releases/bill-eliminating-statue-limitation-sex-crimes-wins-final-senate-passage.

218 "I felt like I was watching a hate crime play out": Angel Ellis in discussion with the author, May 2023.

218 "the criminal justice system in Oklahoma": *Oklahoma v. Castro-Huerta*, 21-429 (US Supreme Court), June 29, 2022, 4.

218 crimes against Native Americans were going unpunished: Matthew L. M. Fletcher, "With Historical Promises in Mind, Justices Weigh State Criminal Jurisdiction in Indian Country," *SOCTUSblog* (blog), Apr. 28, 2022,

https://www.scotusblog.com/2022/04/with-historical-promises-in-mind
-justices-weigh-state-criminal-jurisdiction-in-indian-country/; *Oklahoma v.
Castro-Huerta*, 21-429 (US Supreme Court), Brief of the City of Tulsa, March 7,
2022; *Oklahoma v. Castro-Huerta*, 21-429 (US Supreme Court), Brief of Amici
Curiae, Oklahoma District Attorneys Association, et al., March 7, 2022; *Oklahoma v. Castro-Huerta*, 21-429 (US Supreme Court), Brief of Amicus Curiae,
Oklahoma Association of Chiefs of Police, March 7, 2022.

219   Allison Herrera and I had published: Rebecca Nagle and Allison Herrera, "Where Is Oklahoma Getting Its Numbers from in Its Supreme Court
Case?," *Atlantic*, April 26, 2022.

219   "your figures are grossly exaggerated": *Oklahoma v. Castro-Huerta*, 21-
429 (US Supreme Court), Oral Argument Transcript, April 27, 2022, 26.

219   "the *Wall Street Journal* article earlier this week": *Oklahoma v. Castro-
Huerta*, Oral Argument Transcript, 29–30.

219   "to punish crimes committed within its borders": *Oklahoma v. Castro-
Huerta*, Oral Argument Transcript, 3.

219   unless Congress has taken it away: *Oklahoma v. Castro-Huerta*, 21-429
(US Supreme Court), Brief of Amici Curiae, Federal Indian Law Scholars and
Historians, April 4, 2022; *Oklahoma v Castro-Huerta*, 21-429 (Supreme Court
of the U.S.) Brief for the Petitioner, February 28, 2022.

219   "you're wrong in all but one decade": *Oklahoma v. Castro-Huerta*, Oral
Argument Transcript, 46.

219   "waving a bloody shirt": *Oklahoma v. Castro-Huerta*, Oral Argument
Transcript, 50.

220   "more than 18,000 cases per year": *Oklahoma v. Castro-Huerta*, 21-429
(US Supreme Court), June 29, 2022.

220   was no longer the law: *Oklahoma v. Castro-Huerta*, 5.

220   "would be hard to fathom": *Oklahoma v. Castro-Huerta*, 21-429 (US
Supreme Court), June 29, 2022, Gorsuch Dissenting.

220   the Supreme Court's majority opinion contained factual errors: Ryan
Gabrielson, "It's a Fact: Supreme Court Errors Aren't Hard to Find," *Pro-
Publica*, October 17, 2017.

220   to overturn the results of a democratic election: Peter Stone, "US Dark-
Money Fund Spends Millions to Back Republican Attorneys General," *Guardian*, June 23, 2023; Emma Platoff, "U.S. Supreme Court Throws Out Texas
Lawsuit Contesting 2020 Election Results in Four Battleground States," *Texas
Tribune*, December 11, 2020; Rebecca Shabad, "Six GOP-led states sue Biden
administration over student loan forgiveness plan," *NBC News*, September 29,
2022; Ciara Torres-Spelliscy, "Tracing the Money Behind the Supreme Court

Case Against Obamacare," Brennan Center for Justice August 31, 2020; "GOP States Sue Biden Administration over New Border Policy," Associated Press, January 24, 2023.

221 the norm before the high court: Richard J. Lazarus, "Docket Capture at the High Court," *Yale Law Journal* 119 (2009): 89.

221 campaign finance to consumer protections: "Seila Law LLC v. Consumer Financial Protection Bureau," Oyez, https://www.oyez.org /cases/2019/19-7; "Supreme Court & Appellate Litigation," Paul Weiss, 2023, https://www.paulweiss.com/practices/litigation/supreme-court-appellate -litigation/practice-overview/representative-engagements; "U.S. Supreme Court Strikes Down Restrictions on Corporate and Union Campaign Speech," Gibson Dunn, January 22, 2010, https://www.gibsondunn.com/u-s-supreme -court-strikes-down-restrictions-on-corporate-and-union-campaign-speech/.

221 lowest point in fifty years: Mark Sherman and Emily Swanson, "Trust in Supreme Court Fell to Lowest Point in 50 Years after Abortion Decision, Poll Shows," Associated Press, May 17, 2023.

221 "trust and confidence" in the institution: Steven Greenhouse, "The US Supreme Court Is Facing a Crisis of Legitimacy," *Guardian*, October 5, 2023.

221 their faith in law itself: Daniel Epps and Ganesh Sitaraman, "How to Save the Supreme Court," *Yale Law Journal* 129, no. 1 (2019): 168.

221 "rise and fall of our democratic faith": Robert O. Saunooke, "The Canary in the Coalmine: The Tragic History of the U.S. Government's Policies Toward Native Peoples," *American Bar Association Judges' Journal* 59 (2020): 1.

EPILOGUE

223 There is no marker: Barbara R. and Brett H. Riggs, *Cherokee Heritage Trails Guidebook* (Chapel Hill: University of North Carolina Press, 2003).

223 Including my own: *McGirt v. Oklahoma*, 18–9526 (US Supreme Court), July 9, 2020; Matthew Fletcher in discussion with the author, October 2023.

224 our inherent sovereignty was recognized: *Haaland v. Brackeen*, 21–376 (US Supreme Court), June 15, 2023, 11–13.

224 they were forced to make: Maggie Blackhawk in discussion with the author, January 2023 and March 2021.

225 railroad tribes because it can: *Haaland v. Brackeen*, 21–376 (US Supreme Court), June 15, 2023; *McGirt v. Oklahoma*, 18–9526 (US Supreme Court), July 9, 2020; *Oklahoma v. Castro-Huerta*, 21–429 (US Supreme Court), June 29, 2022; Matthew Fletcher in discussion with the author, October 2023.

225 such atrocities from happening again: Maggie Blackhawk, "Federal Indian Law as Paradigm within Public Law," *Harvard Law Review* 132, no. 7 (2019): 1787.

225 federal Indian law to do so: Maggie Blackhawk, "The Indian Law That Helps Build Walls," *New York Times*, May 26, 2019.

225 But it is foundational: Maggie Blackhawk, "The Constitution of American Colonialism," *Harvard Law Review* 137, no. 1 (2023): 1.

Bibliography

Secondary Sources

Akers, Donna L. "Removing the Heart of the Choctaw People: Indian Removal from a Native Perspective." *American Indian Culture and Research Journal* 23, no. 3 (1999): 63–76.

Alley, John. "Patrick Nagle: A Party Leader." Unpublished paper (n.d.). WHC M-7, Series 2. Western History Collection. University of Oklahoma, Norman, OK.

Berlin, Ira. *The Making of African America: The Four Great Migrations.* New York: Penguin Books, 2010.

Blackhawk, Maggie. "The Constitution of American Colonialism." *Harvard Law Review* 137, no. 1 (2023).

———. "Federal Indian Law as Paradigm within Public Law." *Harvard Law Review* 132, no. 7 (2019): 1787.

Cassity, R. O. Joe, Jr. "The Political Career of Patrick S. Nagle, 'Champion of the Underdog.'" *Chronicles of Oklahoma* 64, no. 4 (Winter 1986–87): 48–67.

Christensen, Grant. "Predicting Supreme Court Behavior in Indian Law Cases." *Michigan Journal of Race and Law* 26, no. 12 (2021).

Clark, Joseph Stanley. *The Oil Century: From the Drake Well to the Conservation Era.* Norman: University of Oklahoma Press, 1958.

Cushman, Ellen. *The Cherokee Syllabary: Writing the People's Perseverance.* Norman: University of Oklahoma Press, 2011.

Debo, Angie. *And Still the Waters Run: The Betrayal of the Five Civilized Tribes.* Princeton, NJ: Princeton University Press, 1940.

———. *The Road to Disappearance: A History of the Creek Indians.* Norman: University of Oklahoma Press, 1979.

Deer, Sarah. "Reclaiming Our Reservation: *Mvskoke Tvstvnvke Hoktvke Tuccenet (Etem) Opunayakes.*" *Tulsa Law Review* 56 (2021): 519.

Duncan, Barbara R. and Brett H. Riggs. *Cherokee Heritage Trails Guidebook.* Chapel Hill: University of North Carolina Press, 2003.

Essery, Roderick C. "The Cherokee Nation in the Nineteenth Century: Racial Tensions and the Loss of Tribal Sovereignty." PhD diss., Flinders University of South Australia, April 2015.

Evans, Charles, and Clinton Orrin Bunn. *Oklahoma Civil Government*. Ardmore, OK: Bunn Brothers Publishers, 1908.

Federalist Society. "Showcase Panel III: Lawyers, the Adversarial System, and Social Justice." 2022 National Lawyers Convention. Video. https://www.youtube.com/watch?v=JuuPCRBxz8g.

Fixico, Donald L. "The Crazy Snake Movement and the Four Mothers Society," *Chronicles of Oklahoma* 100, no. 4 (Winter 2022–2023): 388–409.

Foreman, Grant. *Indian Removal: The Emigration of the Five Civilized Tribes of Indians*. Norman: University of Oklahoma Press, 1974.

Garrison, Tim Alan. *The Legal Ideology of Removal: The Southern Judiciary and the Sovereignty of Native American Nations*. Athens: University of Georgia Press, 2002.

Goldberg, Carole. "Finding the Way to Indian Country: Justice Ruth Bader Ginsburg's Decisions in Indian Law Cases." *Ohio State Law Journal* 70, no. 4 (2009): 1003.

Green, Michael D. *The Politics of Indian Removal: Creek Government and Society in Crisis*. New York: Bedford/St. Martin's Press, 1985.

Haveman, Christopher D. *Rivers of Sand: Creek Indian Emigration, Relocation, and Ethnic Cleansing in the American South*. Lincoln: University of Nebraska Press, 2016.

———. *Bending Their Way Onward: Creek Indian Removal in Documents*. Lincoln: University of Nebraska Press, 2018.

Krakoff, Sarah, "Mark the Plumber v. Tribal Empire, or Non-Indian Anxiety v. Tribal Sovereignty? The Story of *Oliphant v. Suquamish Indian Tribe*." In *Indian Law Stories*, ed. Goldberg, Carole E., Kevin Washburn, and Philip P. Frickey. New York: Foundation Press/Thomson Reuters, 2011.

Krehbiel, Randy. "Watch Now: Gov. Kevin Stitt Says *McGirt* Legal Decision Is State's 'Most Pressing Issue,'" *Tulsa World*, August 27, 2021, video, https://tulsaworld.com/news/state-and-regional/govt-and-politics/watch-now-gov-kevin-stitt-says-mcgirt-legal-decision-is-states-most-pressing-issue/ article_f6d8abac-05df-11ec-8949-9f3194062845.html.

LaVelle, John P. "Beating a Path of Retreat from Treaty Rights and Tribal Sovereignty: The Story of *Montana v. United States*." In *Indian Law Stories*, ed. Goldberg, Carole E., Kevin Washburn, and Philip P. Frickey. New York: Foundation Press/Thomson Reuters, 2011.

Lazarus, Richard J. "Docket Capture at the High Court." *Yale Law Journal* 119, no. 89 (2009): 89.

Miles, Tiya. "'Circular Reasoning': Recentering Cherokee Women in the Antiremoval Campaigns." *American Quarterly* 61, no. 2 (June 2009): 221–43.

———. *Ties That Bind: The Story of an Afro-Cherokee Family in Slavery and Freedom.* Oakland: University of California Press, 2005.

Miller, Robert J., and Robbie Ethridge. *A Promise Kept: The Muscogee (Creek) Nation and McGirt v. Oklahoma.* Norman: University of Oklahoma Press, 2023.

Nagle, Patrick Sarsfield. *The Man on the Section Line: An Argument; Extracts of a Speech of P. S. Nagle; Delivered before an Audience of Farmers in a Country School House in Kingfisher County, Oklahoma.* Kingfisher, OK (n.p., n.d.).

Nagle, Rebecca, and Allison Herrera. "Where Is Oklahoma Getting Its Numbers from in Its Supreme Court Case?" *Atlantic,* April 26, 2022.

Nichols, Roger L. *Massacring Indians: From Horseshoe Bend to Wounded Knee.* Norman: University of Oklahoma Press, 2021.

Nolan, Raymond. "The Midnight Rider: The EPA and Tribal Self-Determination." *American Indian Quarterly* 42, no. 3 (2018): 329.

Owl, Constance. "*Tsalagi Tsulehisanvhi*: Uncovering Cherokee Language Articles from the *Cherokee Phoenix* Newspaper, 1828–1834." Master's thesis, Western Carolina University, 2019.

Perdue, Theda. *Cherokee Women: Gender and Culture Change, 1700–1835.* Lincoln and London: University of Nebraska Press, 1998.

Perdue, Theda, and Michael D. Green. *The Cherokee Nation and the Trail of Tears.* New York: Penguin Books, 2007.

Portnoy, Alisse Theodore. "'Female Petitioners Can Lawfully Be Heard': Negotiating Female Decorum, United States Politics, and Political Agency 1829–1831." *Journal of the Early Republic* 23, no. 4 (2003): 573–610.

Roberts, Alaina E. *I've Been Here All the While: Black Freedom on Native Land.* Philadelphia: University of Pennsylvania Press, 2021.

Robertson, Lindsay. *Conquest by Law: How the Discovery of America Dispossessed Indigenous Peoples of Their Lands.* Oxford and New York: Oxford University Press, 2005.

Roney, Jessica Choppin. "1776, Viewed from the West." *Journal of the Early Republic* 37, no. 4 (2017): 655–700.

Rosay, André B. "Violence against American Indian and Alaska Native Women and Men." *National Institute of Justice Journal* 277 (2016): 38–45.

Royce, C. C. *Indians of North America, Southern States.* Map. Library of Congress, 1884.

Rozema, Vicki, ed. *Voices from the Trail of Tears.* Real Voices, Real History. Winston-Salem, NC: J. F. Blair, 2003.

Saunt, Claudio. *Unworthy Republic: The Dispossession of Native Americans and the Road to Indian Territory.* New York: W. W. Norton & Co., 2020.

Starr, Emmet. *History of the Cherokee Indians and Their Legends and Folk Lore*. Baltimore: Genealogical Publishing Co., 2008.

Strickland, Rennard. *Fire and the Spirits: Cherokee Law from Clan to Court*. Norman: University of Oklahoma Press, 1975.

Thoburn, Joseph B., and Muriel H. Wright. *Oklahoma: A History of the State and Its People*. Vol. 2. New York: Lewis Historical Publishing Co., 1929.

US Department of the Interior, Indian Affairs. "History of Indian Land Consolidation: Roots for Fractionation: The Allotment Policy (1887–1934)." https://www.bia.gov/guide/history-indian-land-consolidation.

Wallace, Anthony F. C. *The Long, Bitter Trail: Andrew Jackson and the Indians*. New York: Hill & Wang, 1993.

Walker, Robert Sparks. *Torchlights to the Cherokees: The Brainerd Mission*. New York: Macmillan Co., 1931.

Weinstein, Henry. "Lisa McCalmont, 49; Lawyer Challenged Execution by Injection." *Los Angeles Times*. November 14, 2007.

Wilkins, Thurman. *Cherokee Tragedy: The Ridge Family and the Decimation of a People*. Norman: University of Oklahoma Press, 1989.

Primary Sources

Alley, John. "Patrick Nagle: A Party Leader." Unpublished paper (n.d.). WHC M-7, Series 2. Western History Collection. University of Oklahoma, Norman, OK.

Barnard, Kate. *Fourth Report of the Commissioner of Charities and Corrections from October 1, 1911 to October 1, 1912*. Oklahoma City: Oklahoma Engraving & Printing Co, 1912.

Battey, George Magruder Jr. *A History of Rome and Floyd County, State of Georgia, United States of America, Including Numerous Incidents of More Than Local Interest, 1540–1922*. Atlanta: Cherokee Publishing Co., 1969.

Bonnin, Gertrude, Charles H. Fabens, and Matthew K. Sniffen. *Oklahoma's Poor Rich Indians: An Orgy of Graft and Exploitation of the Five Civilized Tribes—Legalized Robbery*, Philadelphia: Office of the Indian Rights Association, 1924.

The Brainerd Journal: A Mission to the Cherokees, 1817–1823. Edited by Joyce B. Phillips and Paul Gary Phillips. Lincoln and London: University of Nebraska Press, 1998.

Bruner, William. Interview, Calvin, Oklahoma, October 29, 1937, by Nettie Cain. Oklahoma Federation of Labor Collection, M452, box 5, folder 2. Western History Collection. University of Oklahoma.

Butler, Elizur, to David Greene, August 2, 1838. ABCFM 18.3.1, X-70a. American Board of Commissioners for Foreign Missions Papers. Houghton Library. Harvard University.

Butrick, Daniel S. *Cherokee Removal: The Journal of Rev. Daniel S. Butrick: May 19, 1838–Apr. 1, 1839*. Park Hill, Oklahoma: Trail of Tears Association, Oklahoma Chapter, 1998.

Cherokee Cavaliers: Forty Years of Cherokee History as Told in the Correspondence of the Ridge-Watie-Boudinot Family. Edited by Edward Everett Dale and Gaston Litton. Norman: University of Oklahoma Press, 1939.

Cherokee Editor: The Writings of Elias Boudinot. Edited by Theda Perdue. Athens: University of Georgia Press, 1996.

Constitution and Enabling Act of the State of Oklahoma. Compiled by Clinton O. Bunn and William C. Bunn. Ardmore, OK: Bunn Brothers Publishers, 1907.

Correspondence of Andrew Jackson, Volume 2. Edited by John Spencer Bassett. Washington, DC: Carnegie Institute of Washington, 1926.

Crockett, David. *Davy Crockett's Own Story: As Written by Himself: The Autobiography of America's Great Folk Hero*. New York: Citadel Press, 1955.

Daggett, Herman to Samuel Worcester, December 18, 1818. ABCFM 12.1 II (2nd Series), X-101. American Board of Commissioners for Foreign Missions Papers. Houghton Library. Harvard University.

Dawes, Hon. H. L. "The Indian Territory." In *Proceedings of the Fourteenth Annual Meeting of the Lake Mohonk Conference of Friends of the Indian, 1896*, Lake Mohonk Conference 1897.

Dean, Primus. Interview, Wewoka, Oklahoma, June 28, 1968, by Robert L. Miller. T280, fiche 242–243, vol. 43, Doris Duke American Indian Oral History Collection. Western History Collection. University of Oklahoma.

Draper, Lyman. Manuscript collection. Vol. 4, vol. 30 S, vols. 7 YY, 8 YY, 10 YY, 11 YY, 12 YY, 13 YY. Microfilm. Wisconsin Historical Society.

Harmon-Dawson, Flora. Enrollment jacket, Cherokee card 10756. Oklahoma Historical Society.

Haveman, Christopher D. *Bending Their Way Onward: Creek Indian Removal in Documents*. Lincoln: University of Nebraska Press, 2018.

Indian Affairs: Laws and Treaties, vols. 1, 2, 3. Compiled, annotated, and edited by Charles J. Kappler. Washington, DC: Government Printing Office, 1913.

Jackson, Andrew. *The Papers of Andrew Jackson*. Vol. 3, 1814–1815. Edited by Harold D. Moser, David R. Hoth. Sharon Macpherson, and John H. Reinbold. Knoxville: University of Tennessee Press, 1991.

———. *The Papers of Andrew Jackson*. Vol. 7, 1829. Edited by Daniel Feller, Harold D. Moser, Laura-Eve Moss, and Thomas Coens. Knoxville: University of Tennessee Press, 2007.

————. *The Papers of Andrew Jackson.* Vol. 8, 1830. Edited by Daniel Feller, Laura-Eve Moss, and Thomas Coens. Knoxville: University of Tennessee Press, 2010.

————. *The Papers of Andrew Jackson.* Vol. 9, 1831. Edited by Daniel Feller, Laura-Eve Moss, Thomas Coens, and Erik B. Alexander. Knoxville: University of Tennessee Press, 2013.

Journal of the House of Warriors. Creek National Records. Vol. 2, CRN 7, CRN 8. Microfilm. Oklahoma Historical Society.

Laws of the Cherokee Nations, Adopted by the Council at Various Periods. Knoxville, TN: n.p., 1826.

Leonard, Ryan. Special counsel for the Governor of Oklahoma. Interview by Maddie Stone. June 2022.

Letters of Benjamin Hawkins, 1796–1806. Vol. 2. Savannah: Georgia Historical Society, 1916.

Lumpkin, Wilson. *The Removal of the Cherokee Indians from Georgia, 1827–1841.* Vol. 1. Wormsloe, GA, and New York: Dodd, Mead & Co., 1907.

McKenney, Thomas L., and James Hall. *History of the Indian Tribes of North America with Biographical Sketches and Anecdotes of the Principal Chiefs.* Vol. 1. Philadelphia: E. C. Biddle, 1836.

————. *History of the Indian Tribes of North America with Biographical Sketches and Anecdotes of the Principal Chiefs.* Vol. 3. Edinburgh: John Grant reprint, 1933.

Meserve, Charles F. *The Dawes Commission and the Five Civilized Tribes of Indian Territory.* Philadelphia: Office of the Indian Rights Association, 1896.

The Moravian Springplace Mission to the Cherokees, vol. 1: 1805–1813. Translated by Rowena McClinton. Lincoln and London: University of Nebraska, 2007.

Morse, Jedidiah. *A Report to the Secretary of War of the United States, on Indian Affairs.* New Haven: Davis & Force, 1822.

Naharkey, Moses. Enrollment Jacket, Creek card 4363. Oklahoma Historical Society.

Nagle, Patrick Sarsfield. *The Man on the Section Line: An Argument; Extracts of a Speech of P. S. Nagle; Delivered before an Audience of Farmers in a Country School House in Kingfisher County, Oklahoma.* Kingfisher, OK (n.p., n.d.).

Nichols, Larry. Previous chairman, Devon Energy. Interview by Maddie Stone. August 2023.

The Papers of Chief John Ross. Vol. 1. Edited by Gary E. Moulton. Norman: University of Oklahoma Press, 1985.

Payne, John Howard. *John Howard Payne to His Countrymen.* Athens: University of Georgia Press, 1961.

The Payne-Butrick Papers. Edited by William L. Anderson, Jane L. Brown, and Anne F. Rogers. Lincoln and London: University of Nebraska Press, 2010.

Perdue, Theda, and Michael D. Green. *The Cherokee Removal: A Brief History with Documents.* New York: Bedford/St. Martin's, 2005.

———. *The Cherokee Nation and the Trail of Tears.* New York: Penguin Books, 2007.

Pitman, Laurel. Interview, Muskogee, Oklahoma, October 25, 1937, by Jas. S. Buchanan. Oklahoma Federation of Labor Collection, M452, box 5, folder 2. Western History Collection. University of Oklahoma.

Polson, William Dudley. Enrollment jacket, Cherokee card 2925. Oklahoma Historical Society.

Ramsey, J. G. M. *Annals of Tennessee.* Vols. 1, 2, 3, and 10. Philadelphia: Lippincott, Grambo & Co., 1853.

Records of the Moravians Among the Cherokees: The Anna Rosina Years, Part 2: Warfare on the Horizon. Vol. 4. Edited by C. Daniel Crews and Richard W. Starbuck. Norman: University of Oklahoma Press, 2012.

Ridge, John R. *Poems.* San Francisco: Henry Payot & Co., 1868.

Robson, Joe. Tulsa area developer. Interview by Maddie Stone. June 2022.

The State Records of North Carolina. Edited by Walter Clark. North Carolina Records of the American Revolution, vol. 22, James Martin statement. Goldsboro, NC: Nash Brothers, 1907.

Worcester, Samuel A., to David Greene, June 26, 1839. ABCFM 18.3.1, X-136. American Board of Commissioners for Foreign Missions Papers. Houghton Library, Harvard University.

Government Records

Gales and Seaton's Register of Debates in Congress. Compiled by Joseph Gales and William Seaton. Eighteenth Congress through Twenty-Fifth Congress. Washington, DC: Gales and Seaton, 1824–1837.

Landman, A. M. *Superintendent's Annual Narrative and Statistical Reports from Field Jurisdictions of the Bureau of Indian Affairs, 1907–1938.* Superintendent of Five Civilized Tribes Office Files, RG 75, M1011, 1935. Microfilm.

Millie Naharkey Classified File (MNCF) 29257-1923-175.2-Creek. Central Classified Files, 1907–1939, Entry PI-163 121A, RG 75. National Archives and Records Administration, Washington, DC.

US Department of the Interior. *Annual Report.* "Indian Affairs." Washington, DC: Government Printing Office, 1898.

————. *Annual Report*. "Indian Affairs." Washington, DC: Government Printing Office, 1899.

————. *Annual Report: Report of Agencies in Indian Territory.* "Snake Uprising." Washington, DC: Government Printing Office, 1901.

————. *Annual Report*. "Indian Affairs." Washington, DC: Government Printing Office, 1911.

————. *Annual Report*. "Indian Affairs." Washington, DC: Government Printing Office, 1912.

————. *Annual Report: Report of the Commissioner of Indian Affairs.* Washington, DC: Government Printing Office, 1913.

————. *Annual Report: Report of the Commissioner of Indian Affairs.* Washington, DC: Government Printing Office, 1919.

————. *Annual Report: Report of the Commissioner of Indian Affairs.* Washington, DC: Government Printing Office, 1920.

US Congress. House. *Report of the Select Committee of the House of Representatives, to Which Were Referred the Messages of the President U.S., of the 5th and 8th February, and 2d March, 1827.* 19th Congress, 2nd Session, H.R. Rep. 98. 1827.

————. *Indians-Cherokee: Memorial of a Council Held at Running Waters.* November 28, 1834, 23rd Congress, 2nd Session, H.R. Doc. 91, 1835.

————. *Memorial and Protest of the Cherokee Nation.* 24th Congress, 1st Session, H.R. Doc. 286, 1836.

————. *An Act to Provide for the Allotment of Lands in Severalty to Indians on the Various Reservations, and to Extend the Protection of the Laws of the United States and the Territories over the Indians, and for Other Purposes* (Dawes Act). 49th Congress, 2nd Session, 1886.

————. *Indian Claims Commission Hearings before the Committee on Indian Affairs.* 74th Congress, 1st Session, H.R. 7837, 1935.

US Congress, Senate. *Annals of Congress, Gales and Seaton.* Senate, 21st Congress, 1st Session, 1830.

————. *Senate Record.* Petitions and Memorials, Protection of Indians, Records of the US Senate, SEN21A-G7, NARA, 1831.

————. *Senate Record.* Petitions and Memorials, Protection of Indians, Records of the US Senate, SEN21A-G8, NARA, 1832.

————. *Report from the Secretary of War, in Compliance with a Resolution of the Senate of the 13th October, 1837, in Relation to the Cherokee Treaty of 1835.* 25th Congress, 2nd Session, S. Doc.120. 1838.

————. *Documents in Relation to the Validity of the Cherokee Treaty of 1835*. 25th Congress, 2nd Session, S. Doc. 121. 1838.

————. *Memorial of the Citizens of the Creek Nation*. 43rd Congress, 2nd Session, S. Mis. Doc. 71, 1875.

————. The Dawes Commission. *Report of the Commission Appointed to Negotiate with the Five Civilized Tribes of Indians, Known as the Dawes Commission*. 53rd Congress, 3rd Session, S. Doc. 24, 1894.

————. The Dawes Commission. *Report of the Commission Appointed to Negotiate with the Five Civilized Tribes of Indians, Known as the Dawes Commission*. 54th Congress, 1st Session, S. Doc. 12, 1895.

————. *An Act to Ratify the Agreement Between the Dawes Commission and the Seminole Nation of Indians* (Seminole Allotment Agreement). 55th Congress. 1897.

————. *Agreement with the Five Civilized Tribes. Letter from the Secretary of the Interior, Submitting to Congress, for Its Consideration and Ratification, an Agreement between the Commissioners of the United States to Negotiate with the Five Civilized Tribes and the Commission on the Part of the Muscogee or Creek Nation, Concluded on the 27th day of September, 1897*. 55th Congress, 2nd Session, S. Doc 34. 1897.

————. *An Act for the Protection of the People of the Indian Territory, and for Other Purposes* (Curtis Act). 55th Congress. Statute 495. 1898.

————. *An Act to Ratify and Confirm an Agreement with the Muscogee or Creek Tribe of Indians, and for Other Purposes* (Creek Allotment Agreement). 57th Congress. 1901.

————. *An Act to Provide for the Allotment of the Lands of the Cherokee Nation, for the Disposition of Town Sites Therein, and for Other Purposes* (Cherokee Allotment Agreement). 57th Congress. 1902.

————. *Removal of Restrictions upon the Sale of Surplus Allotments, etc: Memorial from Citizens of Indian Territory*. 58th Congress, 2nd Session, S. Doc 169. 1904.

————. *Report of the Select Committee to Investigate Matters Connected with Affairs in the Indian Territory, with Hearings, November 11, 1906–January 9, 1907*. Includes "Testimony of Pleasant Porter." 59th Congress, 2nd Session. S. Rep. No. 5013. 1907.

————. *Choctaw and Chickasaw Atoka Allotment Agreement* (Atoka Agreement). 60th Congress. 1908.

Treaties and Tribal Nation Constitutions

» Treaty of Hopewell, November 28, 1785.

» Treaty of Fort Jackson, August 9, 1814.

» Constitution of Cherokee Nation, February 21, 1828.

» Treaty of Dancing Rabbit Creek, September 27, 1830.

» Treaty of New Echota, December 29, 1835.

» Confederate States of America Treaty with the Cherokees, October 7, 1861.

» US Treaty with the Creeks, July 19, 1866.

» Constitution of Cherokee Nation, June 26, 1976.

» Constitution of Muscogee (Creek) Nation, October 9, 1979.

Legal and Court Documents

» *Bosse v. Oklahoma*, PCD-2019-124. Opinion Granting Post-Conviction Relief. Oklahoma Court of Criminal Appeals. March 11, 2021.

» *Carpenter v. Murphy*, 17-1107. Oral Argument Transcript. US Supreme Court. November 27, 2018.

» *Hogner v. Oklahoma*, CF- 2015-263. Opinion. Oklahoma Court of Criminal Appeals. March 11, 2021.

» *Matloff v. Wallace*, PR-2021-366. Opinion. Oklahoma Court of Criminal Appeals. August 12, 2021.

» *McGirt v. Oklahoma*, No. 18-9526. Associate Justice Elena Kagan Oral Argument Transcript. November 27, 2018.

» *McGirt v. Oklahoma*, No. 18-9526. Oral Argument Transcript. US Supreme Court. May 11, 2020.

» *Millie Naharkey Classified File (MNCF)* 29257-1923-175.2-Creek, Central Classified Files, 1907–1939, Entry PI-163 121A, RG 75 National Archives and Records Administration, Washington, DC.

» Millie Naharkey Probate Records, Vols. 1–4, 500. Tulsa County, OK.

» *Murphy v. Oklahoma*, PCD-2004-321. Evidentiary Hearing Transcript. McIntosh County District Court. 2004.

» *Oklahoma v. Murphy*, CF-1999-164A. Trial Transcript. McIntosh County District Court. 2000.

» *USA v. McGirt*, 20-CR-50-JFH. Trial Transcript. US District Court, Eastern District of Oklahoma. November 5, 2020.

» *USA v. Murphy*, 20-CR-078-RAW. Trial Transcript. US District Court, Eastern District of Oklahoma. 2021.

BIBLIOGRAPHY   321

» *USA v. Murphy*, 20-CR-078-RAW. Sentencing Hearing Proceedings. US District Court, Eastern District of Oklahoma. 2022.

Responses to Author's FOIA information and Open Records Requests

» Keli Blanchett, executive assistant to Tulsa County district attorney. Email message to author, March 21, 2022.

» Office of the Attorney General of Oklahoma. Response to Open Records Request. In possession of author.

» Office of District Attorney, District 12, Oklahoma. Response to Open Record Request. In possession of author.

» Office of the Governor of Oklahoma. Response to Open Records Request. In possession of author.

» Office of Tulsa County District Attorney. Response to Open Record Request. In possession of author.

» Oklahoma Corporation Commission. Data in possession of author.

» Oklahoma Department of Corrections. Data on Native American Inmate Count by Controlling Offense County. Data in possession of author.

» Oklahoma Department of Corrections. Data on *McGirt v. Oklahoma* Releases. Data in possession of author.

» Oklahoma District Attorneys Council. Data on Cases Filed CY 2019, 2020, and 2021 by Oklahoma county. In possession of author.

» US Department of Transportation. Email correspondence with author.

» US Department of Interior, Office of Surface Mining. Presentation obtained under FOIA from the Reclamation response to FOIA request. In possession of author.

» US Department of the Interior. Response to Freedom of Information Act Request. In possession of author.

Interviews by the Author

Adair, Janelle. Traditional storyteller and citizen of United Keetoowah Band of Cherokee Indians. October 2020.

Bacon, Kara. Choctaw Nation tribal prosecutor. May 2022 and June 2023.

Ballenger, Norma. Patient at Muscogee Nation health facility. March 2019.

Ballenger, Roger. Former Oklahoma state senator. March 2019.

Bird, Sheila. Citizen of the United Keetoowah Band of Cherokee Indians, consultant and historian. April 2019.

Blackhawk, Maggie. Law professor. January 2023 and March 2021.

Blackwell, M. Sharon. Legal expert in service to Patrick Murphy's legal team. November 2021.

Braden, Scott. Former federal public defender and counsel for Patrick Murphy. October 2021.

Butler, Elizabeth, Melody McPerryman, Georgia (Judy) Proctor, and Keli Proctor. Weogufkee Ceremonial Grounds members. February 2023.

Christopher, Kristi. Former federal public defender and counsel for Patrick Murphy. November 2021 and March 2022.

Dalley, Iris. Former Oklahoma State Bureau of Investigation crime-scene investigator. November 2021.

Dellinger, Kevin. Former attorney general of Muscogee Nation. March 2019.

Desiree. Mother of patient at Muscogee Nation health facility. March 2019.

Echohawk, John. Executive director of the Native American Rights Fund. January 2023.

Ellis, Angel. Director of Mvskoke Media. July 2020 and May 2023.

Evans, Roxanne. Family member. February 2022.

Fain, Abi. Choctaw lawyer and signer of open letter. June 2023.

Fields, Anderson, Jr. Community member and witness. December 2021.

Fletcher, Matthew. Law professor. April 2019 and October 2023.

Floyd, James. Former principal chief of Muscogee Nation. March 2019, March 2022, and April 2023.

Gambler, Amelia. Family member. February 2022.

Gershengorn, Ian. Counsel for Patrick Murphy and Jimcy McGirt. April 2022.

Ghezzi, Patti. Former federal public defender and counsel for Patrick Murphy. October 2021.

Giampetroni, David. Counsel for Muscogee Nation. November 2021.

Golden, Brenda. Muscogee lawyer and protest organizer. June 2023.

Gray, Bobby. Former sheriff of McIntosh County. 2022.

Grayson, Rhonda. Board chairwoman, Muscogee Creek Indian Freedmen Band. November 2020.

Guyton, Effie Cato. President, Vernon Charitable Foundation. March 2022.

Harjo, Suzan Shown. Cheyenne and Muscogee policy advocate and writer. March 2022.

Hoskin, Chuck, Jr. Principal chief of Cherokee Nation. June 2023.

Hunter, Mike. Former attorney general of Oklahoma. June 2022.

Kanji, Riyaz. Counsel for Muscogee Nation. November 2021 and May 2023.

Kelough, Eldon. Former officer, Muscogee Nation Lighthorse Tribal Police Department. November 2021.

Kingfisher, Pam. Citizen of Cherokee Nation. April 2019.

Kunzweiler, Stephen. Tulsa County district attorney. March 2022.

Leeds, Stacy. Cherokee legal scholar. June 2023.

Loper, Te'Ata, and Miko Brandon. Citizens of Choctaw Nation. October 2023.

Maxey, Rosemary McCombs. Weogufkee Indian Baptist Church member and Muscogee language teacher. July 2022.

Maxey, Rosemary McCombs, and Liza Proctor. Weogufkee Indian Baptist Church members and Muscogee language teacher. February 2023.

McCoy, Melody. Native American Rights Fund staff attorney. January 2023.

McGirt, Jimcy. Defendant. August 2022.

Murphy, Patrick. Defendant. April 2023.

Peevey, Michael. Millie Naharkey's great-grandson. March 2023.

Peterson, Gary. Former counsel for Patrick Murphy. March 2019 and October 2021.

Ross, John. Cherokee first language speaker and translator. April 2019.

Taylor, Mark. Family member and witness. December 2021.

Terry, Shawn. Secretary of Health for Muscogee Nation. March 2019.

Thomas, J. Miko. Citizen of Chickasaw Nation. October 2023.

Tinker, Philip. Counsel for Muscogee Nation. October 2021, November 2021, and February 2022.

Vann, Marilyn. President of the Descendants of Freedmen of the Five Civilized Tribes. March 2019.

Washburn, Kevin. Law professor. February 2021.

Wermiel, Stephen. Law professor and author at *SCOTUSblog*. June 2019.

Williamson, Doris Burris. Choctaw freedpeople descendant. November 2023.

Wind, Daniel, III. Deputy chief, Muscogee Nation Lighthorse Tribal Police Department. July 2022.

Wind, Sue. Muscogee Nation citizen and Seminole descendant. July 2023.

Yeatman, Darla. Millie Naharkey's granddaughter. April 2023.

Credits and Permissions

Page 8: Photograph taken by the author

Page 14: Illustration by Keli Gonzales

Page 27: Charles Bird King, MAJOR RIDGE, A CHEROKEE CHIEF, from *History of the Indian Tribes of North America*, ca. 1838, Smithsonian American Art Museum

Page 29: Illustration by Keli Gonzales

Pages 48–49: Photograph by Brittany Bendabout

Page 52: Courtesy of Scott Braden

Page 58: Illustration by Keli Gonzales

Page 61: Charles Bird King, JOHN RIDGE, A CHEROKEE, from *History of the Indian Tribes of North America*, ca. 1838, Smithsonian American Art Museum

Page 63: Charles Bird King, OPOTHLE YOHOLO, A CREEK CHIEF, from *History of the Indian Tribes of North America*, ca. 1837, Smithsonian American Art Museum

Page 64: Charles Bird King, WILLIAM MCINTOSH, A CREEK CHIEF, from *History of the Indian Tribes of North America*, ca. 1838, National Portrait Gallery, Smithsonian Institution

Page 68: Photograph of a painting of Elias Boudinot, 1802–1839, a Cherokee, Oklahoma Historical Society Glass Plate Collection, No. 19615.43, courtesy of the Oklahoma Historical Society

Page 71: Illustration by Keli Gonzales

Page 81: Photograph by Brittany Bendabout

Page 117: Photograph by Cody Hammer

Page 135: Illustration by Keli Gonzales

Page 142: National Anthropological Archives, Smithsonian Institution [BAE GN 01139A]

Page 144: Map showing progress of allotment in the Creek Nation, courtesy of Library of Congress Geography and Map Division

Page 145: Map showing progress of allotment in the Muscogee Nation, Dana, C. H. Creek & Seminole Nations, Indian territory: compiled from the United States Survey / compiled and drawn by C. H. Dana (Washington, D.C.)

Page 154: Oil rigs in Glenn Pool Field, published by Tulsa Indian Trading Company, Albertype Collection, No. 18827.082, courtesy of the Oklahoma Historical Society

Page 160: Courtesy of Austin American-Statesman—USA TODAY NETWORK

Page 181: Photograph by Brittany Bendabout

Page 200: Photograph by Brittany Bendabout

Index

Note: page numbers in *italics* indicate photographs.

About the Author

Rebecca Nagle is an award-winning journalist and a citizen of Cherokee Nation. She is the writer and host of the podcast *This Land*. Her writing on Native representation, federal Indian law, and tribal sovereignty has been featured in the *Atlantic*, the *Washington Post*, the *Guardian*, *USA Today*, *Indian Country Today*, and other publications. She is a Peabody Award nominee and the recipient of the American Mosaic Journalism Prize, the Women's Media Center Exceptional Journalism Award, and numerous honors from the Native American Journalists Association. Nagle lives in Tahlequah, Oklahoma.

Indigenous communities deserve the same standard of journalism as the rest of the country, but rarely receive it from non-Native media outlets. Nagle's journalism seeks to correct this.